SHINOBU OHTAKA

It's Magi, volume 36!

MAGI

Volume 36

Shonen Sunday Edition

Story and Art by
SHINOBU OHTAKA

MAGI Vol.36
by Shinobu OHTAKA
© 2009 Shinobu OHTAKA
All rights reserved.
Original Japanese edition published by SHOGAKUKAN.
English translation rights in the United States of America, Canada, the United Kingdom,
Ireland, Australia and New Zealand arranged with SHOGAKUKAN.

ORIGINAL COVER DESIGN / Yasuo SHIMURA+Bay Bridge Studio

Translation & English Adaptation ◆ John Werry

Touch-up Art & Lettering ◆ Stephen Dutro

Editor ◆ Mike Montesa

Printed in Canada

Published by VIZ Media, LLC
P.O. Box 77010
San Francisco, CA 94107

10 9 8 7 6 5 4 3 2 1
First printing, June 2019

WWW.SHONENSUNDAY.COM

viz.com

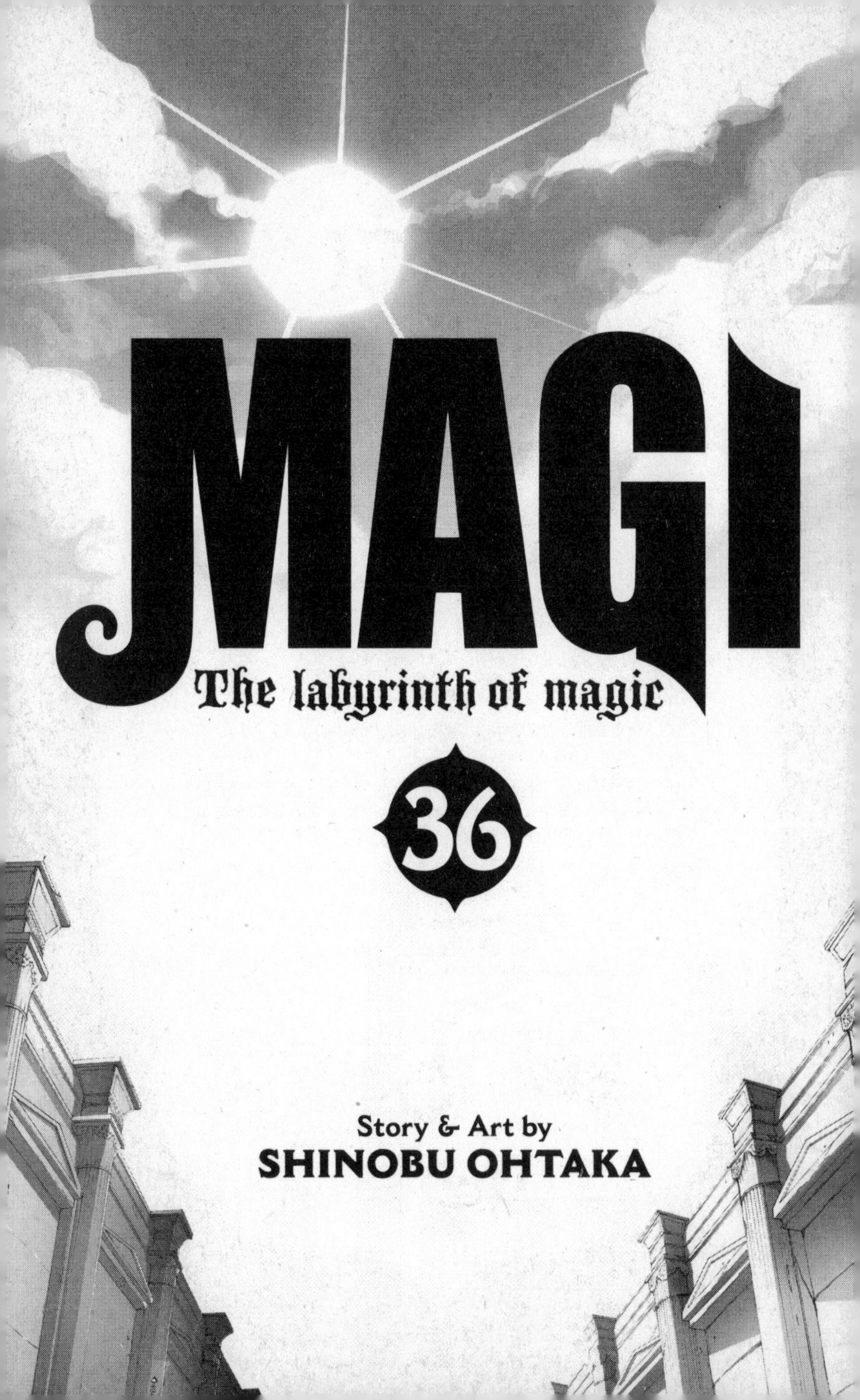

MAGI

The labyrinth of magic

36

Story & Art by

SHINOBU OHTAKA

MAGI
The labyrinth of magic

36

CONTENTS

NIGHT 350 A Great and Impossible Endeavor   5

NIGHT 351 The Spell of Remaking the World   23

NIGHT 352 The Key to the Sacred Palace   41

NIGHT 353 Reaping the Rukh   59

NIGHT 354 Defending the Earth   77

NIGHT 355 The Hierarchy of Gods   95

NIGHT 356 Guidance   113

NIGHT 357 A Part of this World   131

NIGHT 358 Different Fates   149

NIGHT 359 Metal Vessels for Today   167

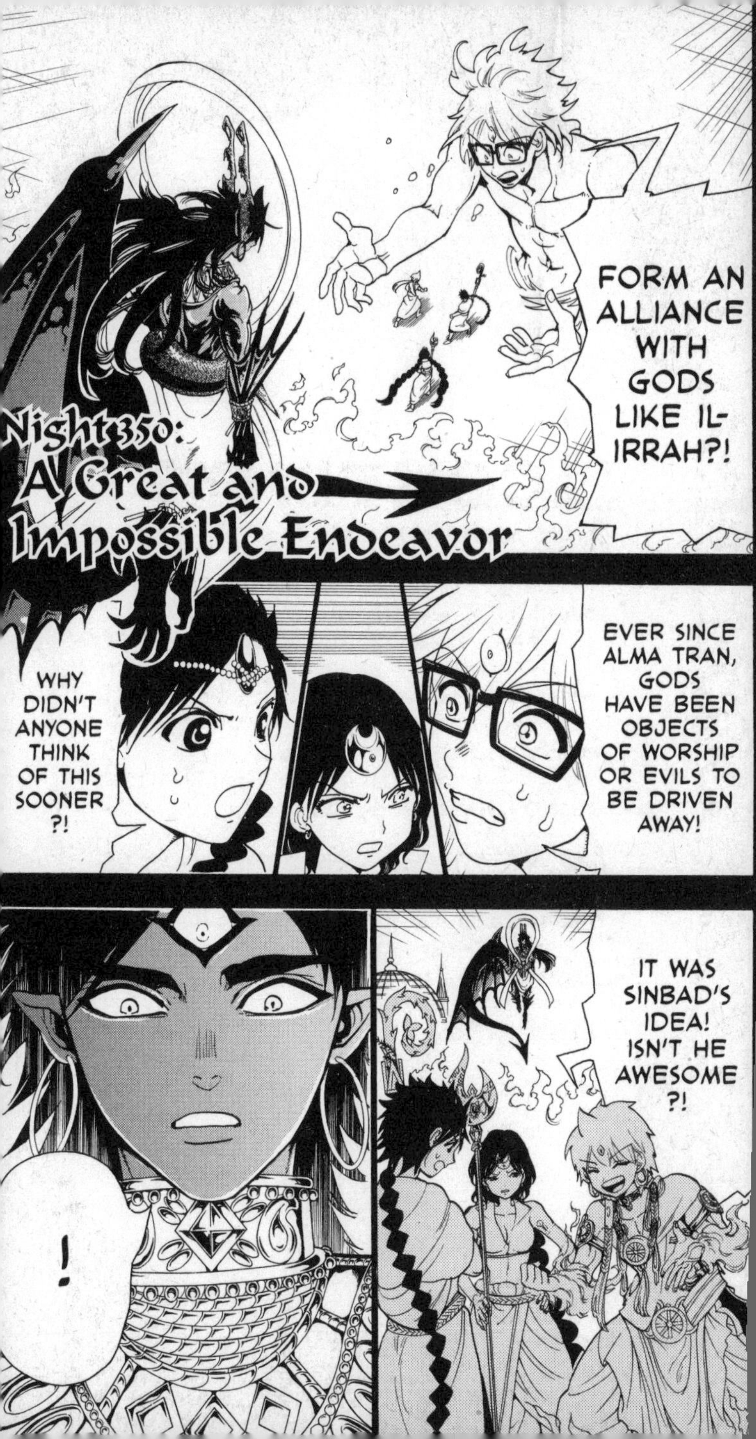
FORM AN ALLIANCE WITH GODS LIKE IL-IRRAH?!
Night 350: A Great and Impossible Endeavor
EVER SINCE ALMA TRAN, GODS HAVE BEEN OBJECTS OF WORSHIP OR EVILS TO BE DRIVEN AWAY!
WHY DIDN'T ANYONE THINK OF THIS SOONER?!
IT WAS SINBAD'S IDEA! ISN'T HE AWESOME?!
!

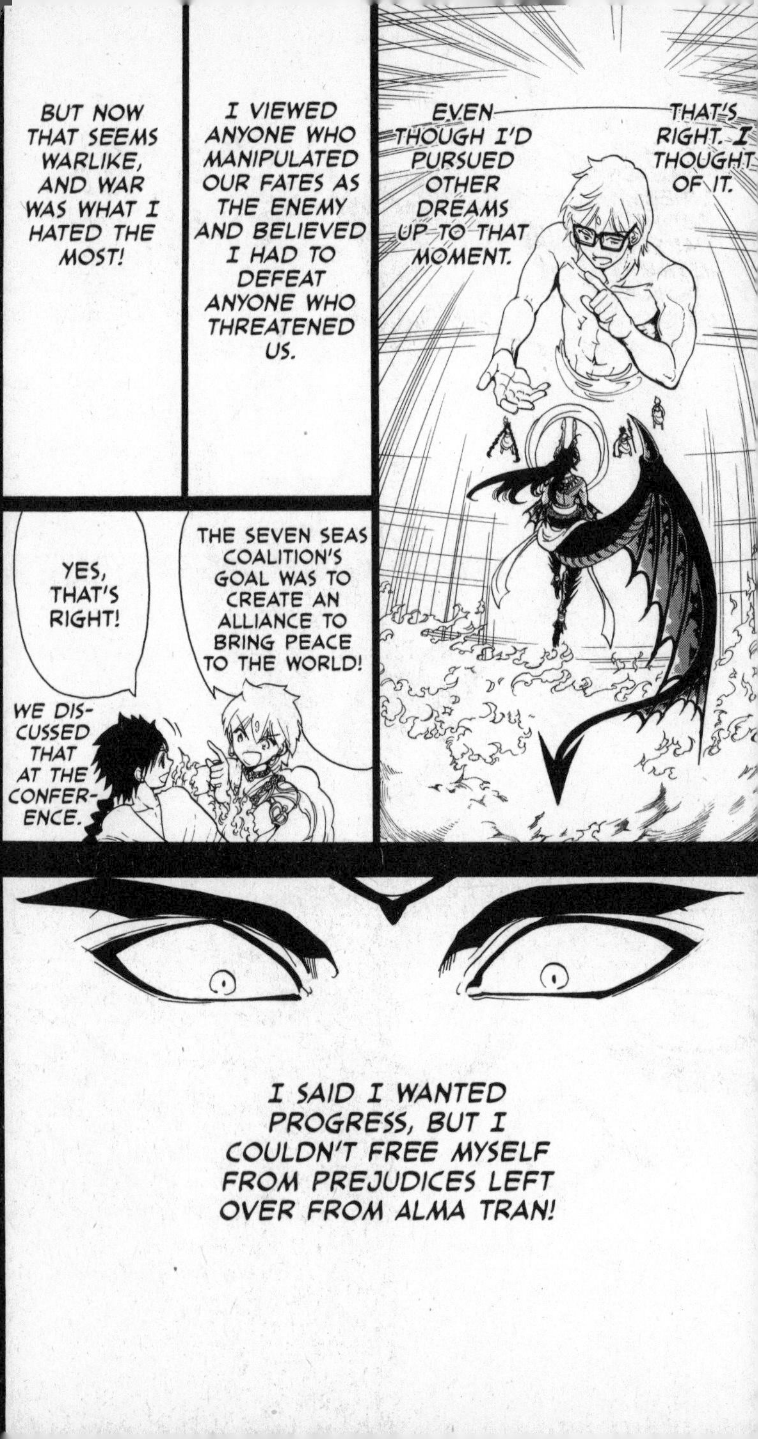
THAT'S RIGHT. I THOUGHT OF IT.
EVEN THOUGH I'D PURSUED OTHER DREAMS UP TO THAT MOMENT.
I VIEWED ANYONE WHO MANIPULATED OUR FATES AS THE ENEMY AND BELIEVED I HAD TO DEFEAT ANYONE WHO THREATENED US.
BUT NOW THAT SEEMS WARLIKE, AND WAR WAS WHAT I HATED THE MOST!
THE SEVEN SEAS COALITION'S GOAL WAS TO CREATE AN ALLIANCE TO BRING PEACE TO THE WORLD!
YES, THAT'S RIGHT!
WE DISCUSSED THAT AT THE CONFERENCE.
I SAID I WANTED PROGRESS, BUT I COULDN'T FREE MYSELF FROM PREJUDICES LEFT OVER FROM ALMA TRAN!

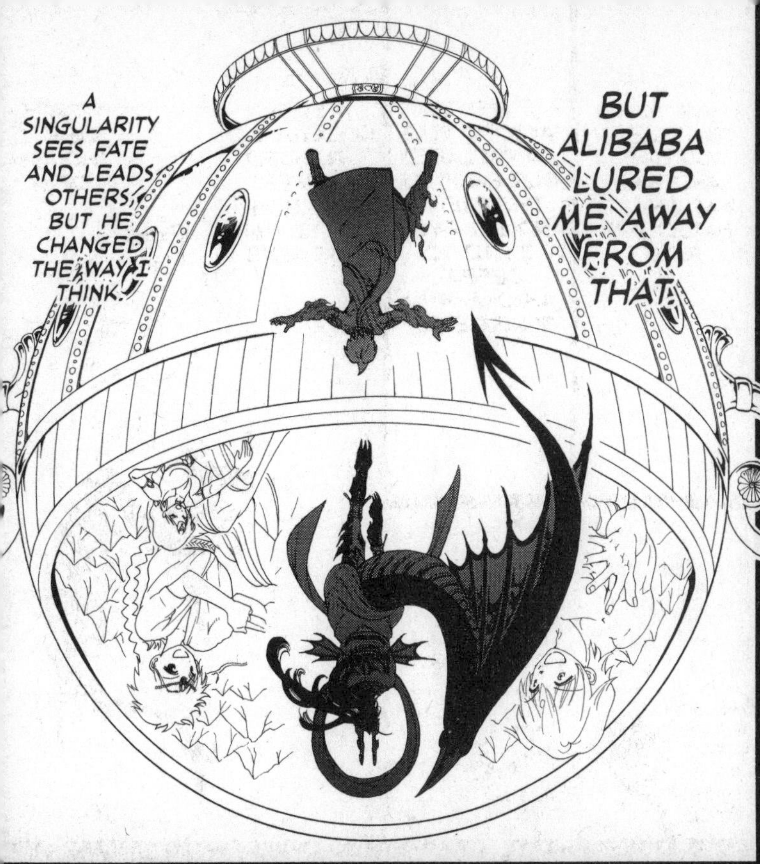
BUT ALIBABA LURED ME AWAY FROM THAT.
A SINGULARITY SEES FATE AND LEADS OTHERS, BUT HE CHANGED THE WAY I THINK.
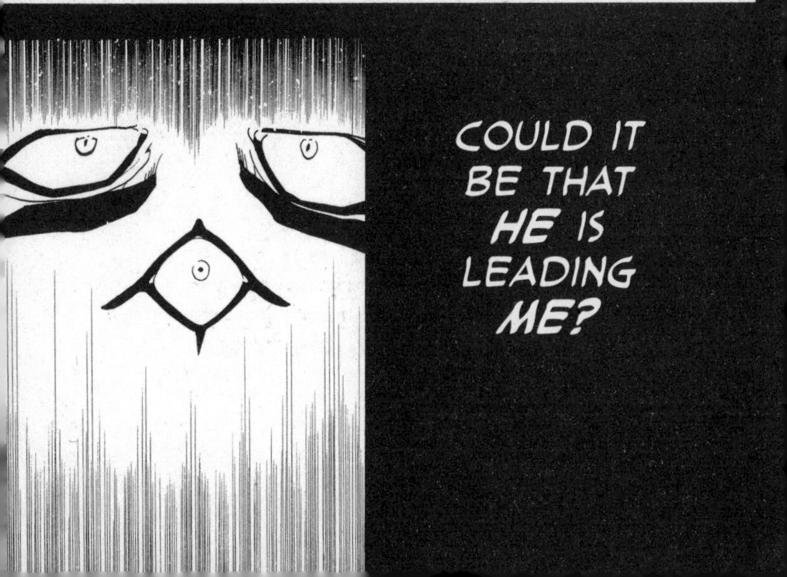
COULD IT BE THAT HE IS LEADING ME?

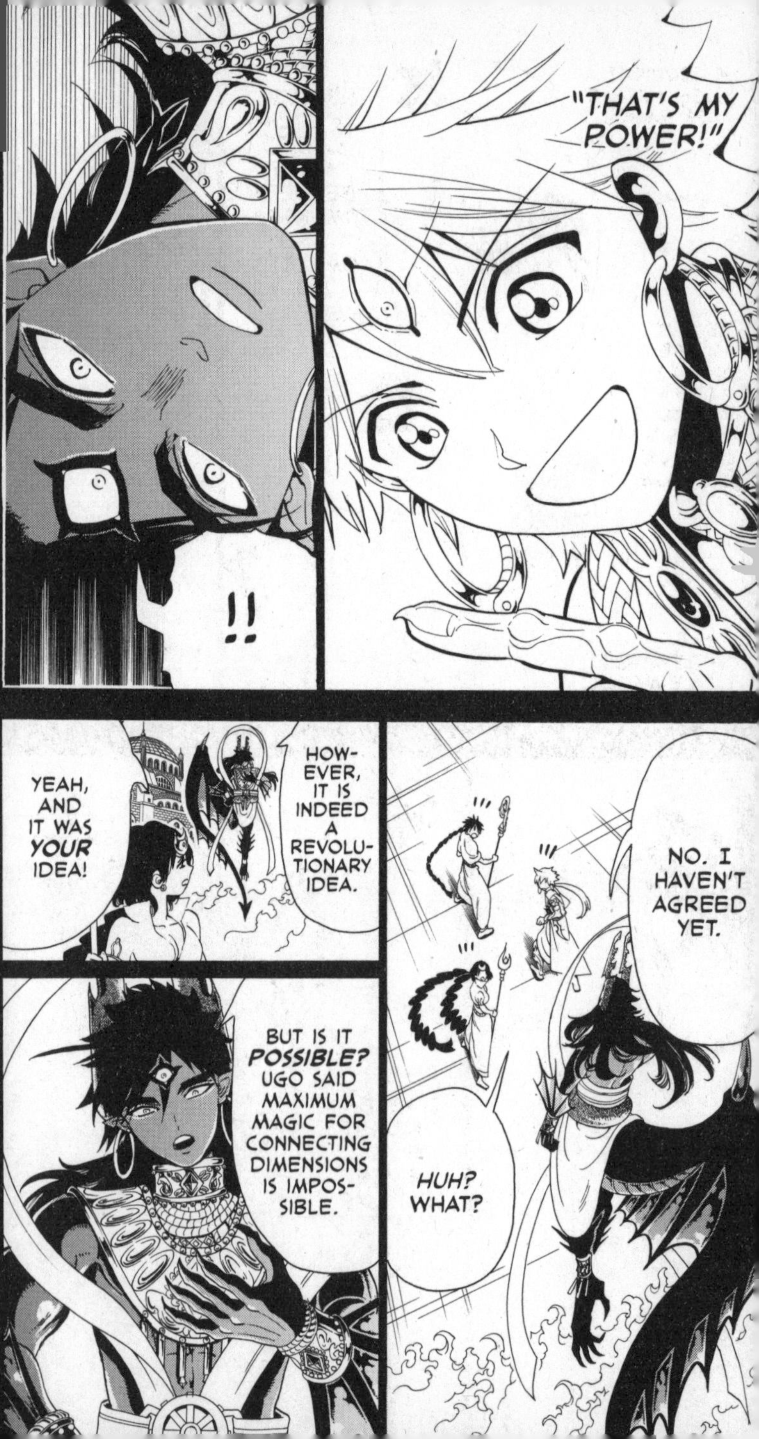
"THAT'S MY POWER!"
!!
NO. I HAVEN'T AGREED YET.
HUH? WHAT?
HOW-EVER, IT IS INDEED A REVOLU-TIONARY IDEA.
YEAH, AND IT WAS *YOUR* IDEA!
BUT IS IT ***POSSIBLE?*** UGO SAID MAXIMUM MAGIC FOR CONNECTING DIMENSIONS IS IMPOS-SIBLE.

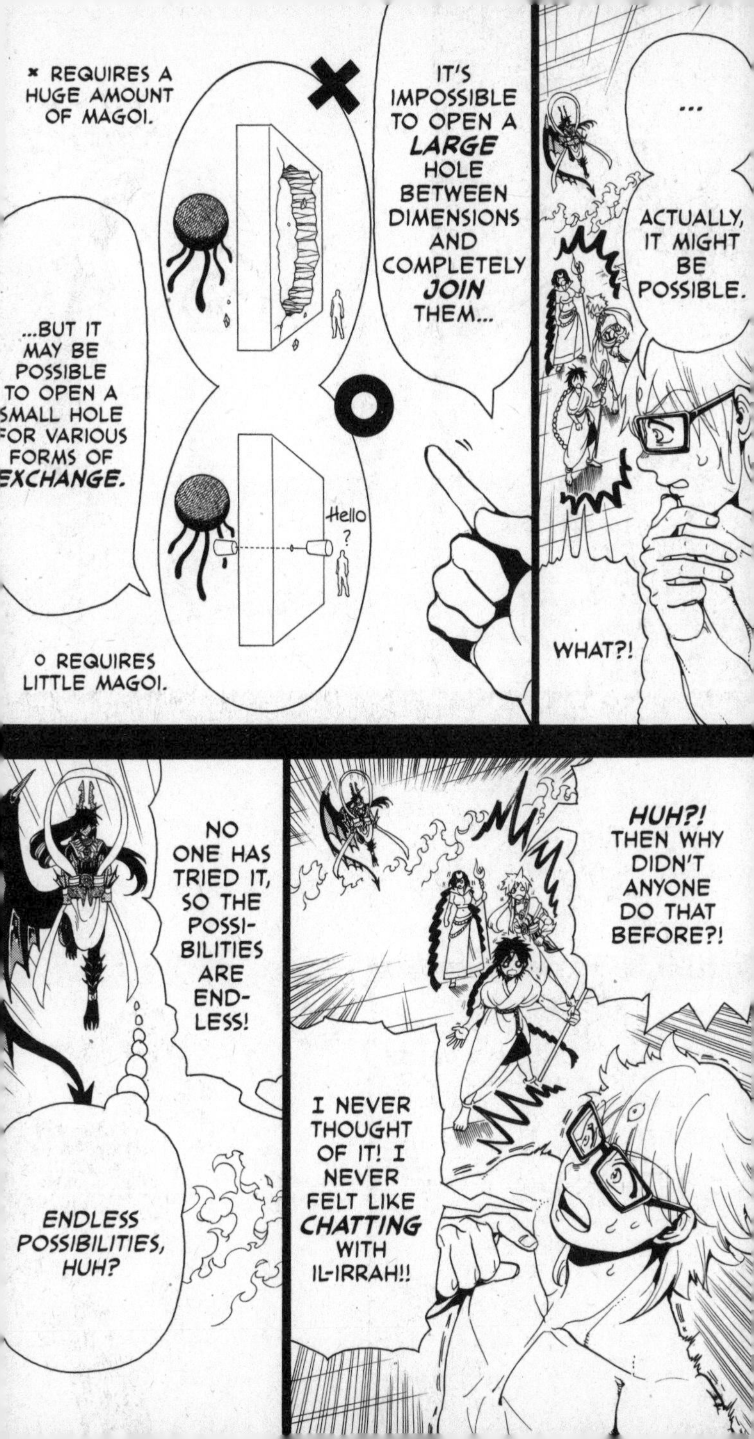
...
ACTUALLY, IT MIGHT BE POSSIBLE.
WHAT?!
IT'S IMPOSSIBLE TO OPEN A LARGE HOLE BETWEEN DIMENSIONS AND COMPLETELY JOIN THEM...
× REQUIRES A HUGE AMOUNT OF MAGOI.
...BUT IT MAY BE POSSIBLE TO OPEN A SMALL HOLE FOR VARIOUS FORMS OF EXCHANGE.
Hello?
○ REQUIRES LITTLE MAGOI.
HUH?! THEN WHY DIDN'T ANYONE DO THAT BEFORE?!
I NEVER THOUGHT OF IT! I NEVER FELT LIKE CHATTING WITH IL-IRRAH!!
NO ONE HAS TRIED IT, SO THE POSSIBILITIES ARE ENDLESS!
ENDLESS POSSIBILITIES, HUH?

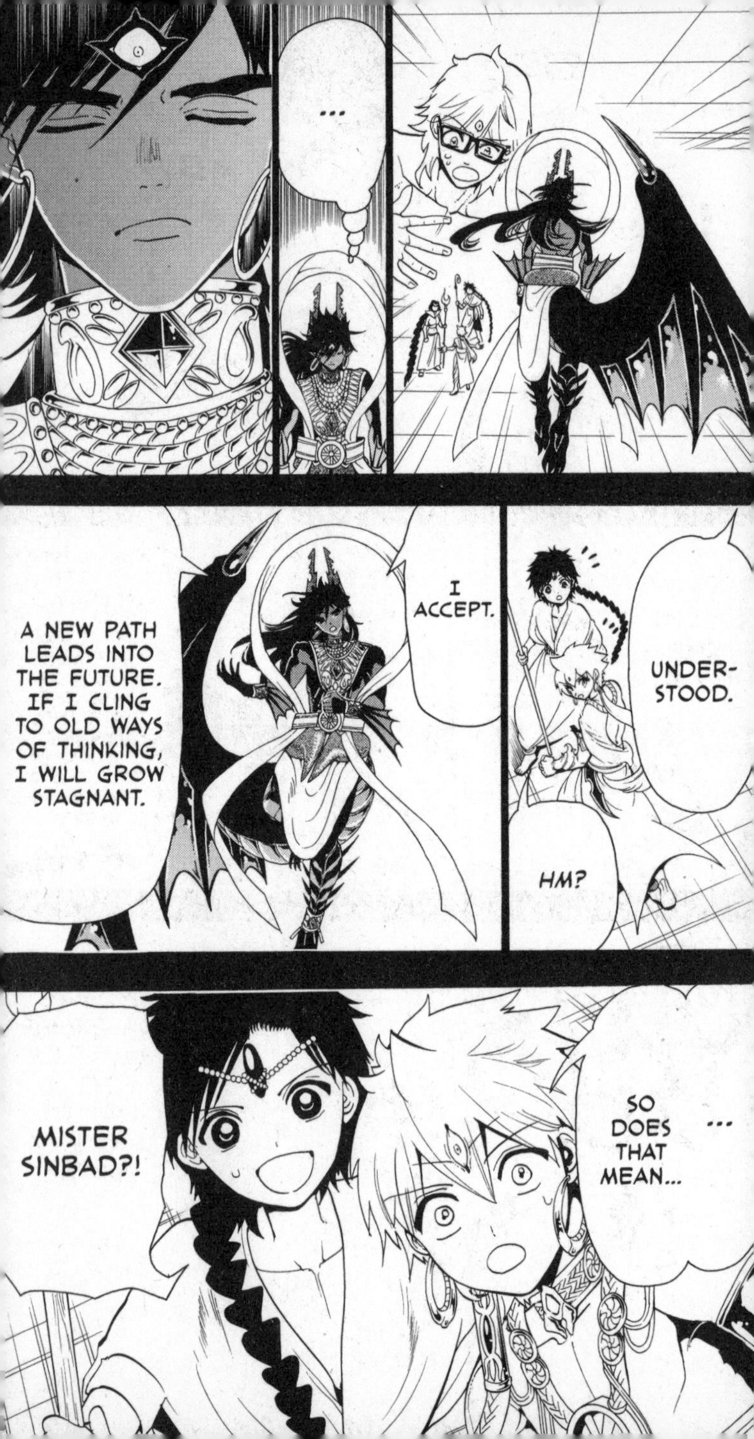
...
UNDER-STOOD.
HM?
I ACCEPT.
A NEW PATH LEADS INTO THE FUTURE. IF I CLING TO OLD WAYS OF THINKING, I WILL GROW STAGNANT.
...
SO DOES THAT MEAN...
MISTER SINBAD?!

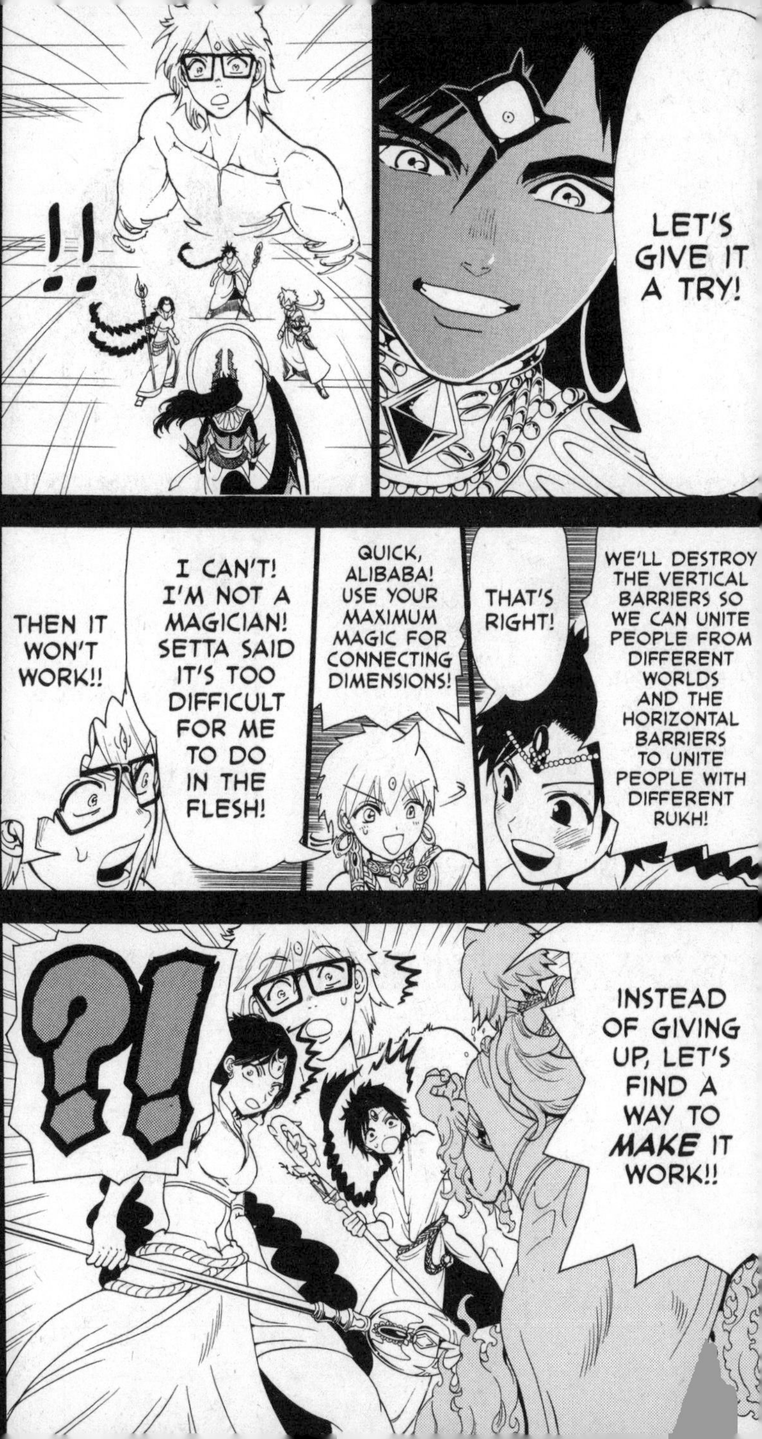
LET'S GIVE IT A TRY!
!!
WE'LL DESTROY THE VERTICAL BARRIERS SO WE CAN UNITE PEOPLE FROM DIFFERENT WORLDS AND THE HORIZONTAL BARRIERS TO UNITE PEOPLE WITH DIFFERENT RUKH!
THAT'S RIGHT!
QUICK, ALIBABA! USE YOUR MAXIMUM MAGIC FOR CONNECTING DIMENSIONS!
I CAN'T! I'M NOT A MAGICIAN! SETTA SAID IT'S TOO DIFFICULT FOR ME TO DO IN THE FLESH!
THEN IT WON'T WORK!!
INSTEAD OF GIVING UP, LET'S FIND A WAY TO *MAKE* IT WORK!!
?!

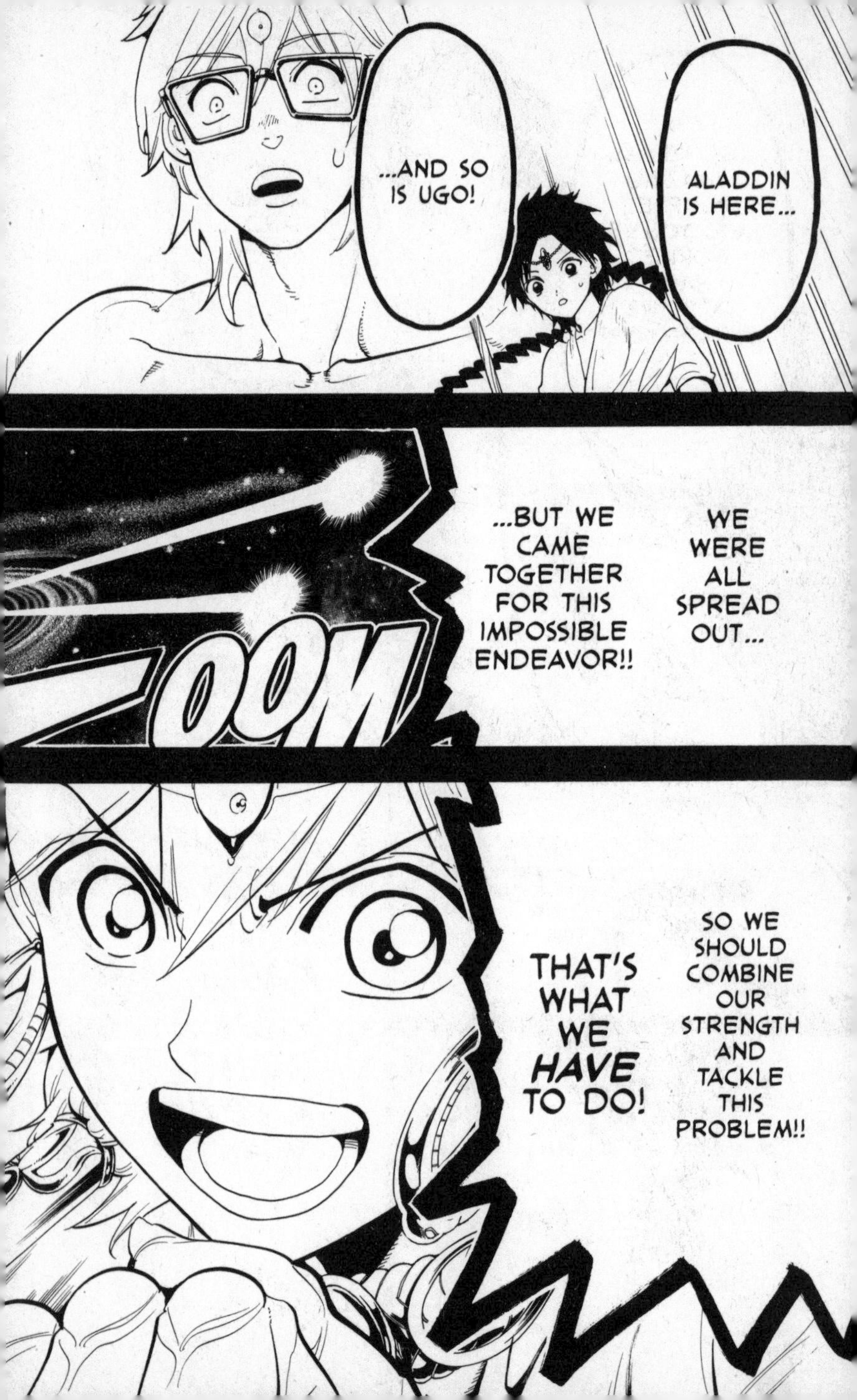
ALADDIN IS HERE...
...AND SO IS UGO!
WE WERE ALL SPREAD OUT...
...BUT WE CAME TOGETHER FOR THIS IMPOSSIBLE ENDEAVOR!!
ZOOM
SO WE SHOULD COMBINE OUR STRENGTH AND TACKLE THIS PROBLEM!!
THAT'S WHAT WE *HAVE* TO DO!

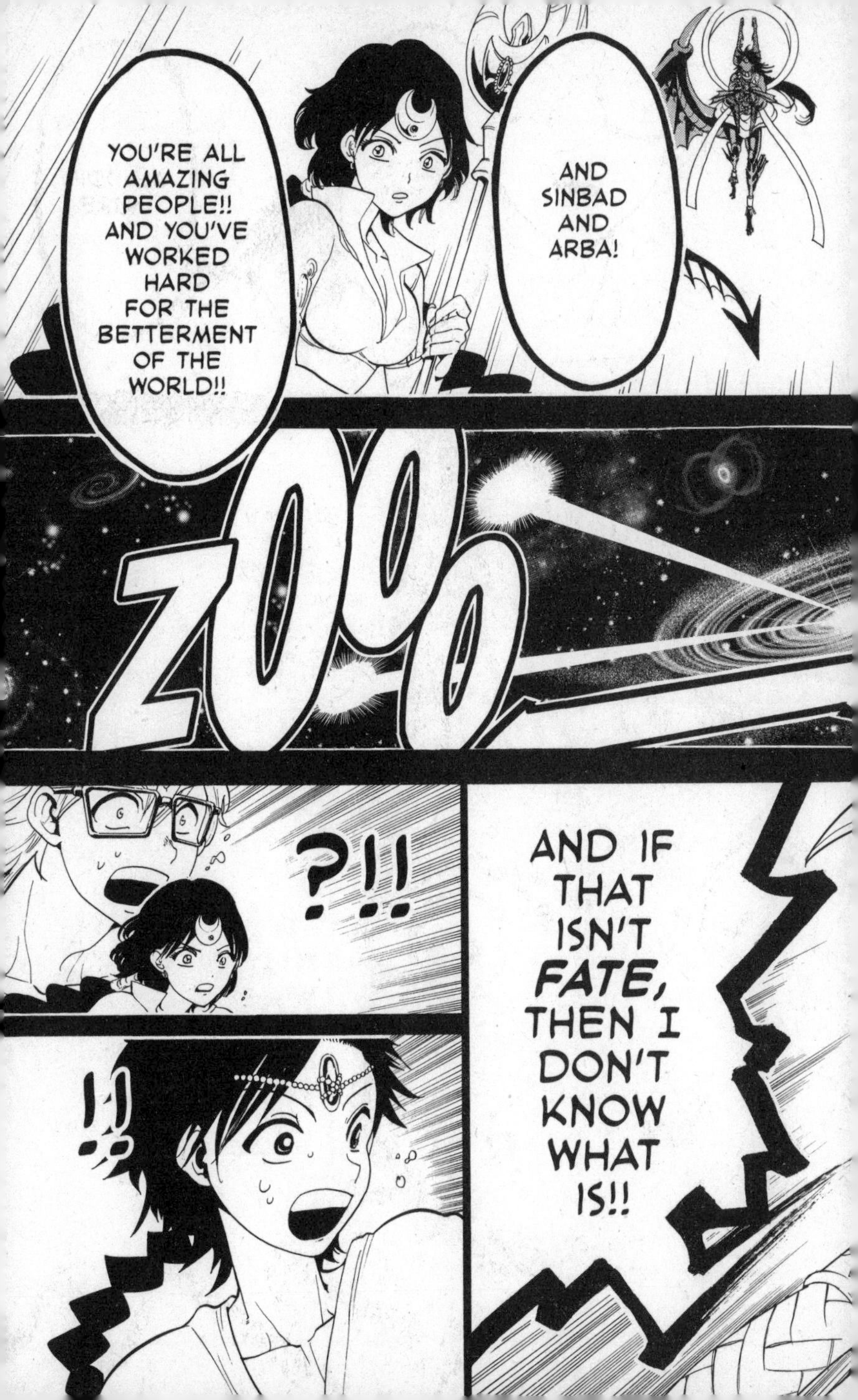
AND SINBAD AND ARBA!
YOU'RE ALL AMAZING PEOPLE!! AND YOU'VE WORKED HARD FOR THE BETTERMENT OF THE WORLD!!
ZOOO
AND IF THAT ISN'T *FATE*, THEN I DON'T KNOW WHAT IS!!
?!!
!!

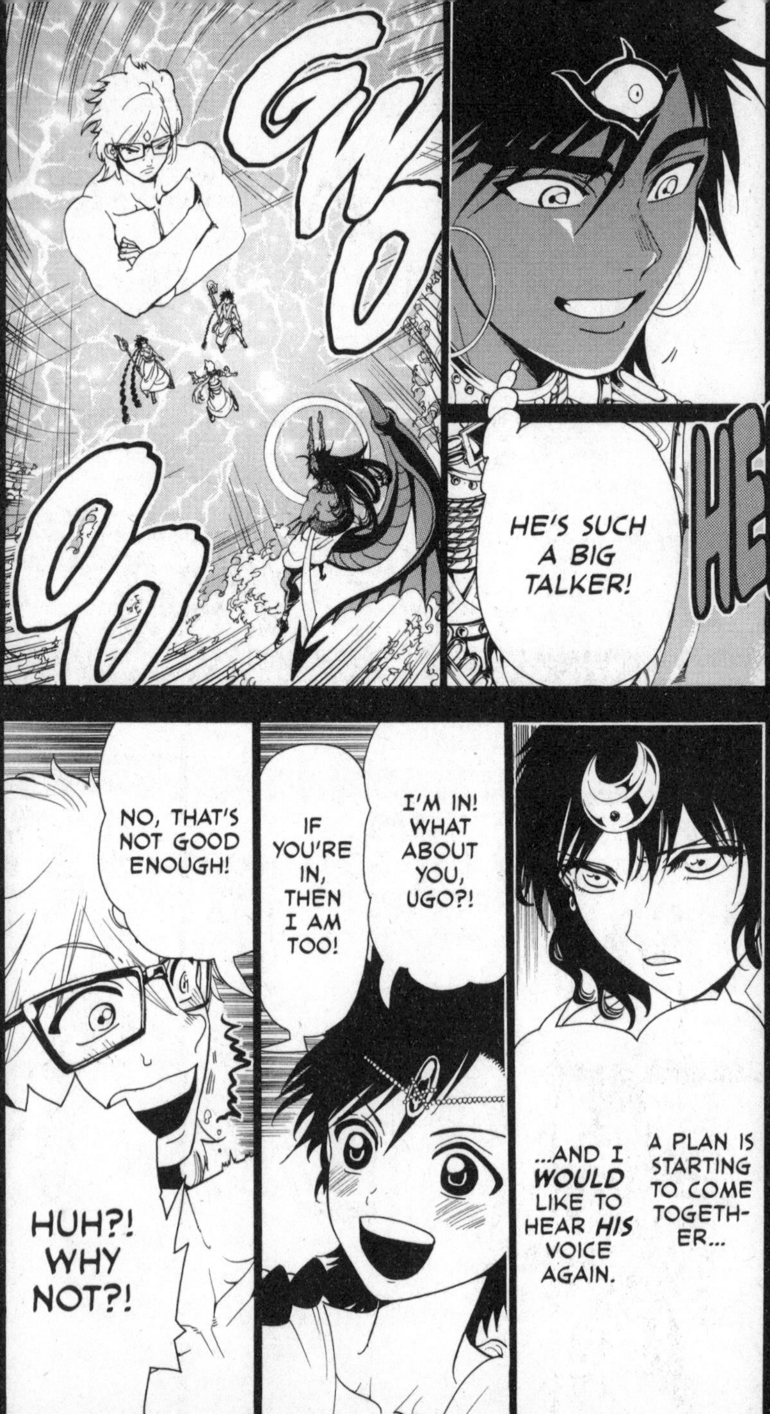
HE'S SUCH A BIG TALKER!
HEH
GWOOOO
A PLAN IS STARTING TO COME TOGETH-ER...
...AND I *WOULD* LIKE TO HEAR *HIS* VOICE AGAIN.
I'M IN! WHAT ABOUT YOU, UGO?!
IF YOU'RE IN, THEN I AM TOO!
NO, THAT'S NOT GOOD ENOUGH!
HUH?! WHY NOT?!

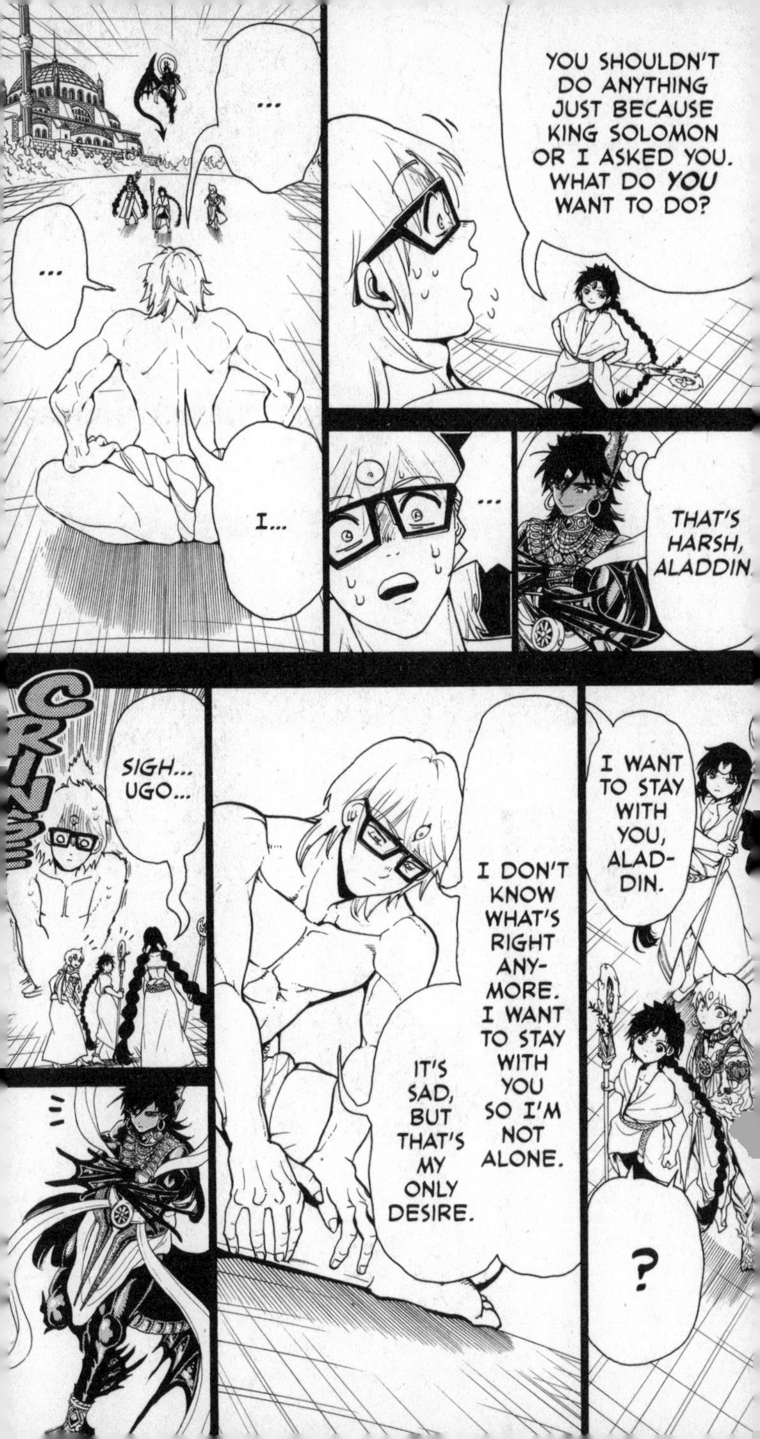
YOU SHOULDN'T DO ANYTHING JUST BECAUSE KING SOLOMON OR I ASKED YOU. WHAT DO *YOU* WANT TO DO?
THAT'S HARSH, ALADDIN.
...
...
...
I...
I WANT TO STAY WITH YOU, ALAD-DIN.
?
I DON'T KNOW WHAT'S RIGHT ANY-MORE. I WANT TO STAY WITH YOU SO I'M NOT ALONE.
IT'S SAD, BUT THAT'S MY ONLY DESIRE.
SIGH... UGO...

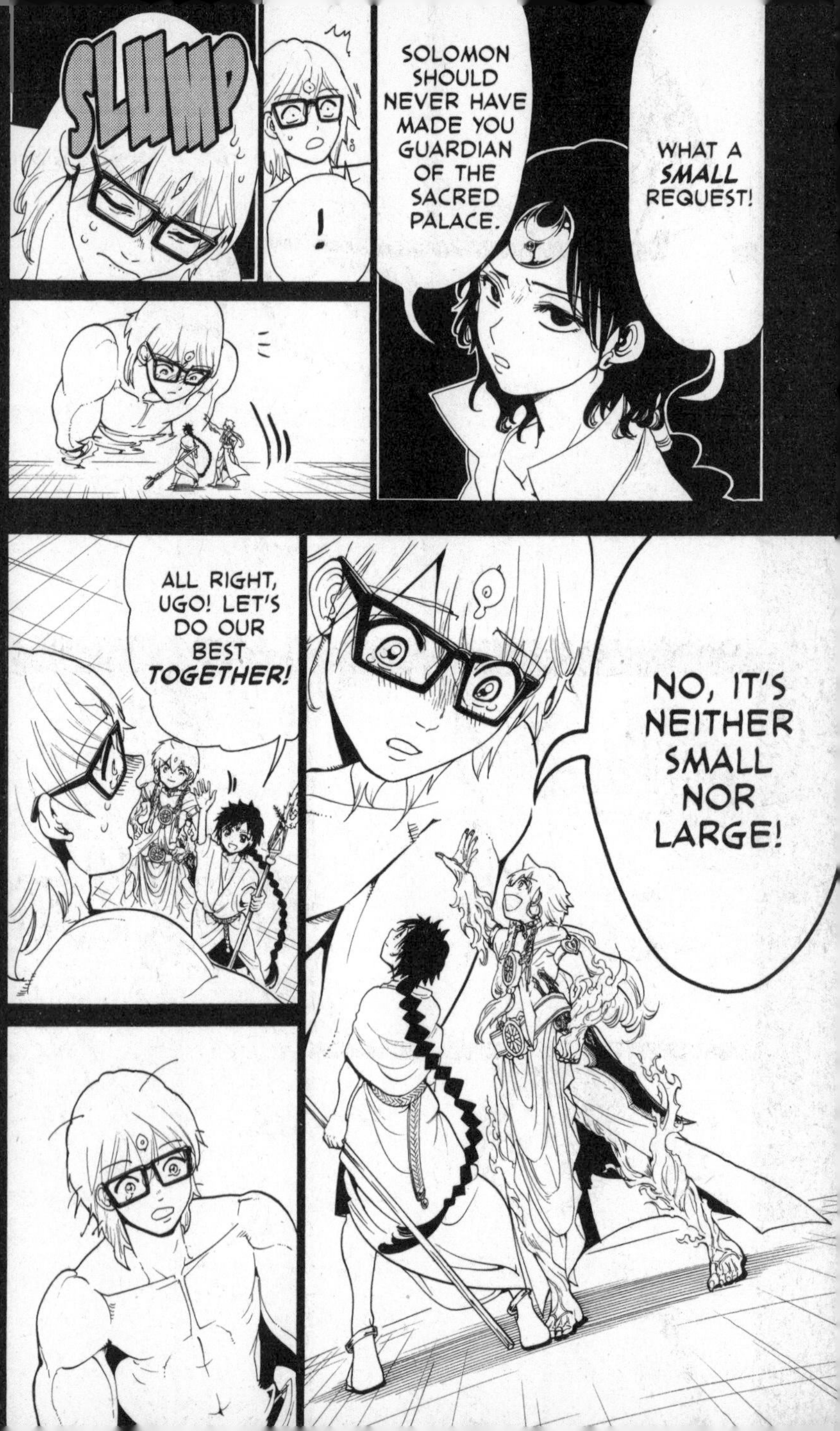
WHAT A SMALL REQUEST!
SOLOMON SHOULD NEVER HAVE MADE YOU GUARDIAN OF THE SACRED PALACE.
!
SLUMP
NO, IT'S NEITHER SMALL NOR LARGE!
ALL RIGHT, UGO! LET'S DO OUR BEST TOGETHER!

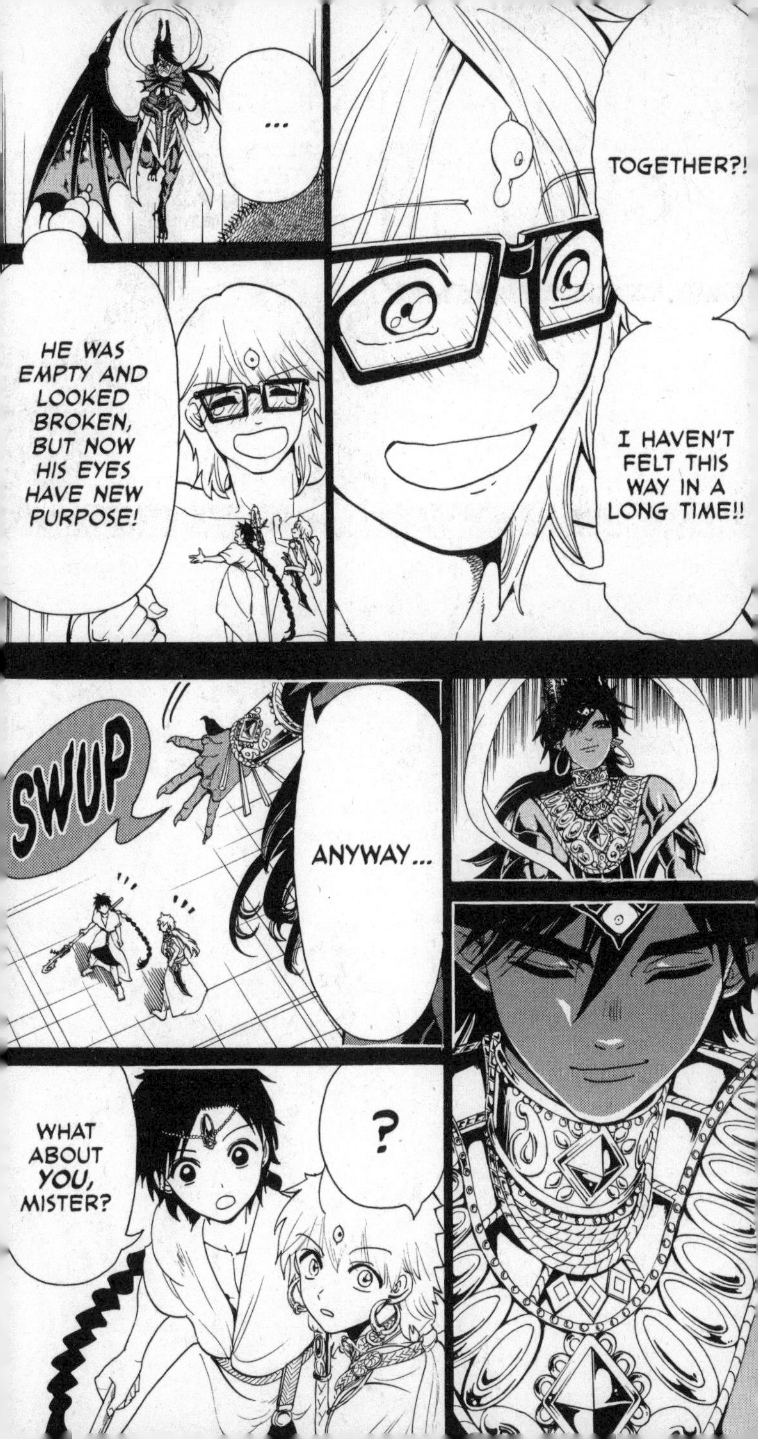
TOGETHER?!
I HAVEN'T FELT THIS WAY IN A LONG TIME!!
...
HE WAS EMPTY AND LOOKED BROKEN, BUT NOW HIS EYES HAVE NEW PURPOSE!
ANYWAY...
SWUP
?
WHAT ABOUT YOU, MISTER?

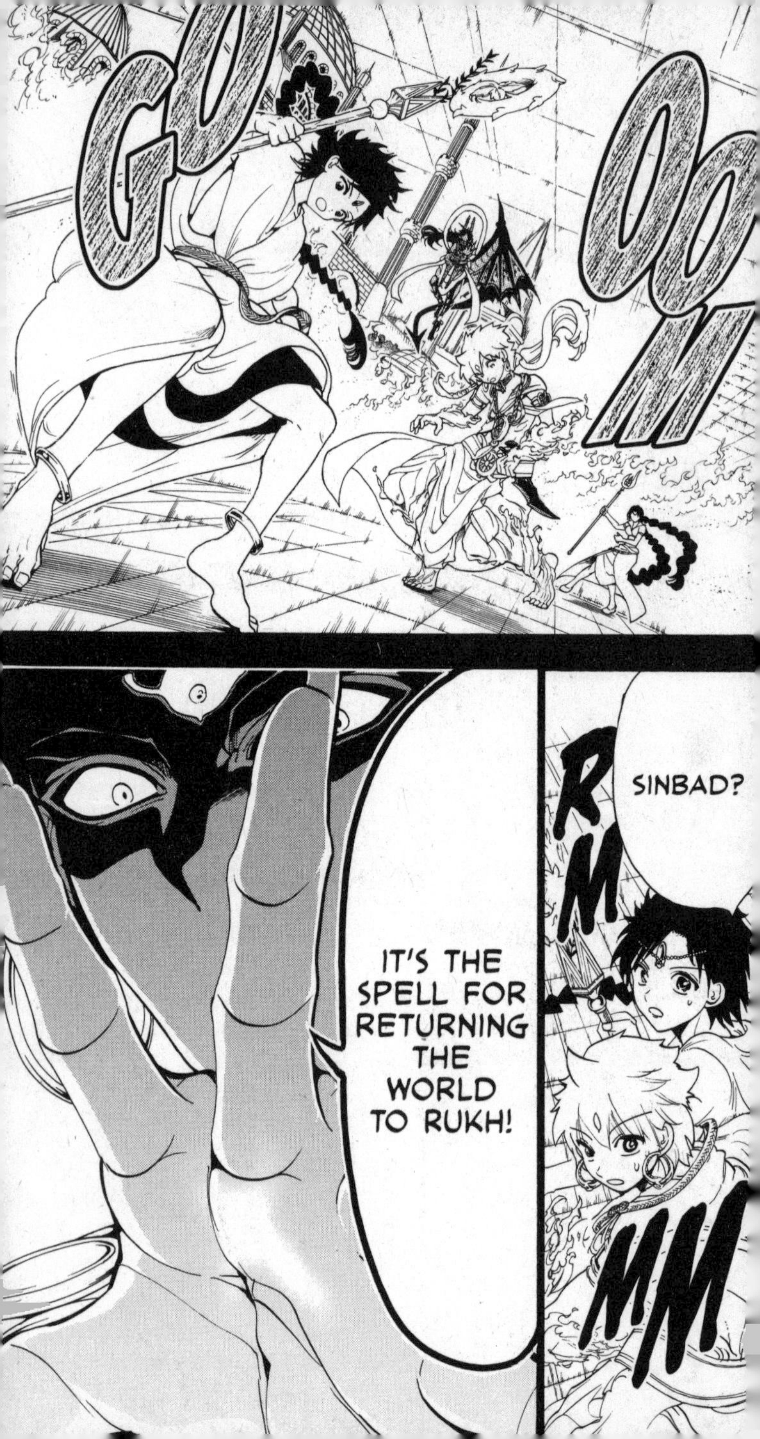
GOOON
RMMMM
SINBAD?
IT'S THE SPELL FOR RETURNING THE WORLD TO RUKH!

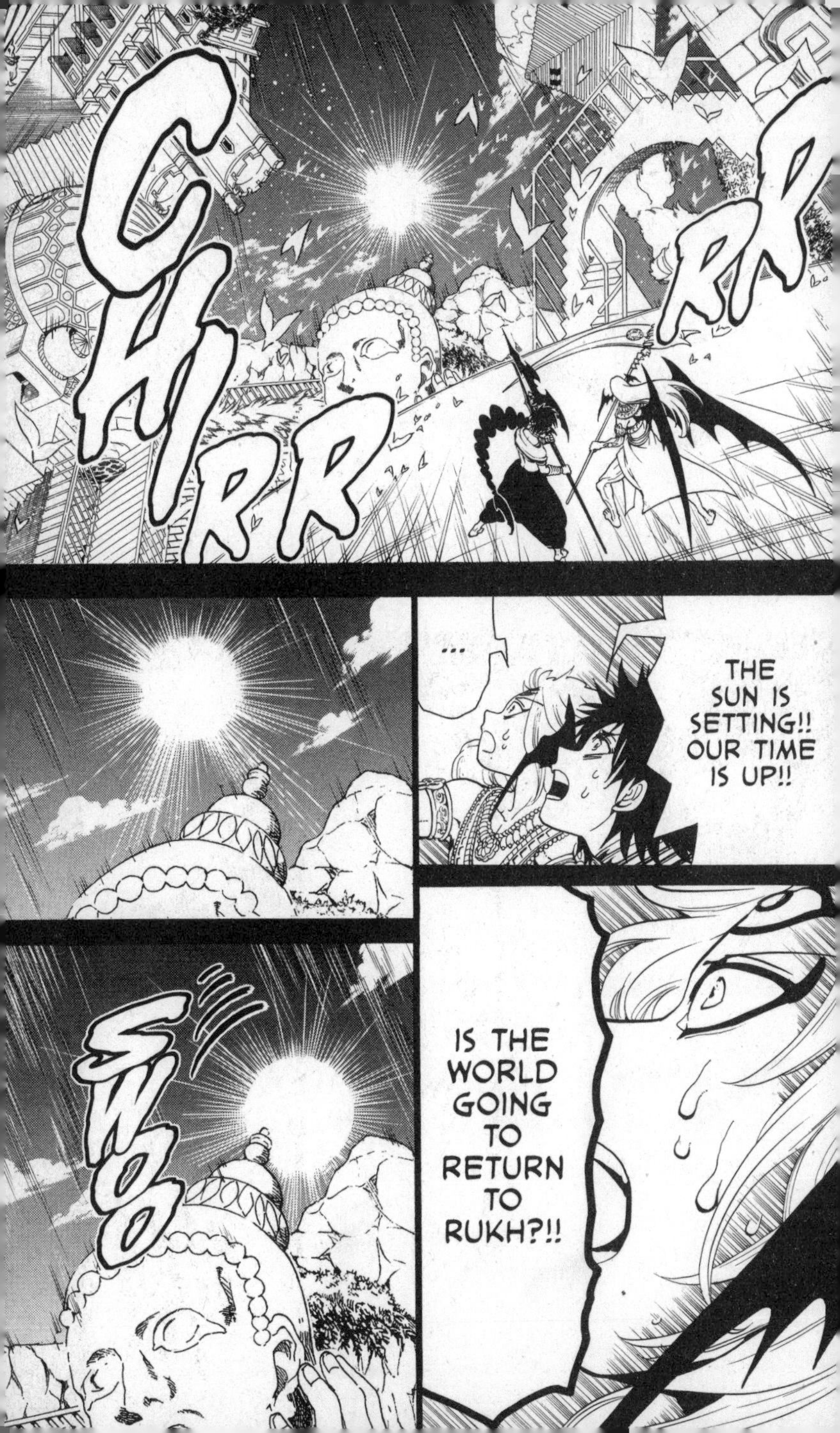
CHIRR
...
THE SUN IS SETTING!! OUR TIME IS UP!!
IS THE WORLD GOING TO RETURN TO RUKH?!!
SWOO

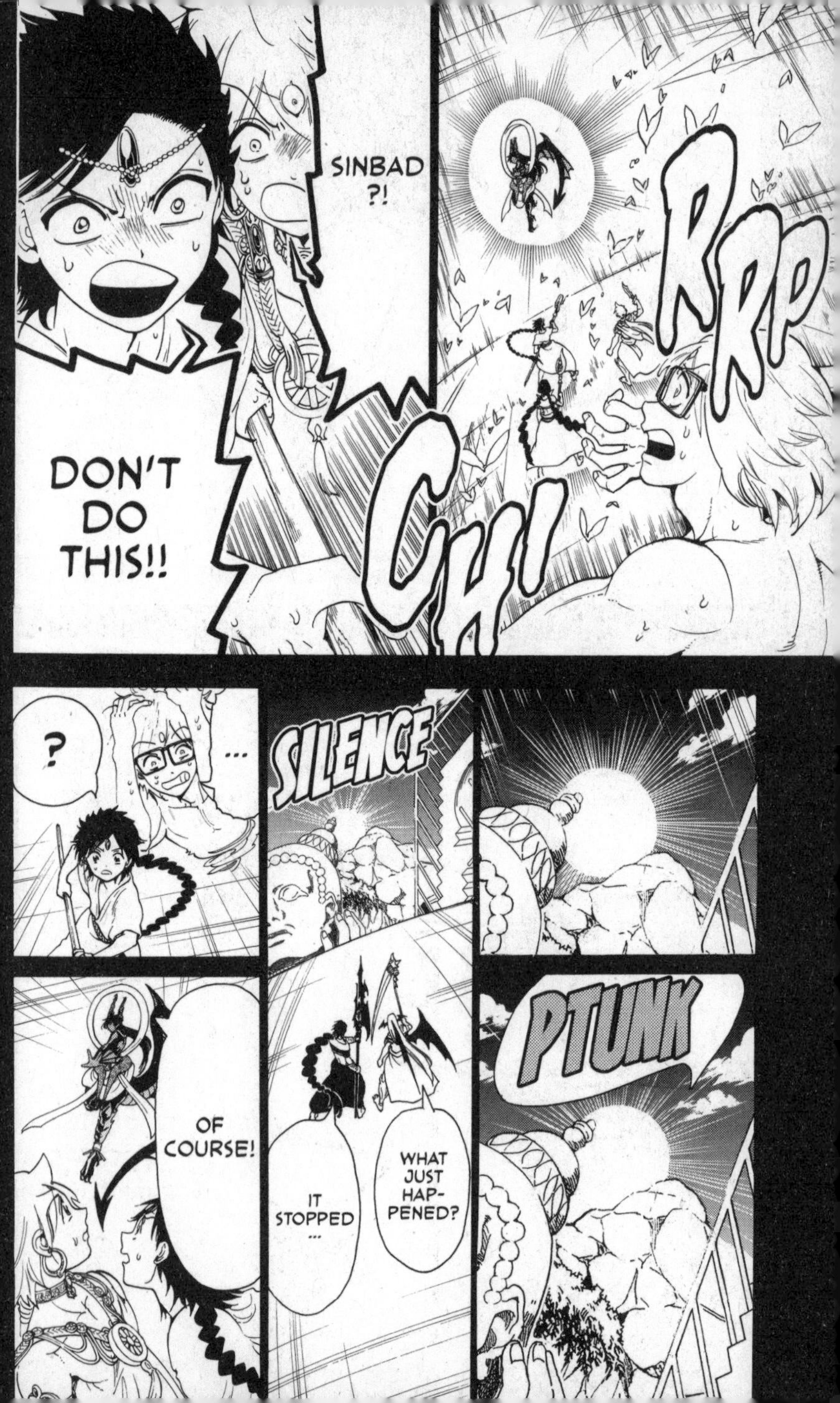
CHI
RRP
SINBAD?!
DON'T DO THIS!!
SILENCE
?
...
PTUNK
WHAT JUST HAP-PENED?
IT STOPPED...
OF COURSE!

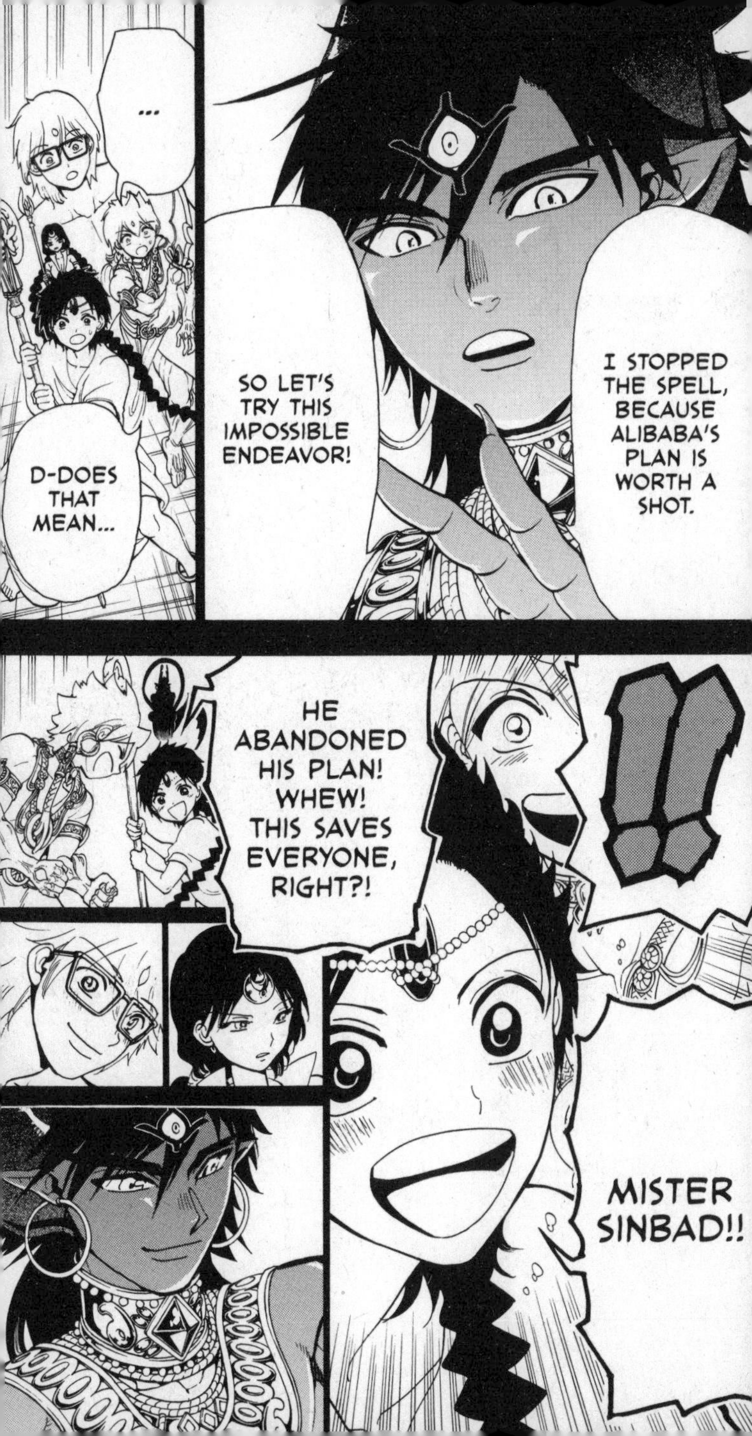
I STOPPED THE SPELL, BECAUSE ALIBABA'S PLAN IS WORTH A SHOT.
SO LET'S TRY THIS IMPOSSIBLE ENDEAVOR!
...
D-DOES THAT MEAN...
!!
HE ABANDONED HIS PLAN! WHEW! THIS SAVES EVERYONE, RIGHT?!
MISTER SINBAD!!

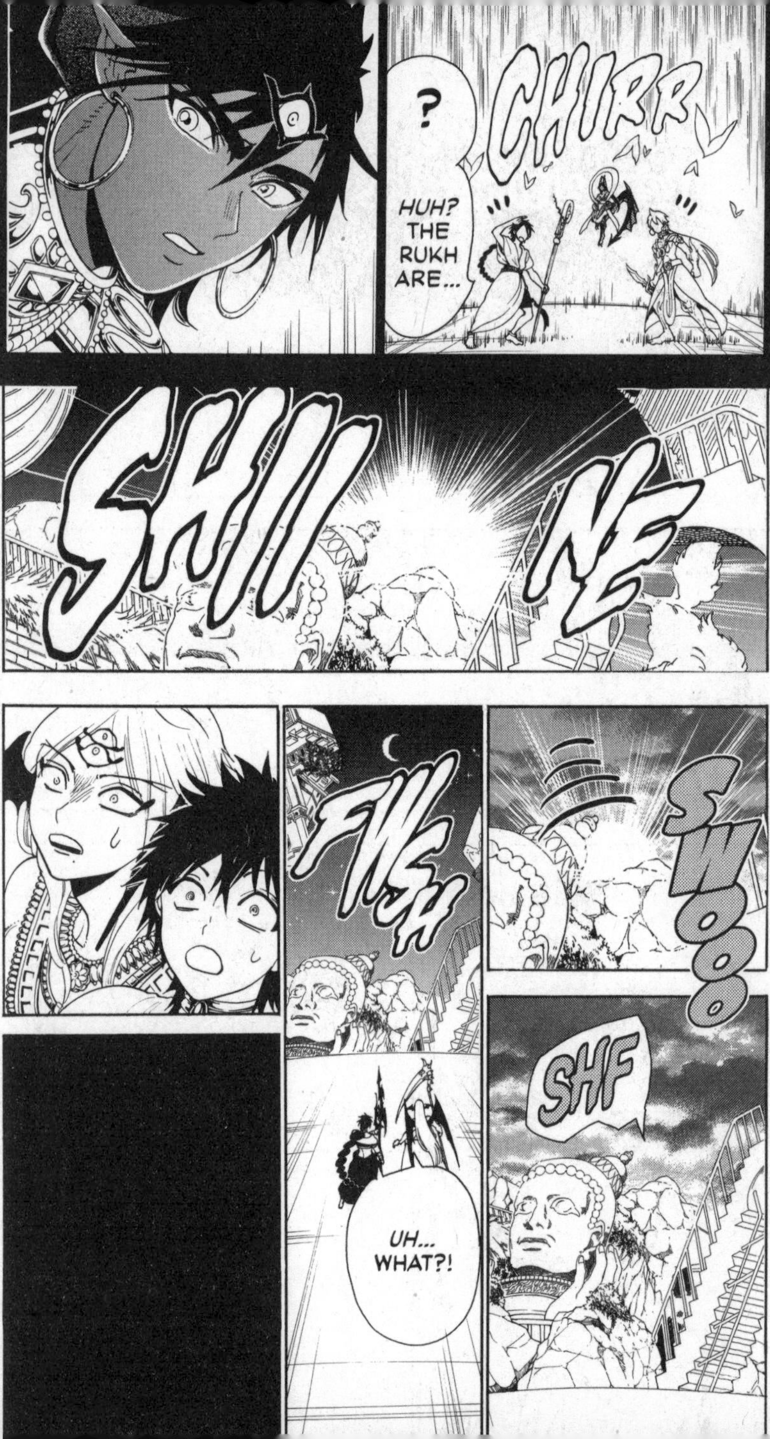

?
CHIRR
HUH? THE RUKH ARE...
SHIINE
SWOOOO
SHF
FWSH
UH... WHAT?!

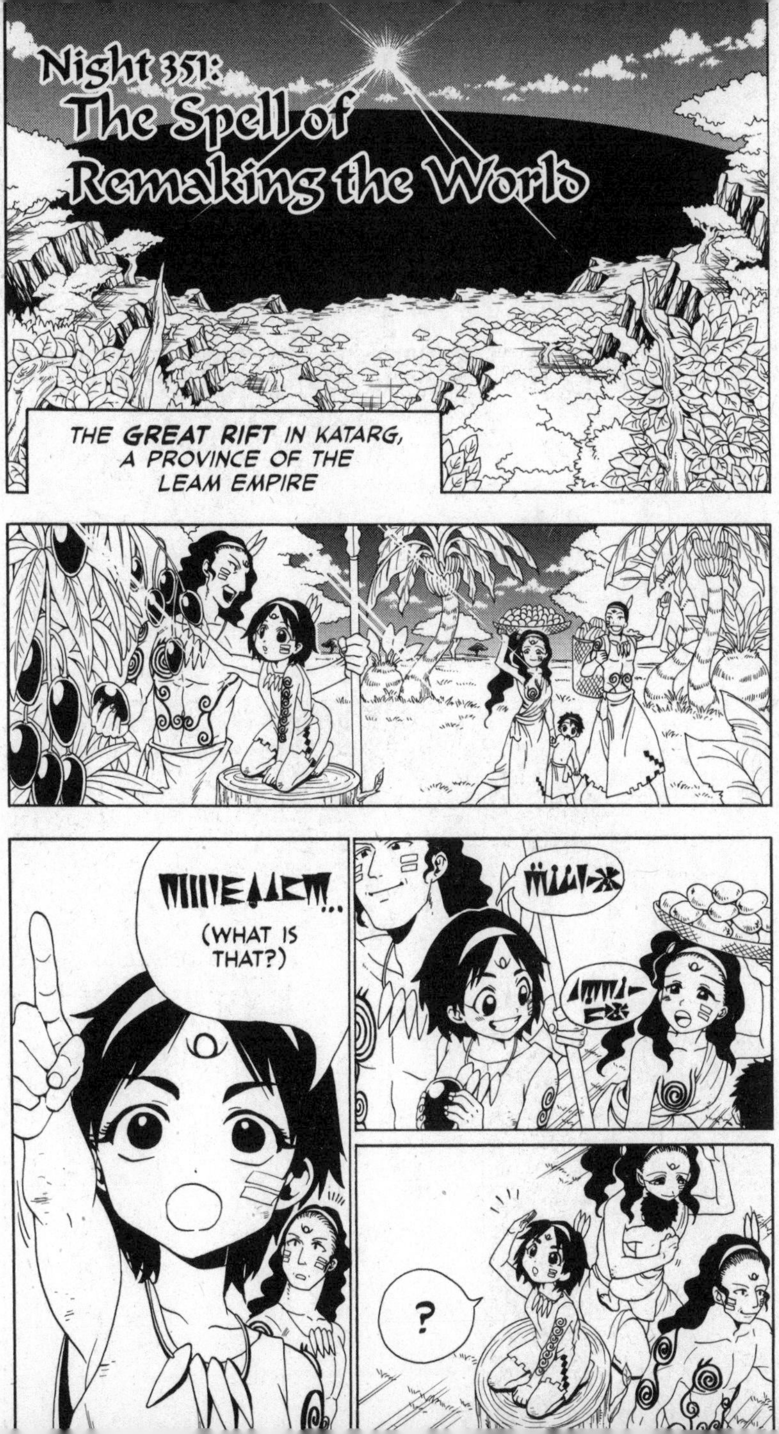
Night 351: The Spell of Remaking the World
THE GREAT RIFT IN KATARG, A PROVINCE OF THE LEAM EMPIRE
?
(WHAT IS THAT?)

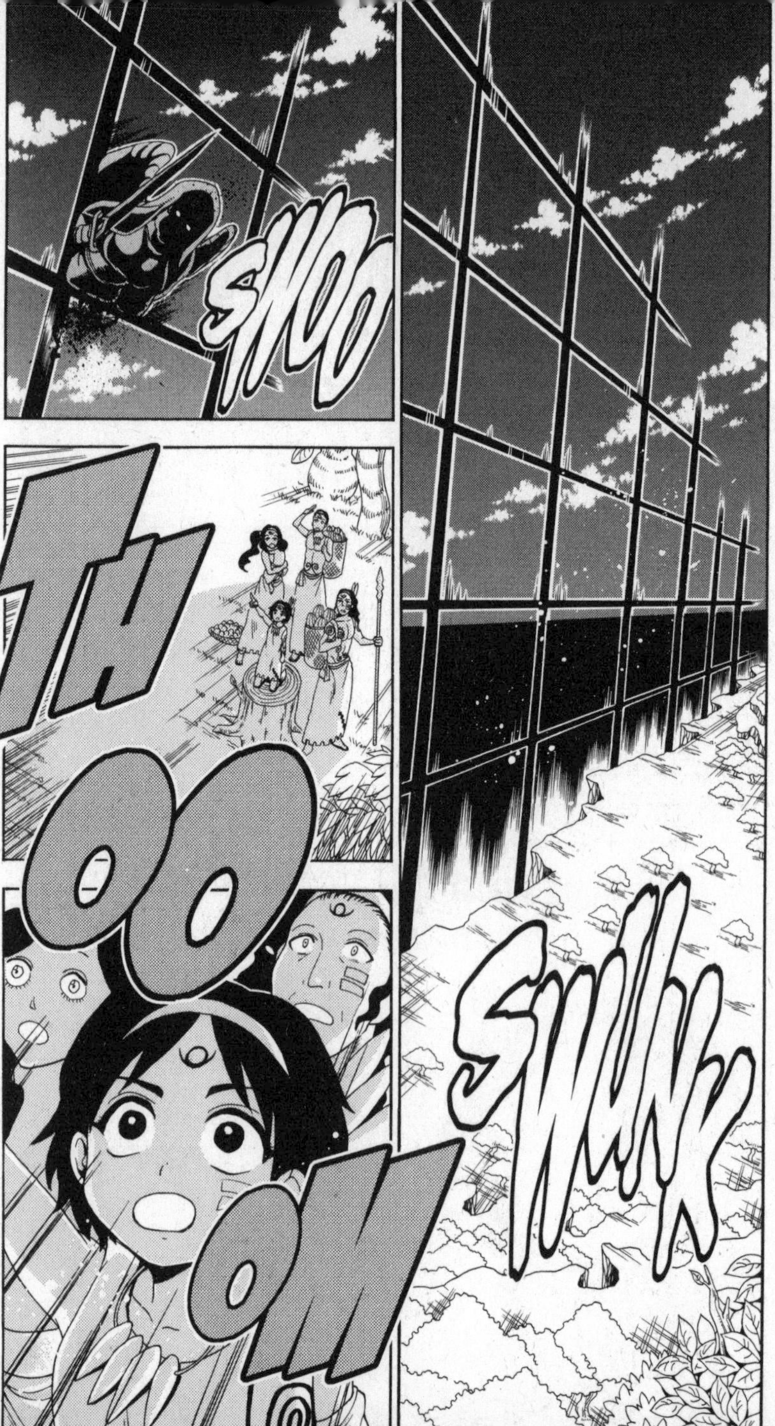
SHUNK
SHOO
THOOOM

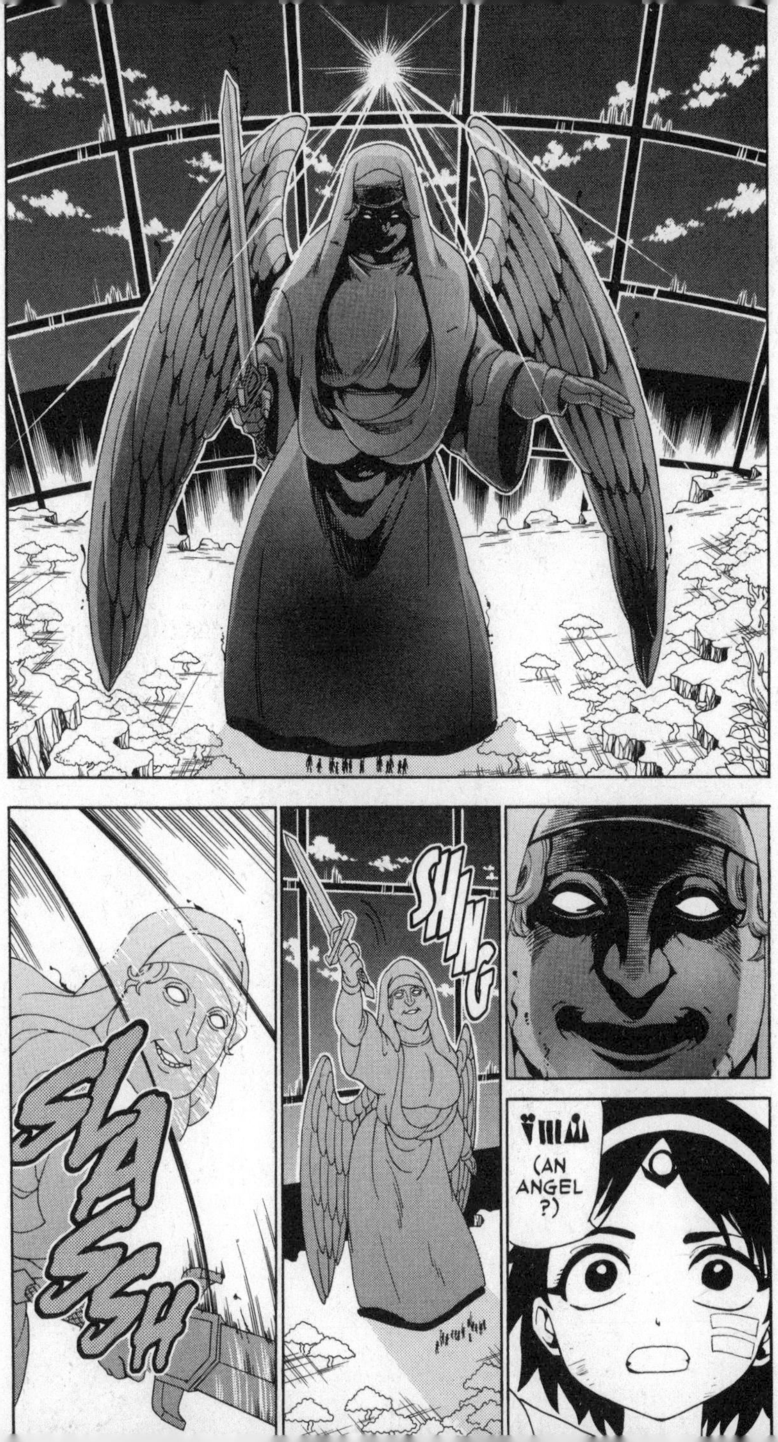
(AN ANGEL ?)
SHING
SLASSH

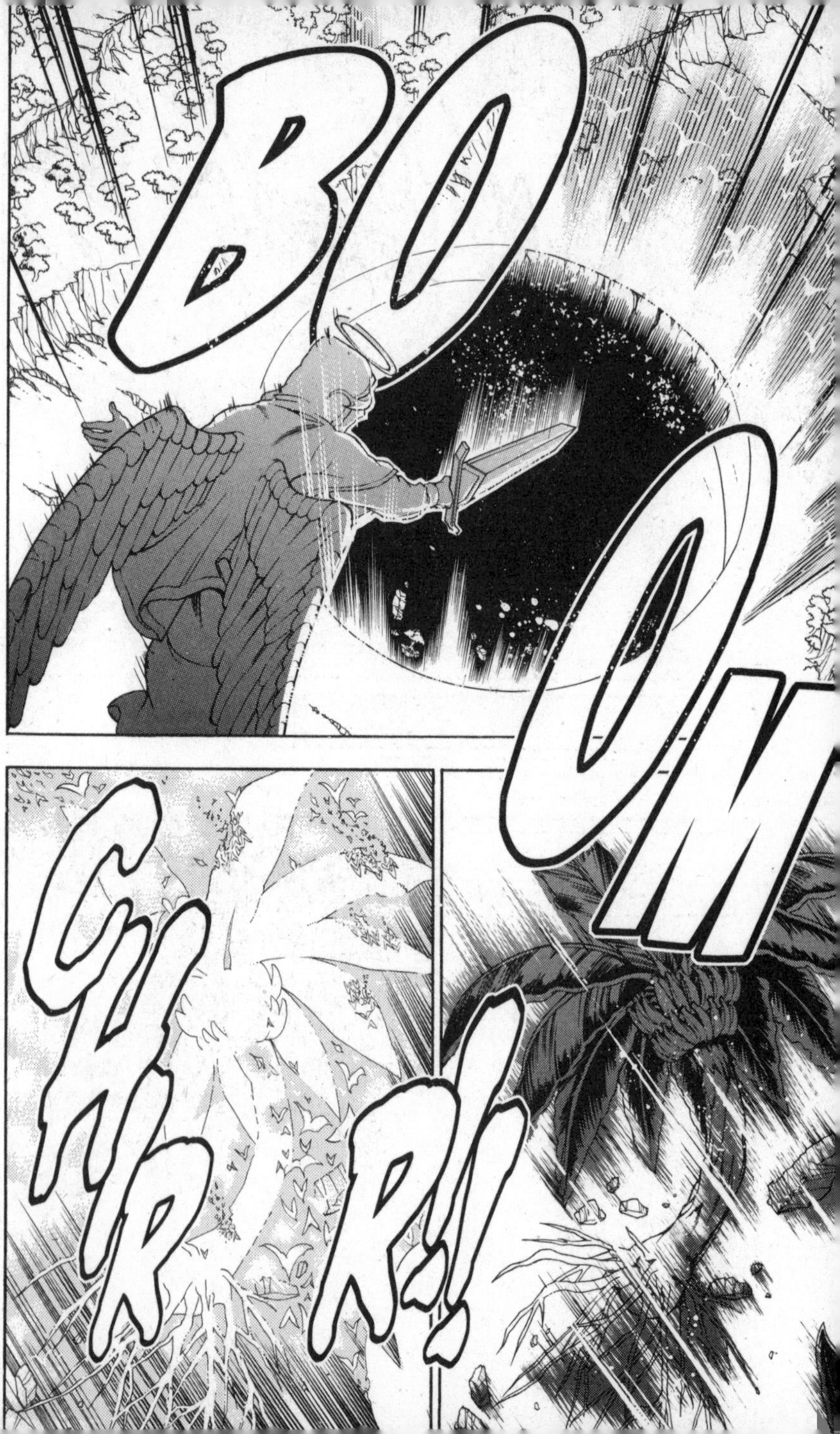
BOOM
GHRR!!

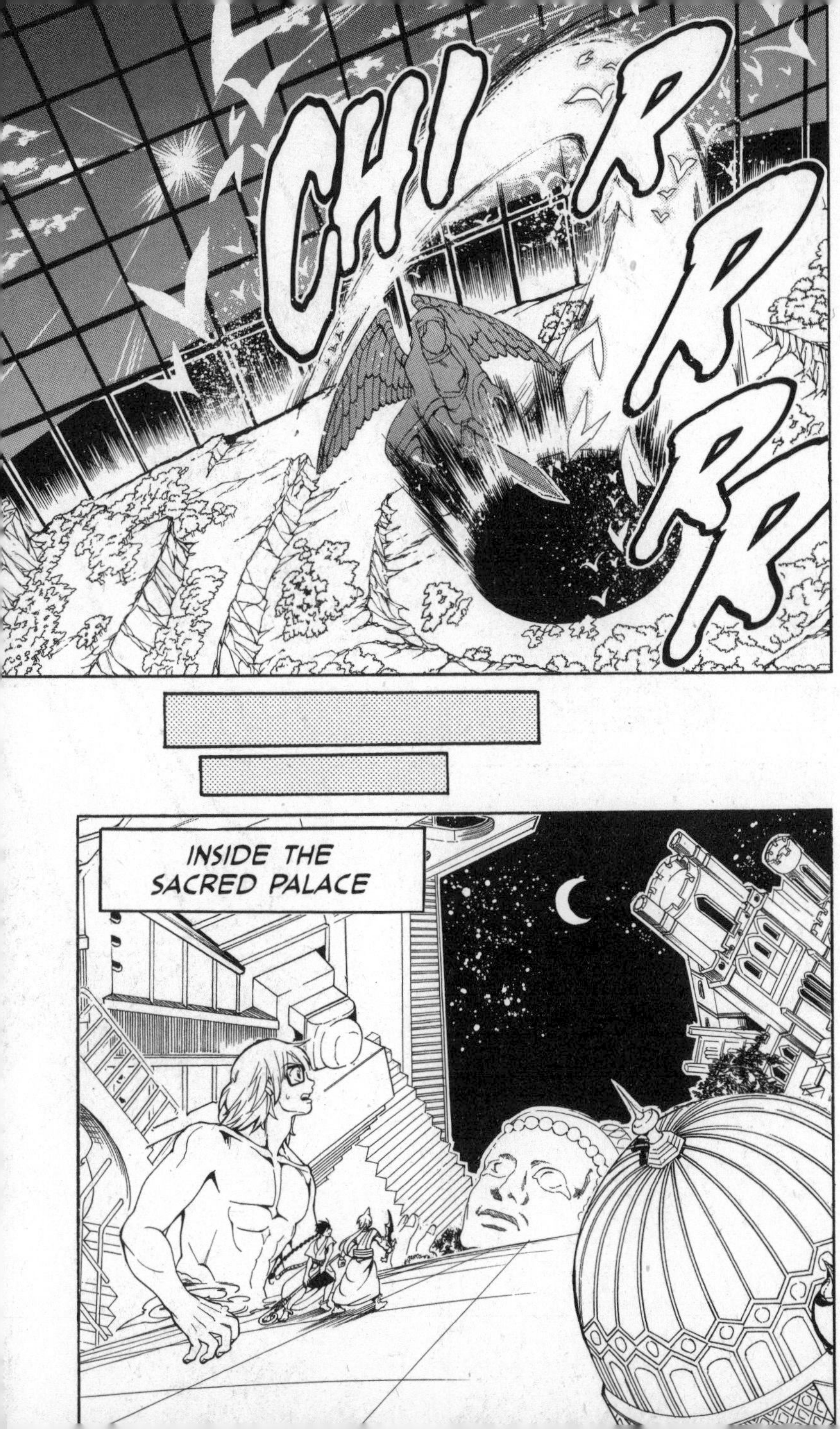
CHIRRRR
INSIDE THE SACRED PALACE

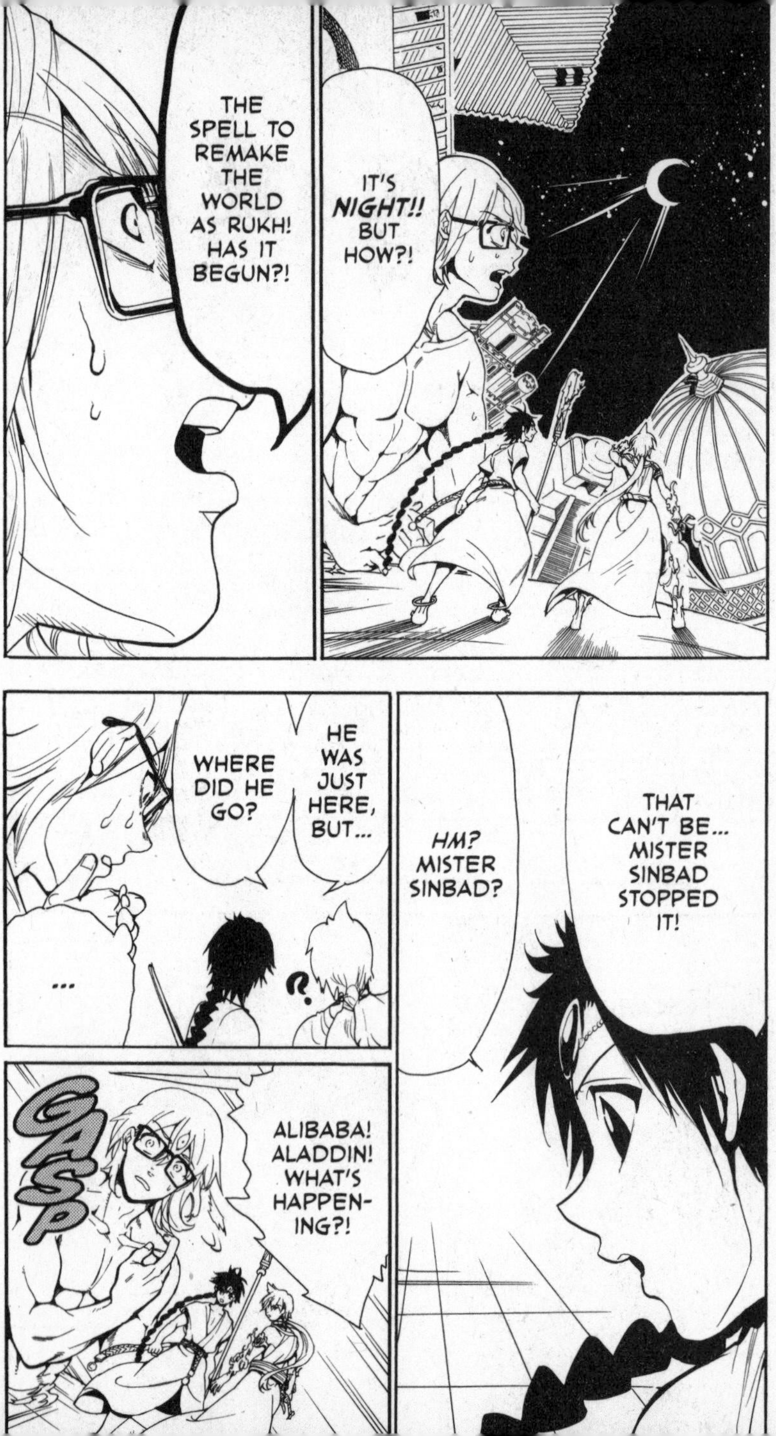
IT'S NIGHT!! BUT HOW?!
THE SPELL TO REMAKE THE WORLD AS RUKH! HAS IT BEGUN?!
THAT CAN'T BE... MISTER SINBAD STOPPED IT!
HM? MISTER SINBAD?
HE WAS JUST HERE, BUT...
WHERE DID HE GO?
...
?
ALIBABA! ALADDIN! WHAT'S HAPPEN-ING?!
GASP

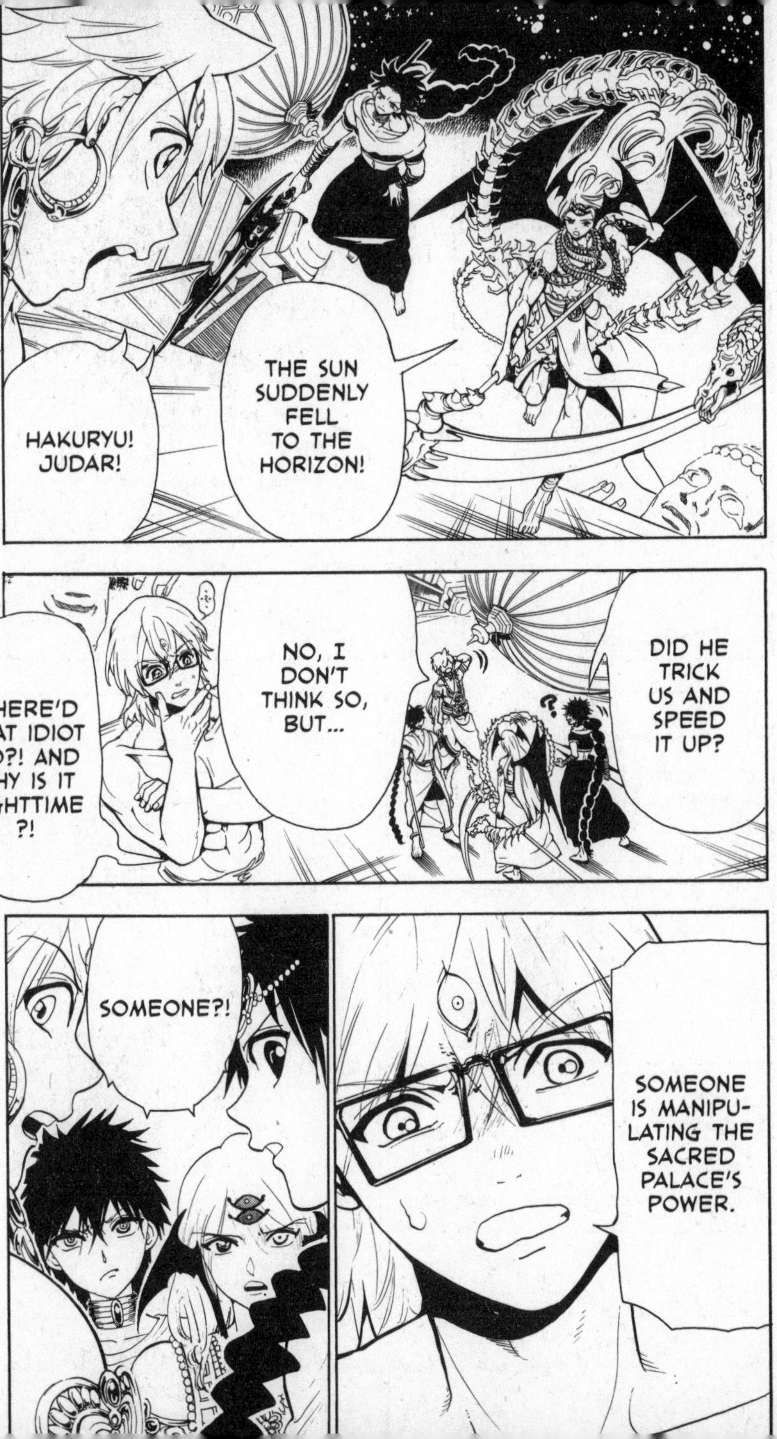
THE SUN SUDDENLY FELL TO THE HORIZON!
HAKURYU! JUDAR!
DID HE TRICK US AND SPEED IT UP?
NO, I DON'T THINK SO, BUT...
WHERE'D THAT IDIOT GO?! AND WHY IS IT NIGHTTIME?!
SOMEONE IS MANIPULATING THE SACRED PALACE'S POWER.
SOMEONE?!

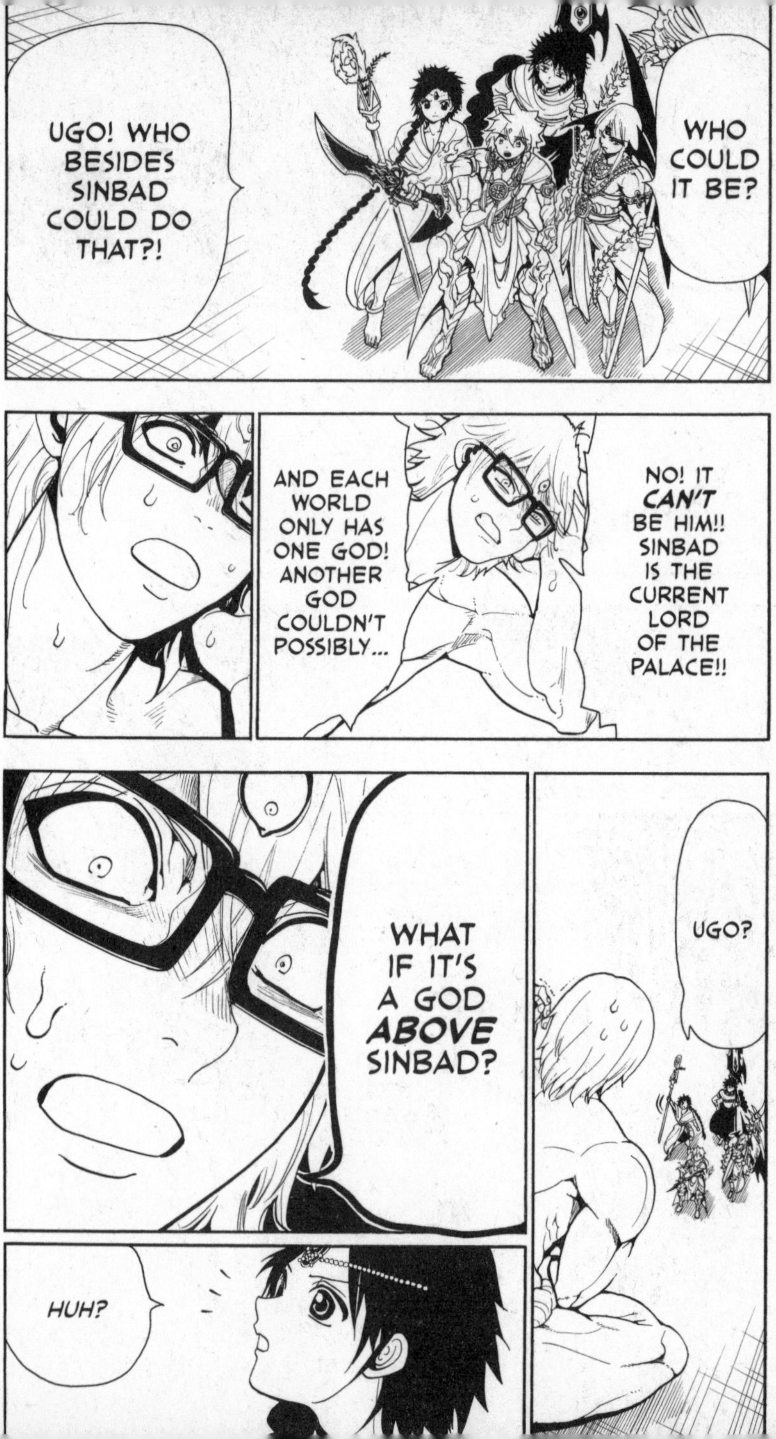
WHO COULD IT BE?
UGO! WHO BESIDES SINBAD COULD DO THAT?!
NO! IT *CAN'T* BE HIM!! SINBAD IS THE CURRENT LORD OF THE PALACE!!
AND EACH WORLD ONLY HAS ONE GOD! ANOTHER GOD COULDN'T POSSIBLY...
UGO?
WHAT IF IT'S A GOD *ABOVE* SINBAD?
HUH?

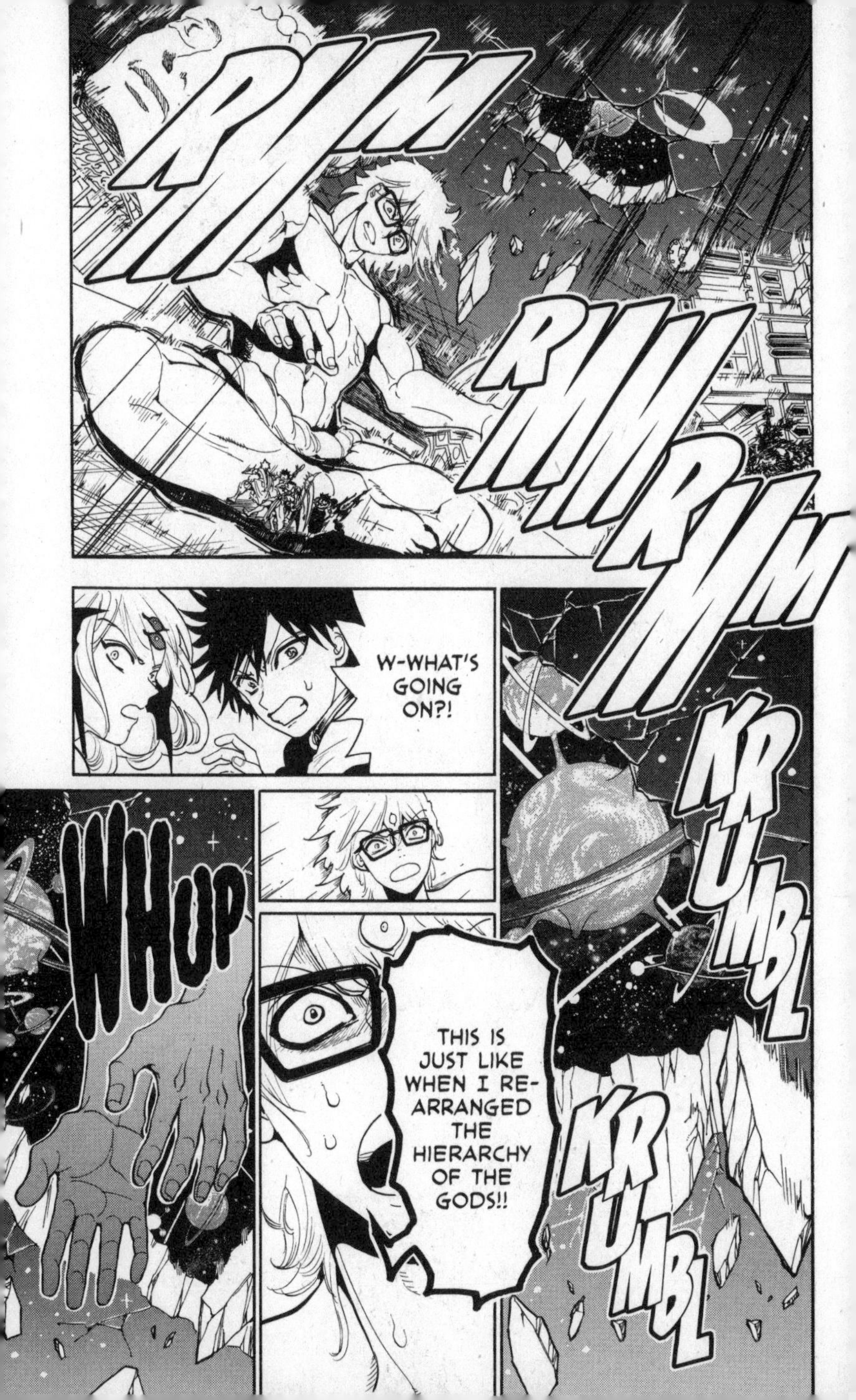
RMM
RMMRMM
KRUMBL
W-WHAT'S GOING ON?!
KRUMBL
THIS IS JUST LIKE WHEN I RE-ARRANGED THE HIERARCHY OF THE GODS!!
WHUP

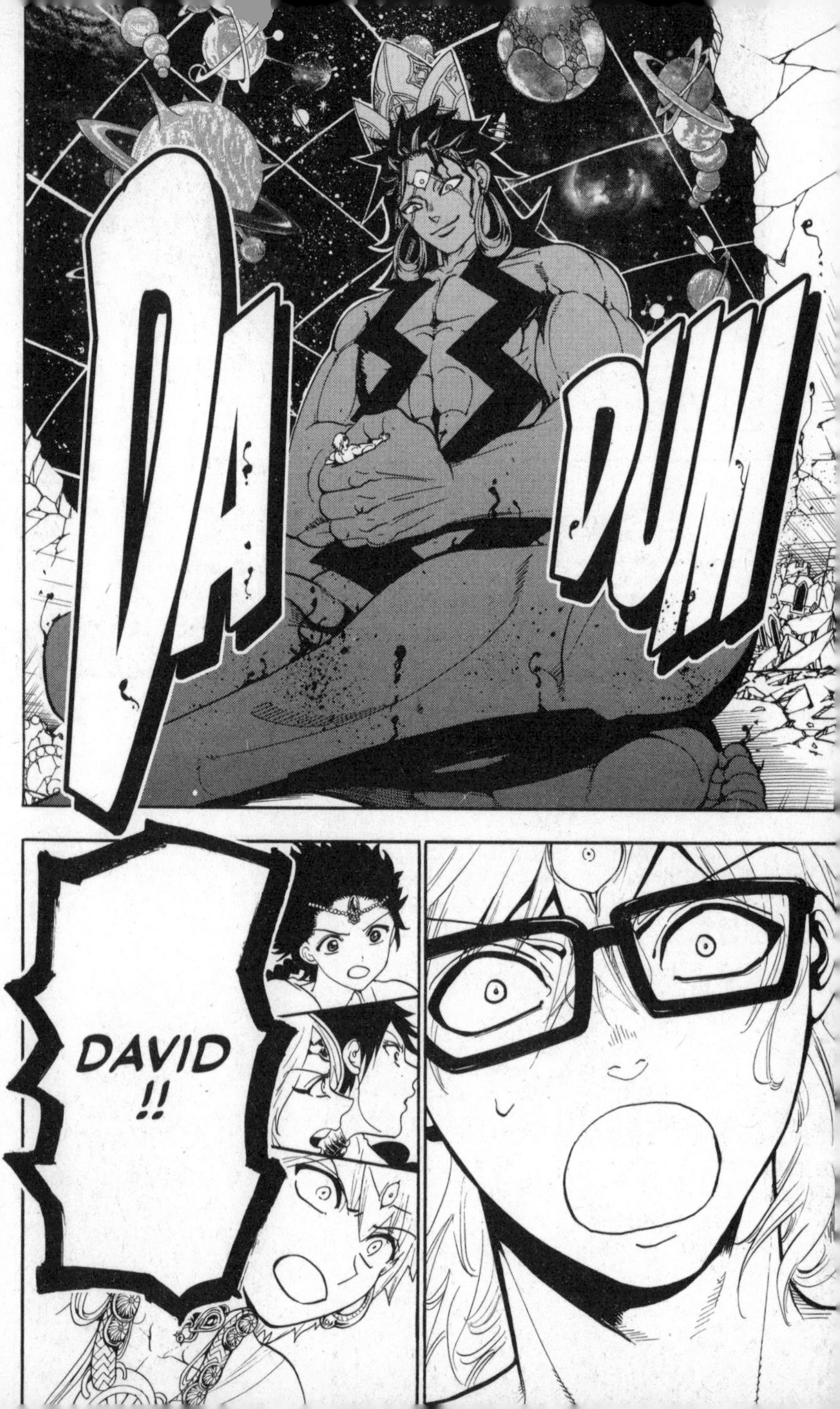
DA DUM
DAVID !!

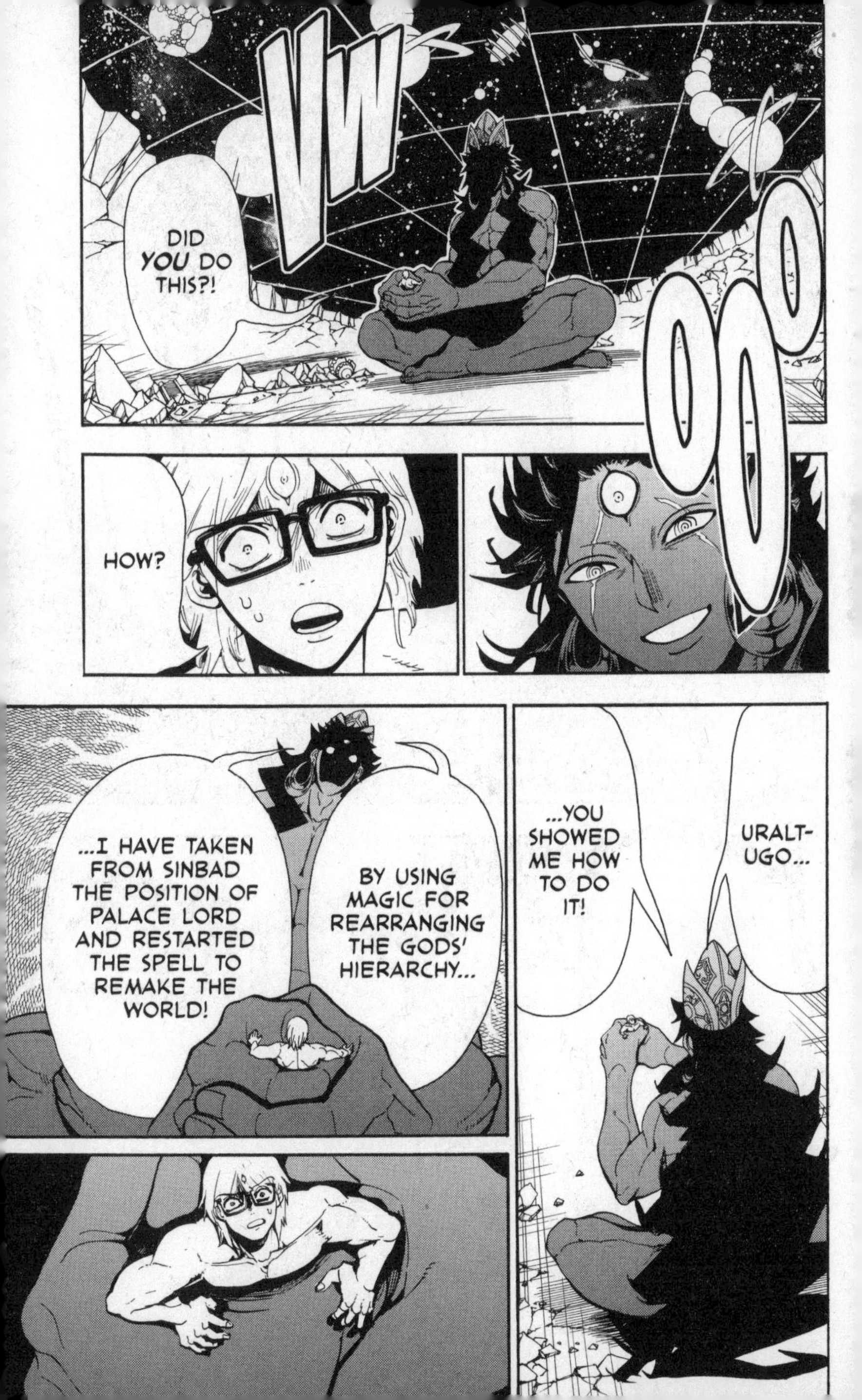
VW
DID YOU DO THIS?!
HOW?
URALT-UGO...
...YOU SHOWED ME HOW TO DO IT!
BY USING MAGIC FOR REARRANGING THE GODS' HIERARCHY...
...I HAVE TAKEN FROM SINBAD THE POSITION OF PALACE LORD AND RESTARTED THE SPELL TO REMAKE THE WORLD!

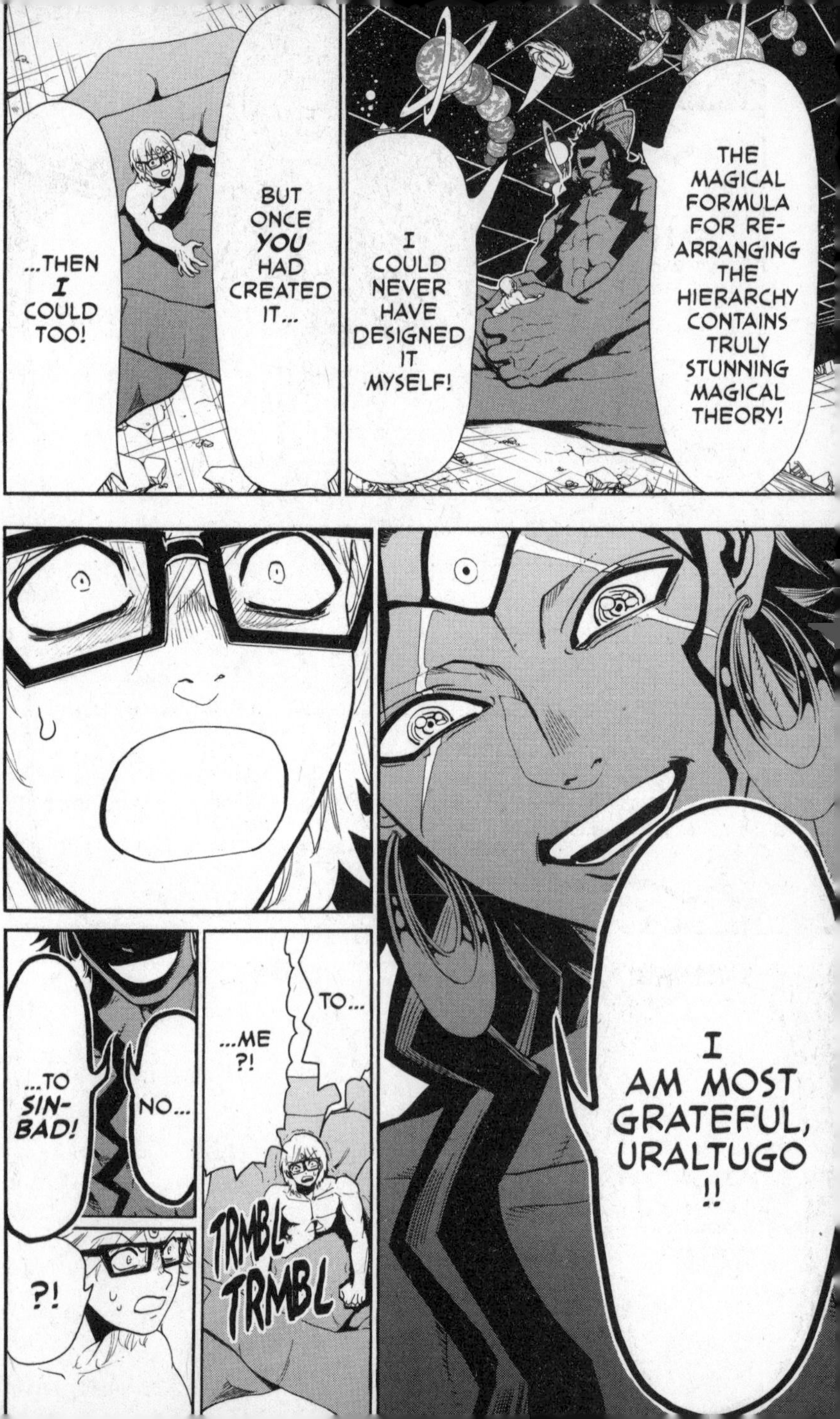
THE MAGICAL FORMULA FOR RE-ARRANGING THE HIERARCHY CONTAINS TRULY STUNNING MAGICAL THEORY!
I COULD NEVER HAVE DESIGNED IT MYSELF!
BUT ONCE YOU HAD CREATED IT...
...THEN I COULD TOO!
I AM MOST GRATEFUL, URALTUGO !!
TO...
...ME ?!
NO...
...TO SIN-BAD!
TRMBL TRMBL
?!

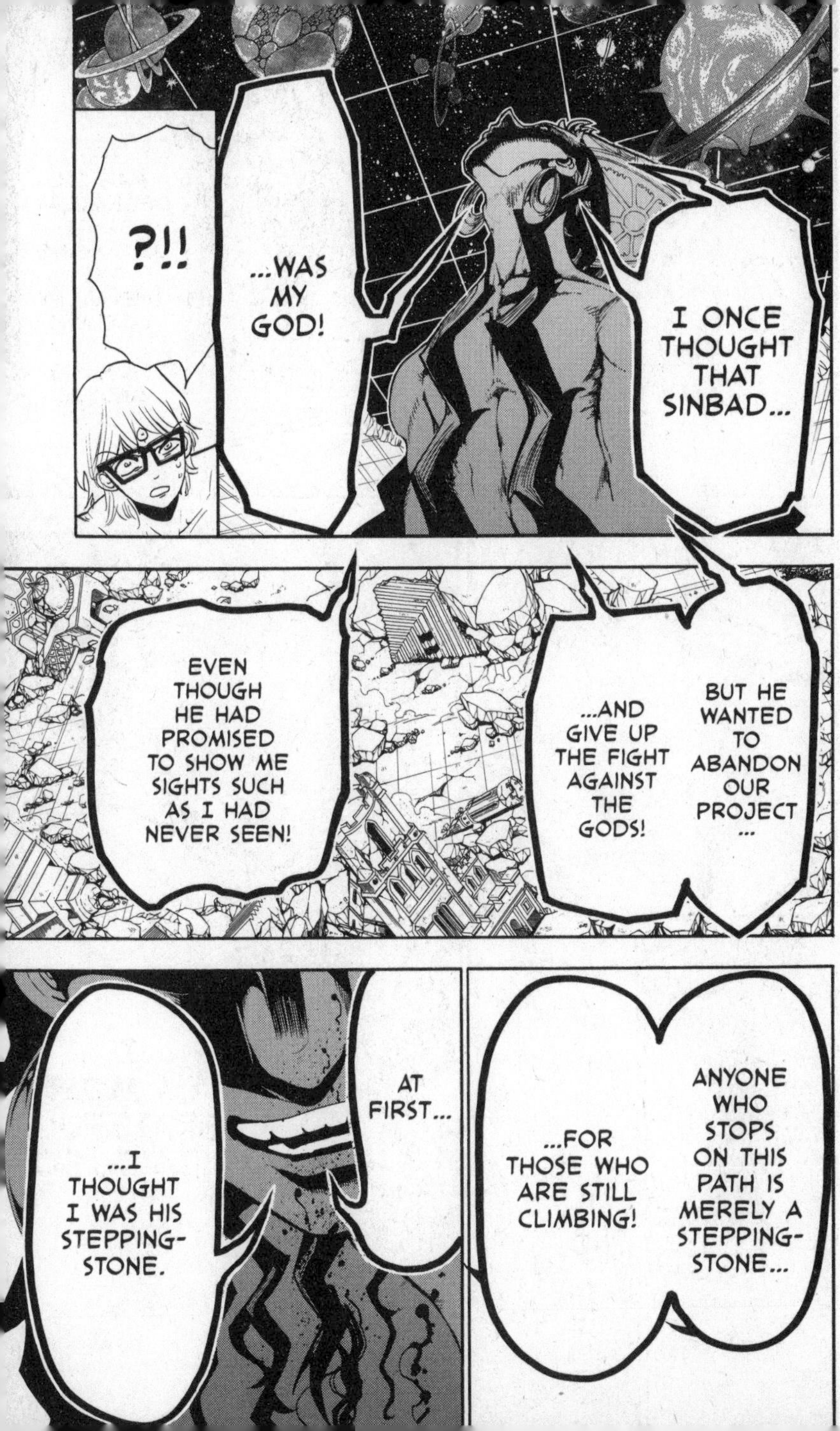
I ONCE THOUGHT THAT SINBAD...
...WAS MY GOD!
?!!
BUT HE WANTED TO ABANDON OUR PROJECT...
...AND GIVE UP THE FIGHT AGAINST THE GODS!
EVEN THOUGH HE HAD PROMISED TO SHOW ME SIGHTS SUCH AS I HAD NEVER SEEN!
ANYONE WHO STOPS ON THIS PATH IS MERELY A STEPPING-STONE...
...FOR THOSE WHO ARE STILL CLIMBING!
AT FIRST...
...I THOUGHT I WAS HIS STEPPING-STONE.

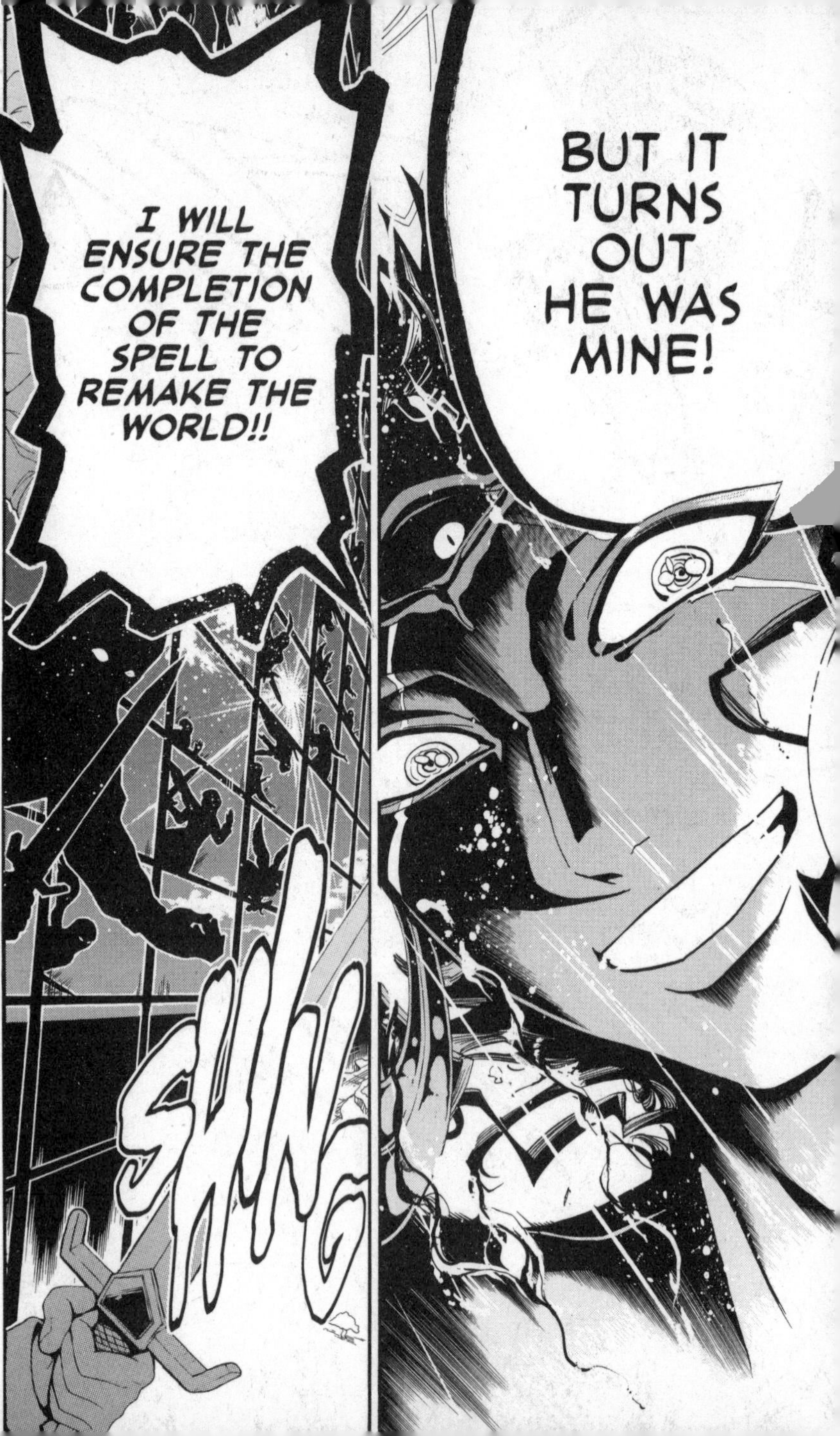
BUT IT TURNS OUT HE WAS MINE!
I WILL ENSURE THE COMPLETION OF THE SPELL TO REMAKE THE WORLD!!
SHING

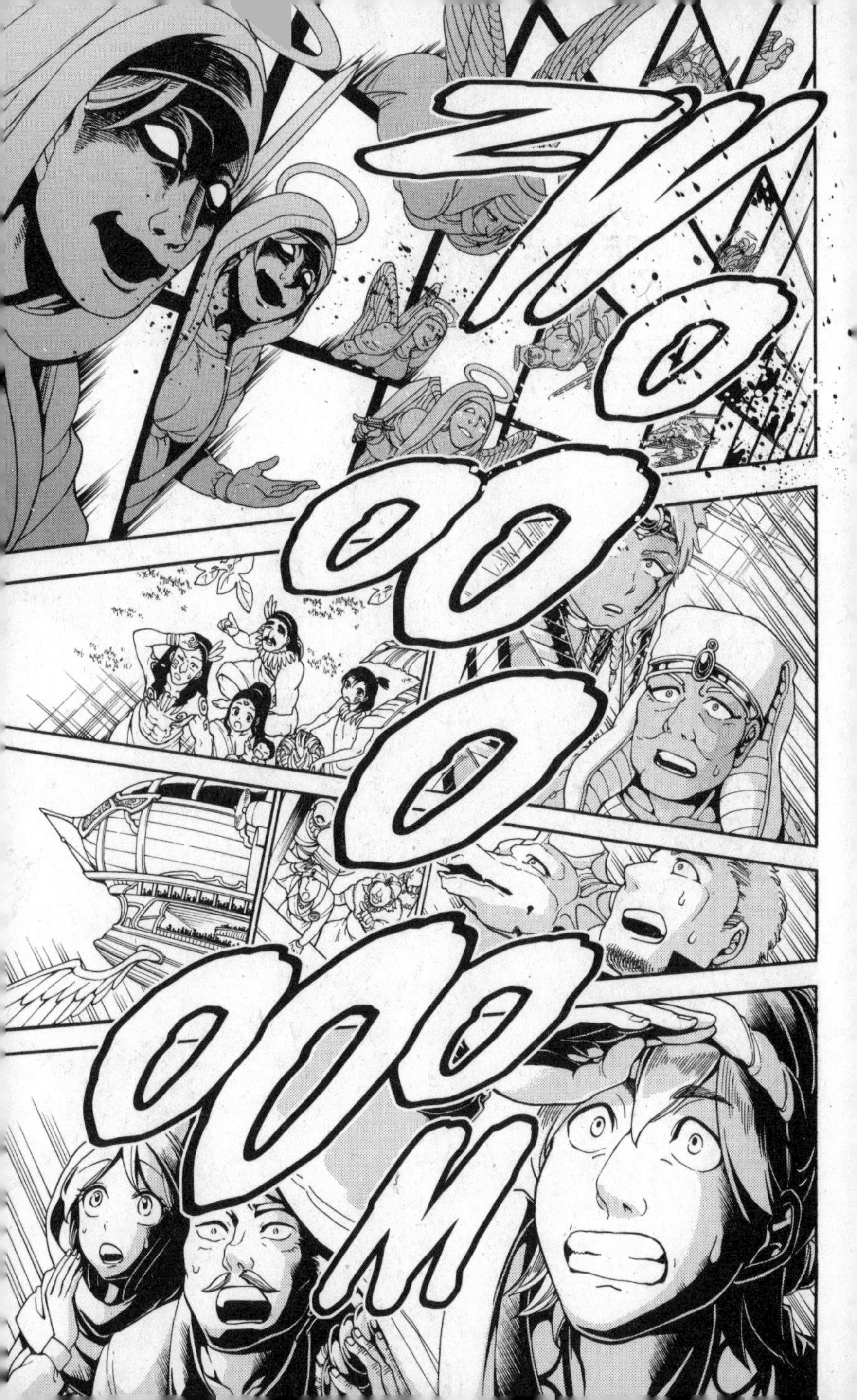
ZWOOOOOOM

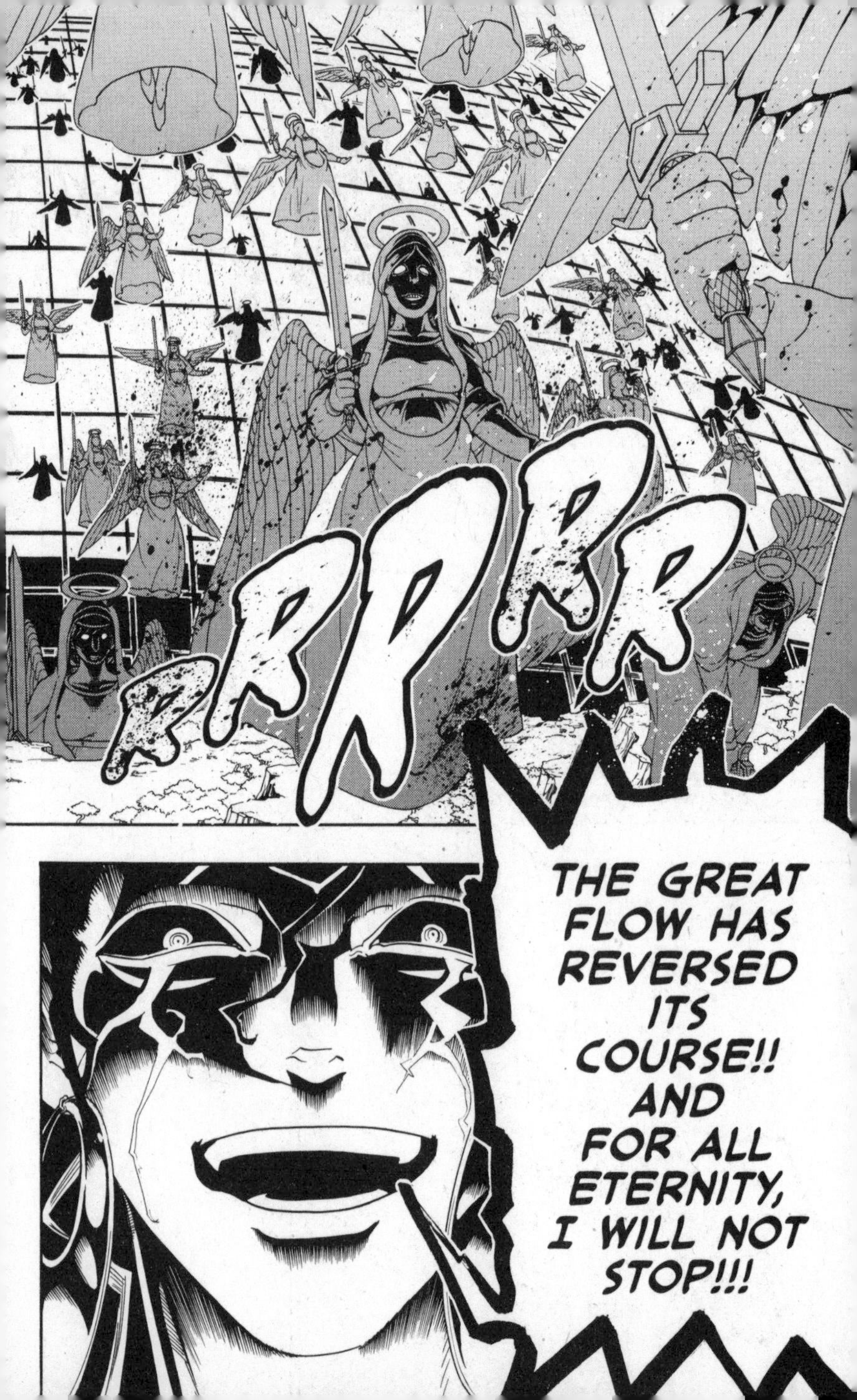
RRRR
THE GREAT FLOW HAS REVERSED ITS COURSE!! AND FOR ALL ETERNITY, I WILL NOT STOP!!!

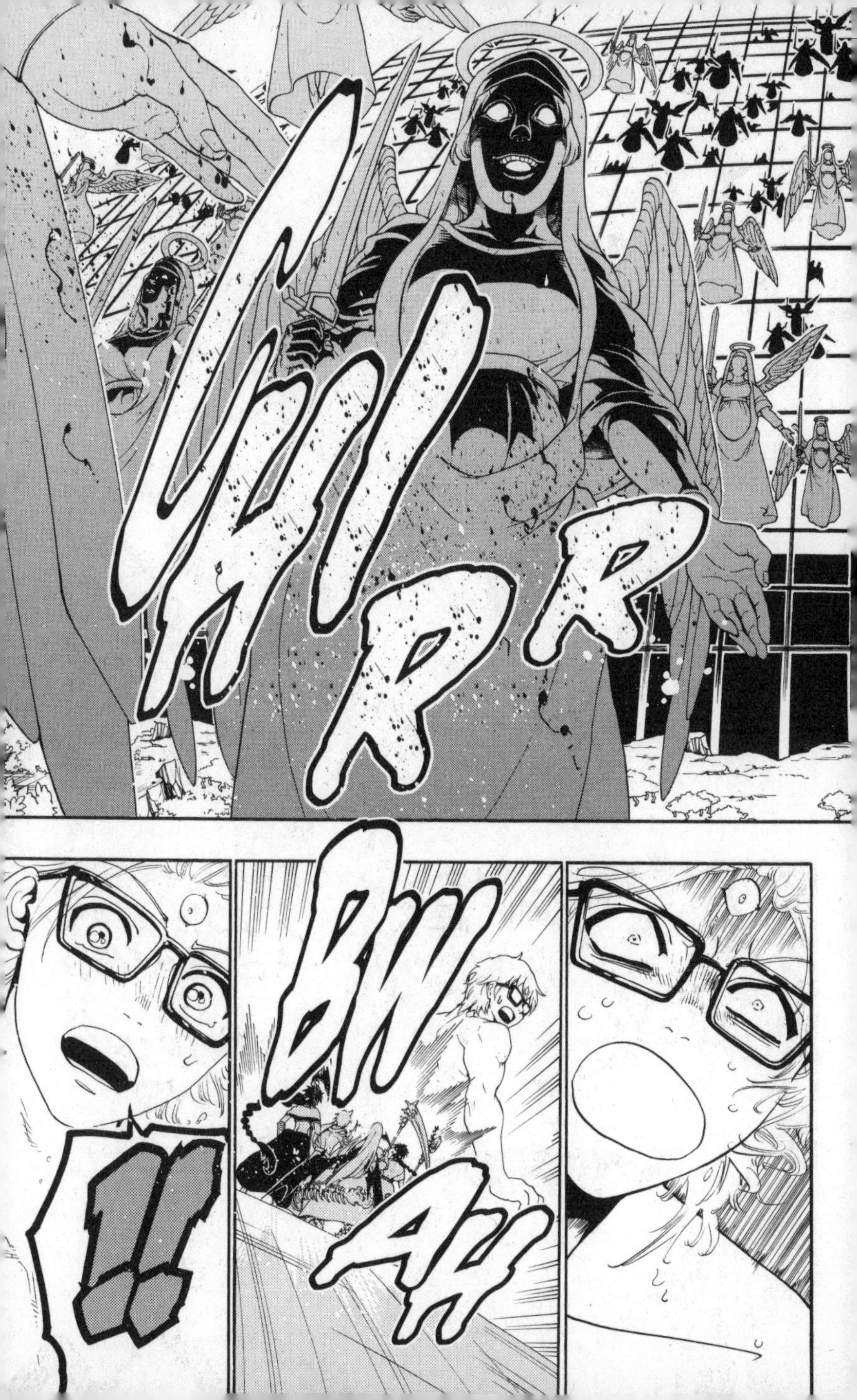
WHIRR
BWAH
!!

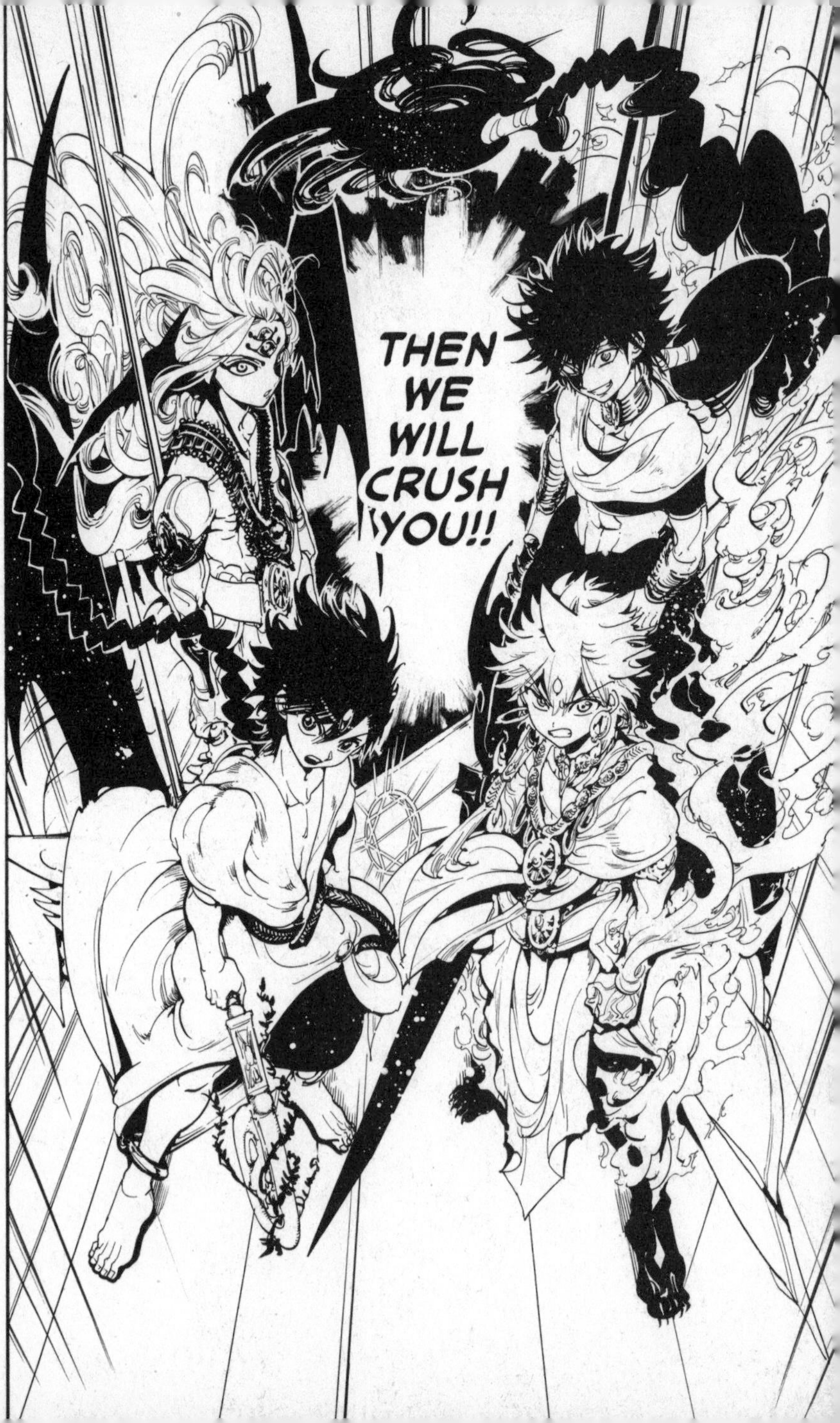
THEN WE WILL CRUSH YOU!!

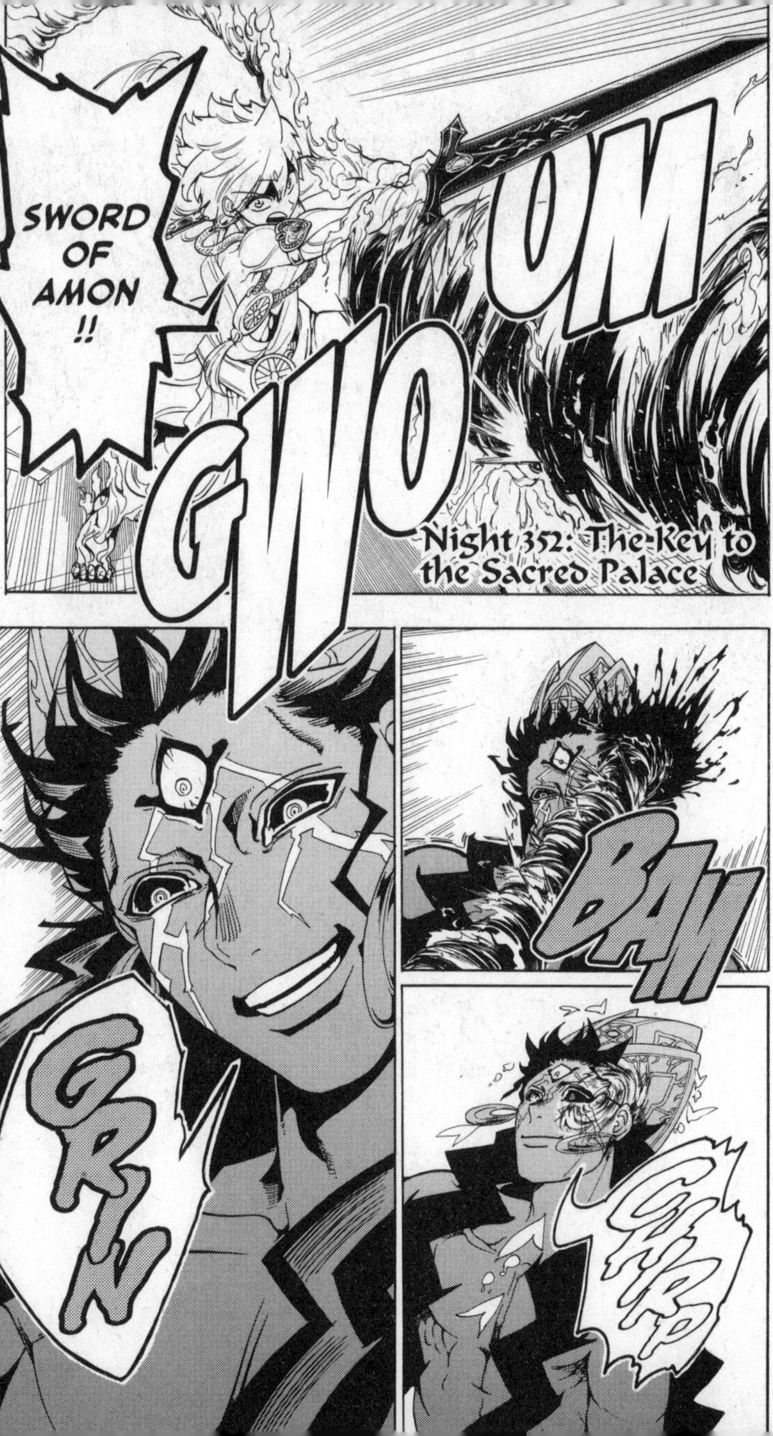
SWORD OF AMON !!
GWOOM
Night 352: The Key to the Sacred Palace
BAM
GRIN

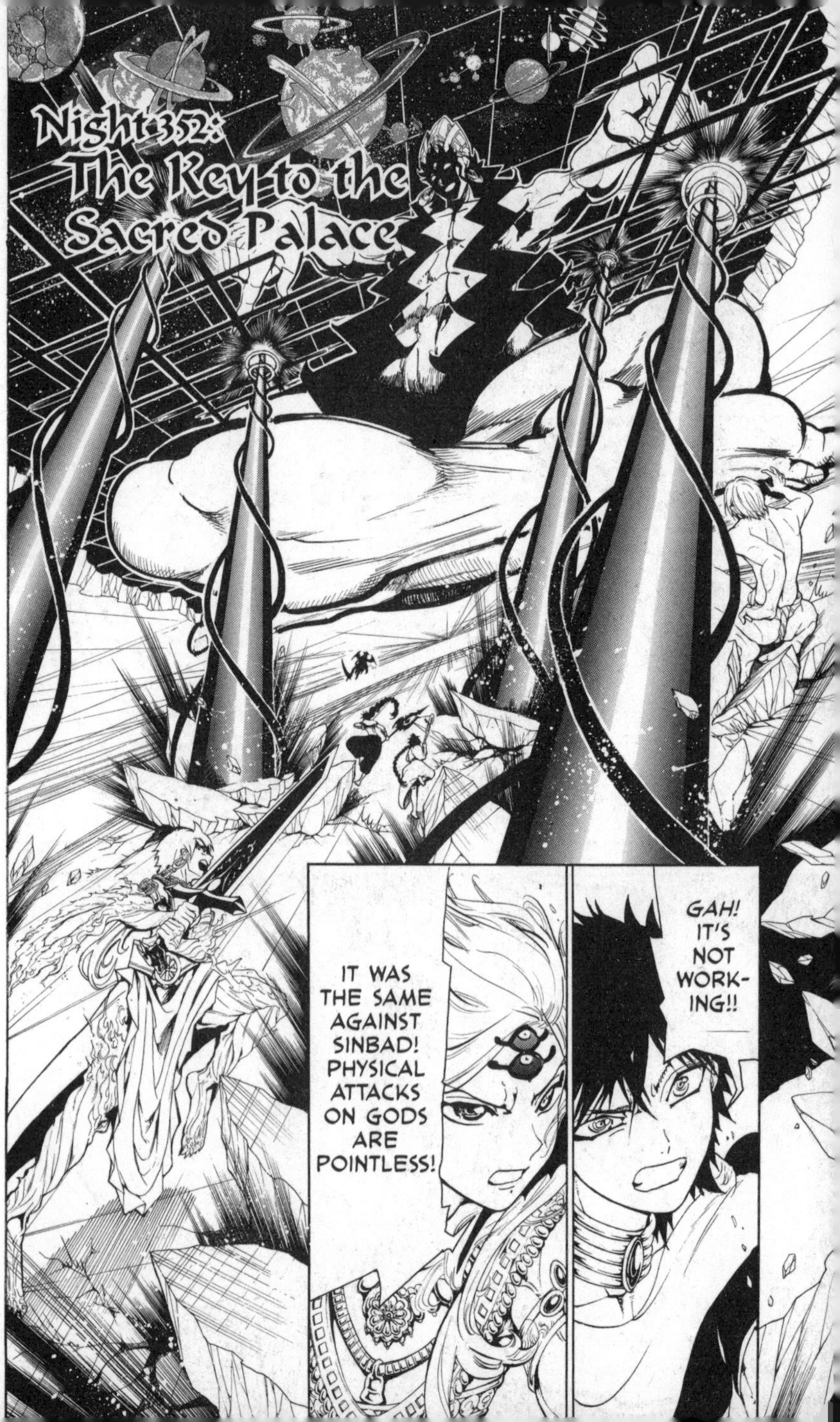
Night 352: The Key to the Sacred Palace
GAH! IT'S NOT WORKING!!
IT WAS THE SAME AGAINST SINBAD! PHYSICAL ATTACKS ON GODS ARE POINTLESS!

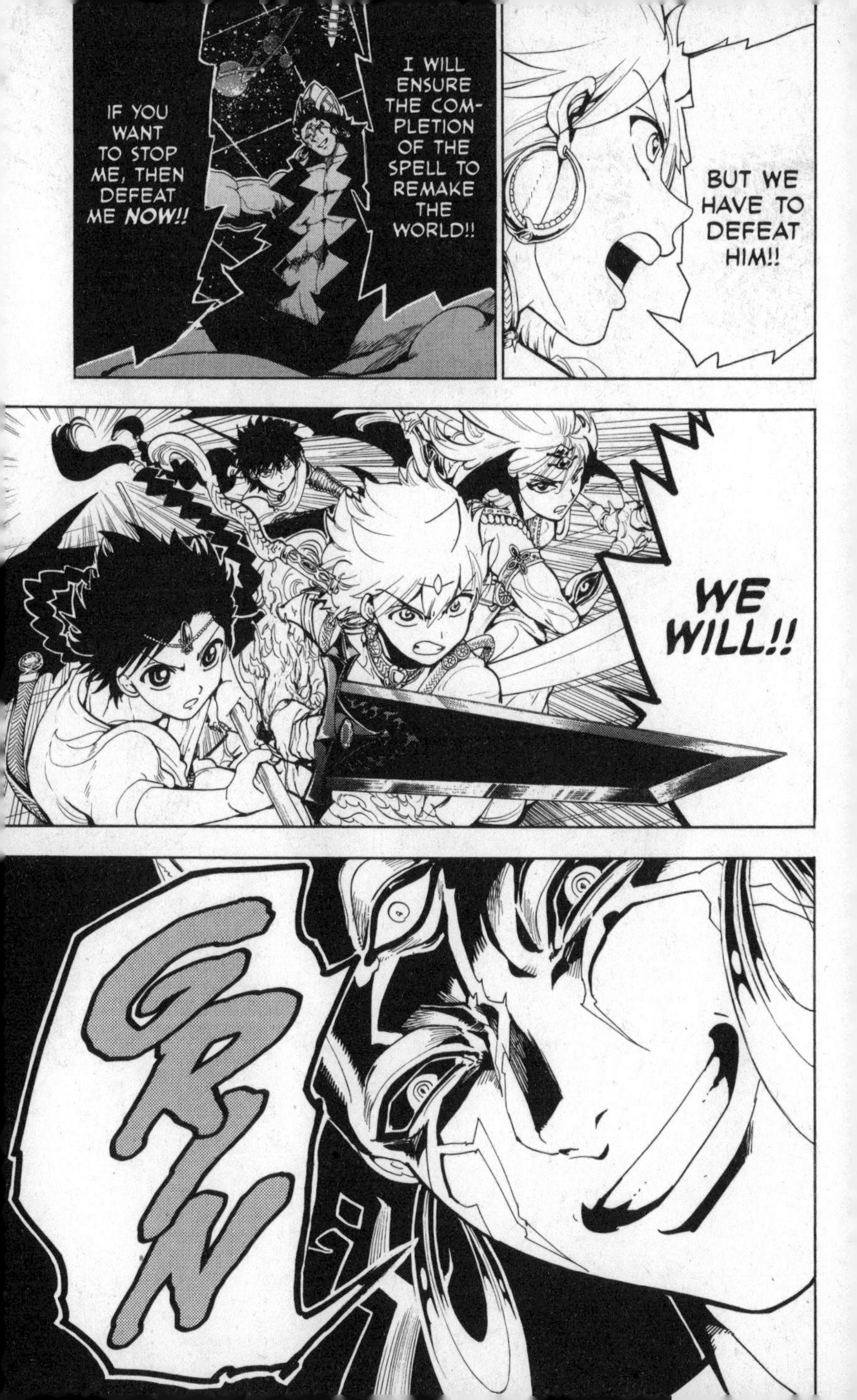
BUT WE HAVE TO DEFEAT HIM!!
I WILL ENSURE THE COMPLETION OF THE SPELL TO REMAKE THE WORLD!!
IF YOU WANT TO STOP ME, THEN DEFEAT ME *NOW*!!
WE WILL!!

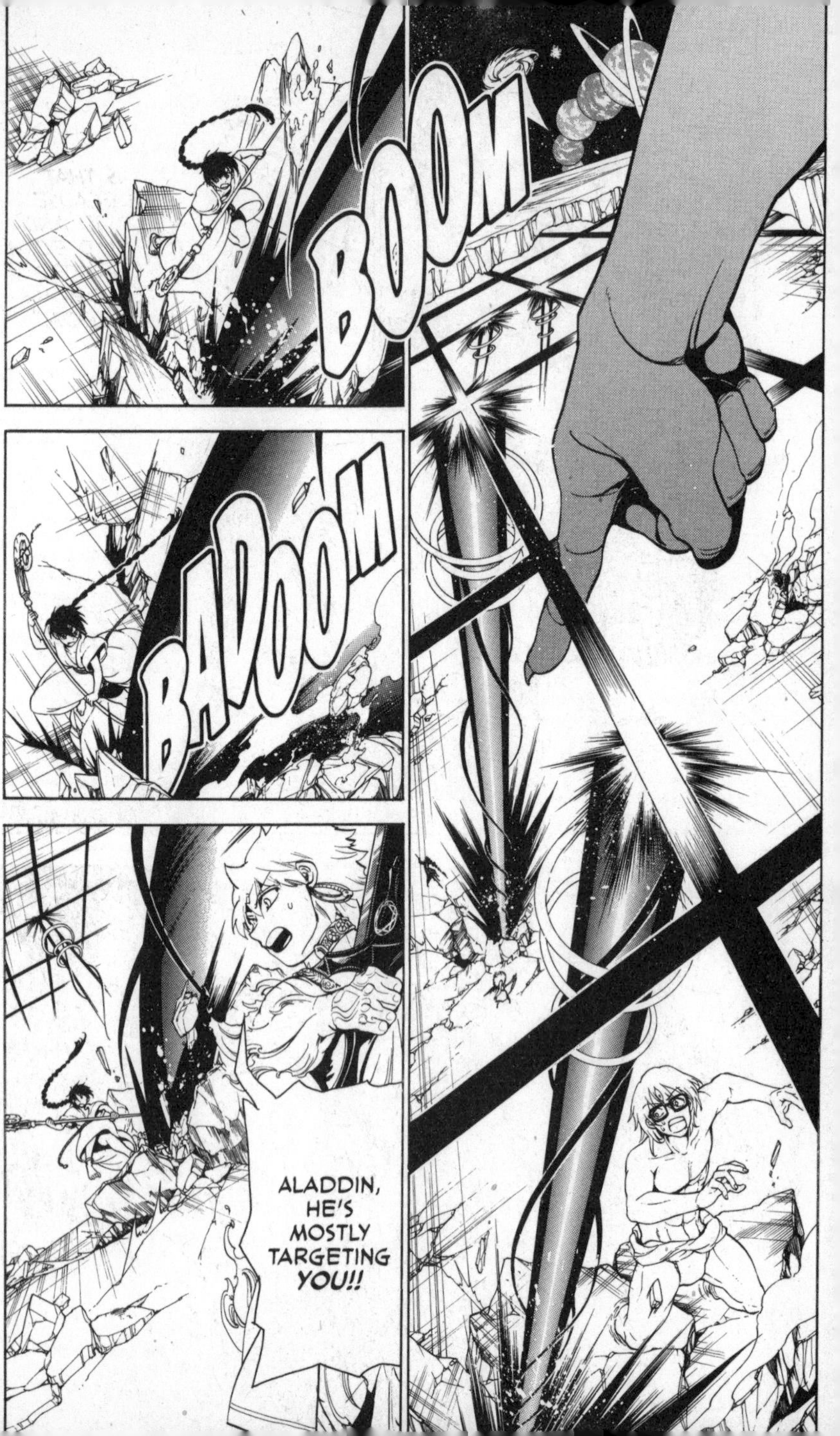
BOOM
BADOOM
ALADDIN, HE'S MOSTLY TARGETING YOU!!

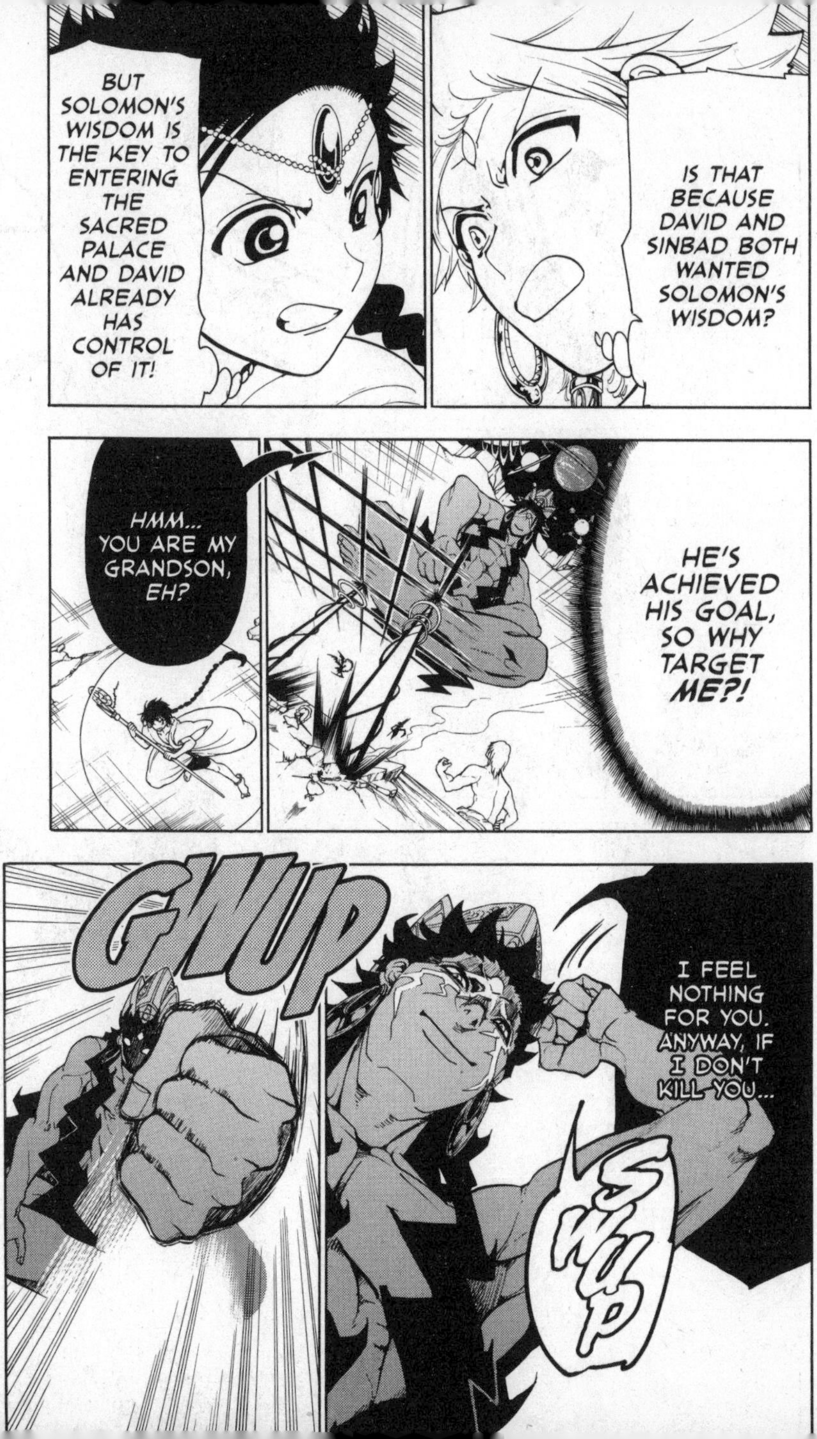
IS THAT BECAUSE DAVID AND SINBAD BOTH WANTED SOLOMON'S WISDOM?
BUT SOLOMON'S WISDOM IS THE KEY TO ENTERING THE SACRED PALACE AND DAVID ALREADY HAS CONTROL OF IT!
HE'S ACHIEVED HIS GOAL, SO WHY TARGET *ME?!*
HMM... YOU ARE MY GRANDSON, EH?
I FEEL NOTHING FOR YOU. ANYWAY, IF I DON'T KILL YOU...
GWUP
SWUP

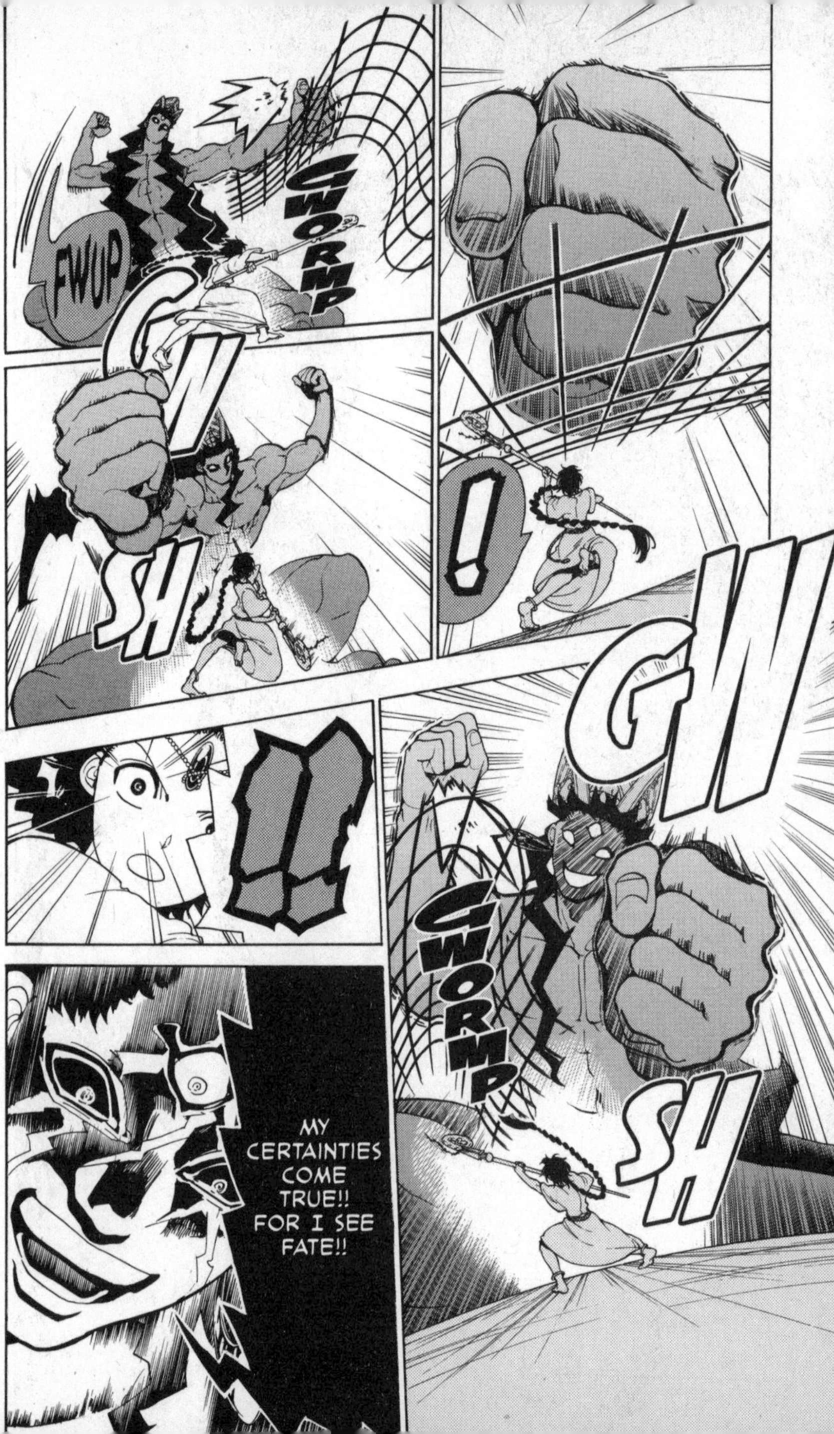
FWUP
GWORMP
!
GN
SH
GN
GWORMP
SH
!!
MY CERTAINTIES COME TRUE!! FOR I SEE FATE!!

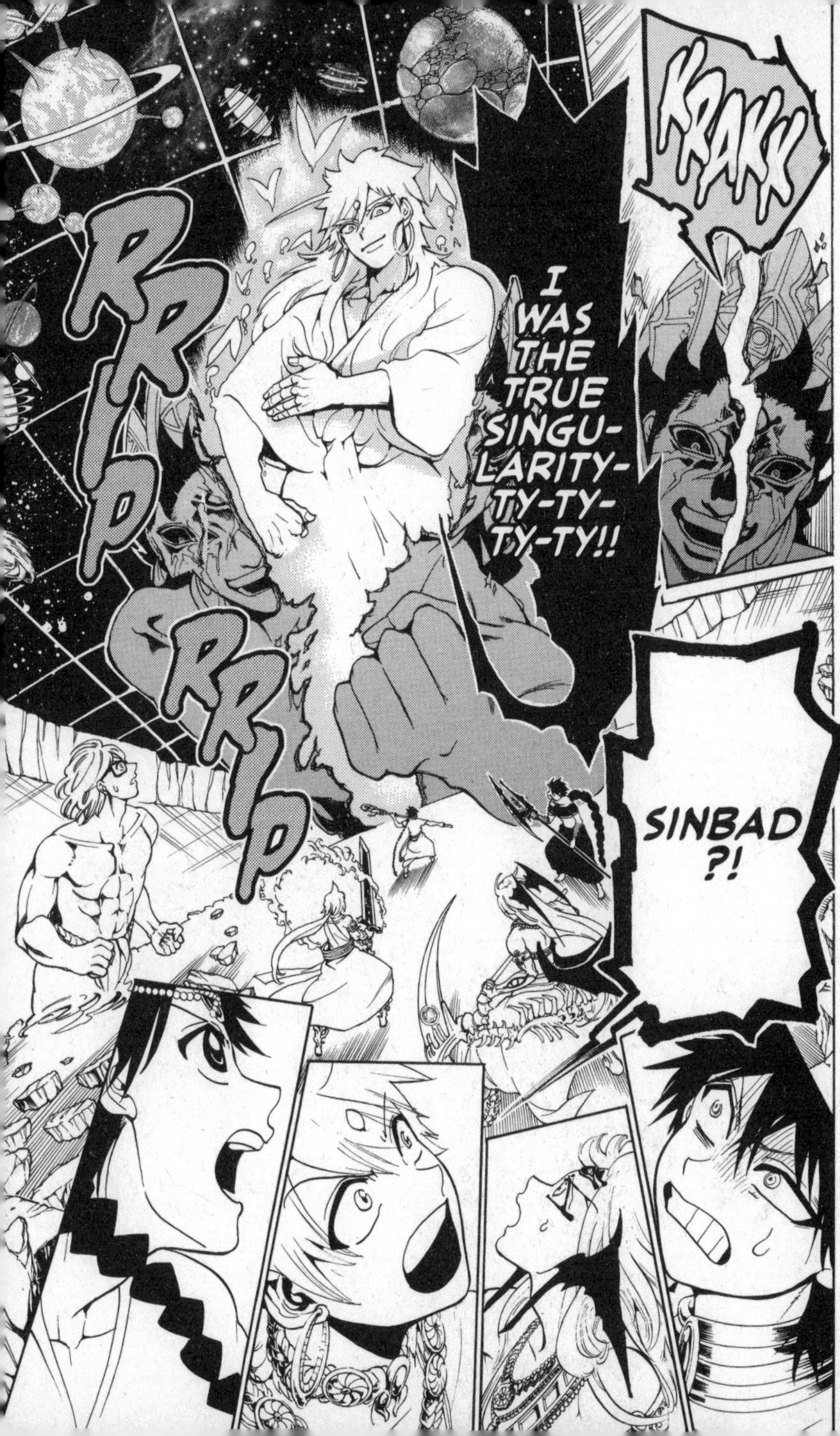
KRAKK
I WAS THE TRUE SINGU-LARITY-TY-TY-TY-TY!!
RRIP
CRRRIP
SINBAD?!

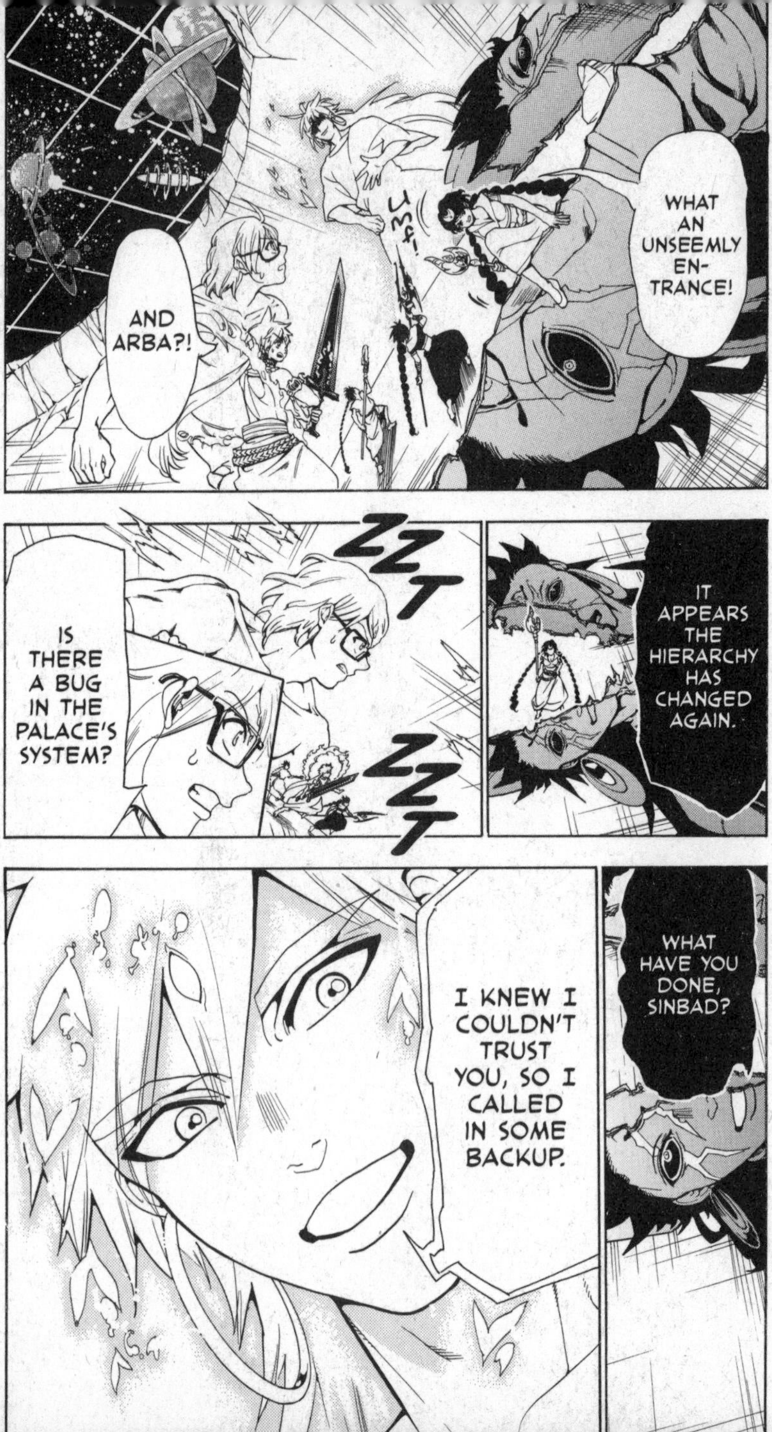
WHAT AN UNSEEMLY EN- TRANCE!
UMF!
AND ARBA?!
IT APPEARS THE HIERARCHY HAS CHANGED AGAIN.
ZZZT
IS THERE A BUG IN THE PALACE'S SYSTEM?
ZZZT
WHAT HAVE YOU DONE, SINBAD?
I KNEW I COULDN'T TRUST YOU, SO I CALLED IN SOME BACKUP.

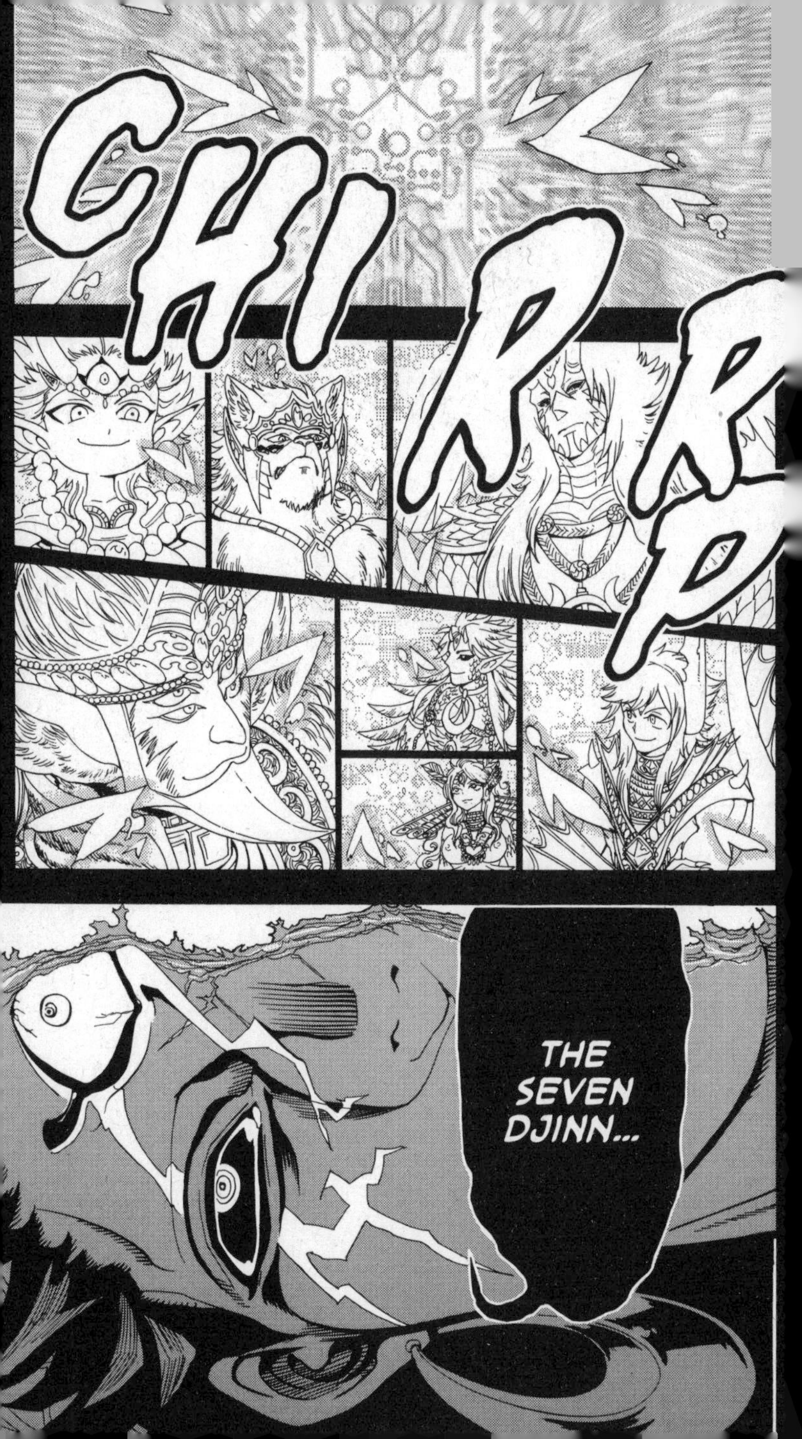
CHIRRP
THE SEVEN DJINN...

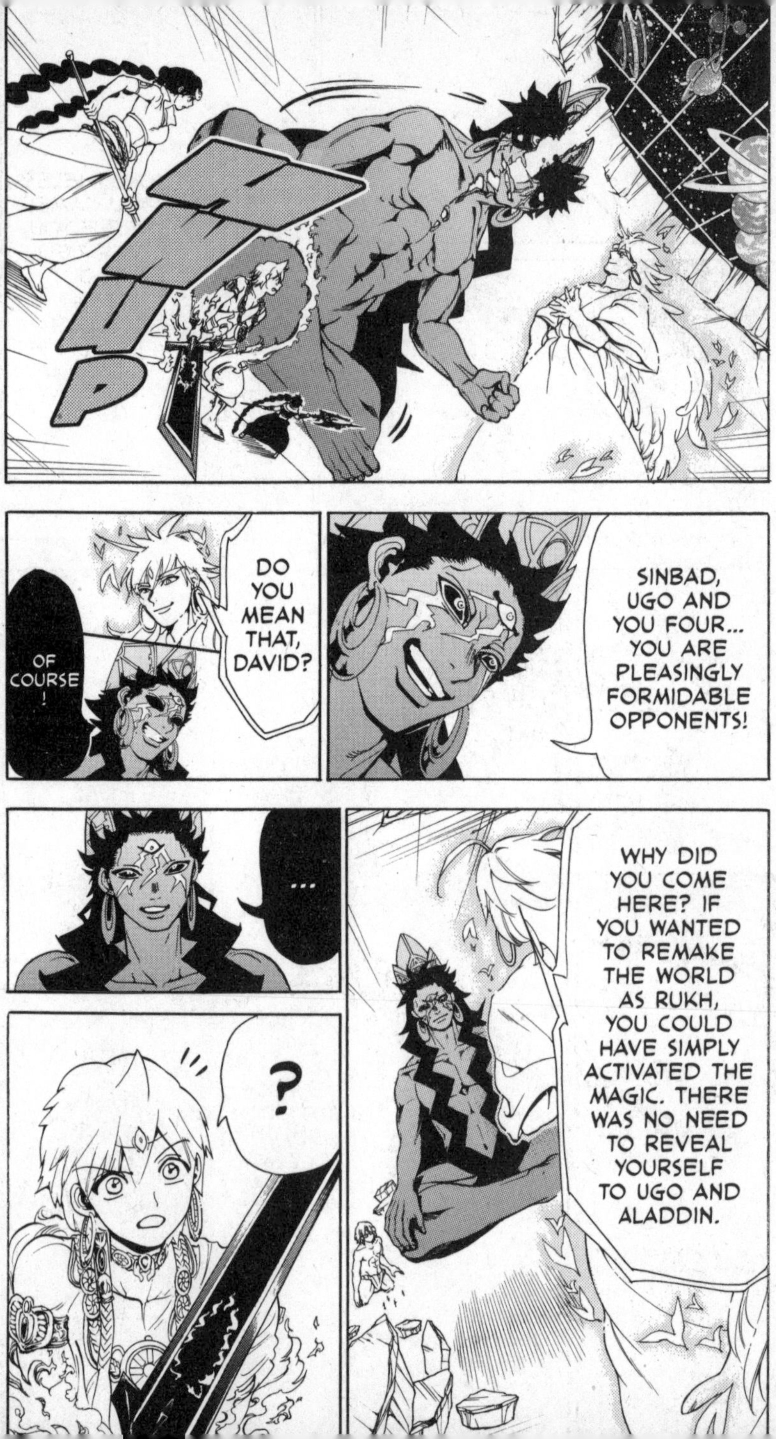
SINBAD, UGO AND YOU FOUR... YOU ARE PLEASINGLY FORMIDABLE OPPONENTS!
DO YOU MEAN THAT, DAVID?
OF COURSE!
WHY DID YOU COME HERE? IF YOU WANTED TO REMAKE THE WORLD AS RUKH, YOU COULD HAVE SIMPLY ACTIVATED THE MAGIC. THERE WAS NO NEED TO REVEAL YOURSELF TO UGO AND ALADDIN.
...
?

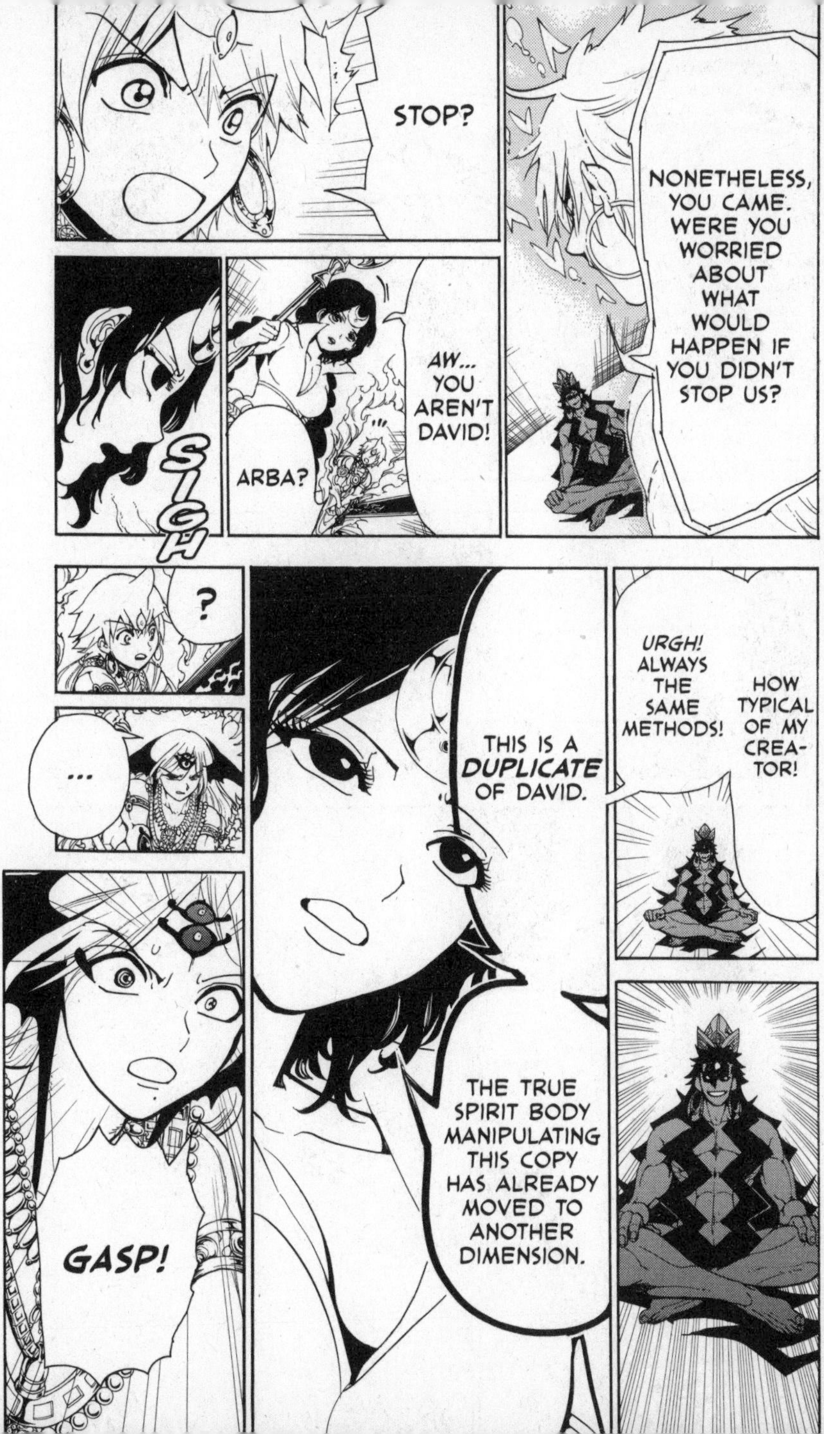
NONETHELESS, YOU CAME. WERE YOU WORRIED ABOUT WHAT WOULD HAPPEN IF YOU DIDN'T STOP US?
STOP?
AW... YOU AREN'T DAVID!
ARBA?
...
SIGH
HOW TYPICAL OF MY CREATOR!
URGH! ALWAYS THE SAME METHODS!
THIS IS A *DUPLICATE* OF DAVID.
THE TRUE SPIRIT BODY MANIPULATING THIS COPY HAS ALREADY MOVED TO ANOTHER DIMENSION.
?
...
GASP!

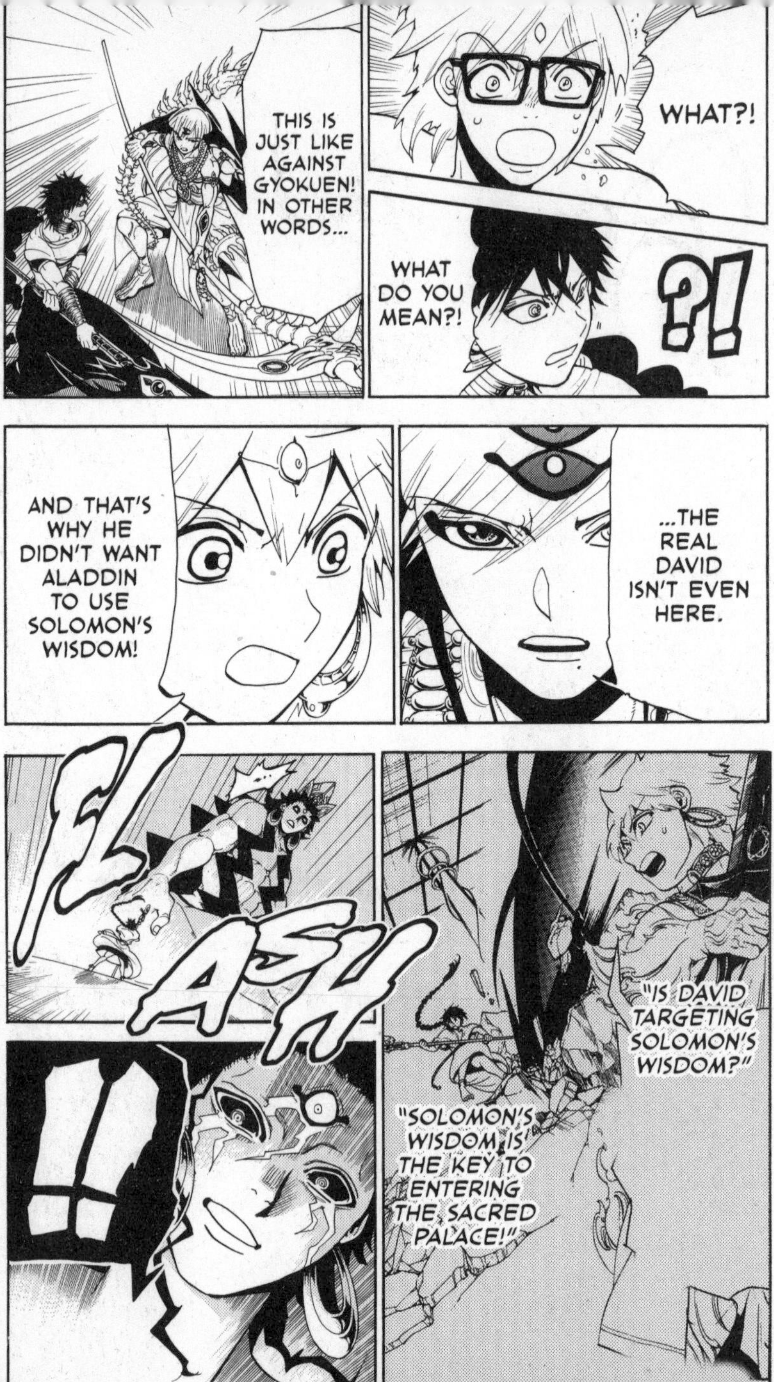
WHAT?!
WHAT DO YOU MEAN?!
?!
THIS IS JUST LIKE AGAINST GYOKUEN! IN OTHER WORDS...
...THE REAL DAVID ISN'T EVEN HERE.
AND THAT'S WHY HE DIDN'T WANT ALADDIN TO USE SOLOMON'S WISDOM!
"IS DAVID TARGETING SOLOMON'S WISDOM?"
"SOLOMON'S WISDOM IS THE KEY TO ENTERING THE SACRED PALACE!"
FLASH
!!

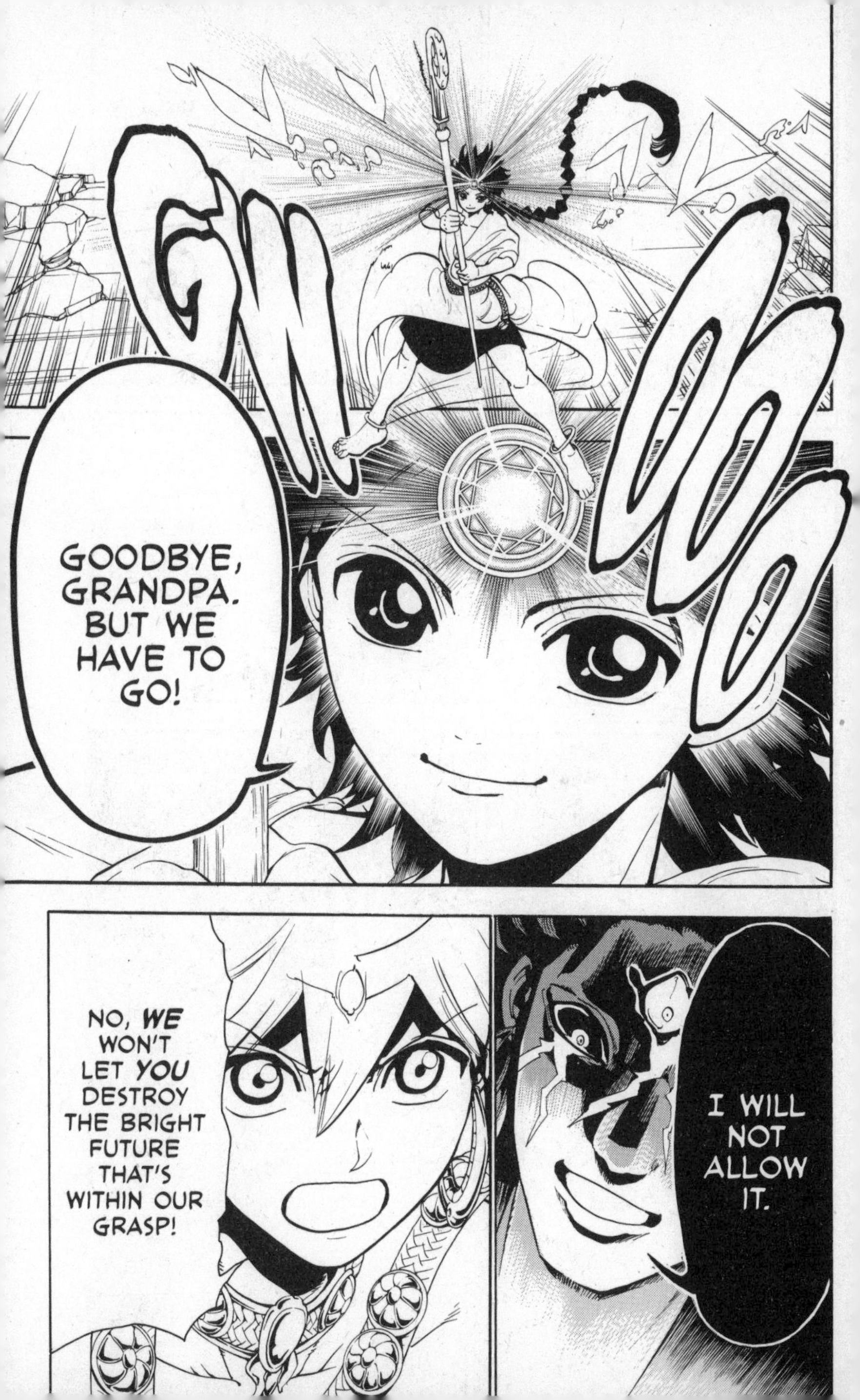
GOODBYE, GRANDPA. BUT WE HAVE TO GO!
I WILL NOT ALLOW IT.
NO, WE WON'T LET YOU DESTROY THE BRIGHT FUTURE THAT'S WITHIN OUR GRASP!

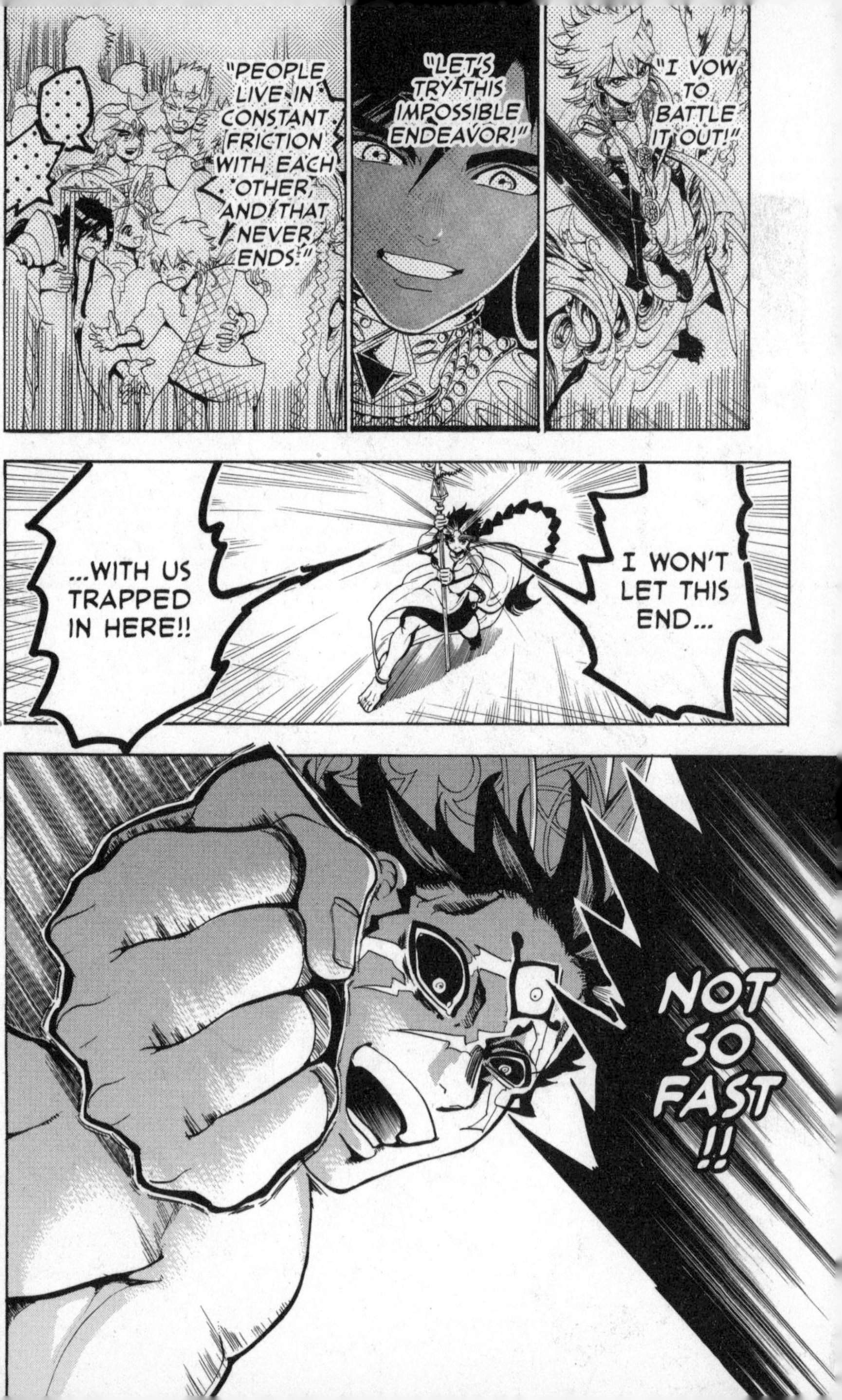
"I VOW TO BATTLE IT OUT!"
"LET'S TRY THIS IMPOSSIBLE ENDEAVOR!"
"PEOPLE LIVE IN CONSTANT FRICTION WITH EACH OTHER, AND THAT NEVER ENDS."
I WON'T LET THIS END...
...WITH US TRAPPED IN HERE!!
NOT SO FAST!!

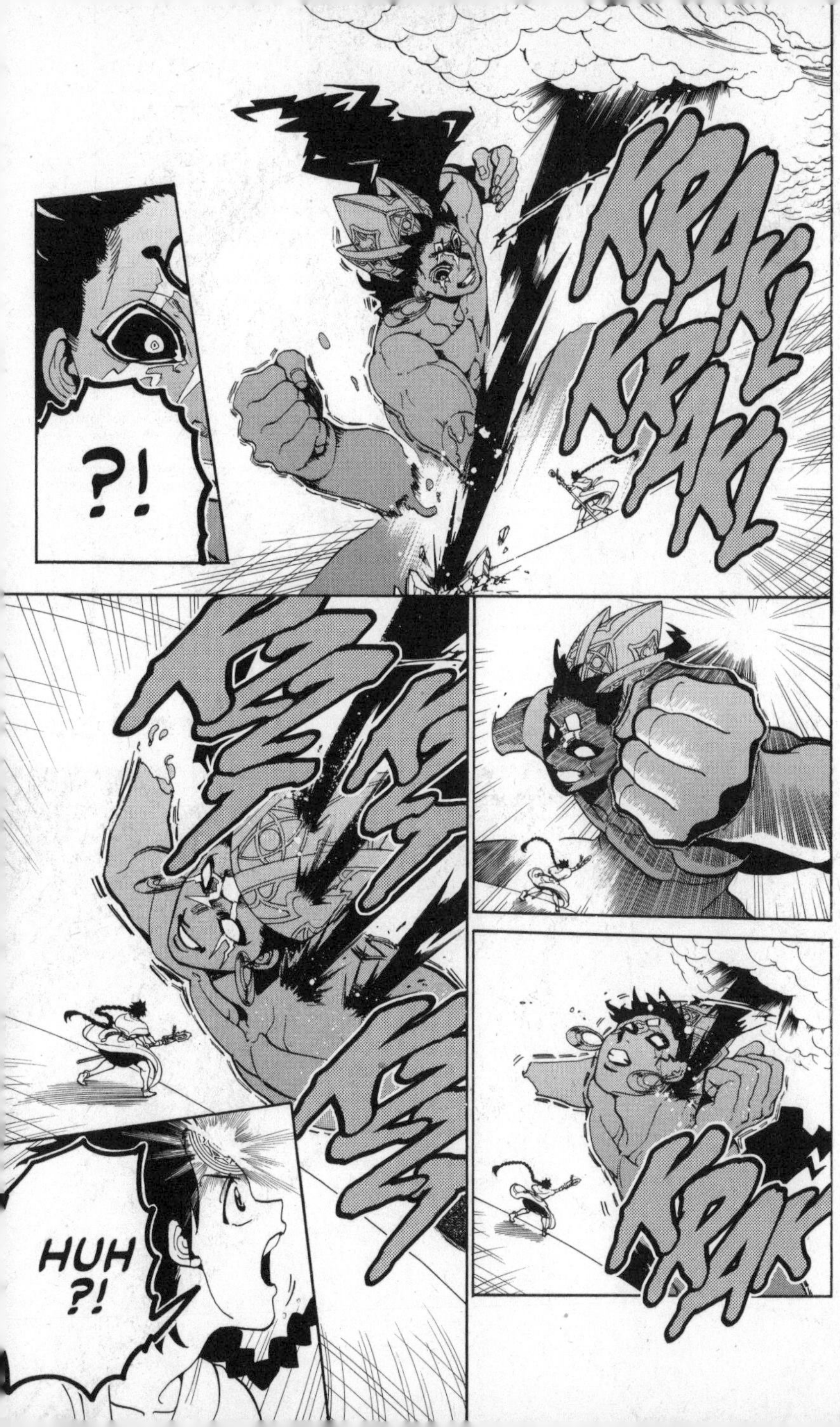
KRAKL KRAKL KRAKL
?!
KRAK
HUH ?!

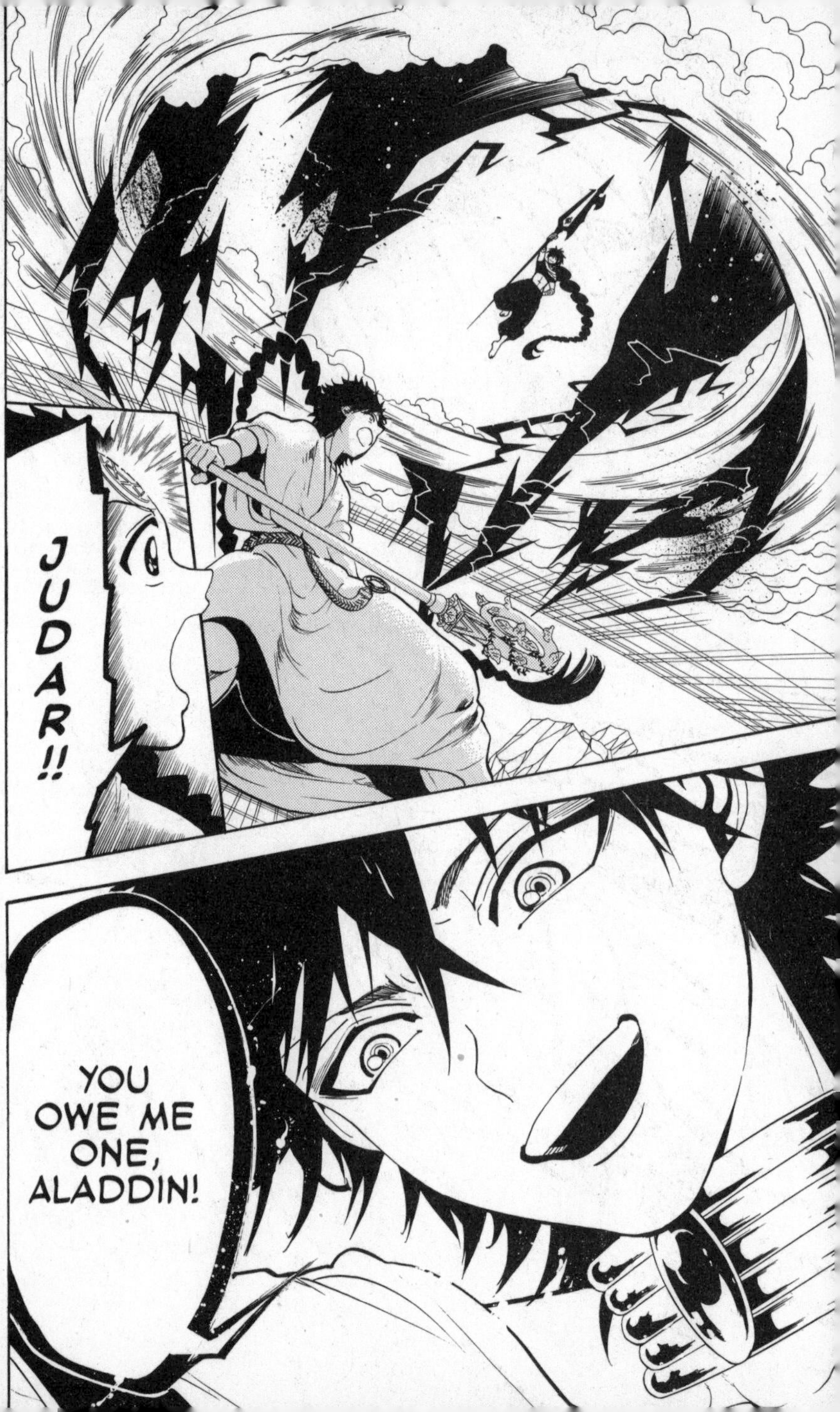
JUDAR!!
YOU OWE ME ONE, ALADDIN!

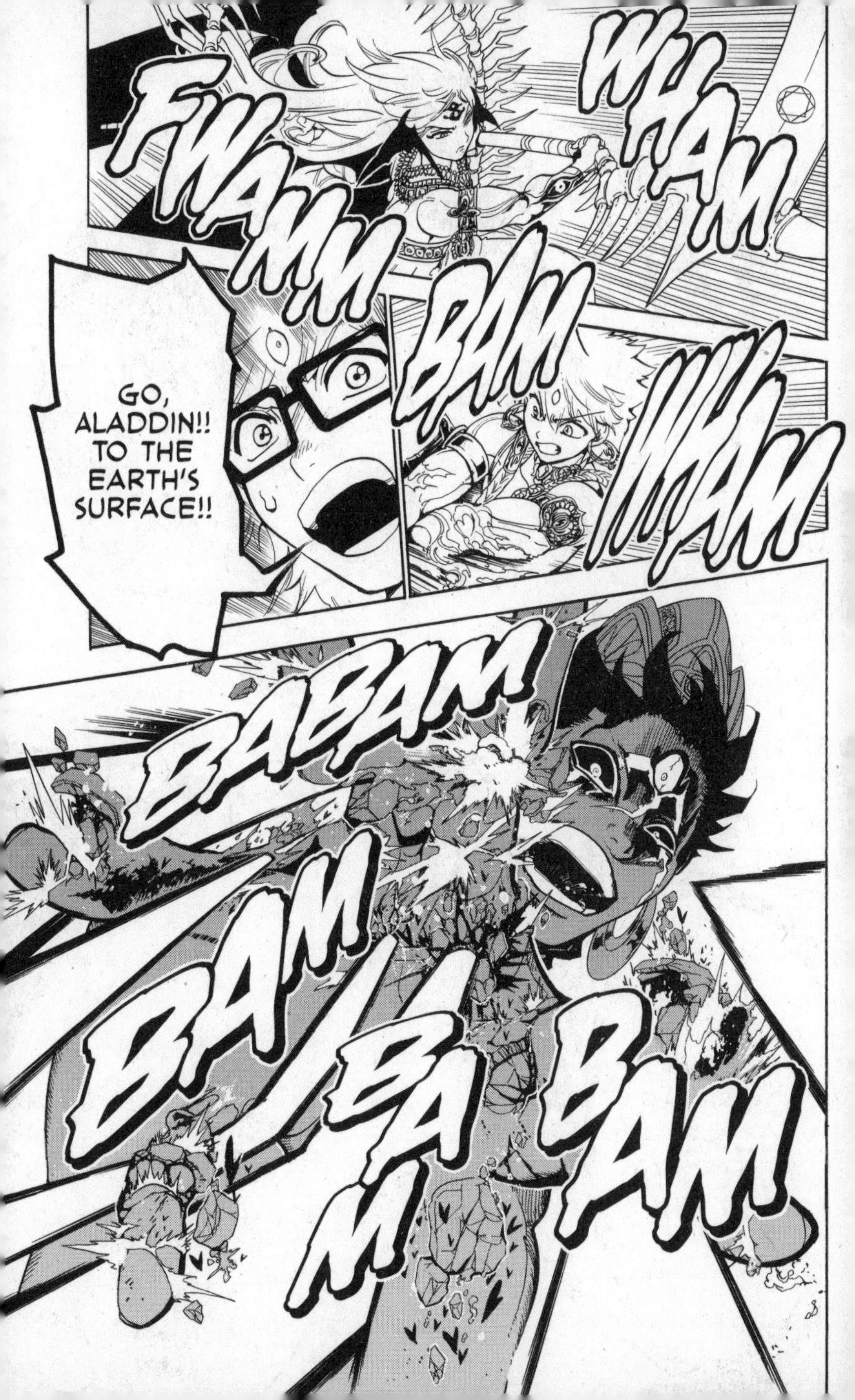
WHAM
FWAMM
BAM
WHAM
GO, ALADDIN!! TO THE EARTH'S SURFACE!!
BABAM
BAM
BAM
BAM

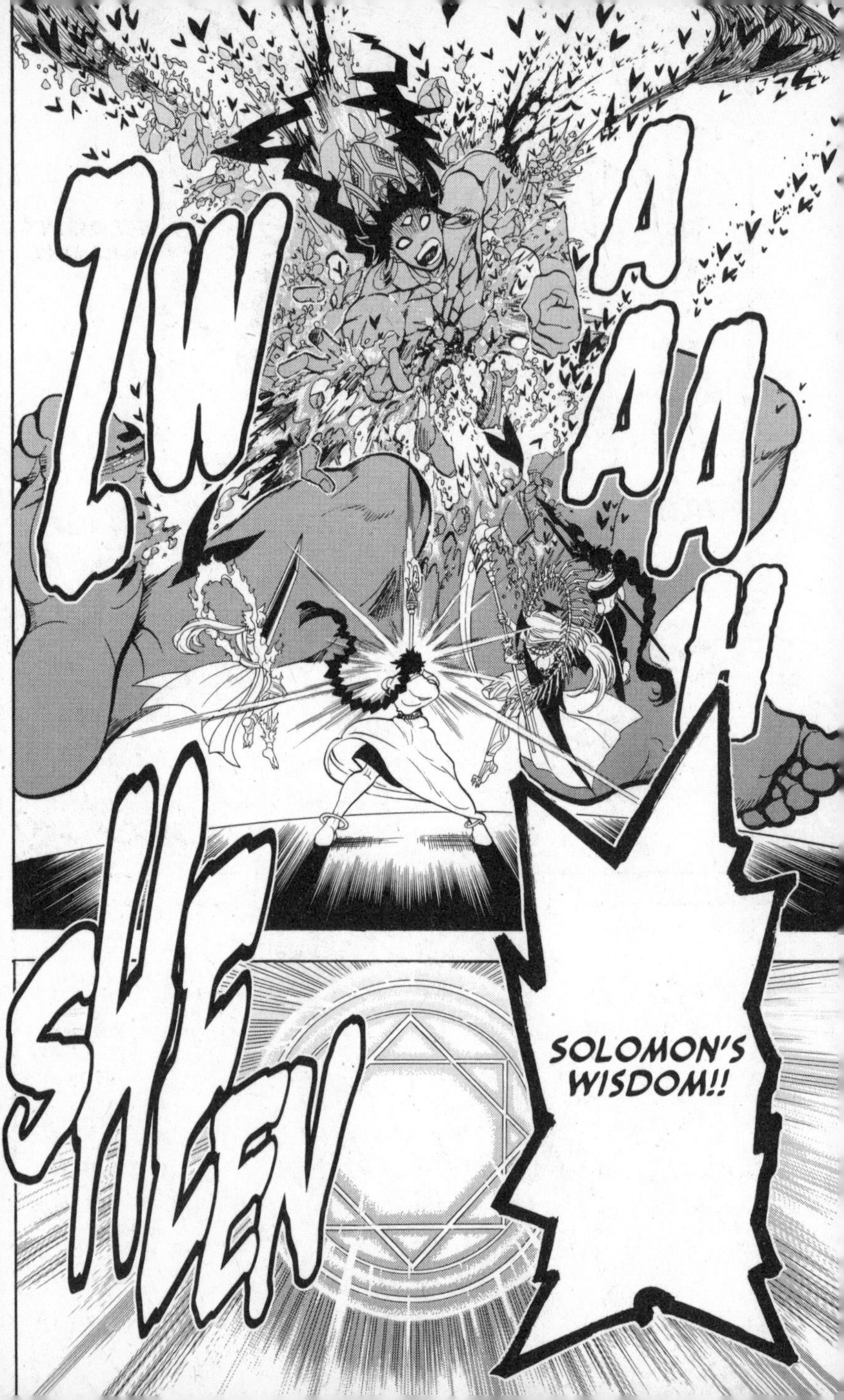
SOLOMON'S WISDOM!!

Night 353: Reaping the Rukh

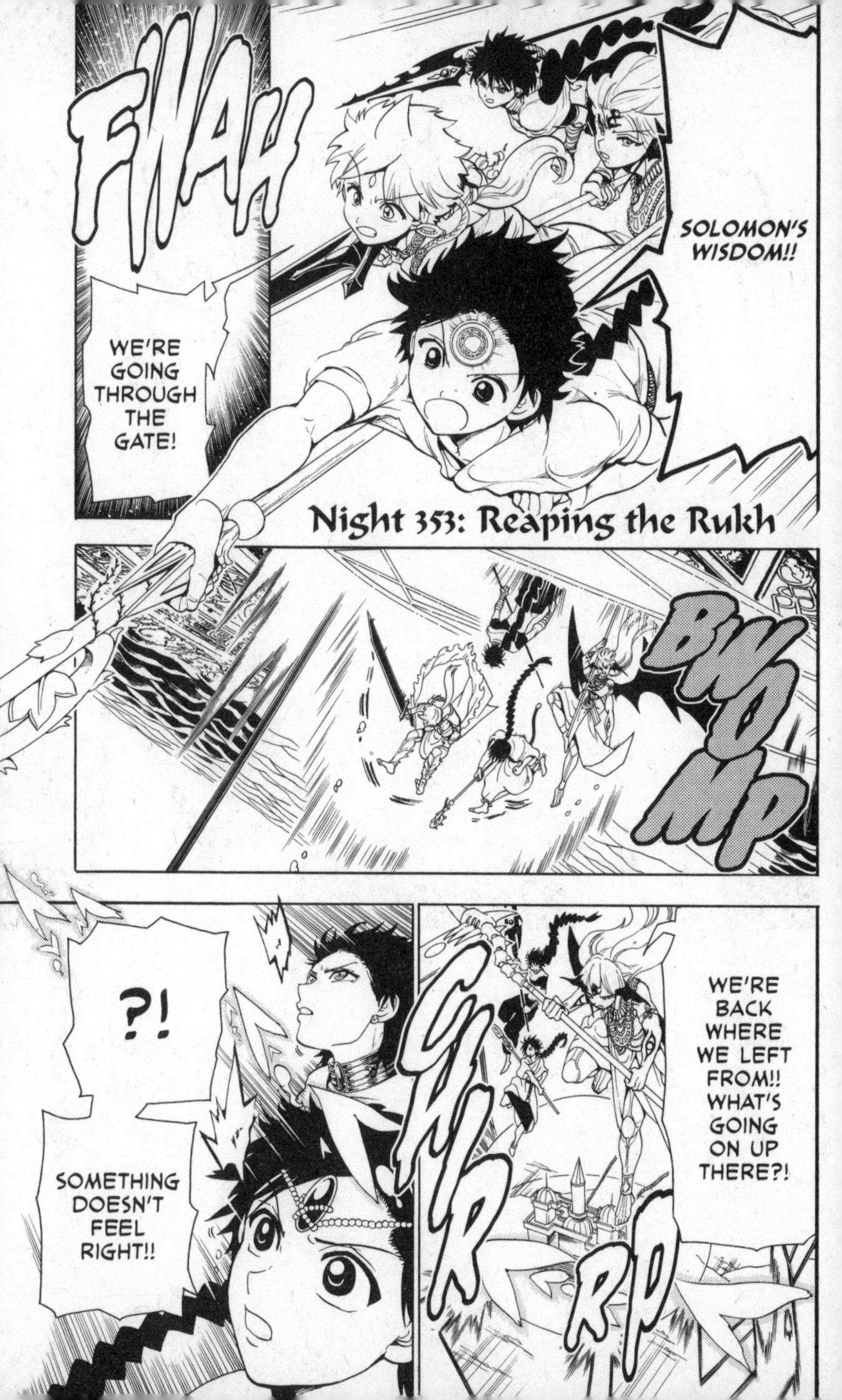
SOLOMON'S WISDOM!!
FWAH
WE'RE GOING THROUGH THE GATE!
BWOMP
WE'RE BACK WHERE WE LEFT FROM!! WHAT'S GOING ON UP THERE?!
?!
SOMETHING DOESN'T FEEL RIGHT!!

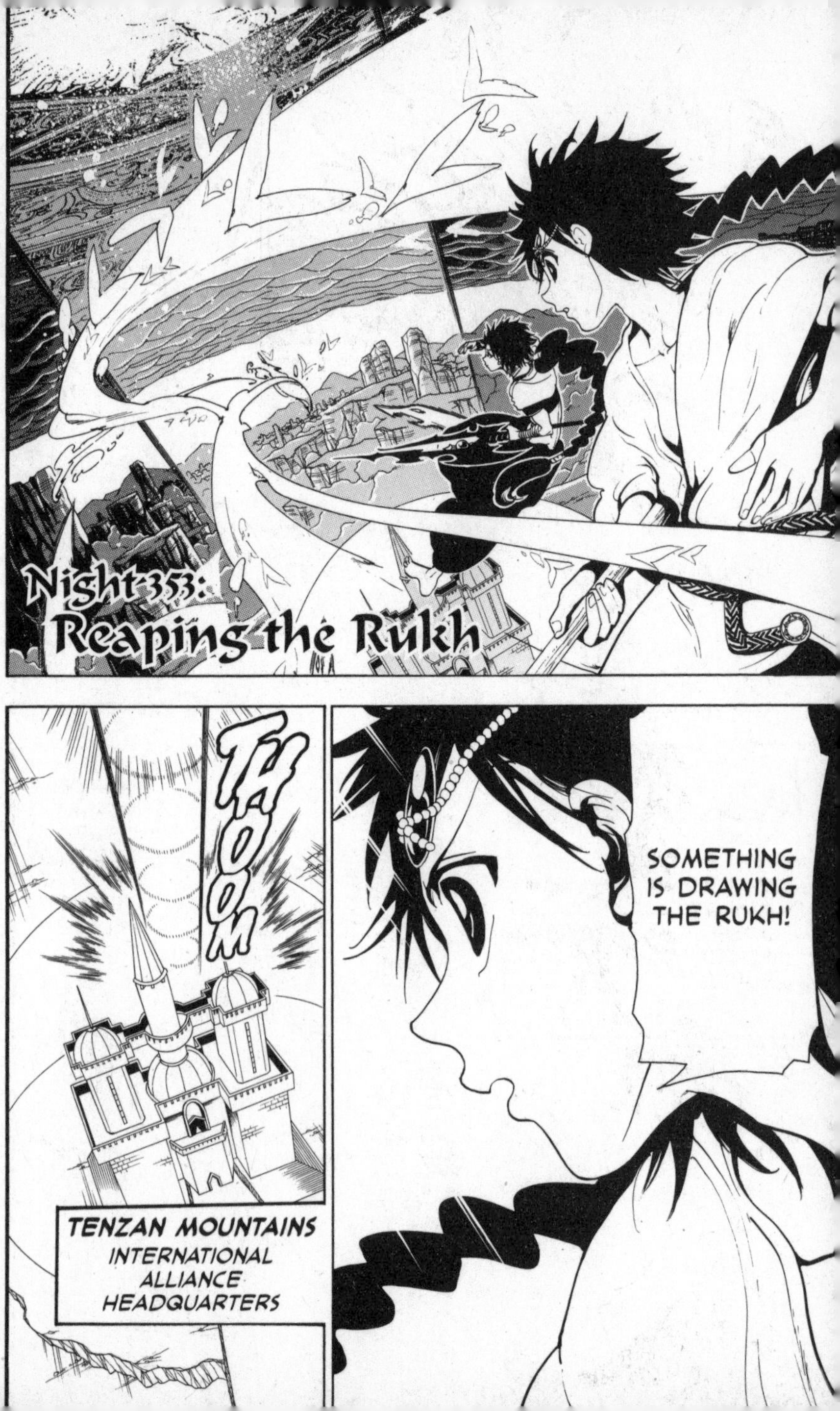
Night 353:
Reaping the Rukh
SOMETHING IS DRAWING THE RUKH!
THOOOM
TENZAN MOUNTAINS
INTERNATIONAL ALLIANCE HEADQUARTERS

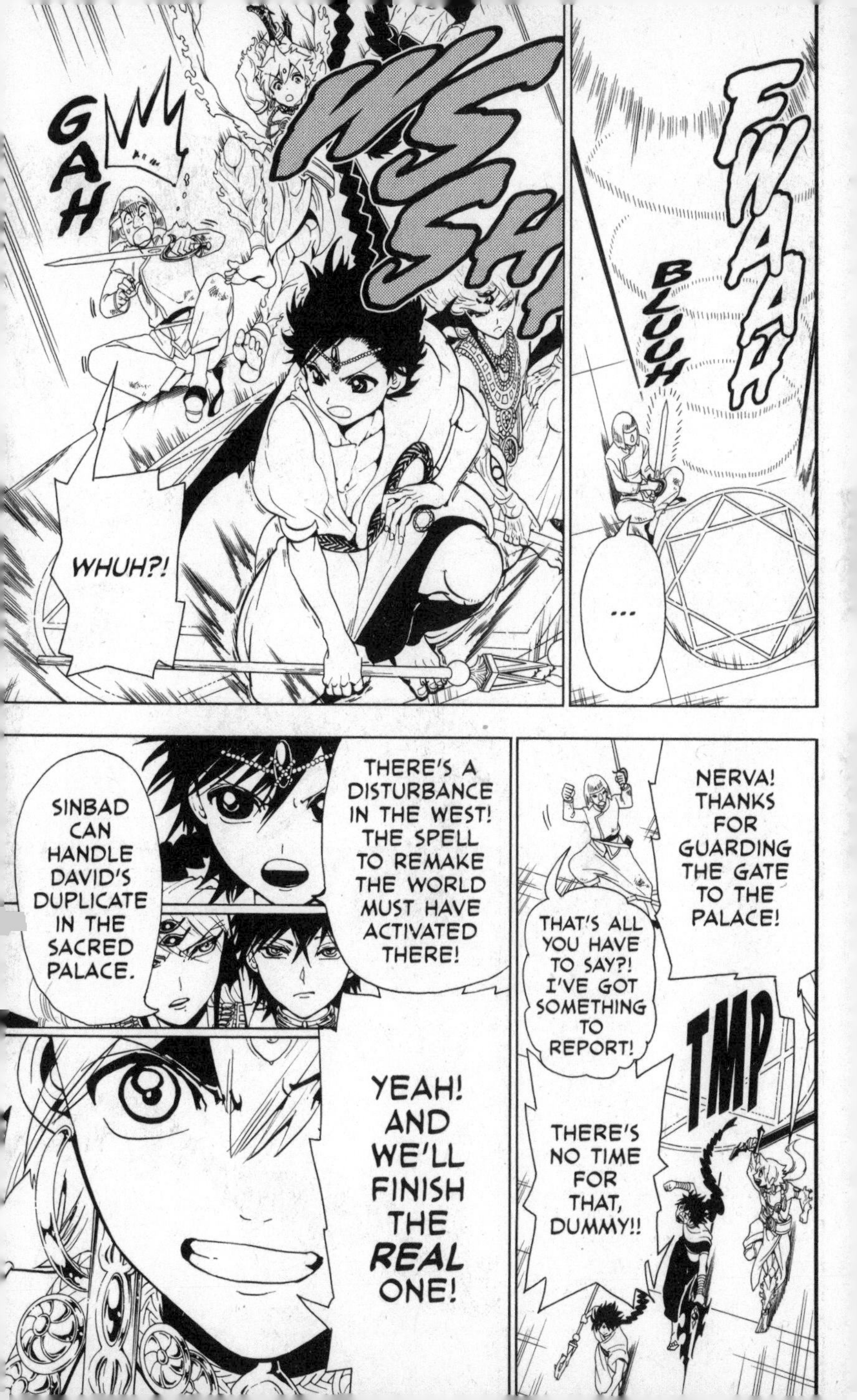
FWAAAH
BLUUH
...
WHSH
GAH
WHUH?!
NERVA! THANKS FOR GUARDING THE GATE TO THE PALACE!
THAT'S ALL YOU HAVE TO SAY?! I'VE GOT SOMETHING TO REPORT!
TMP
THERE'S NO TIME FOR THAT, DUMMY!!
THERE'S A DISTURBANCE IN THE WEST! THE SPELL TO REMAKE THE WORLD MUST HAVE ACTIVATED THERE!
SINBAD CAN HANDLE DAVID'S DUPLICATE IN THE SACRED PALACE.
YEAH! AND WE'LL FINISH THE REAL ONE!

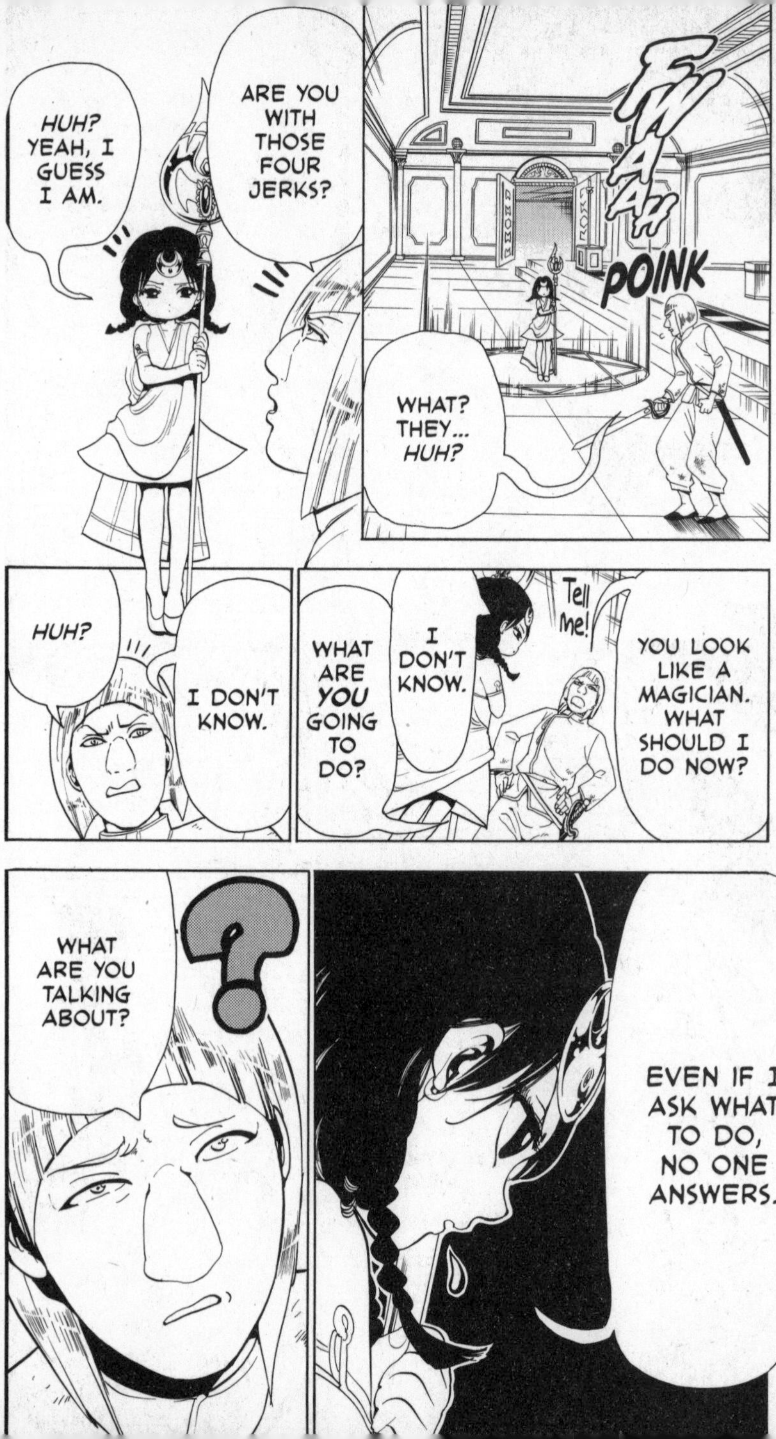
FWAAH
POINK
WHAT? THEY... *HUH?*
ARE YOU WITH THOSE FOUR JERKS?
HUH? YEAH, I GUESS I AM.
Tell me!
YOU LOOK LIKE A MAGICIAN. WHAT SHOULD I DO NOW?
I DON'T KNOW.
WHAT ARE *YOU* GOING TO DO?
I DON'T KNOW.
HUH?
EVEN IF I ASK WHAT TO DO, NO ONE ANSWERS.
WHAT ARE YOU TALKING ABOUT?

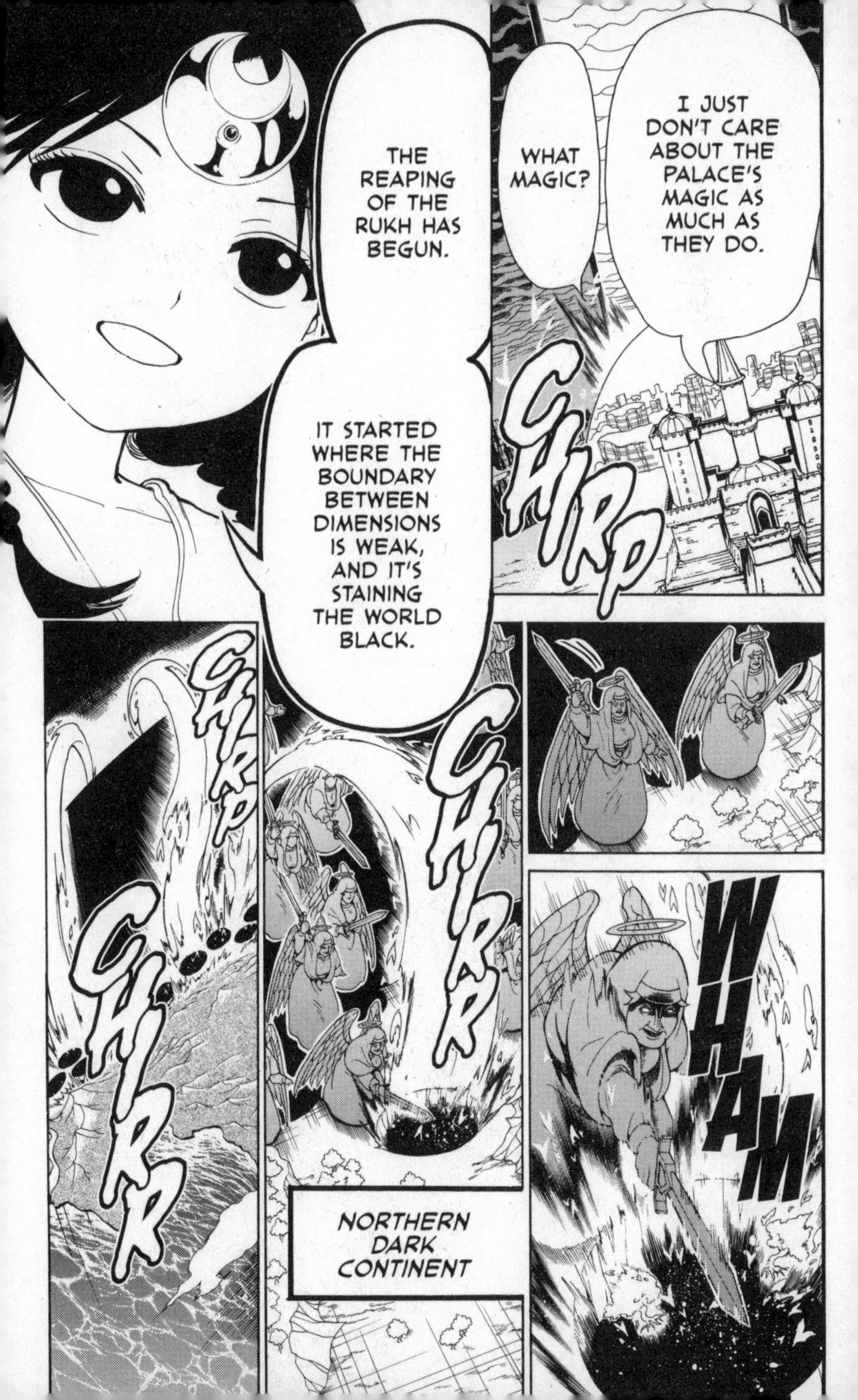
I JUST DON'T CARE ABOUT THE PALACE'S MAGIC AS MUCH AS THEY DO.
WHAT MAGIC?
CHIRP
THE REAPING OF THE RUKH HAS BEGUN.
IT STARTED WHERE THE BOUNDARY BETWEEN DIMENSIONS IS WEAK, AND IT'S STAINING THE WORLD BLACK.
WHAM
CHIRRP
NORTHERN DARK CONTINENT
CHIRP
CHIRRR

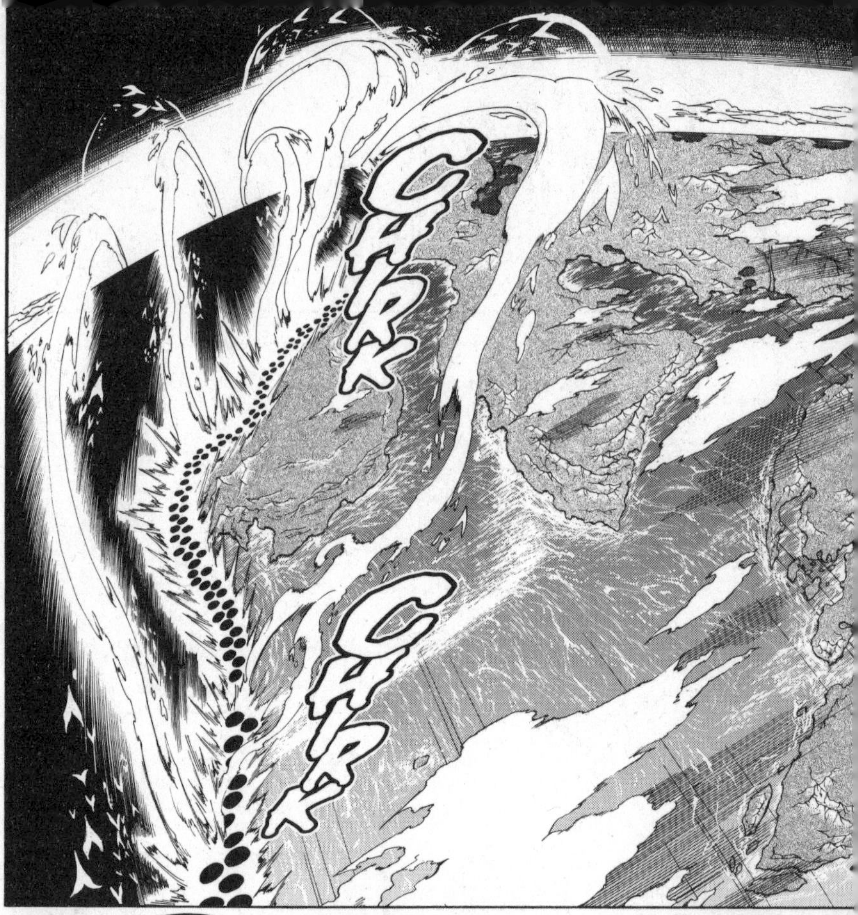
CHAK
CHAK

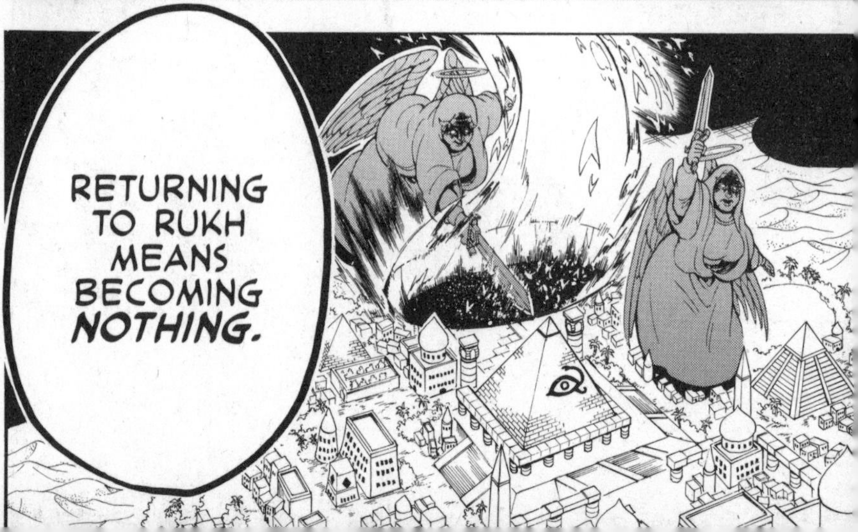
RETURNING TO RUKH MEANS BECOMING NOTHING.

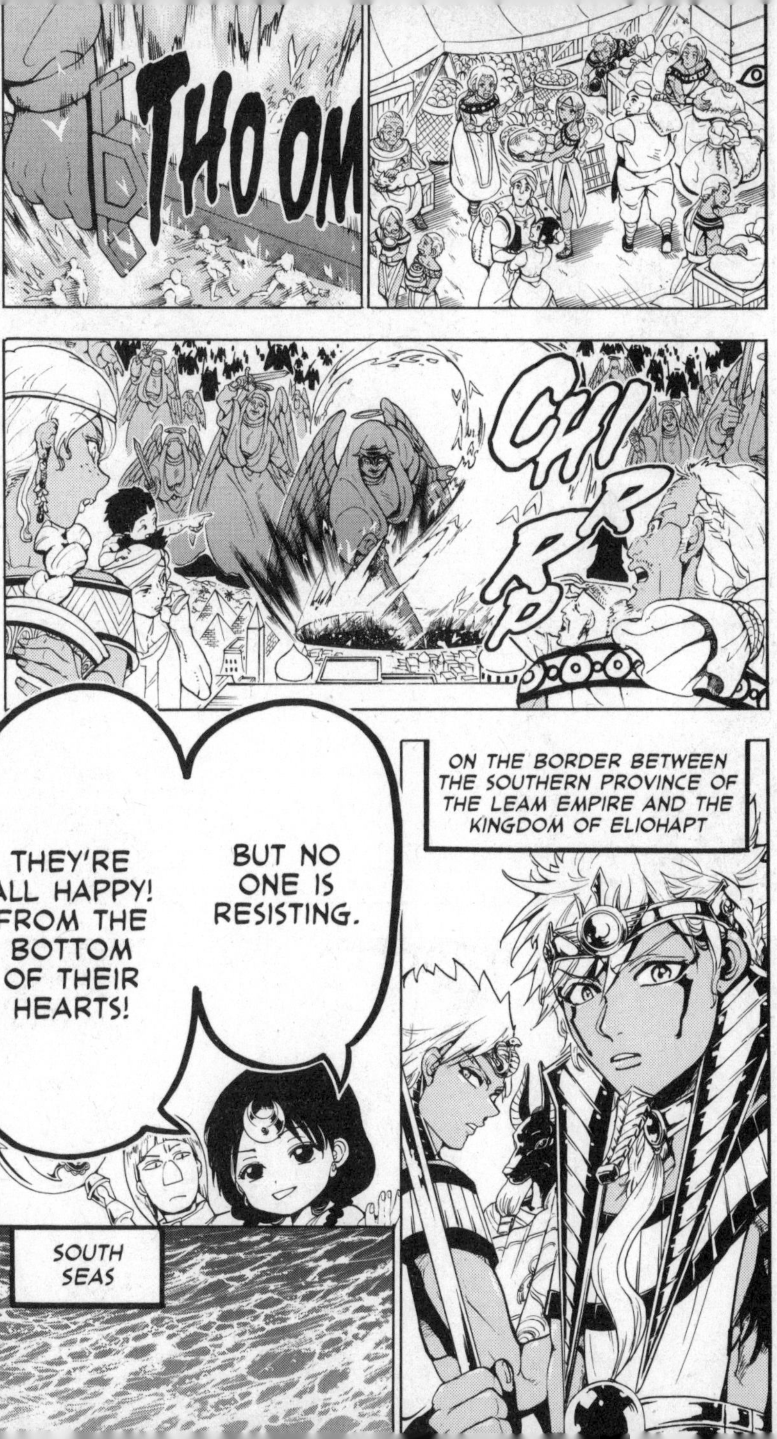
THOOM
CHIRRP
ON THE BORDER BETWEEN THE SOUTHERN PROVINCE OF THE LEAM EMPIRE AND THE KINGDOM OF ELIOHAPT
BUT NO ONE IS RESISTING.
THEY'RE ALL HAPPY! FROM THE BOTTOM OF THEIR HEARTS!
SOUTH SEAS

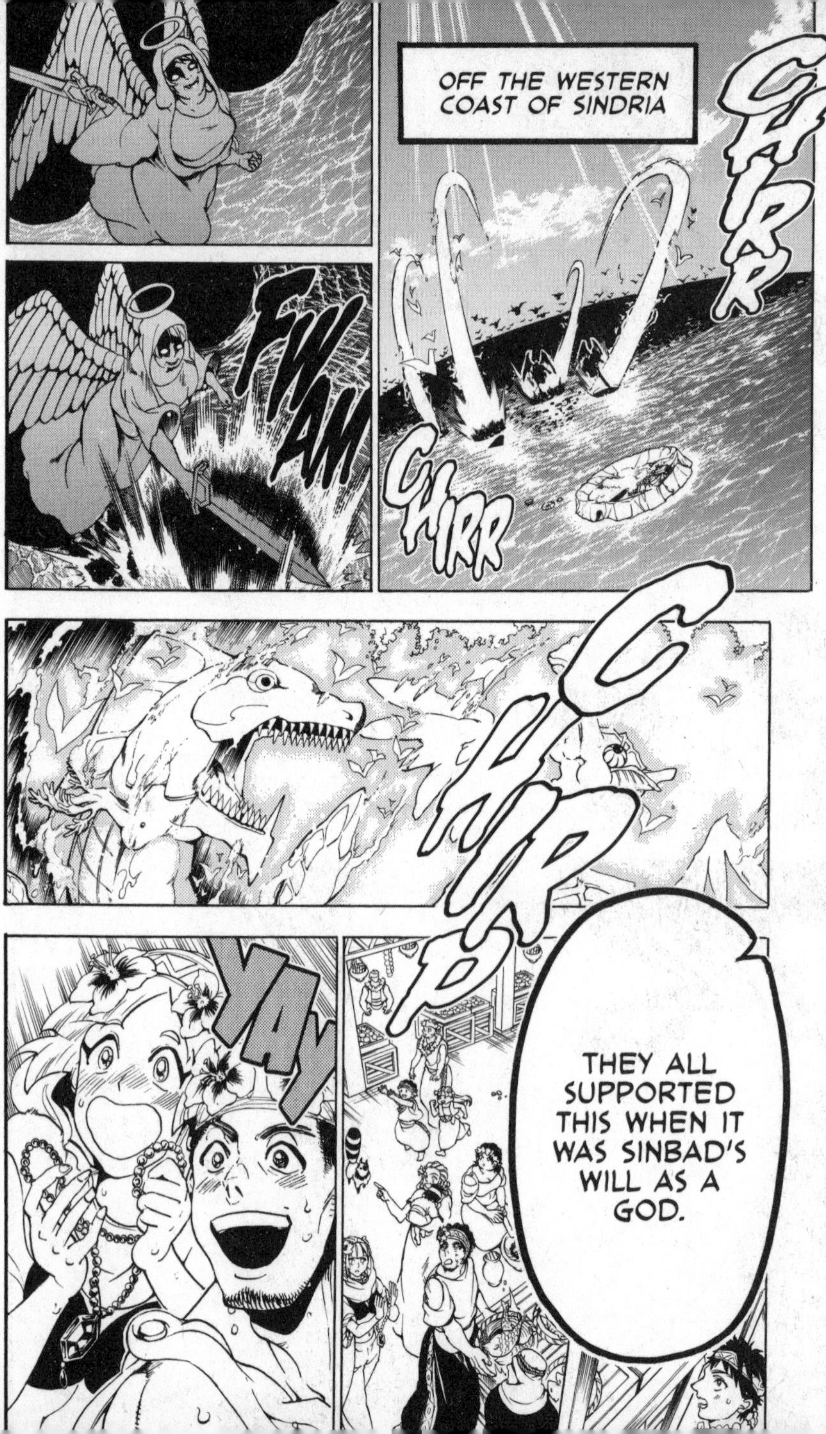
OFF THE WESTERN COAST OF SINDRIA
CHIRR
CHIRR
FWAM
CHIRP
THEY ALL SUPPORTED THIS WHEN IT WAS SINBAD'S WILL AS A GOD.
YAY

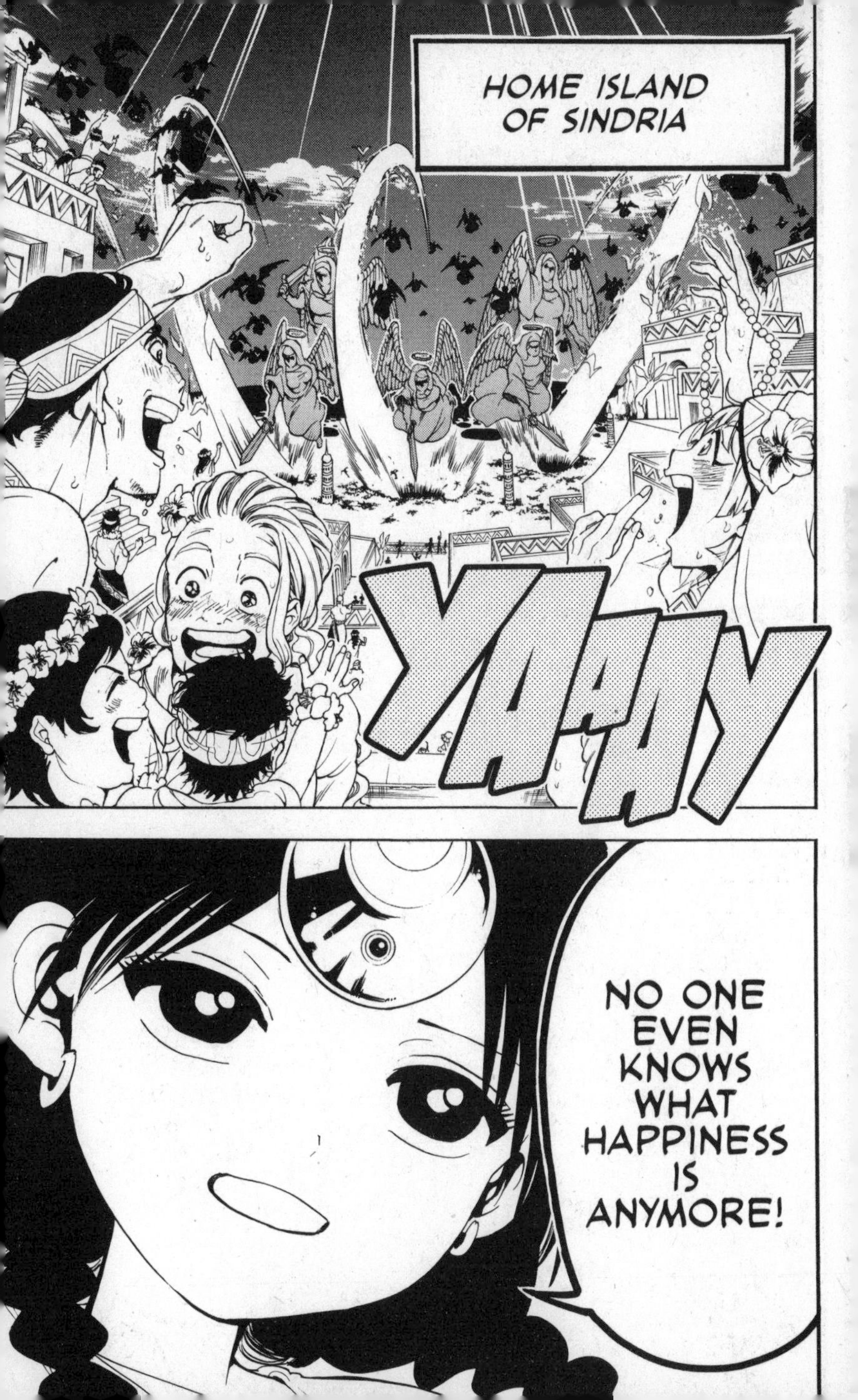
HOME ISLAND OF SINDRIA
YAAAY
NO ONE EVEN KNOWS WHAT HAPPINESS IS ANYMORE!

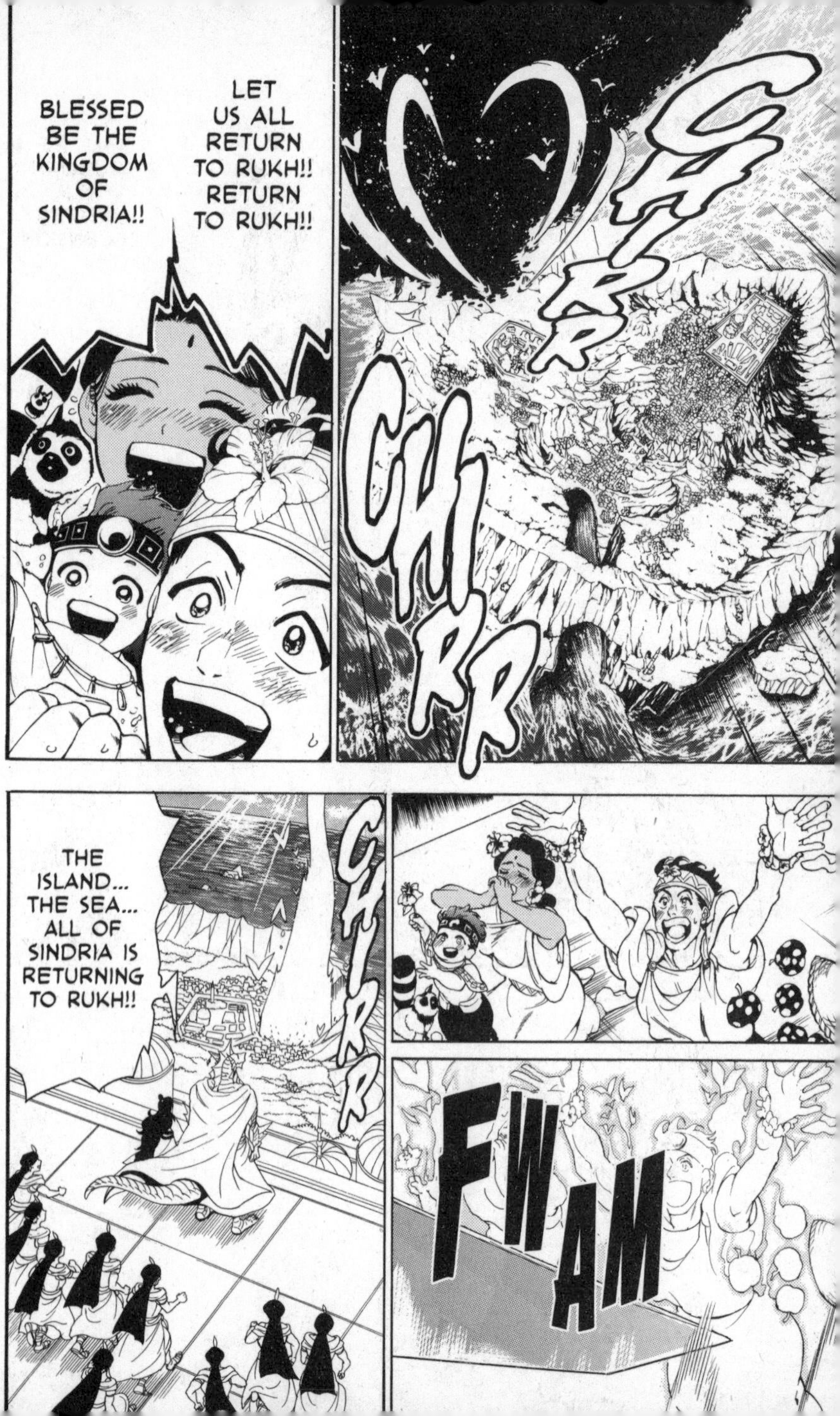
CHIRR
CHIRR
LET US ALL RETURN TO RUKH!! RETURN TO RUKH!!
BLESSED BE THE KINGDOM OF SINDRIA!!
FWAM
THE ISLAND... THE SEA... ALL OF SINDRIA IS RETURNING TO RUKH!!
CHIRR

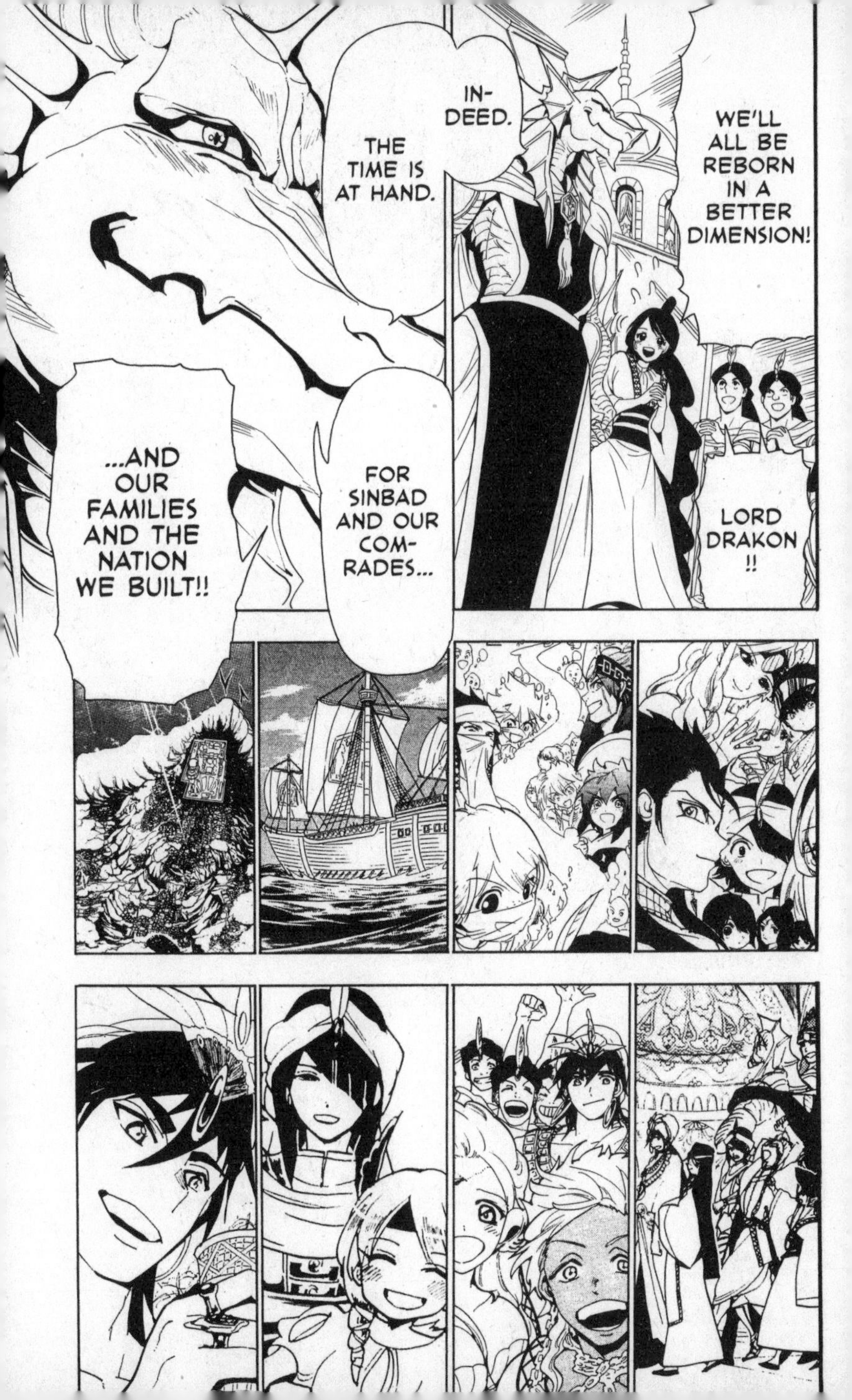
WE'LL ALL BE REBORN IN A BETTER DIMENSION!
LORD DRAKON!!
IN-DEED.
THE TIME IS AT HAND.
FOR SINBAD AND OUR COM-RADES...
...AND OUR FAMILIES AND THE NATION WE BUILT!!

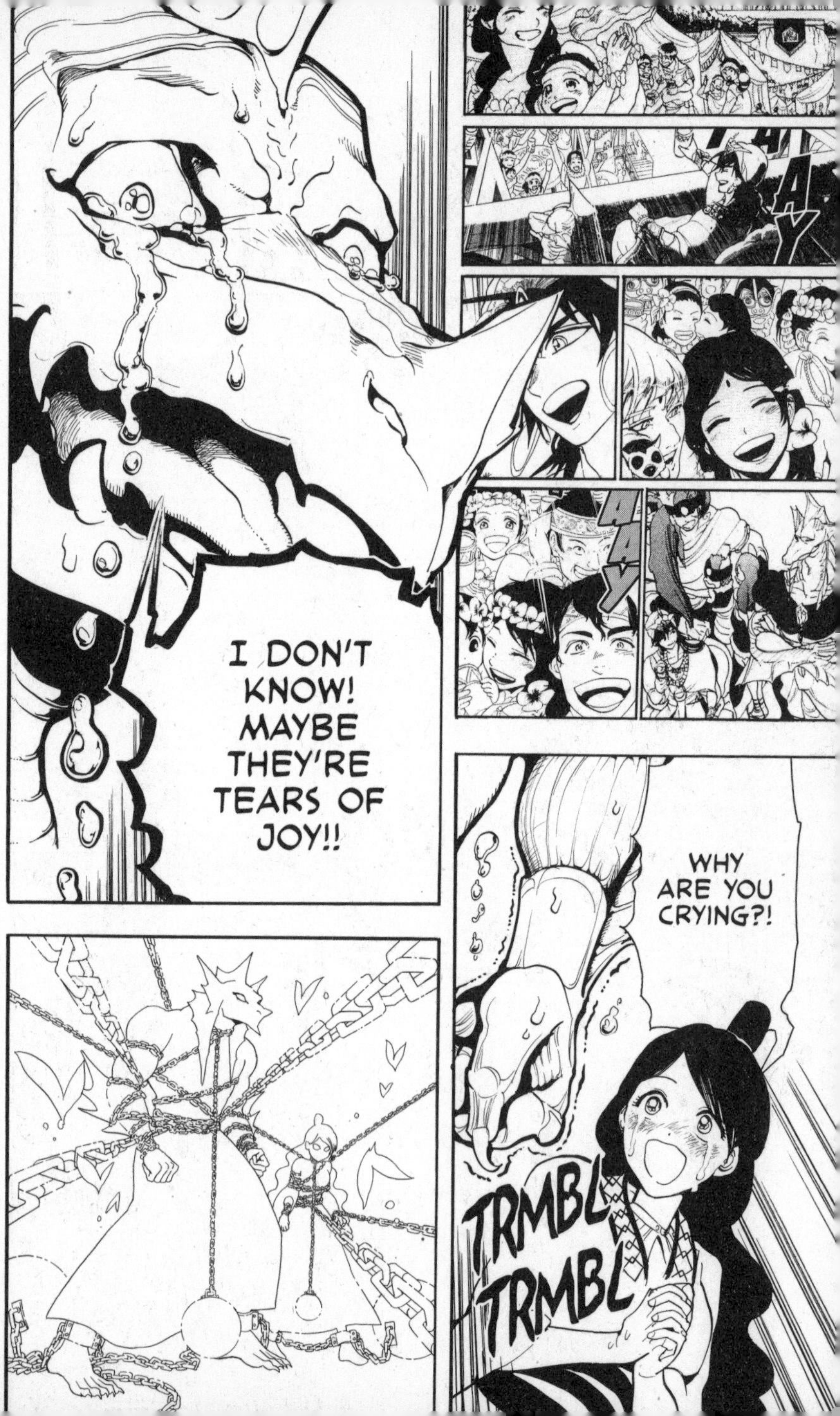

WHY ARE YOU CRYING?!
TRMBL TRMBL
I DON'T KNOW! MAYBE THEY'RE TEARS OF JOY!!

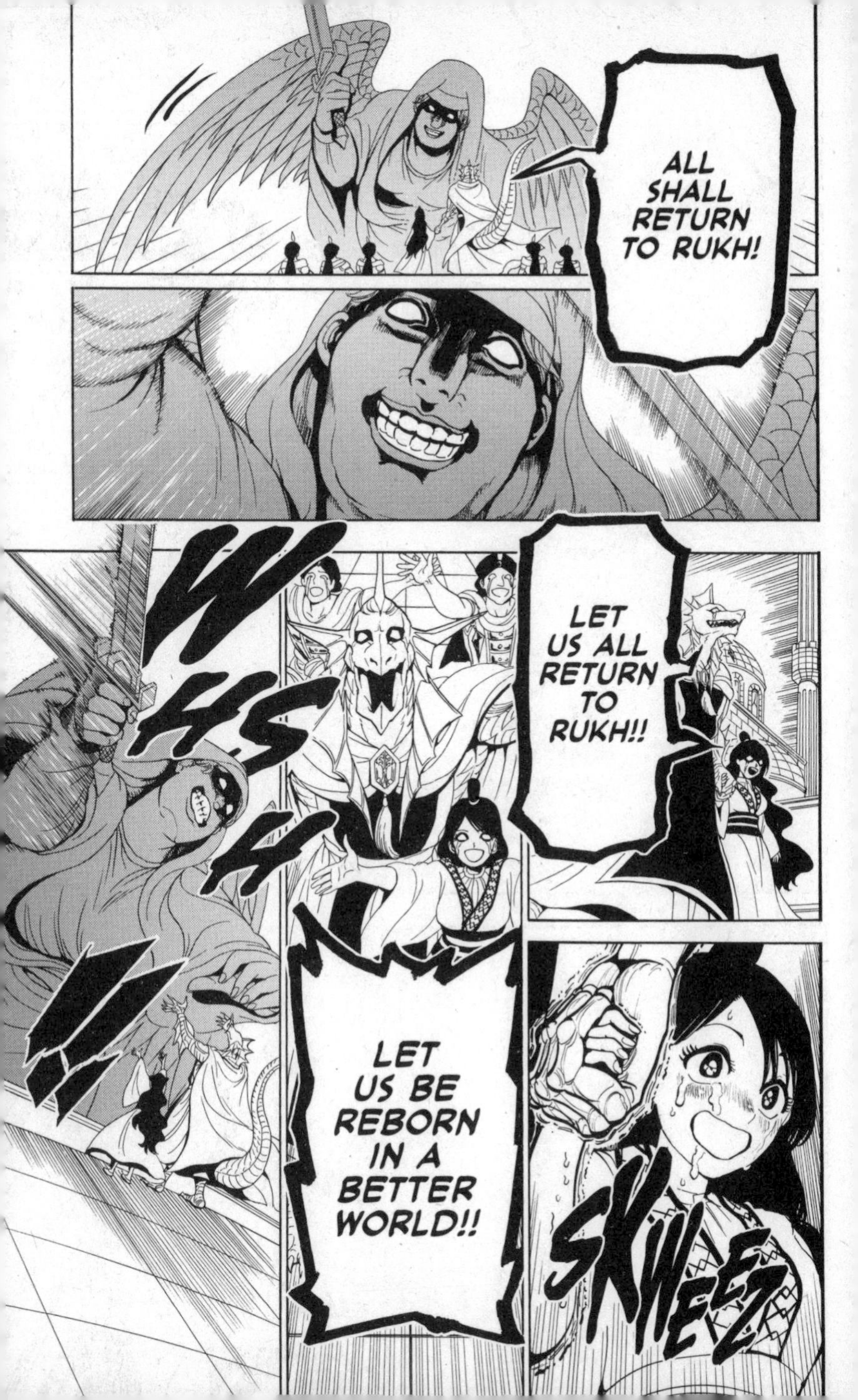
ALL SHALL RETURN TO RUKH!
LET US ALL RETURN TO RUKH!!
SKWEEZ
LET US BE REBORN IN A BETTER WORLD!!
WHSH
!!

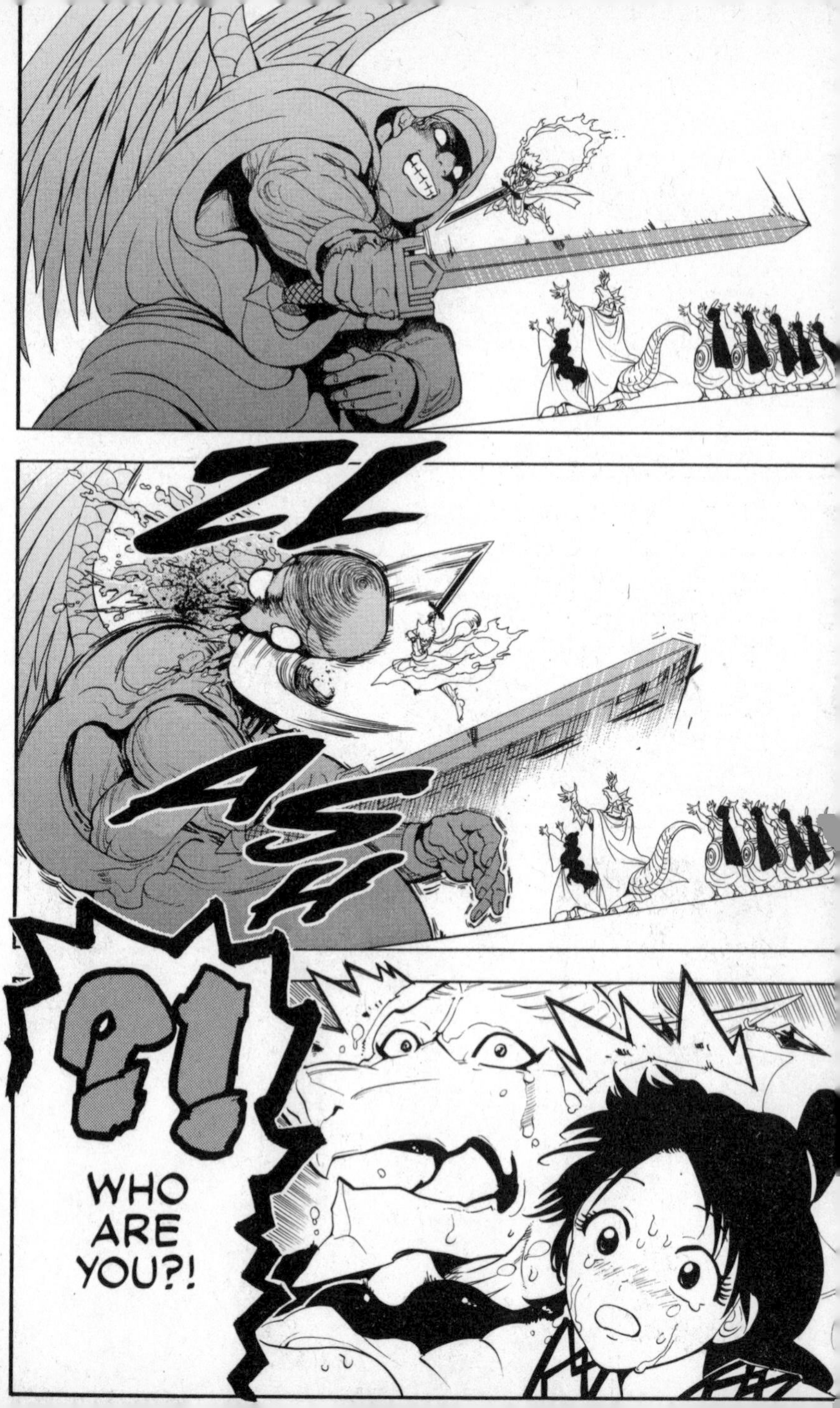
ZZASH
?!
WHO ARE YOU?!

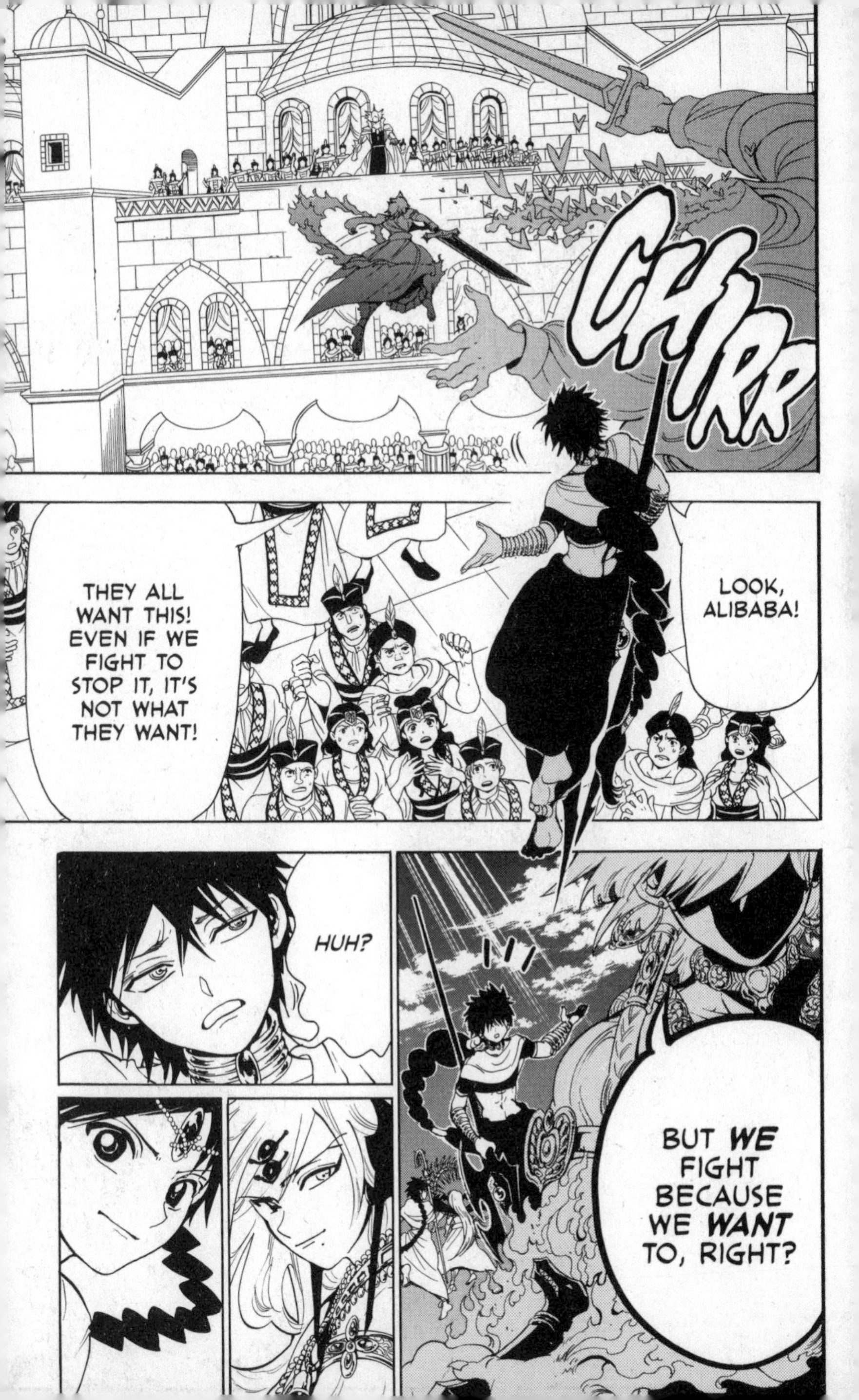
CHIRR
LOOK, ALIBABA!
THEY ALL WANT THIS! EVEN IF WE FIGHT TO STOP IT, IT'S NOT WHAT THEY WANT!
BUT **WE** FIGHT BECAUSE WE **WANT** TO, RIGHT?
HUH?

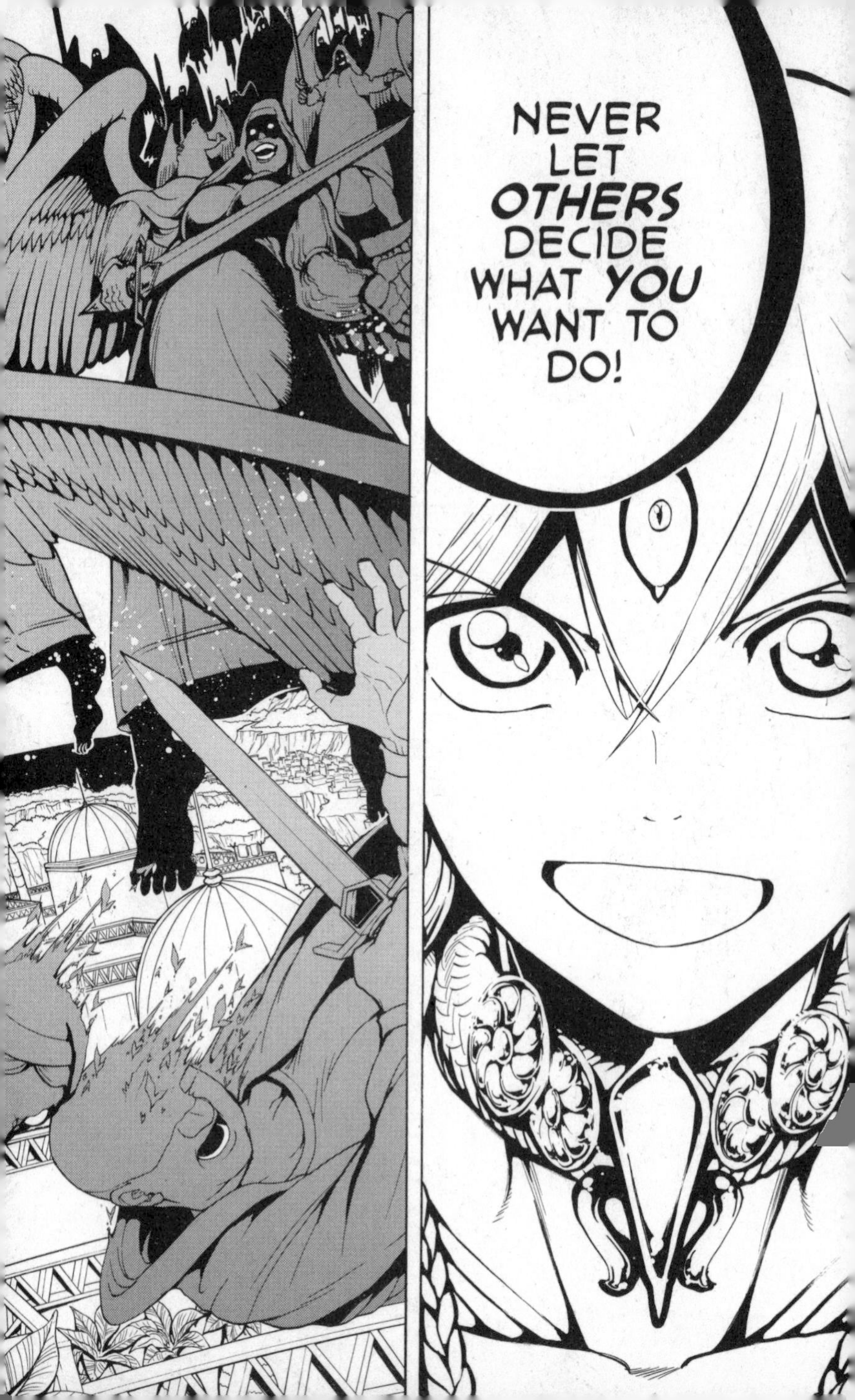
NEVER LET OTHERS DECIDE WHAT YOU WANT TO DO!

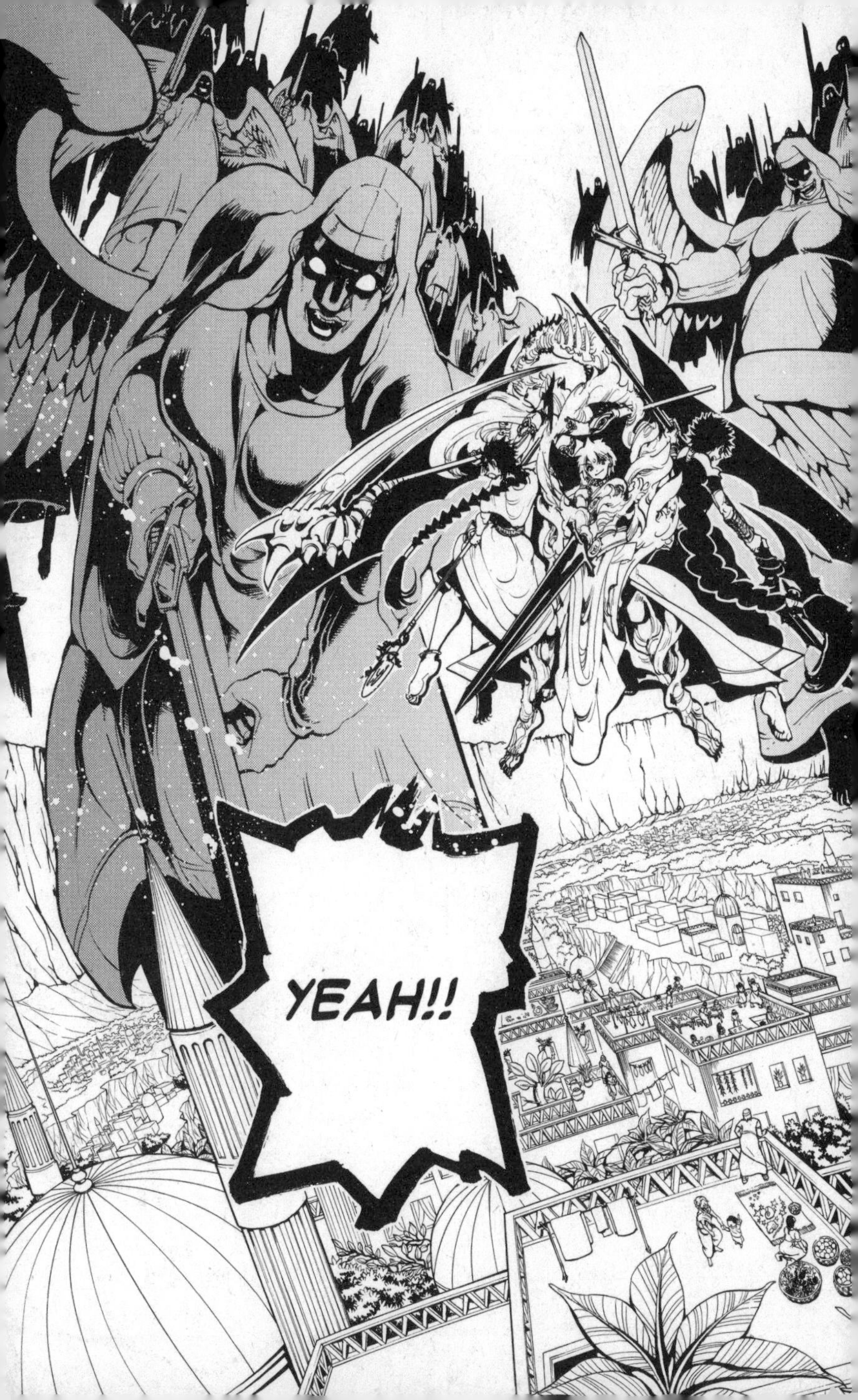
YEAH!!

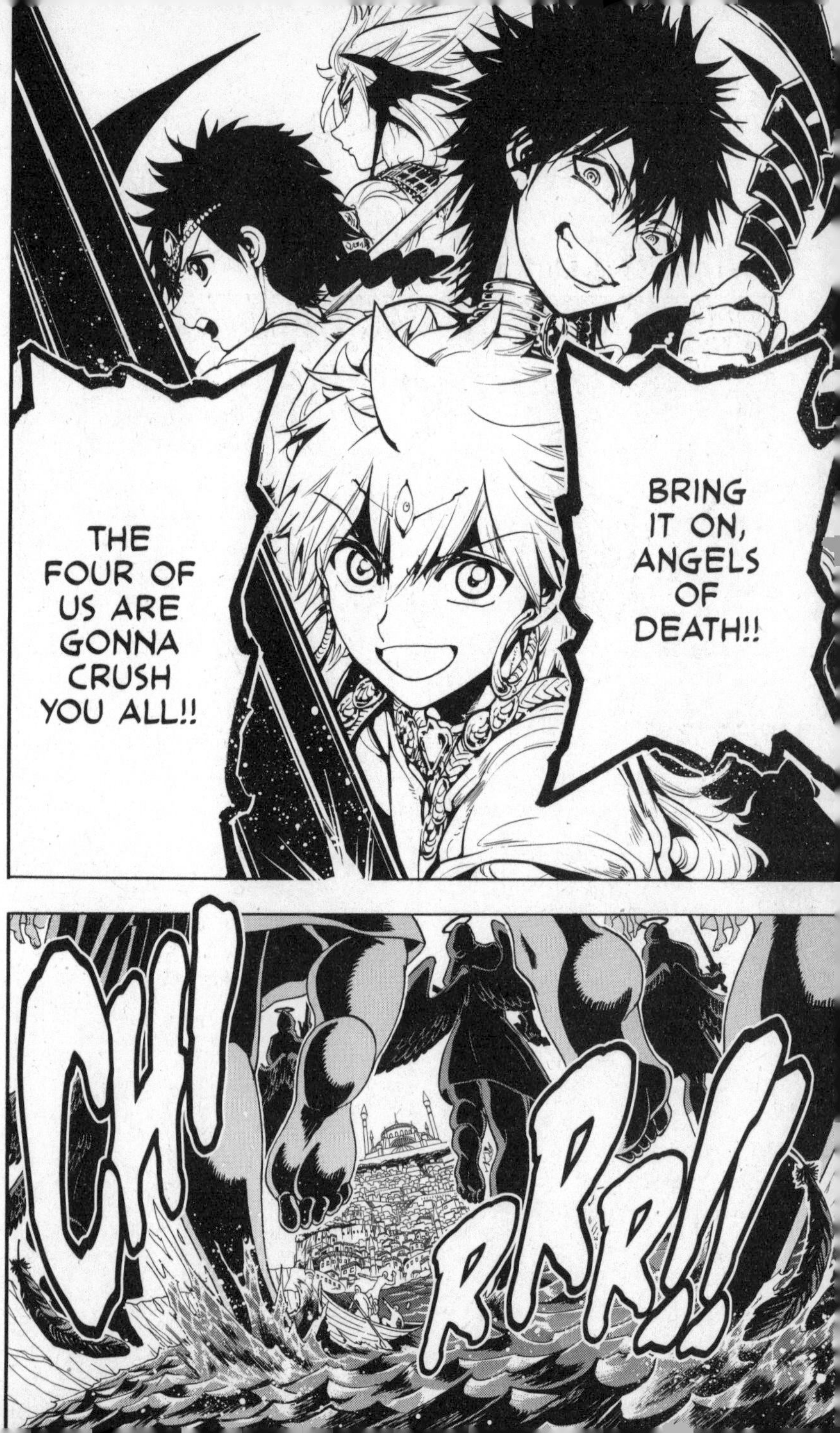
BRING IT ON, ANGELS OF DEATH!!
THE FOUR OF US ARE GONNA CRUSH YOU ALL!!
CHIRRR!!

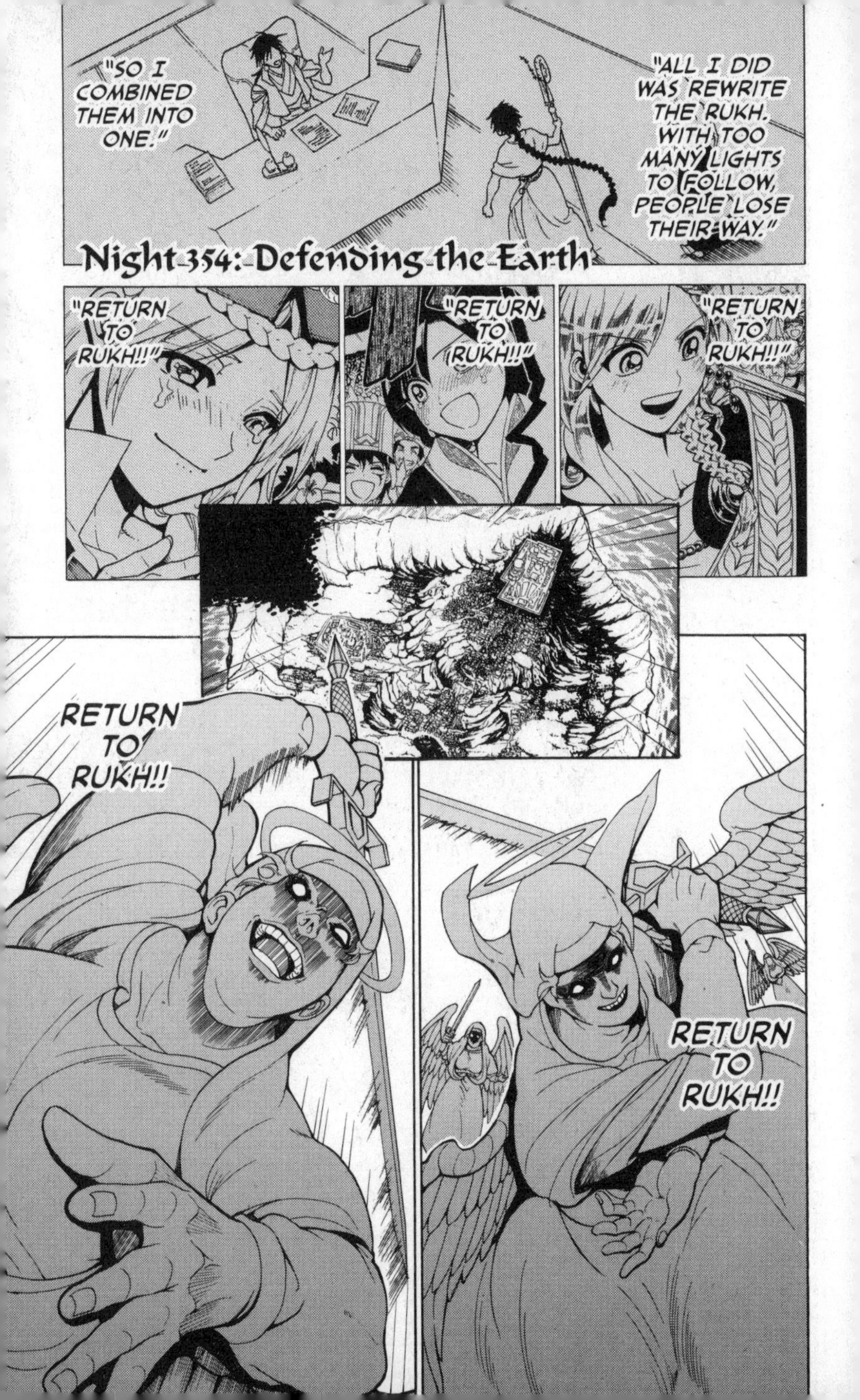
"ALL I DID WAS REWRITE THE RUKH. WITH TOO MANY LIGHTS TO FOLLOW, PEOPLE LOSE THEIR WAY."
"SO I COMBINED THEM INTO ONE."
Night 354: Defending the Earth
"RETURN TO RUKH!!"
"RETURN TO RUKH!!"
"RETURN TO RUKH!!"
RETURN TO RUKH!!
RETURN TO RUKH!!

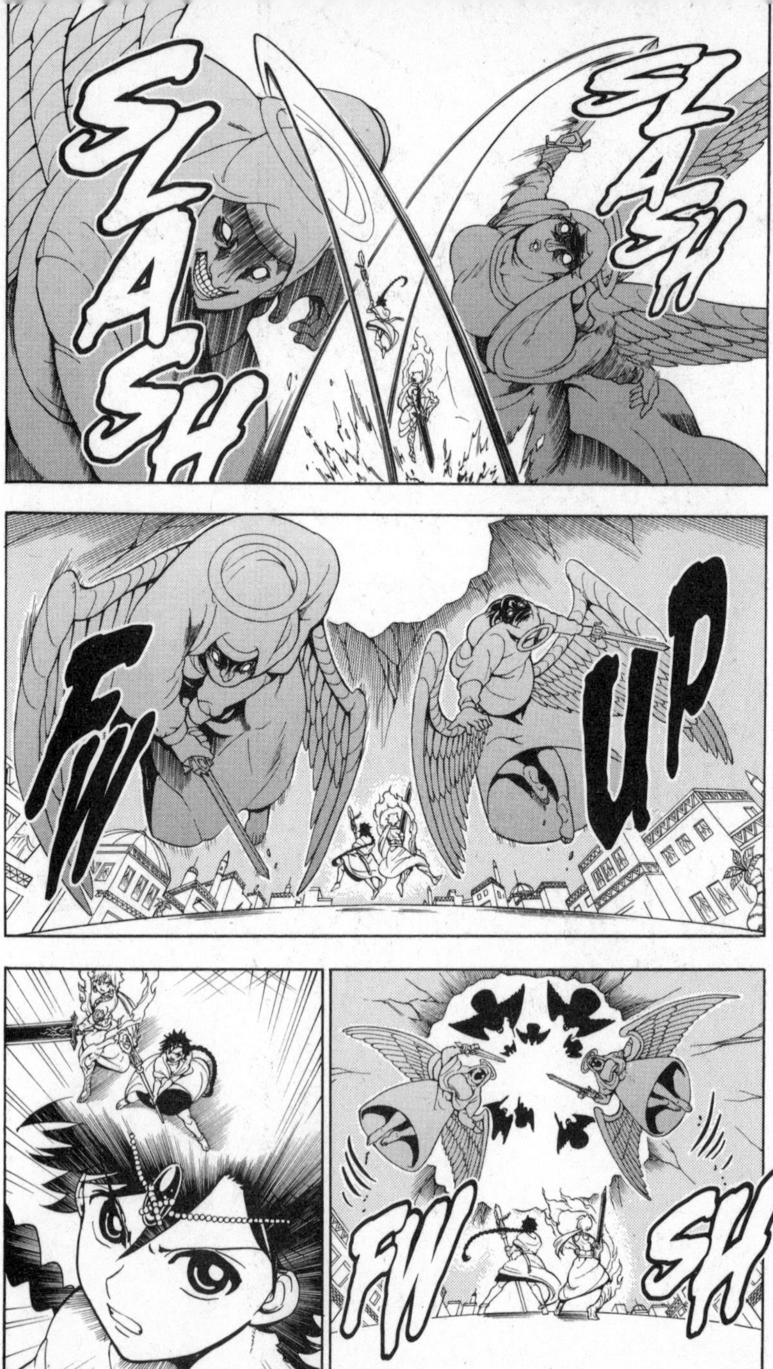
SLASH
SLASH
FWUP
FWSH

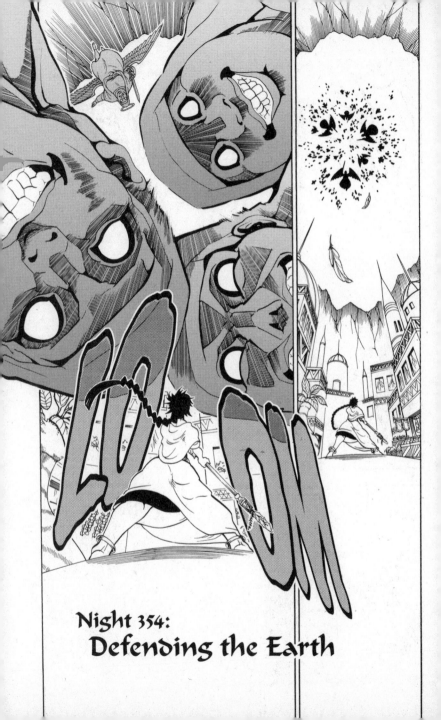

Night 354:
Defending the Earth

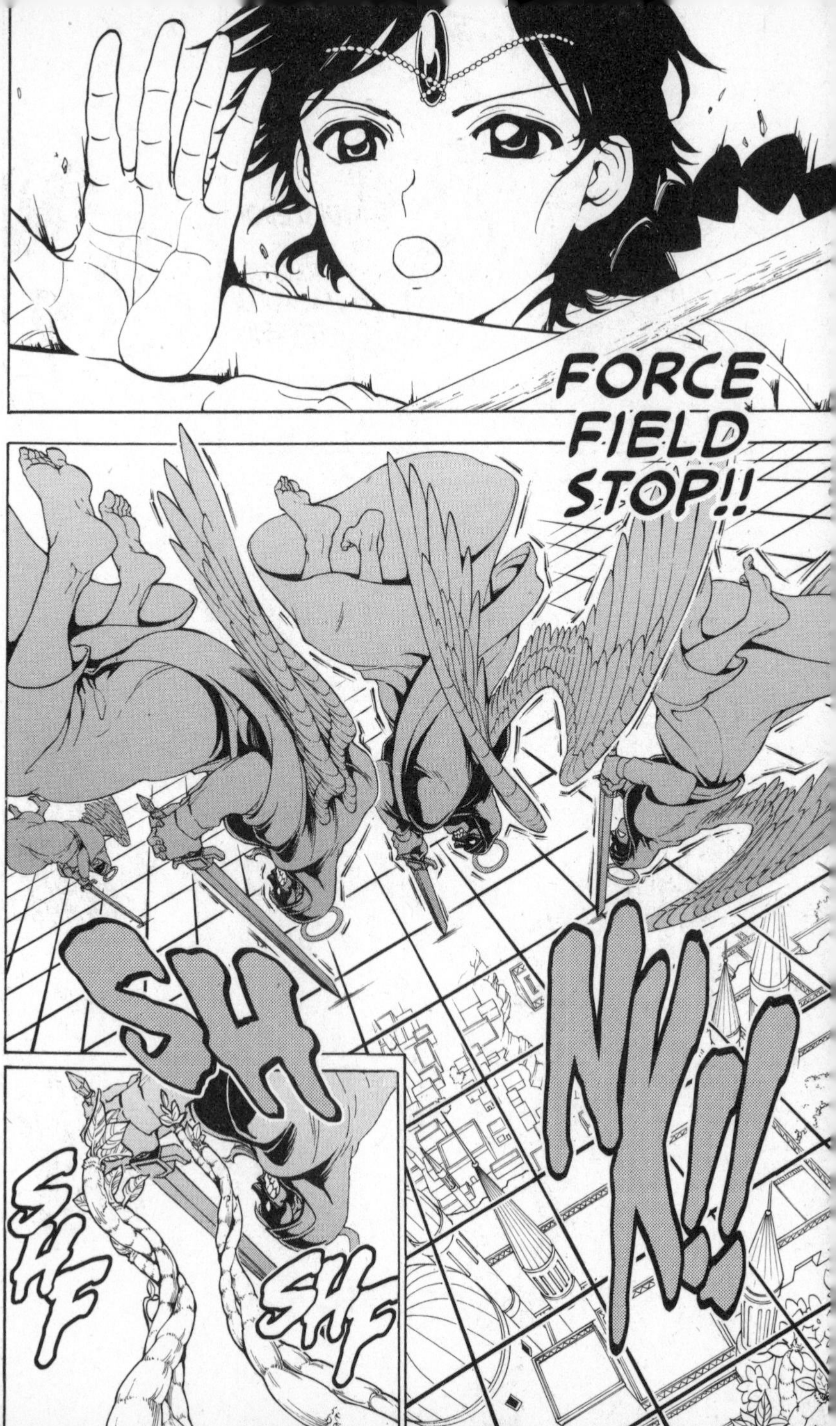
FORCE FIELD STOP!!
SHNK!!
SHF
SHF

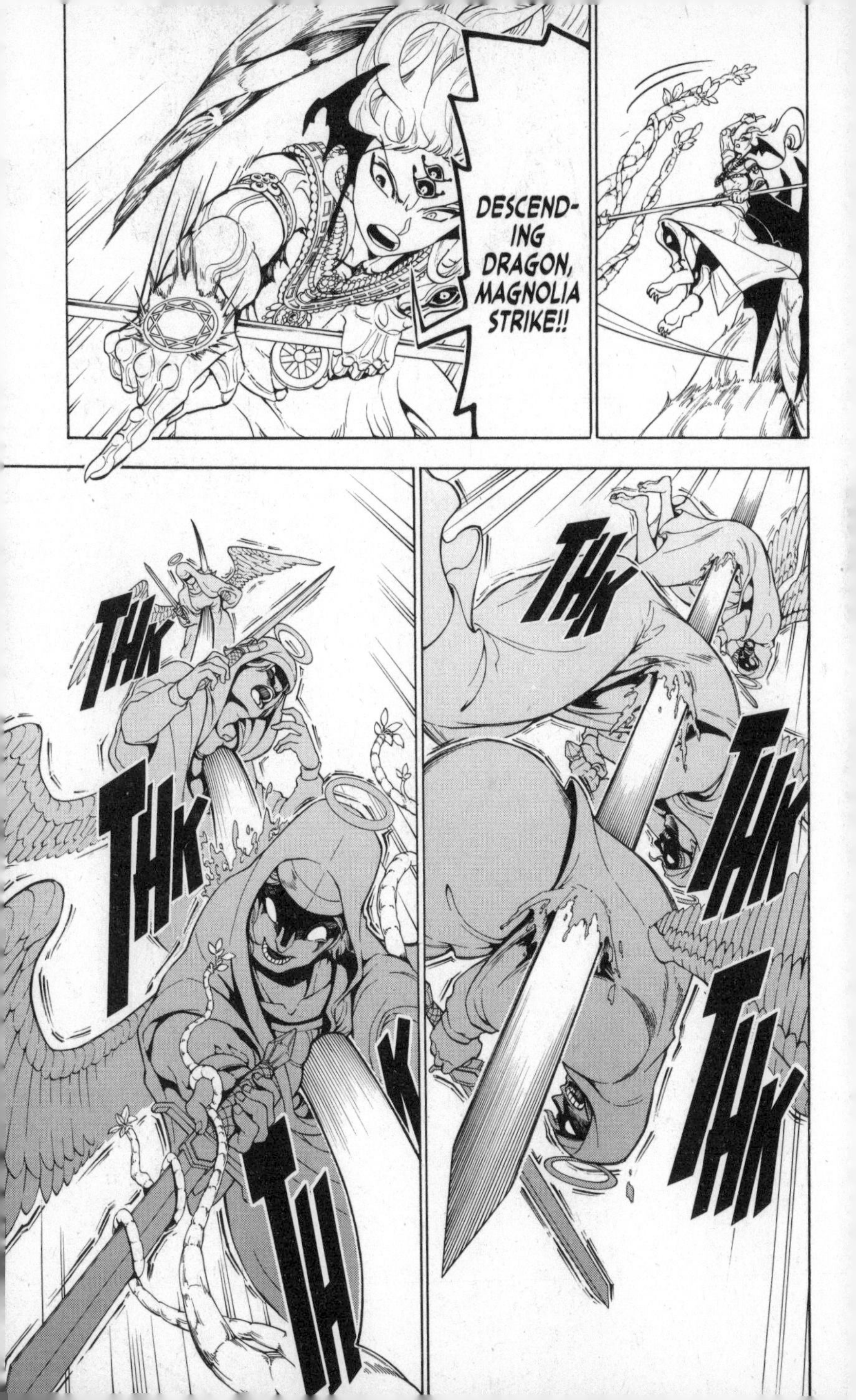
DESCEND-ING DRAGON, MAGNOLIA STRIKE!!
THK
THK
THK
THK
THK
THK

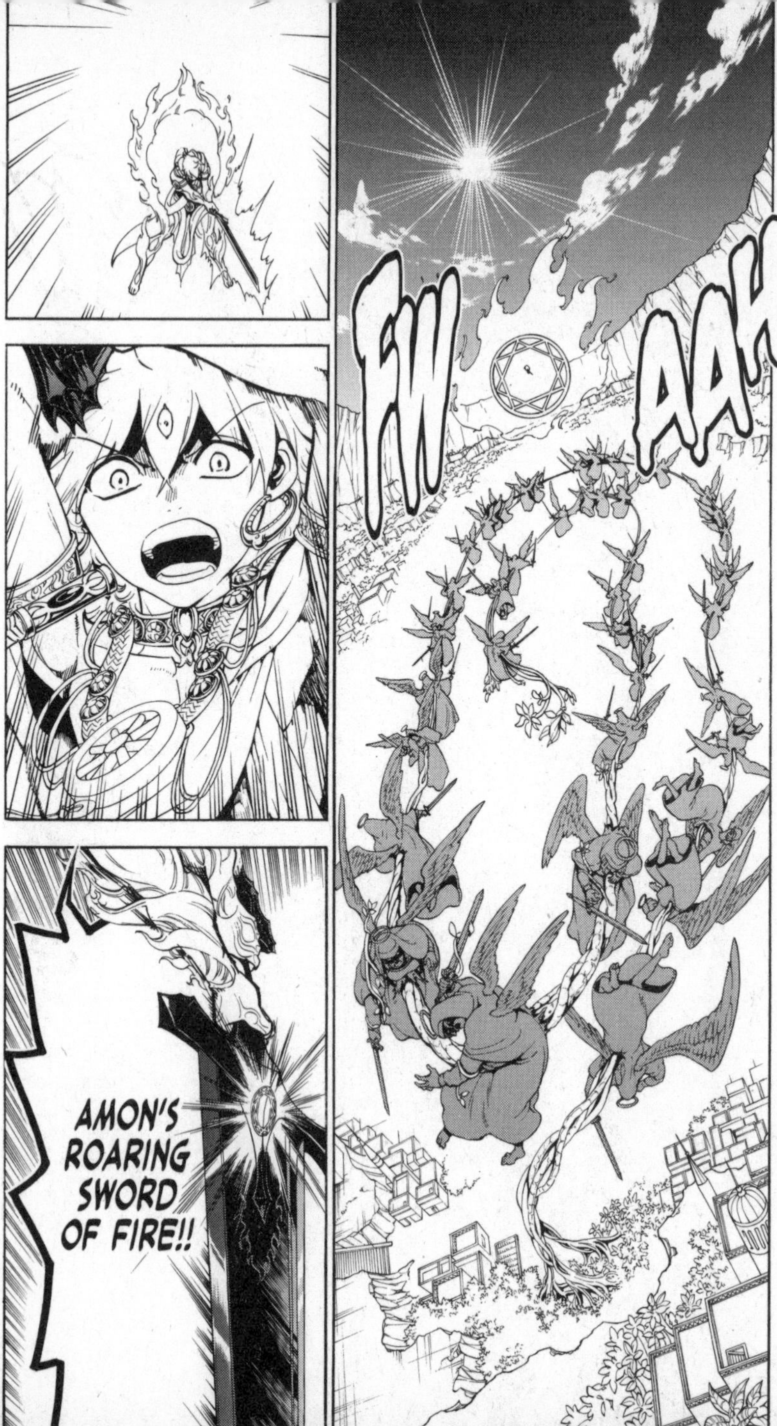
FW AAH
AMON'S ROARING SWORD OF FIRE!!

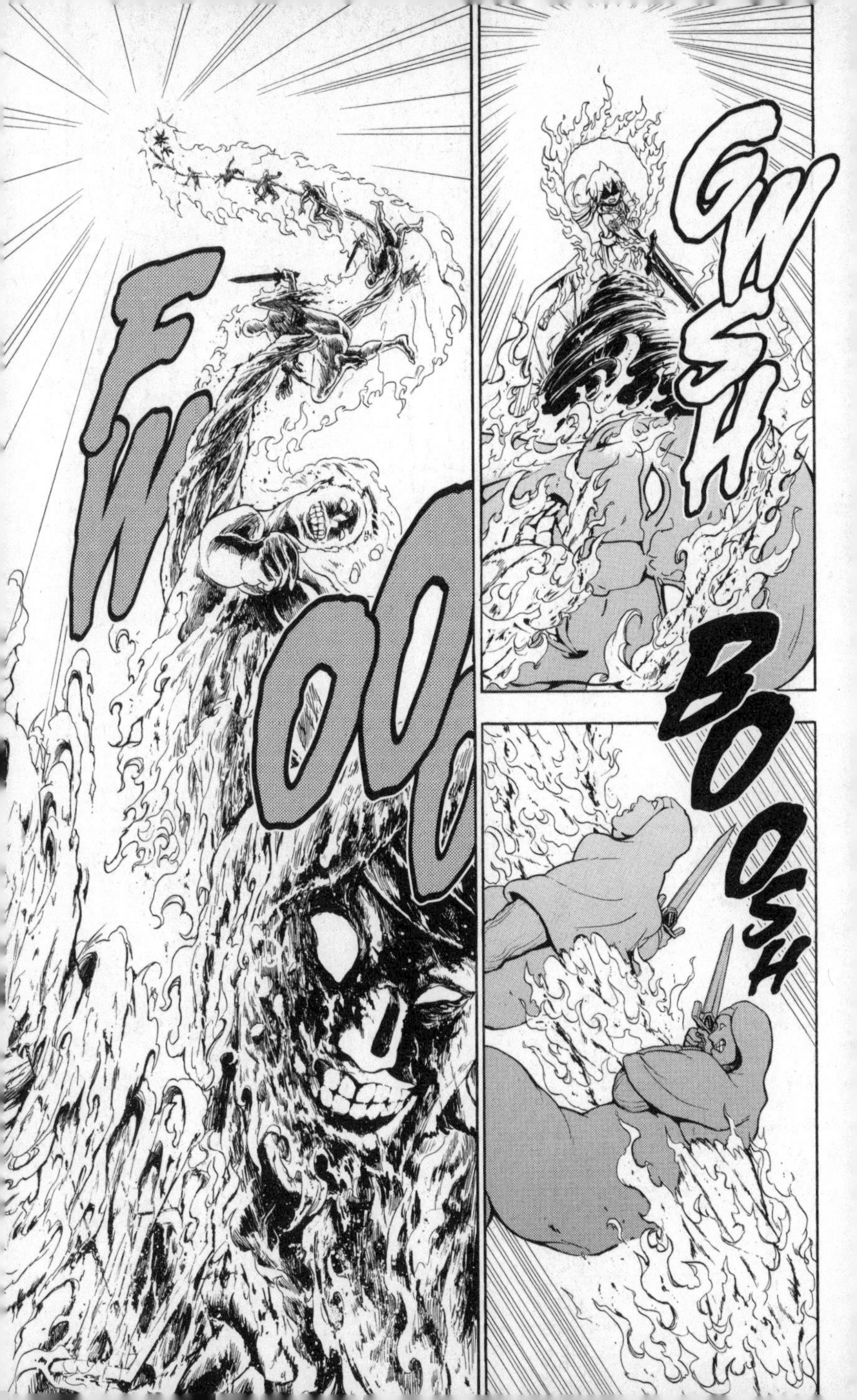
GWSH
BOOOSH
FWOOO

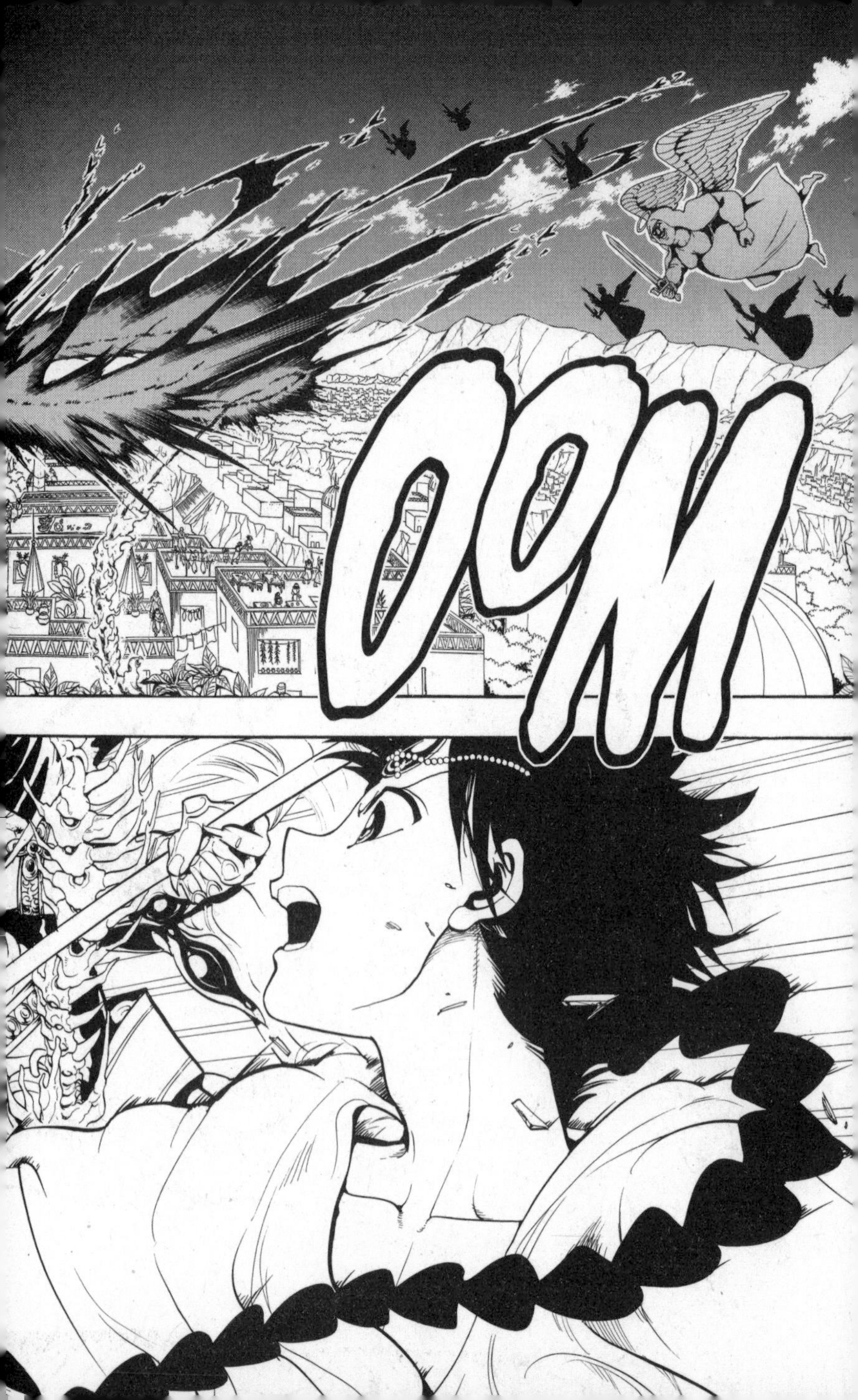
OOM

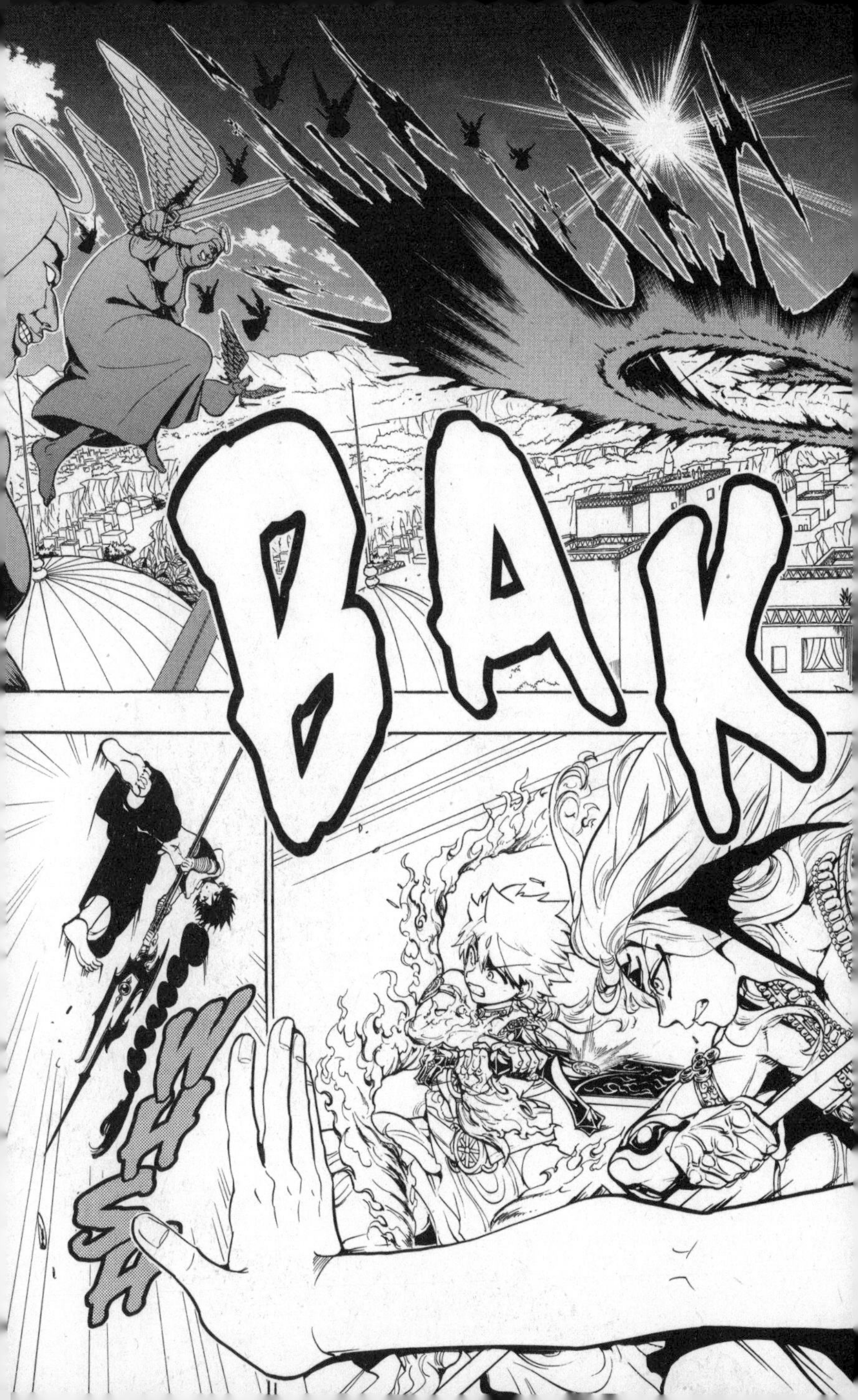
BAK

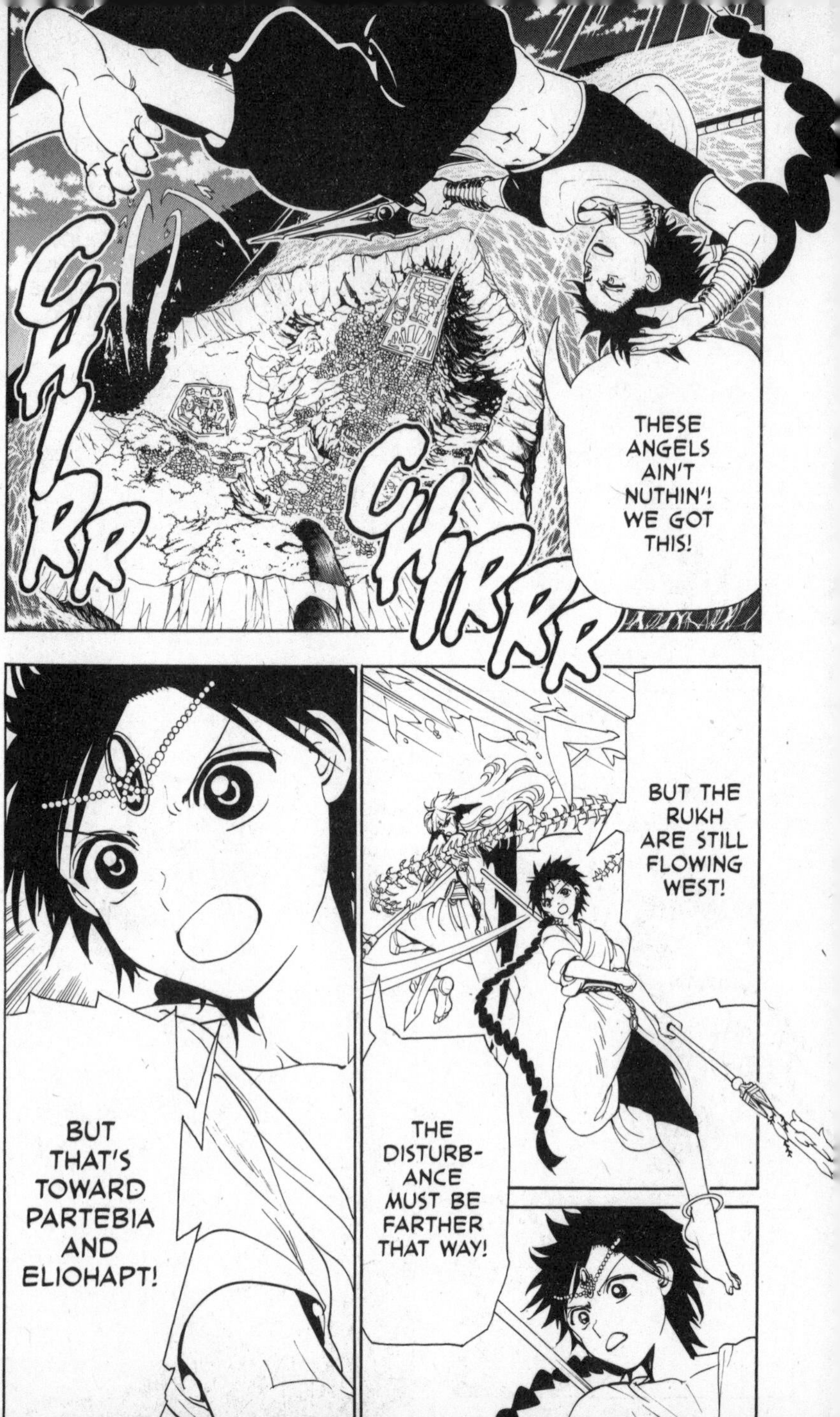
THESE ANGELS AIN'T NUTHIN'! WE GOT THIS!
CHIRR
CHIRRR
BUT THE RUKH ARE STILL FLOWING WEST!
THE DISTURB-ANCE MUST BE FARTHER THAT WAY!
BUT THAT'S TOWARD PARTEBIA AND ELIOHAPT!

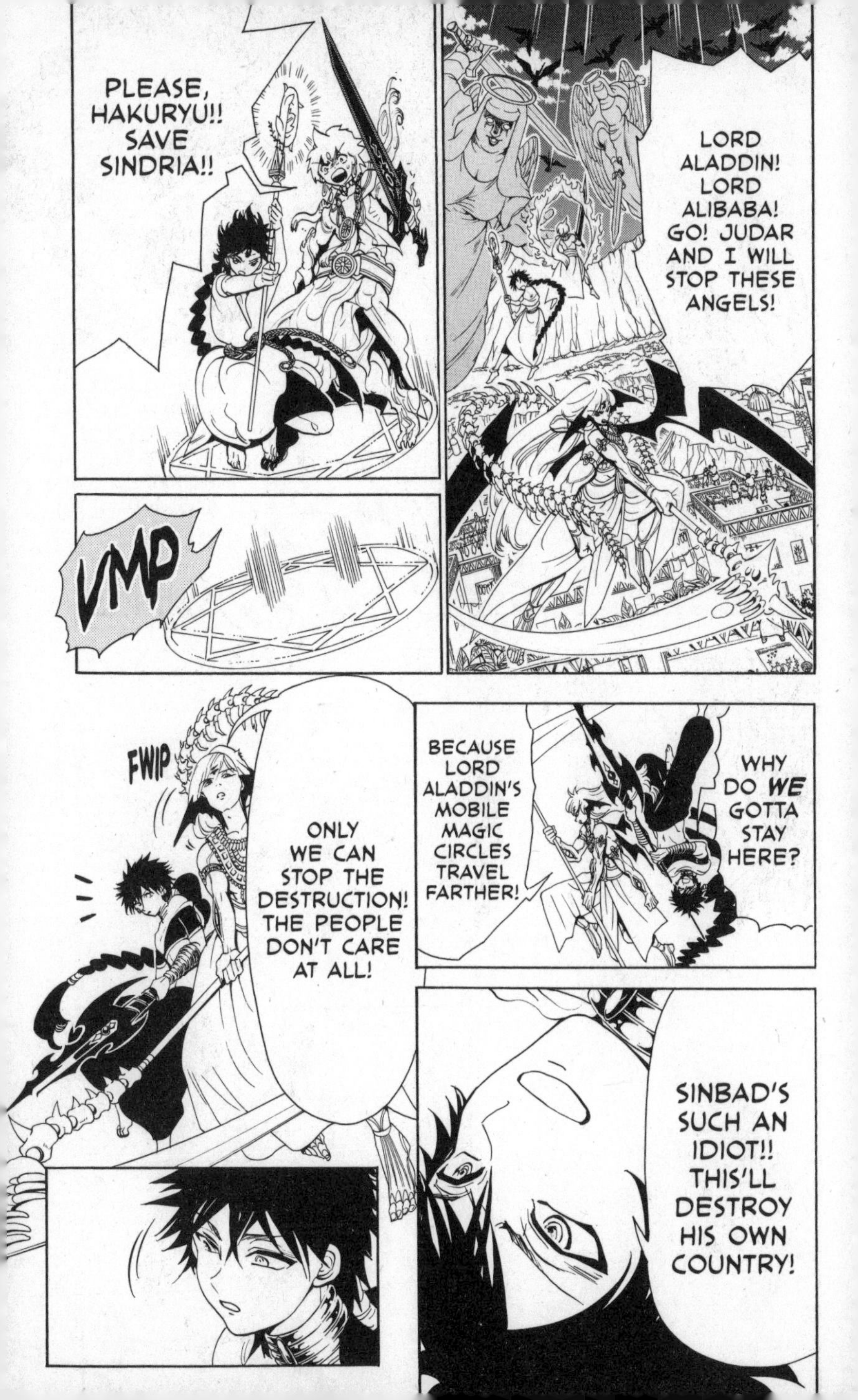
LORD ALADDIN! LORD ALIBABA! GO! JUDAR AND I WILL STOP THESE ANGELS!
PLEASE, HAKURYU!! SAVE SINDRIA!!
VMP
WHY DO *WE* GOTTA STAY HERE?
BECAUSE LORD ALADDIN'S MOBILE MAGIC CIRCLES TRAVEL FARTHER!
SINBAD'S SUCH AN IDIOT!! THIS'LL DESTROY HIS OWN COUNTRY!
FWIP
ONLY WE CAN STOP THE DESTRUCTION! THE PEOPLE DON'T CARE AT ALL!

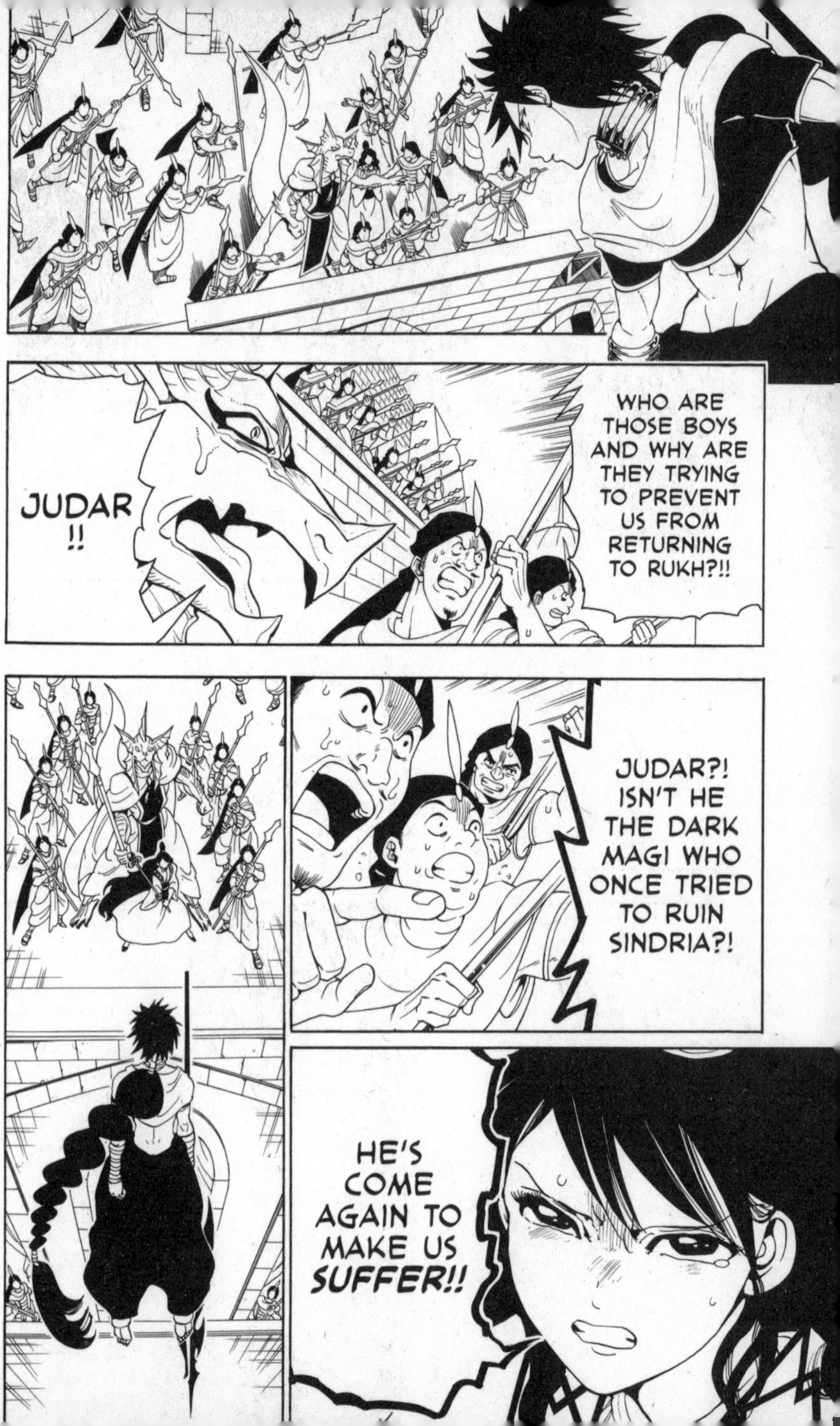
WHO ARE THOSE BOYS AND WHY ARE THEY TRYING TO PREVENT US FROM RETURNING TO RUKH?!!
JUDAR !!
JUDAR?! ISN'T HE THE DARK MAGI WHO ONCE TRIED TO RUIN SINDRIA?!
HE'S COME AGAIN TO MAKE US SUFFER!!

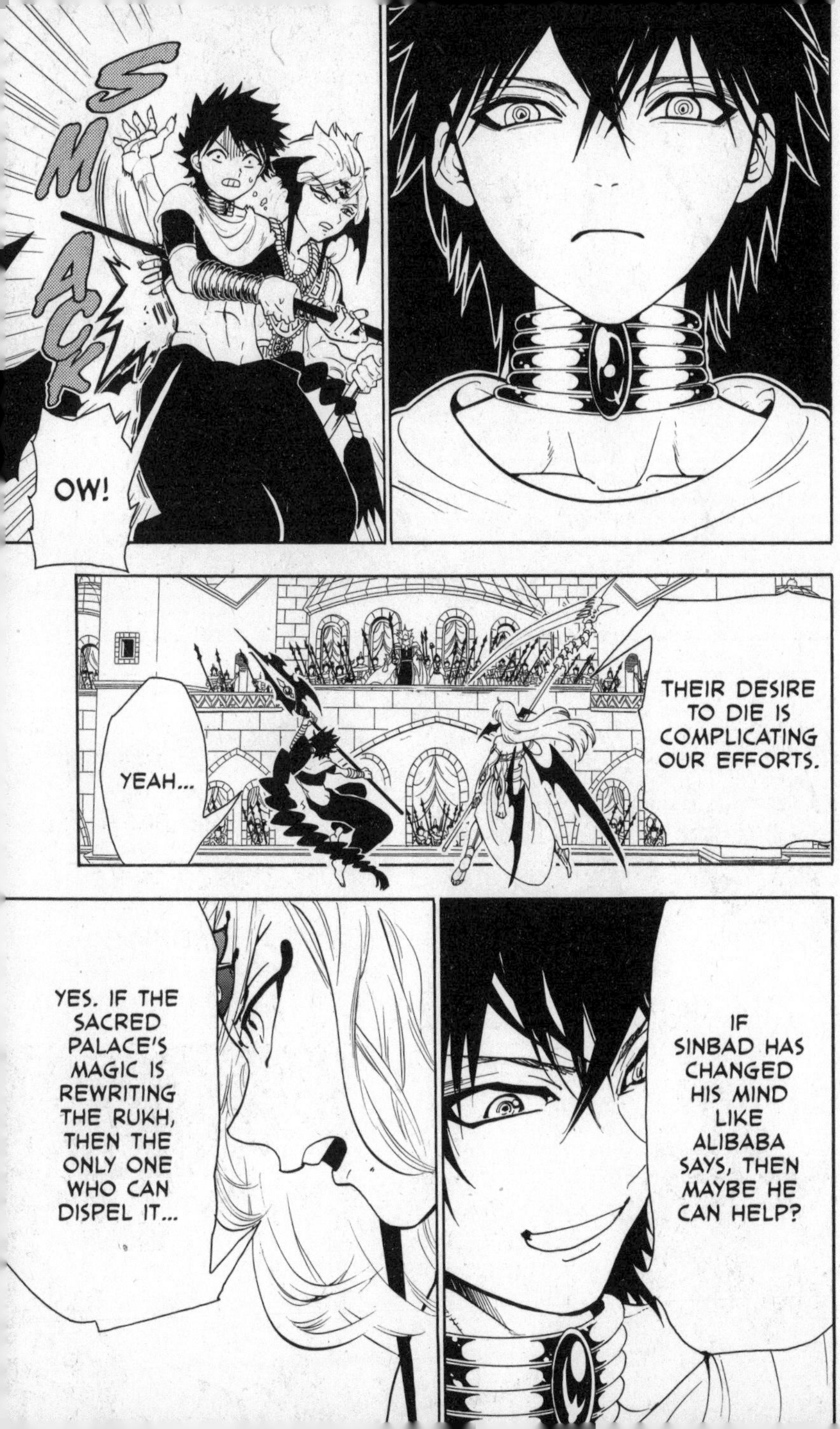
SMACK
OW!
THEIR DESIRE TO DIE IS COMPLICATING OUR EFFORTS.
YEAH...
IF SINBAD HAS CHANGED HIS MIND LIKE ALIBABA SAYS, THEN MAYBE HE CAN HELP?
YES. IF THE SACRED PALACE'S MAGIC IS REWRITING THE RUKH, THEN THE ONLY ONE WHO CAN DISPEL IT...

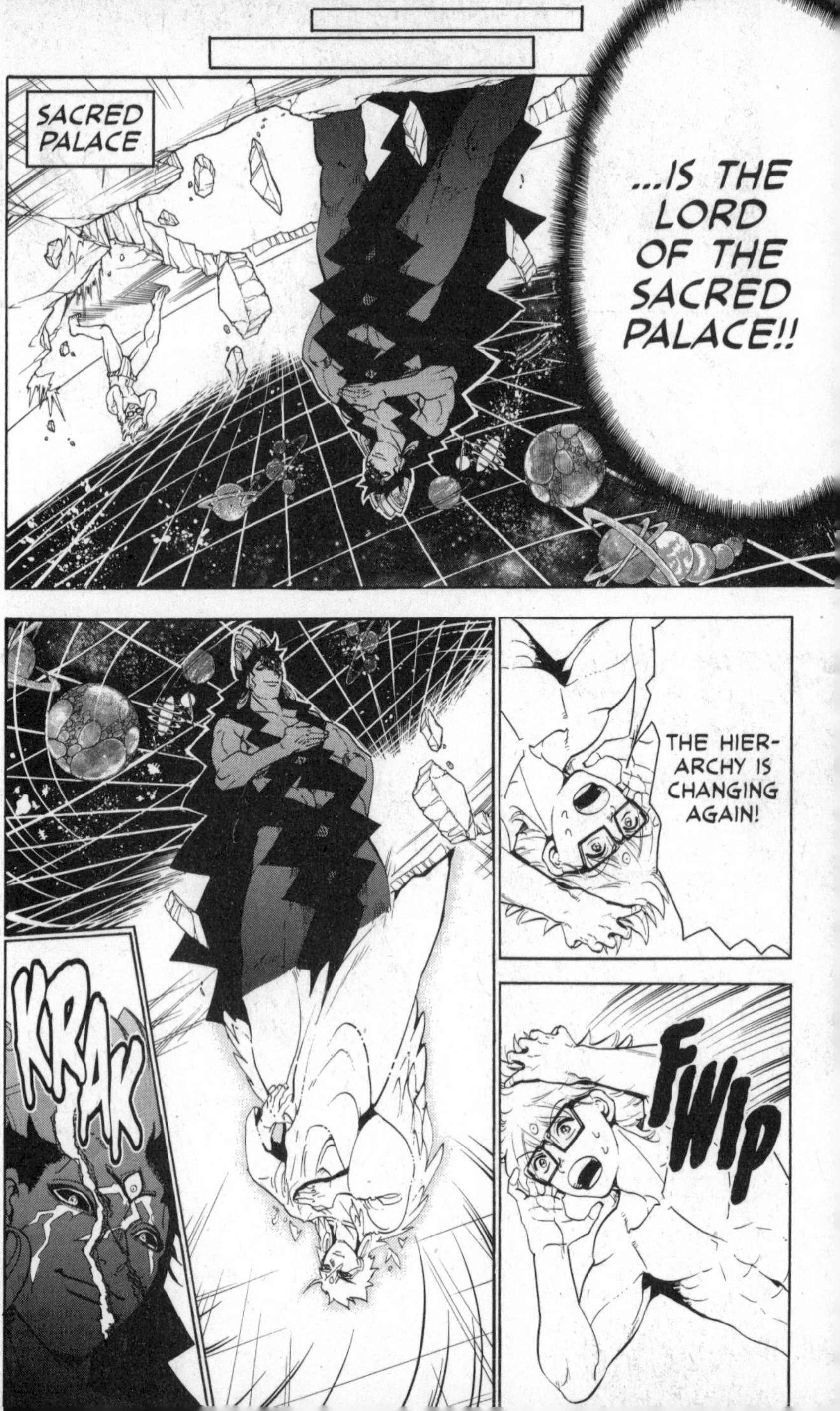
...IS THE LORD OF THE SACRED PALACE!!
SACRED PALACE
THE HIER-ARCHY IS CHANGING AGAIN!
FWIP
KRAK

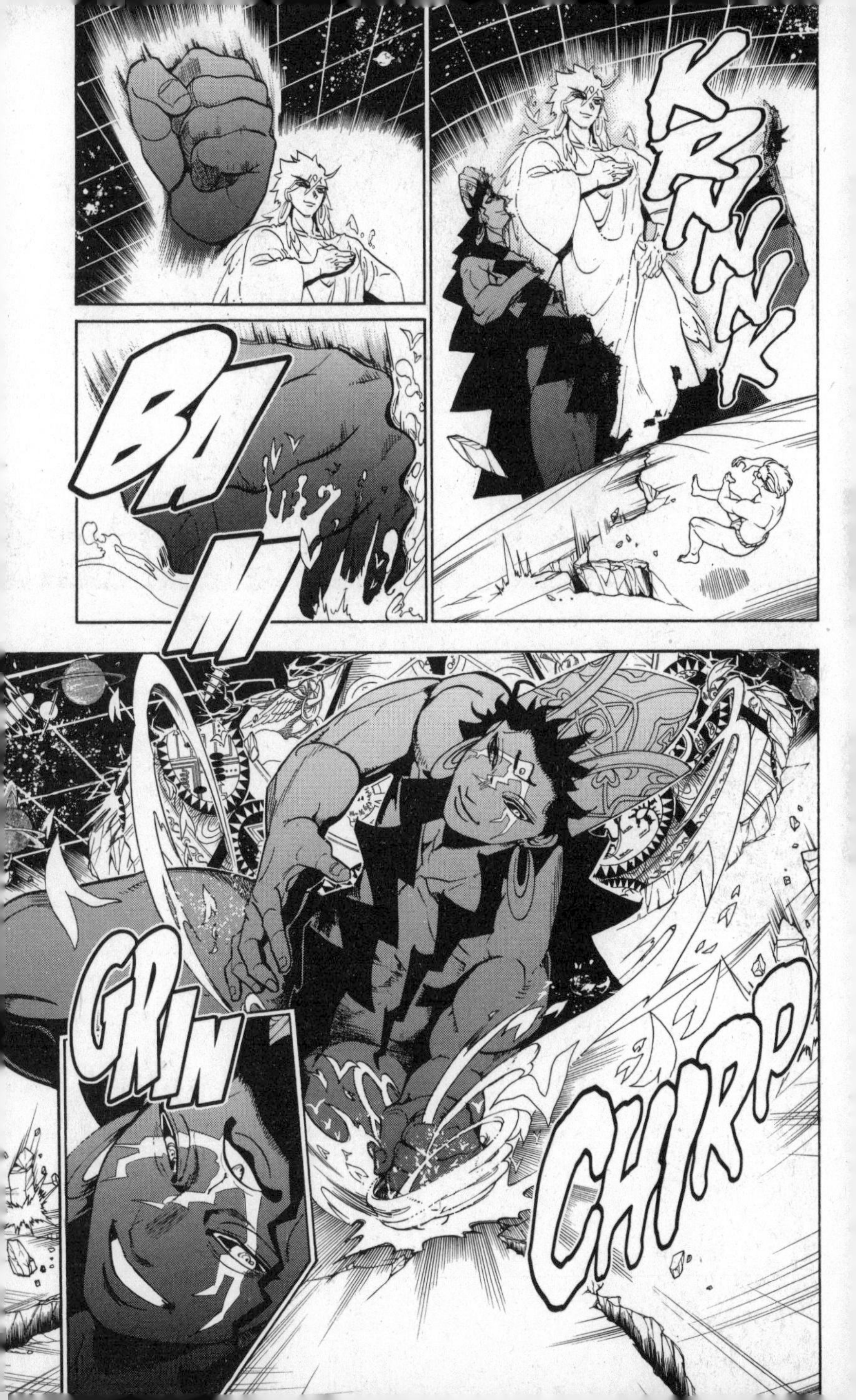
KRNNK
BAM
CHIRP
GRIN

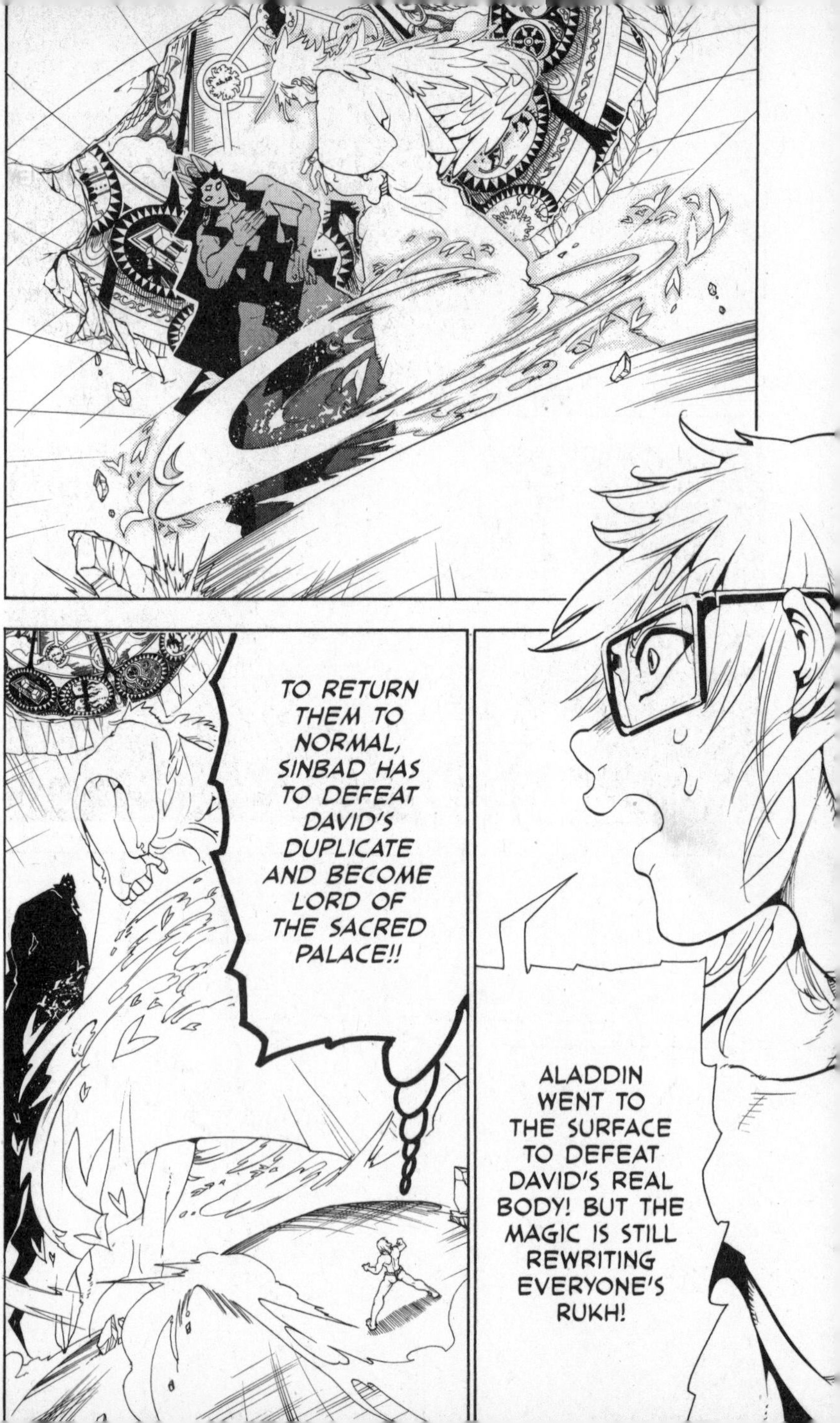
ALADDIN WENT TO THE SURFACE TO DEFEAT DAVID'S REAL BODY! BUT THE MAGIC IS STILL REWRITING EVERYONE'S RUKH!
TO RETURN THEM TO NORMAL, SINBAD HAS TO DEFEAT DAVID'S DUPLICATE AND BECOME LORD OF THE SACRED PALACE!!

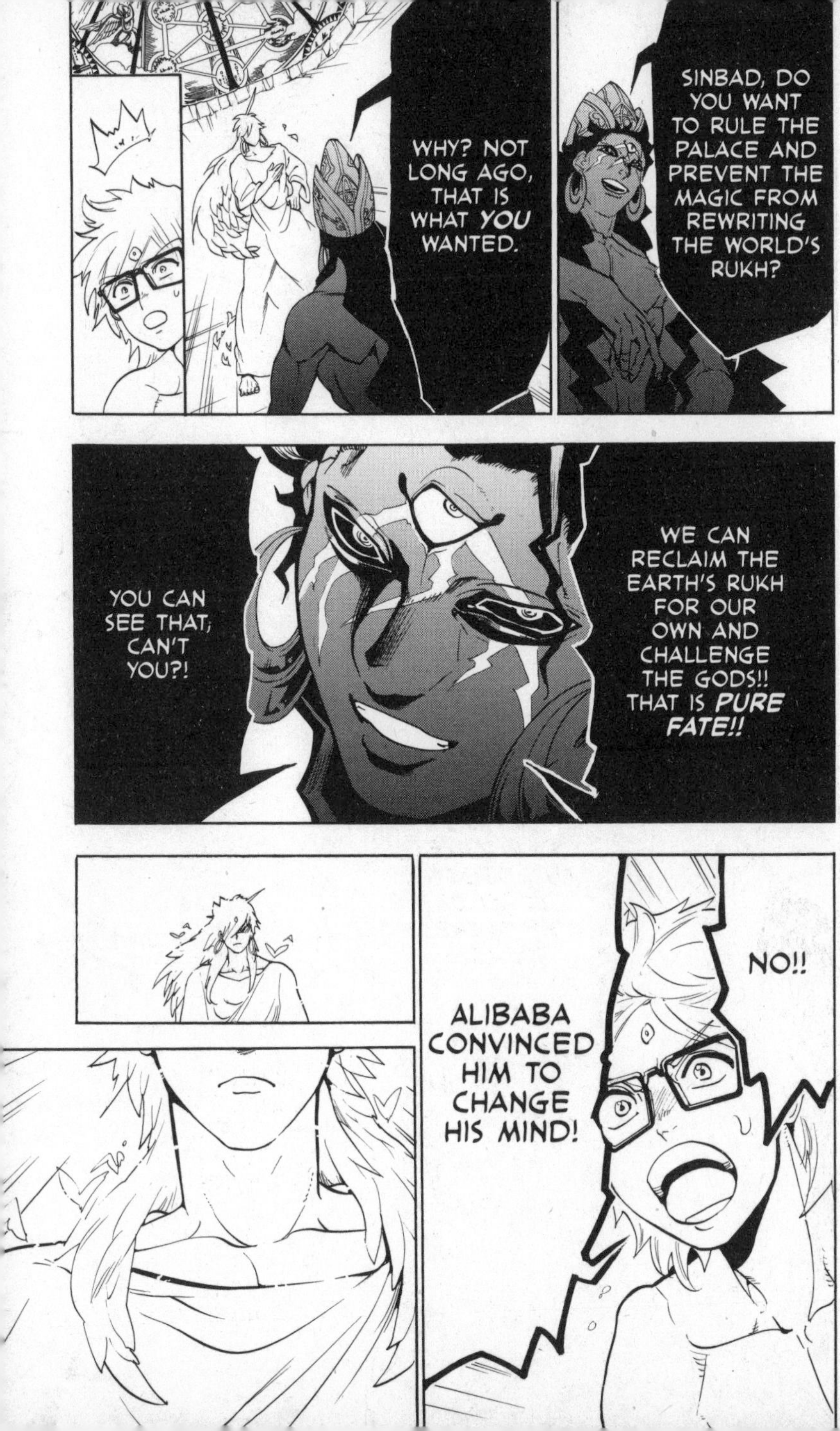
SINBAD, DO YOU WANT TO RULE THE PALACE AND PREVENT THE MAGIC FROM REWRITING THE WORLD'S RUKH?
WHY? NOT LONG AGO, THAT IS WHAT *YOU* WANTED.
WE CAN RECLAIM THE EARTH'S RUKH FOR OUR OWN AND CHALLENGE THE GODS!! THAT IS *PURE FATE!!*
YOU CAN SEE THAT, CAN'T YOU?!
NO!!
ALIBABA CONVINCED HIM TO CHANGE HIS MIND!

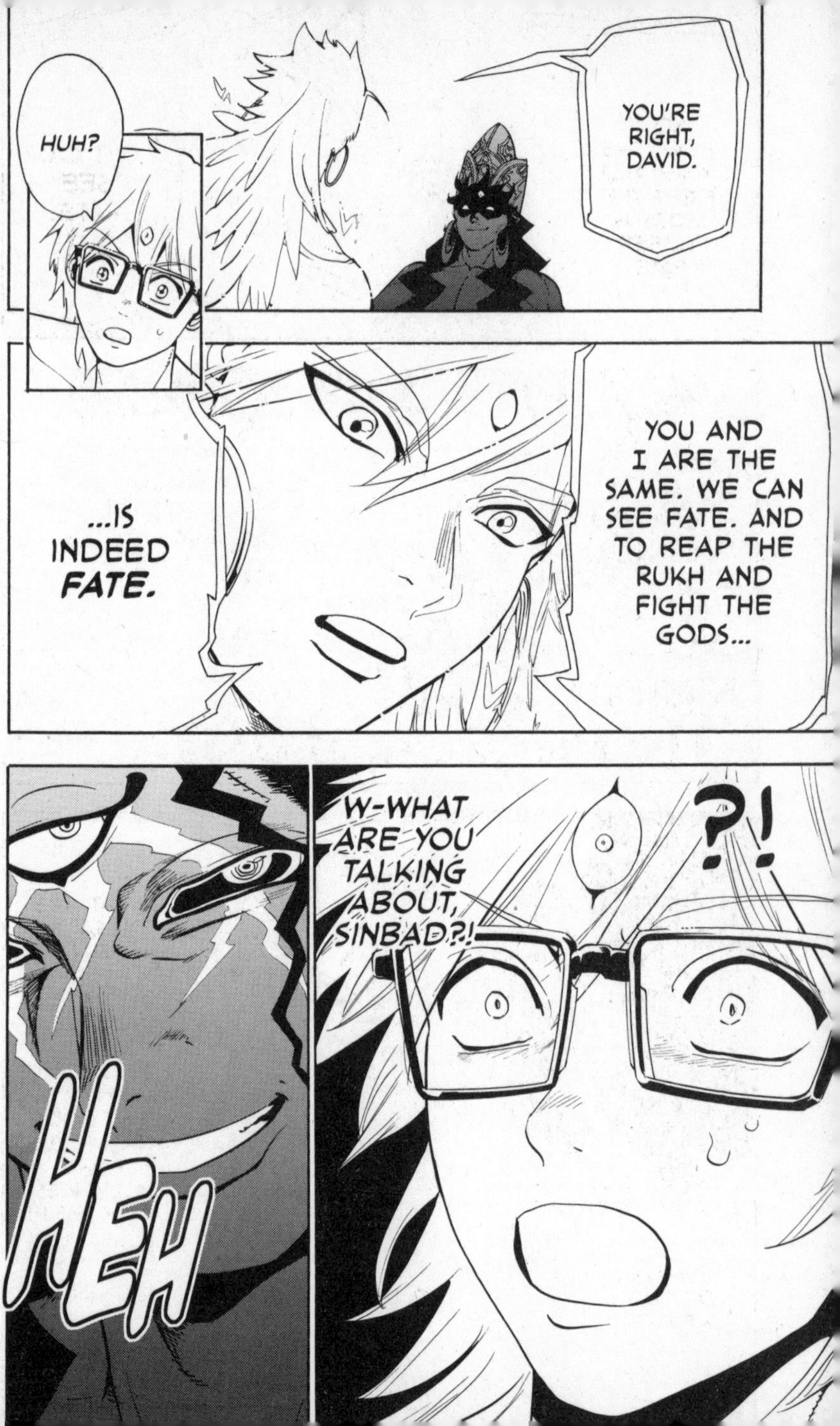
YOU'RE RIGHT, DAVID.
HUH?
YOU AND I ARE THE SAME. WE CAN SEE FATE. AND TO REAP THE RUKH AND FIGHT THE GODS...
...IS INDEED FATE.
?!
W-WHAT ARE YOU TALKING ABOUT, SINBAD?!
HEH

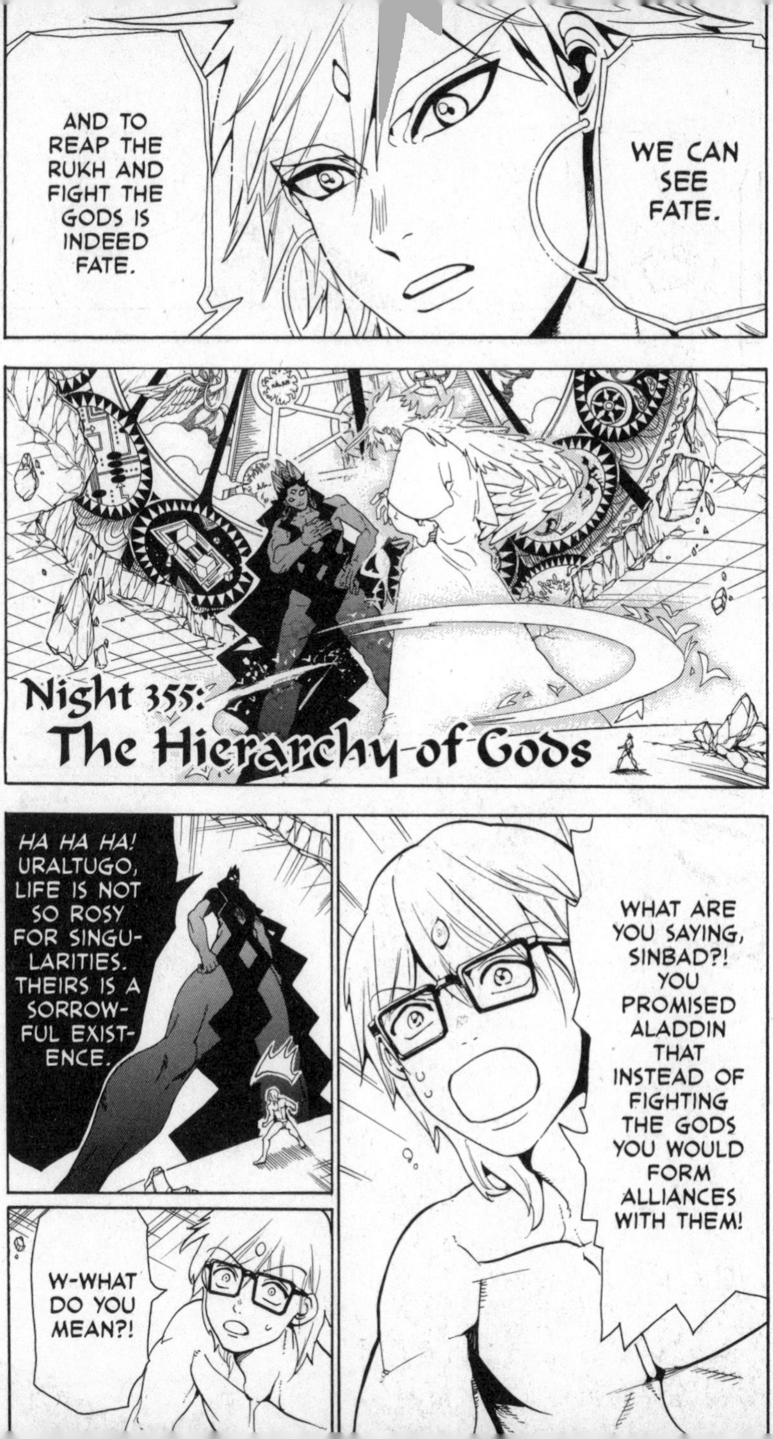
WE CAN SEE FATE.
AND TO REAP THE RUKH AND FIGHT THE GODS IS INDEED FATE.
Night 355: The Hierarchy of Gods
WHAT ARE YOU SAYING, SINBAD?! YOU PROMISED ALADDIN THAT INSTEAD OF FIGHTING THE GODS YOU WOULD FORM ALLIANCES WITH THEM!
HA HA HA! URALTUGO, LIFE IS NOT SO ROSY FOR SINGU-LARITIES. THEIRS IS A SORROW-FUL EXIST-ENCE.
W-WHAT DO YOU MEAN?!

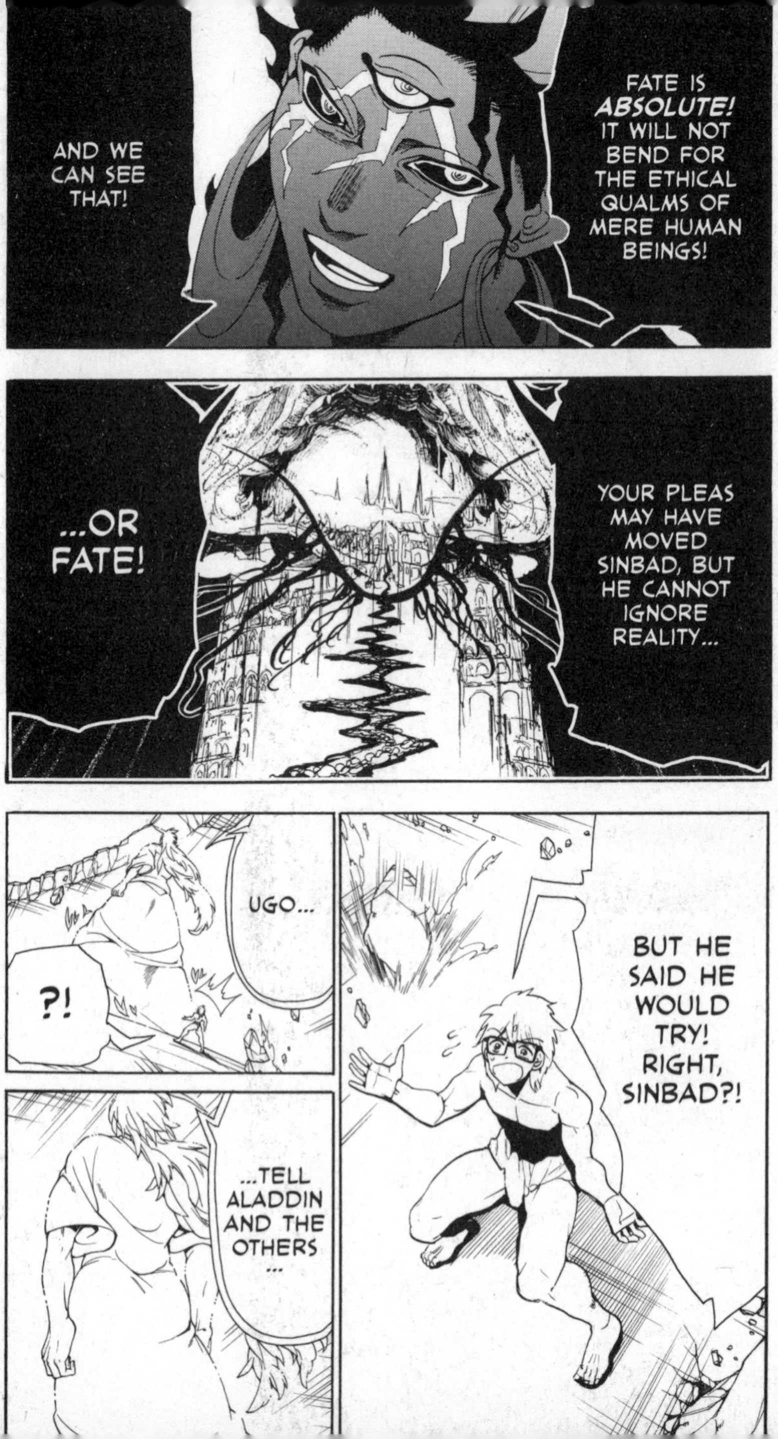
FATE IS ABSOLUTE! IT WILL NOT BEND FOR THE ETHICAL QUALMS OF MERE HUMAN BEINGS!
AND WE CAN SEE THAT!
YOUR PLEAS MAY HAVE MOVED SINBAD, BUT HE CANNOT IGNORE REALITY...
...OR FATE!
BUT HE SAID HE WOULD TRY! RIGHT, SINBAD?!
UGO...
?!
...TELL ALADDIN AND THE OTHERS ...

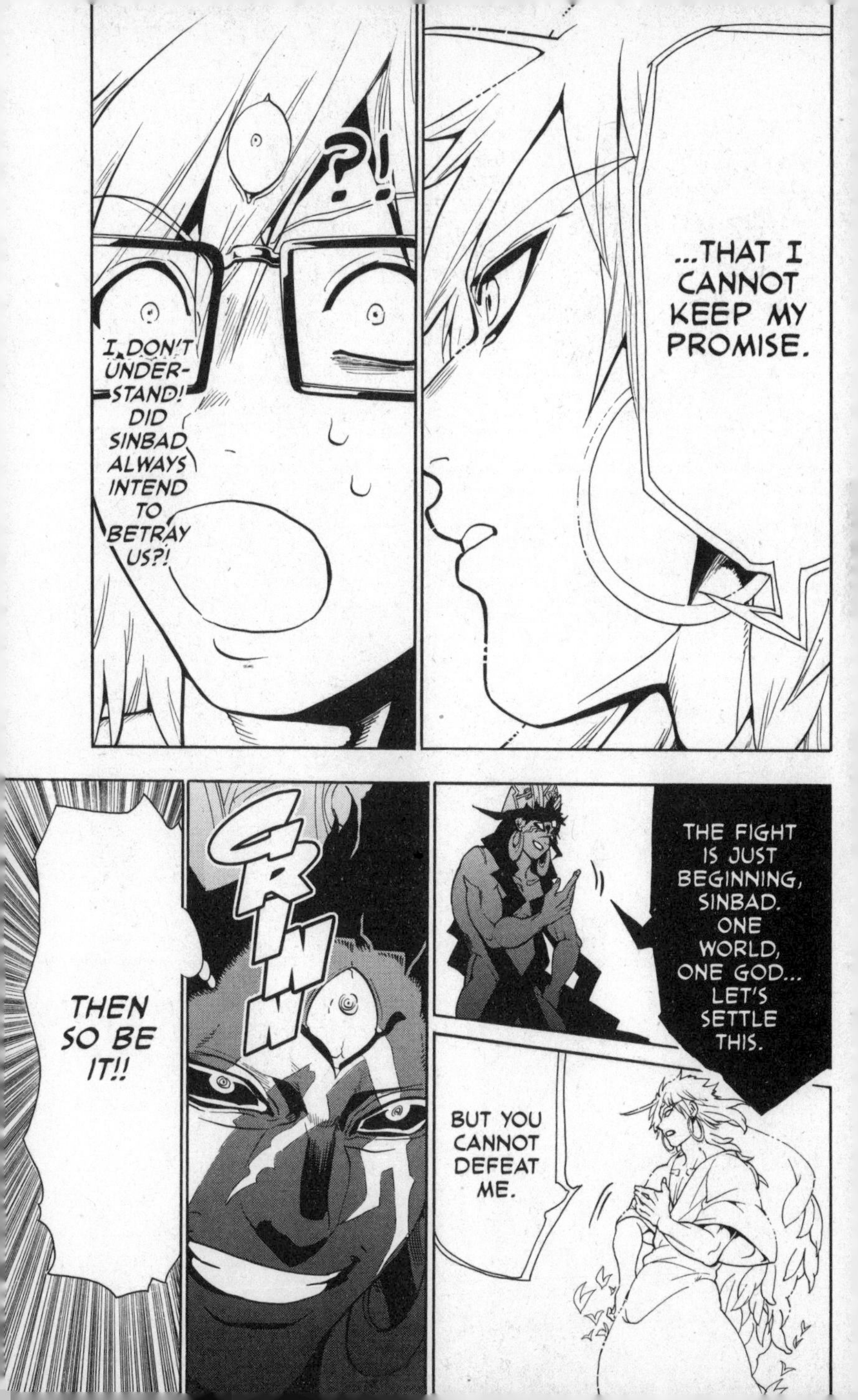
...THAT I CANNOT KEEP MY PROMISE.
?!
I DON'T UNDERSTAND! DID SINBAD ALWAYS INTEND TO BETRAY US?!
THE FIGHT IS JUST BEGINNING, SINBAD. ONE WORLD, ONE GOD... LET'S SETTLE THIS.
BUT YOU CANNOT DEFEAT ME.
GRINN
THEN SO BE IT!!

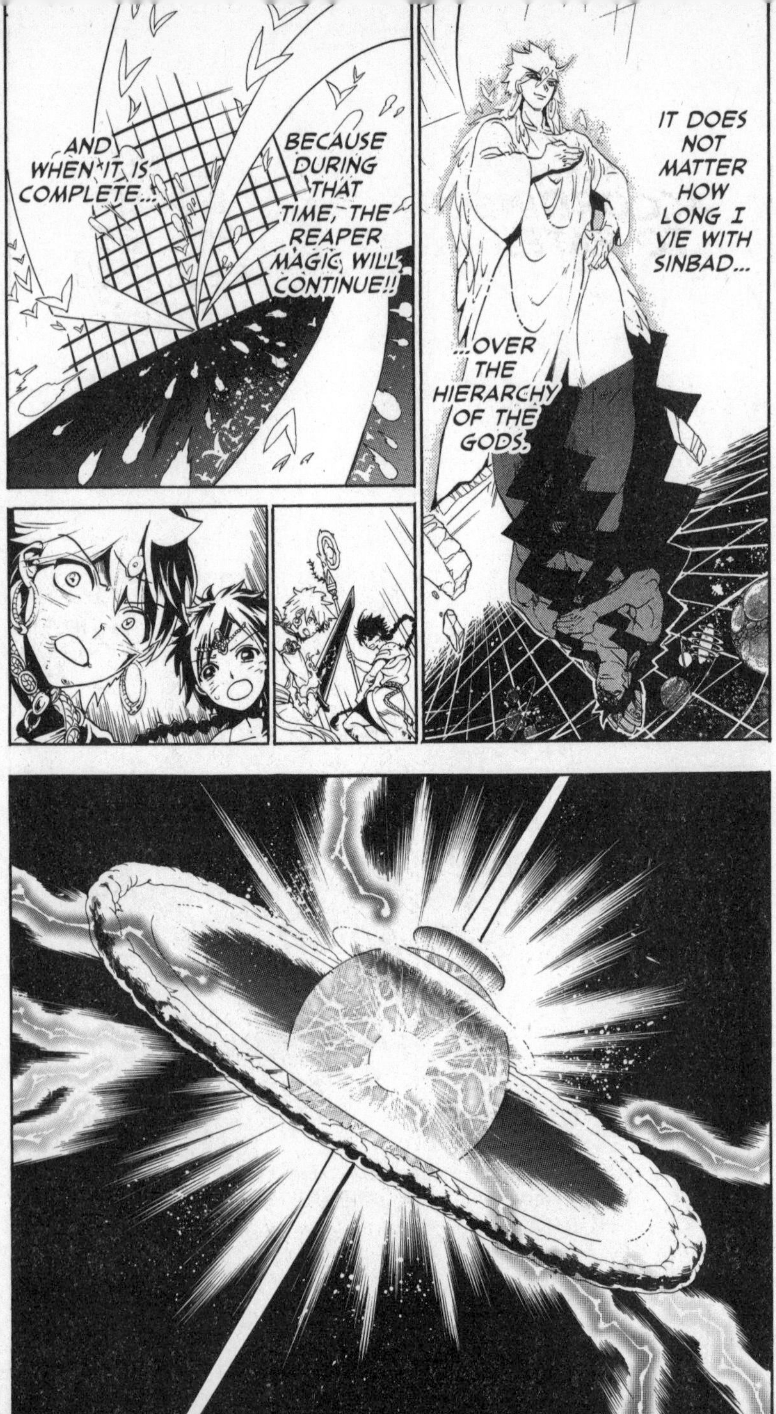
IT DOES NOT MATTER HOW LONG I VIE WITH SINBAD...
...OVER THE HIERARCHY OF THE GODS.
BECAUSE DURING THAT TIME, THE REAPER MAGIC WILL CONTINUE!!
AND WHEN IT IS COMPLETE...

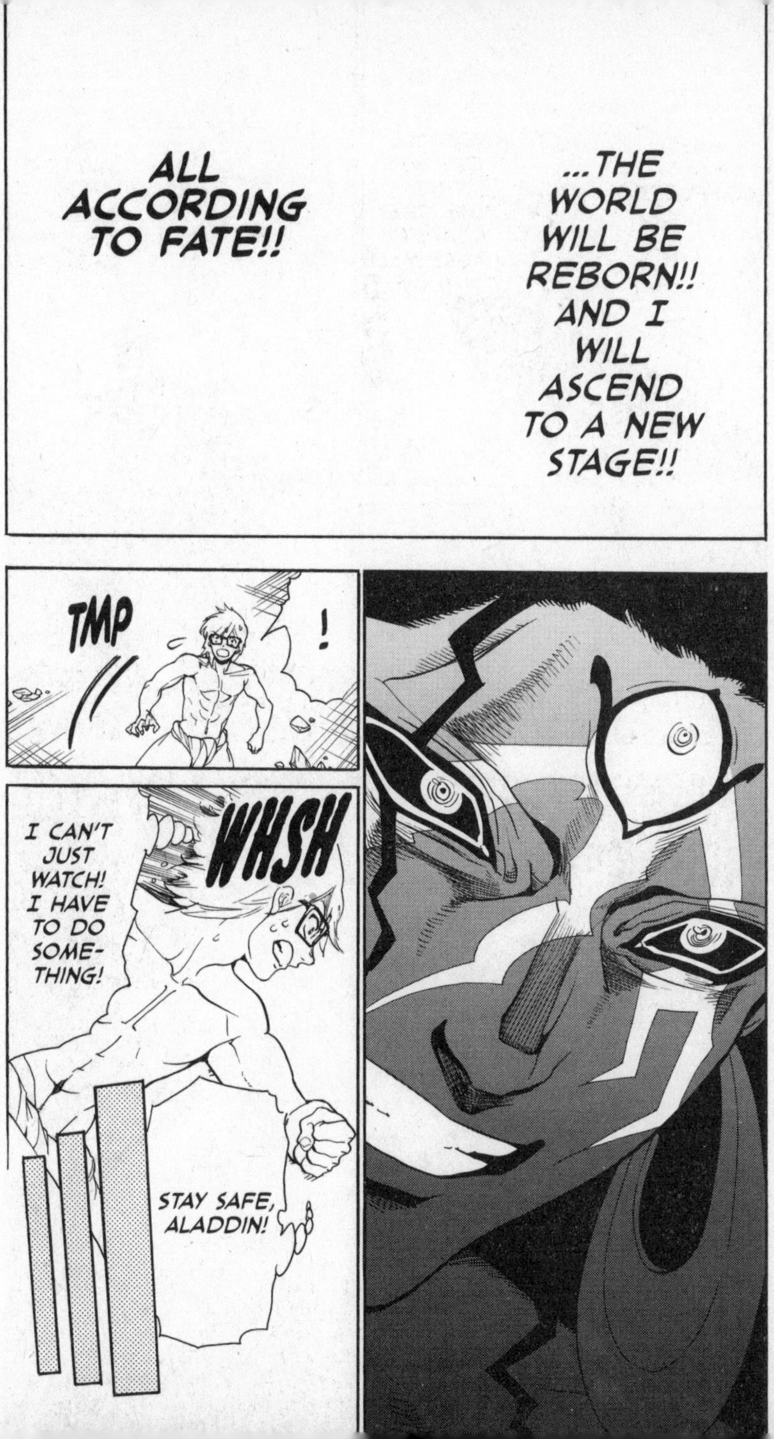
...THE WORLD WILL BE REBORN!! AND I WILL ASCEND TO A NEW STAGE!!
ALL ACCORDING TO FATE!!
!
TMP
WHSH
I CAN'T JUST WATCH! I HAVE TO DO SOME-THING!
STAY SAFE, ALADDIN!

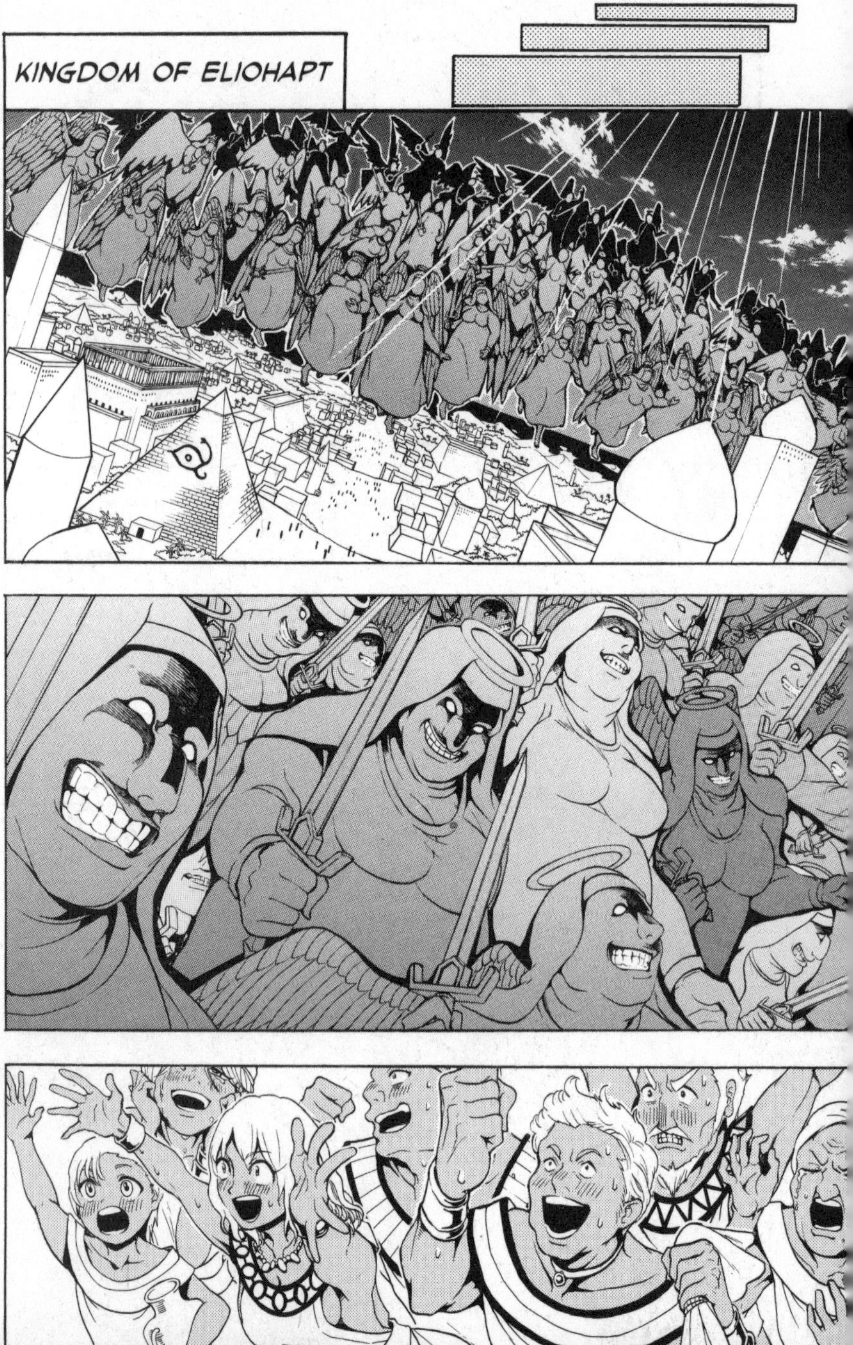
KINGDOM OF ELIOHAPT

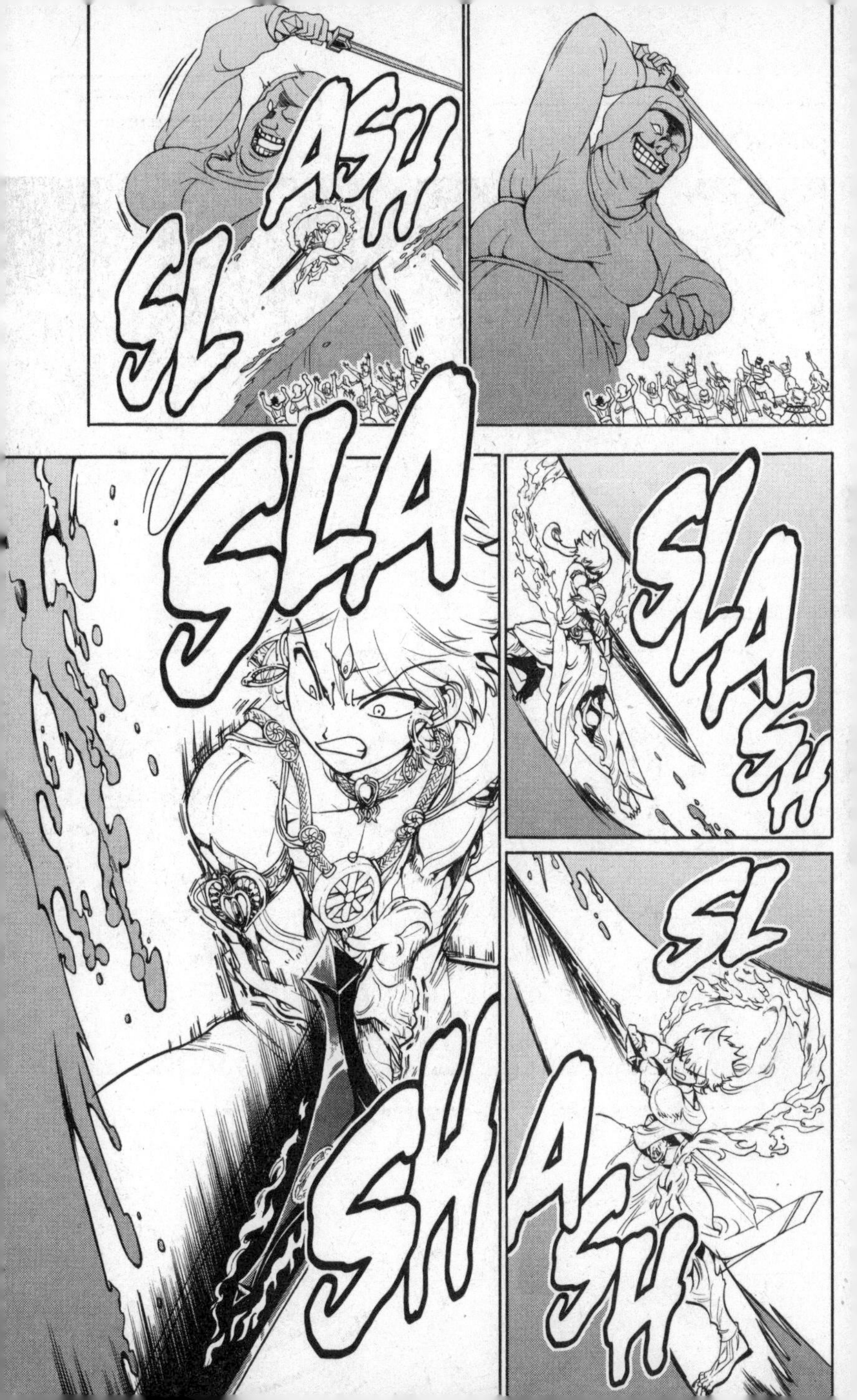
SLASH
SLASH
SLASH
SLASH

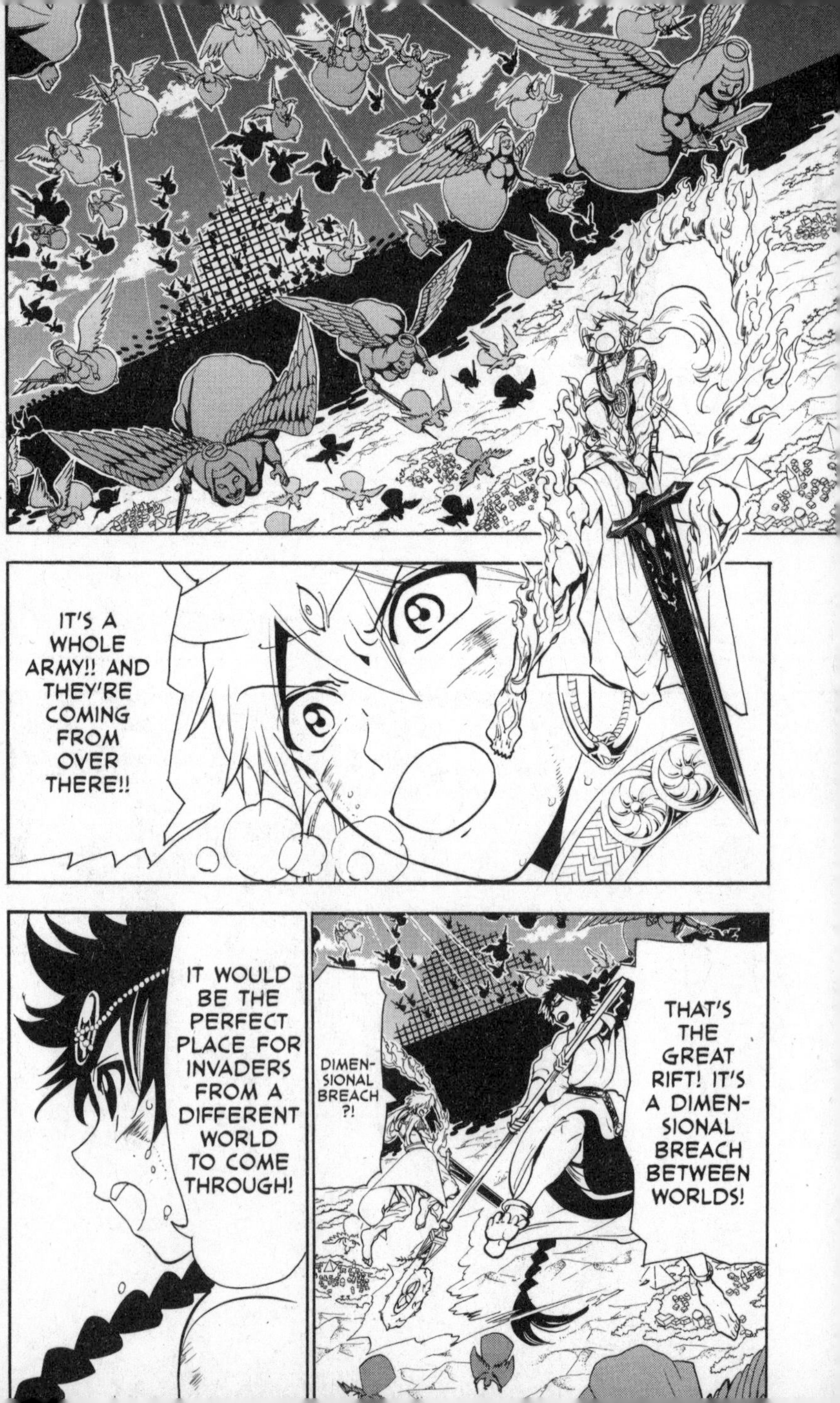
IT'S A WHOLE ARMY!! AND THEY'RE COMING FROM OVER THERE!!
THAT'S THE GREAT RIFT! IT'S A DIMEN-SIONAL BREACH BETWEEN WORLDS!
DIMEN-SIONAL BREACH?!
IT WOULD BE THE PERFECT PLACE FOR INVADERS FROM A DIFFERENT WORLD TO COME THROUGH!

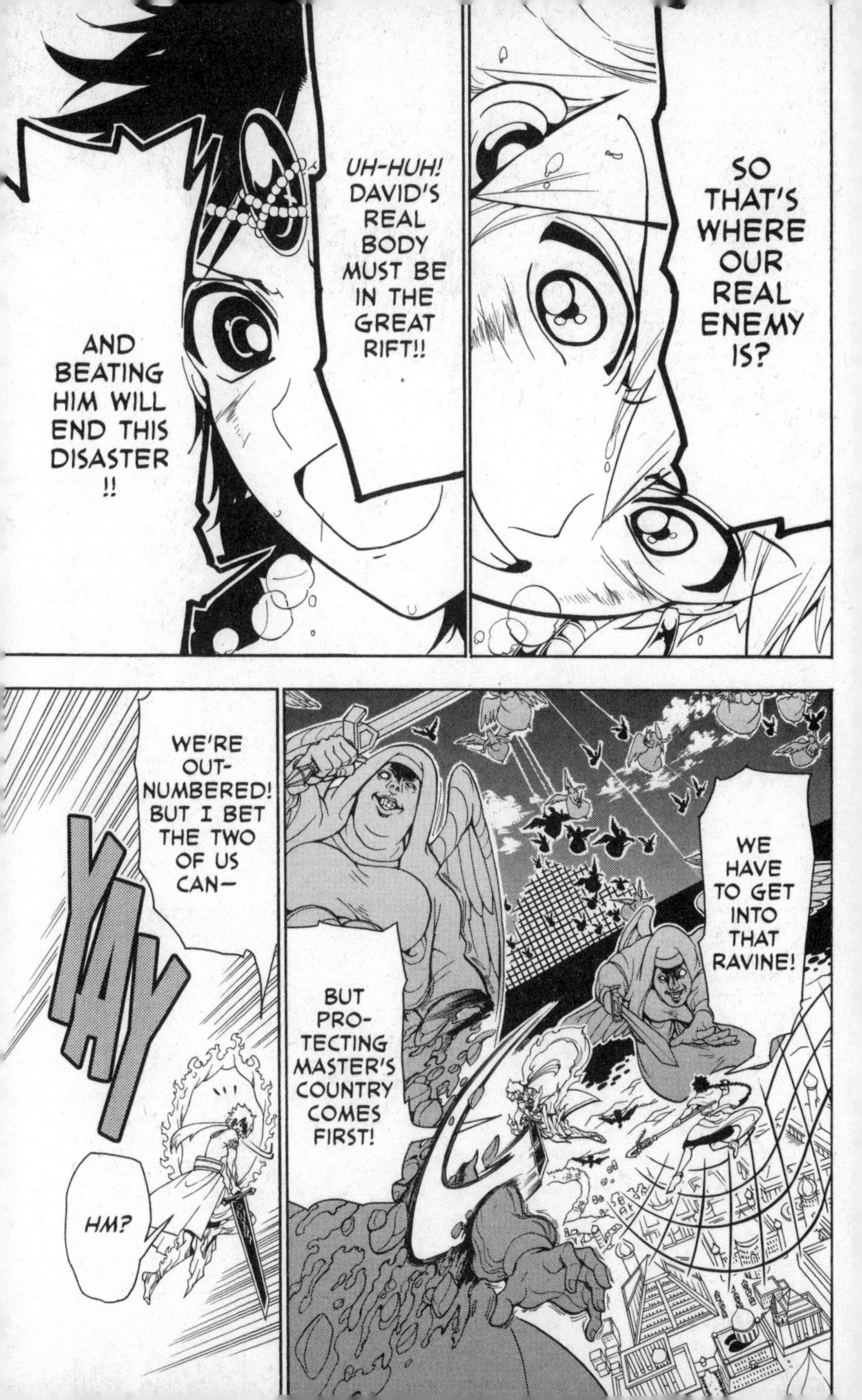
SO THAT'S WHERE OUR REAL ENEMY IS?
UH-HUH! DAVID'S REAL BODY MUST BE IN THE GREAT RIFT!!
AND BEATING HIM WILL END THIS DISASTER!!
WE HAVE TO GET INTO THAT RAVINE!
BUT PROTECTING MASTER'S COUNTRY COMES FIRST!
WE'RE OUT-NUMBERED! BUT I BET THE TWO OF US CAN—
HM?

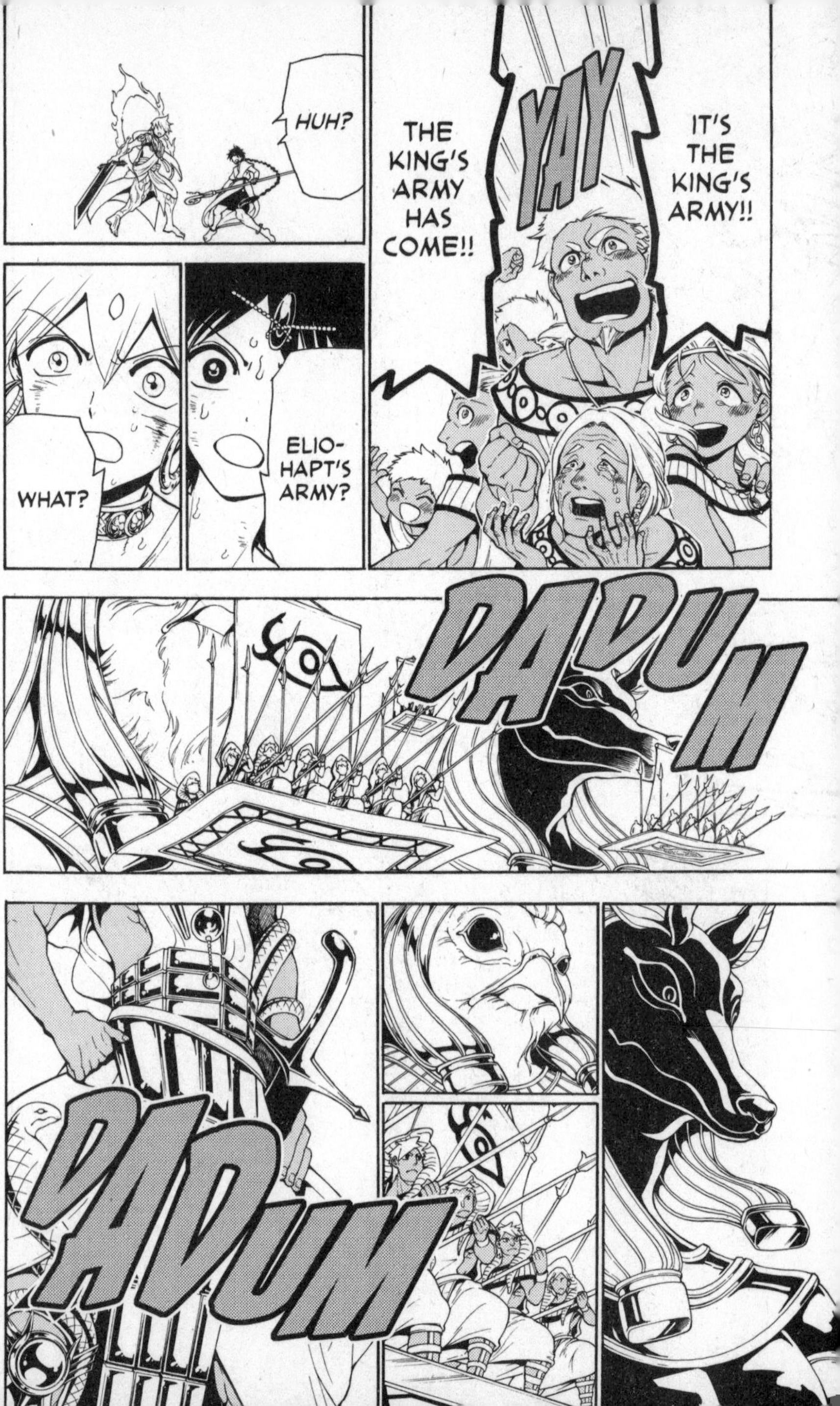
IT'S THE KING'S ARMY!!
YAY
THE KING'S ARMY HAS COME!!
HUH?
ELIO-HAPT'S ARMY?
WHAT?
DADUM
DADUM

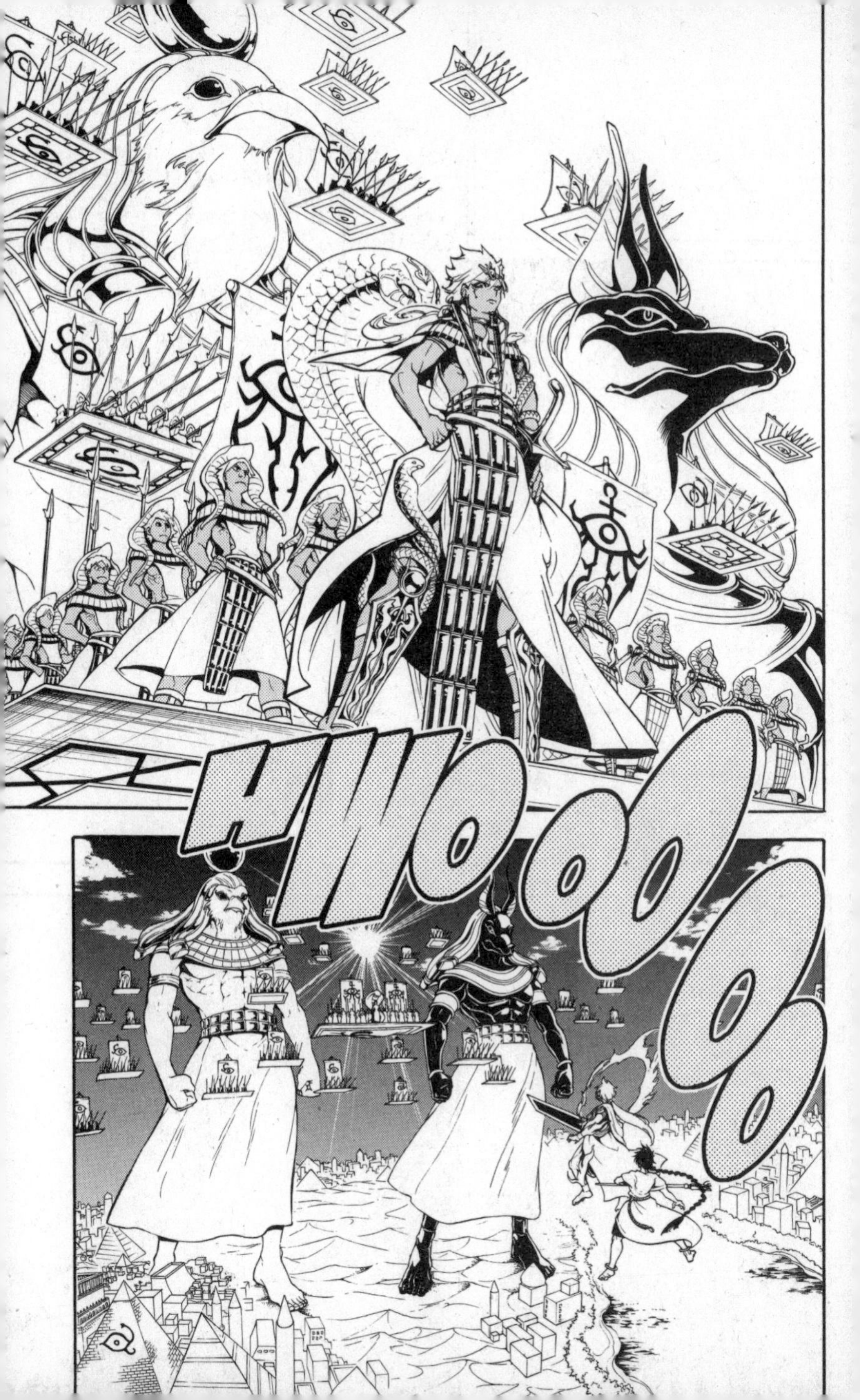
WHOOOOO

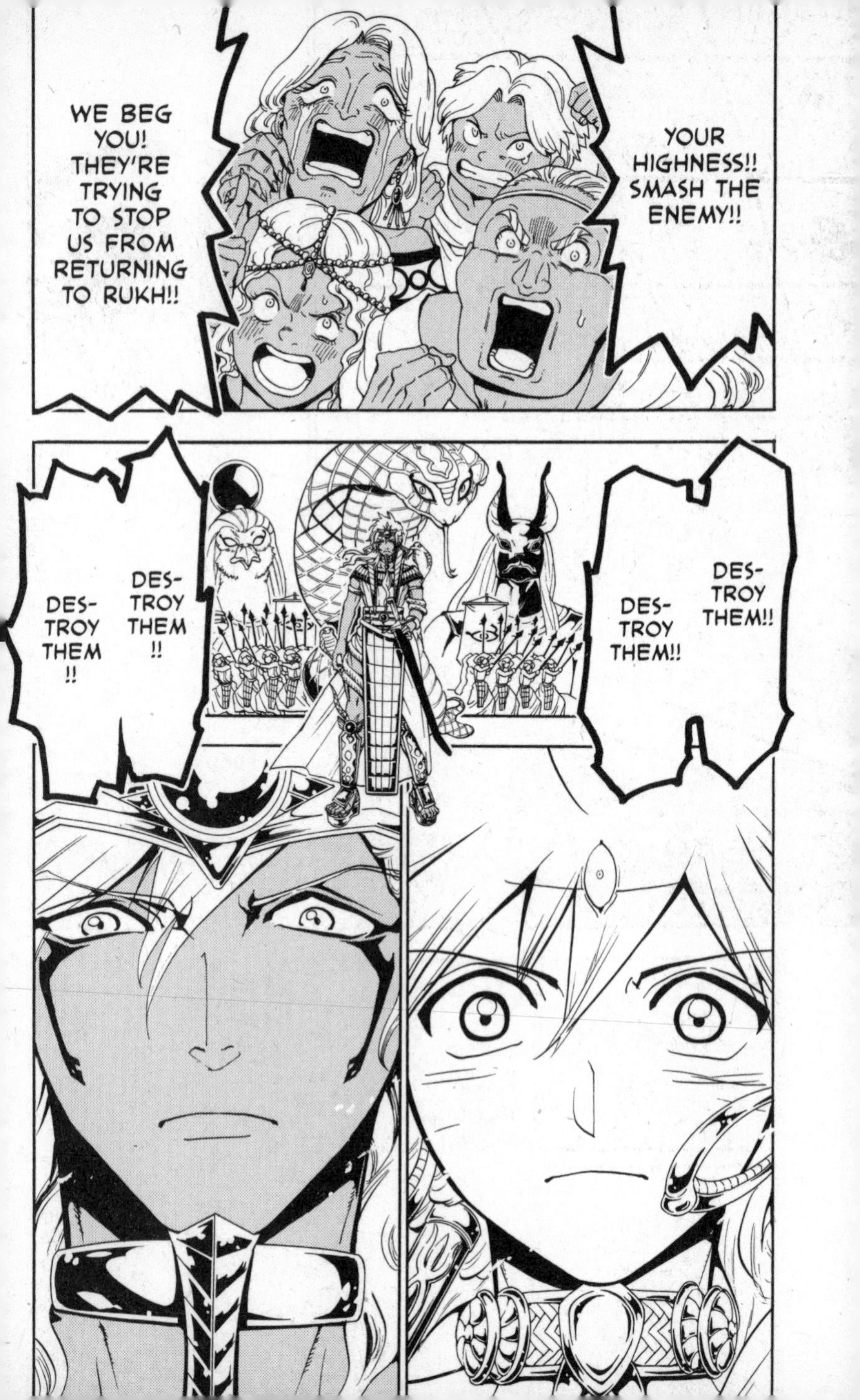
YOUR HIGHNESS!! SMASH THE ENEMY!!
WE BEG YOU! THEY'RE TRYING TO STOP US FROM RETURNING TO RUKH!!
DES-TROY THEM!!
DES-TROY THEM!!
DES-TROY THEM !!
DES-TROY THEM !!

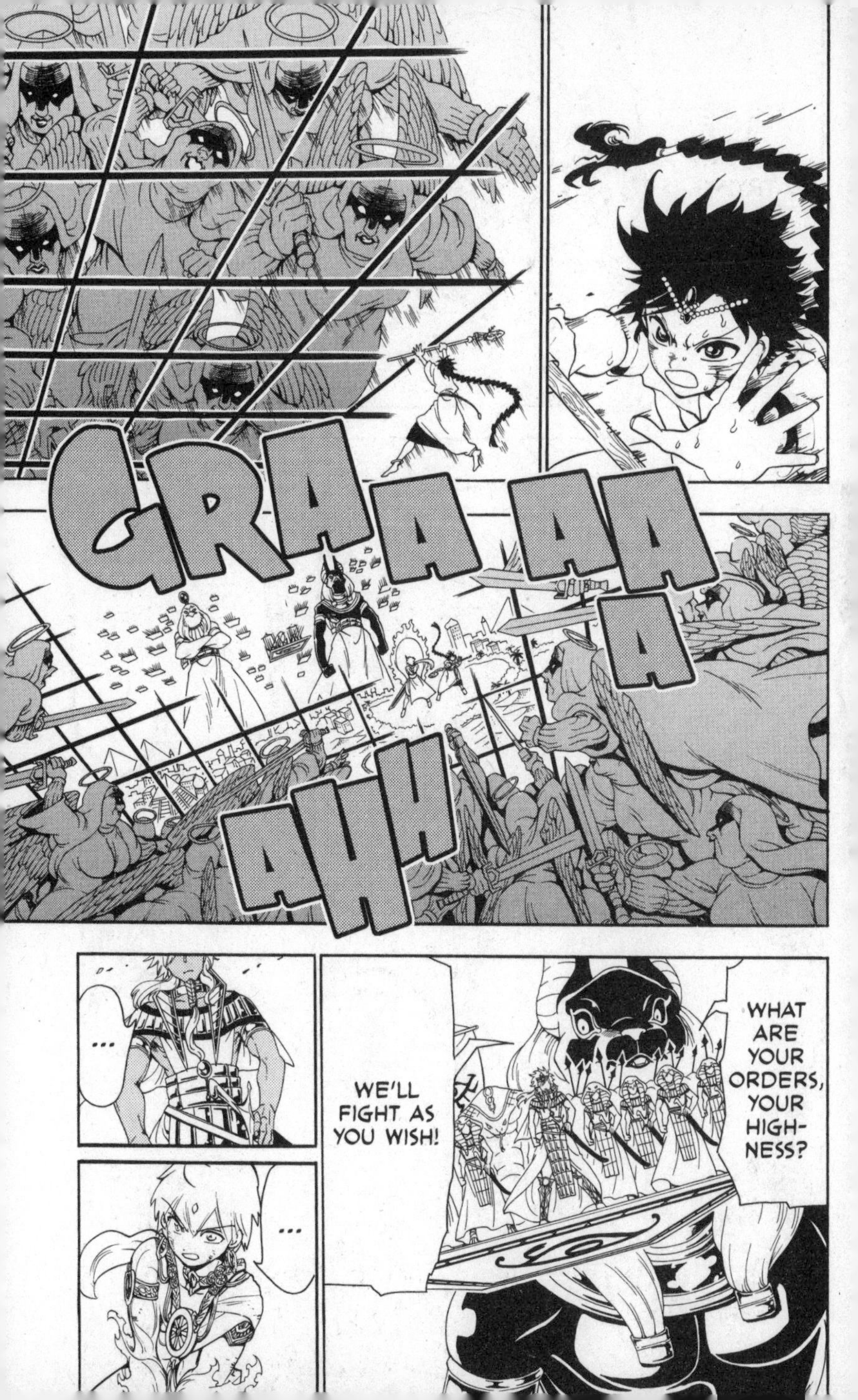
GRAAAAAAHH
WHAT ARE YOUR ORDERS, YOUR HIGHNESS?
WE'LL FIGHT AS YOU WISH!
...
...

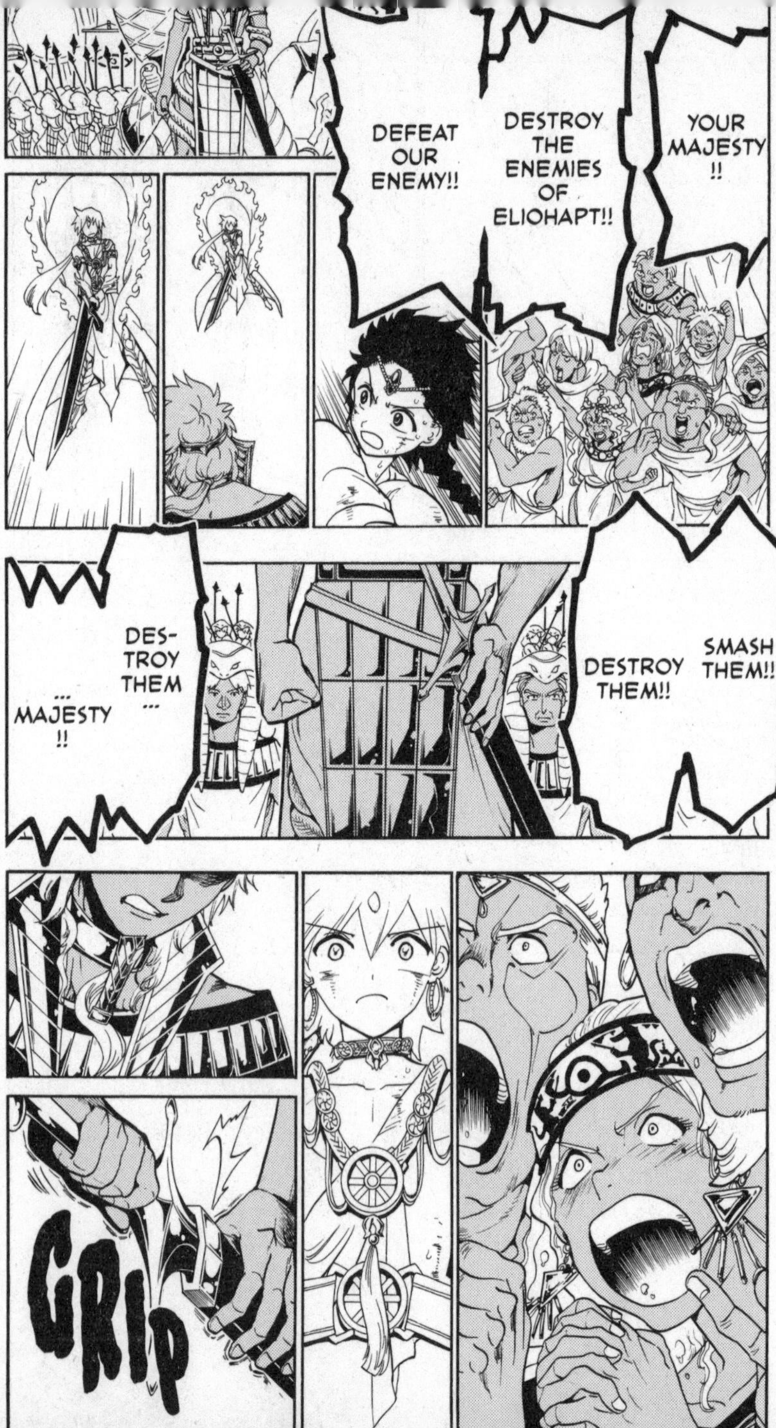
YOUR MAJESTY!!
DESTROY THE ENEMIES OF ELIOHAPT!!
DEFEAT OUR ENEMY!!
SMASH THEM!!
DESTROY THEM!!
DES-TROY THEM...
...MAJESTY!!
GRIP

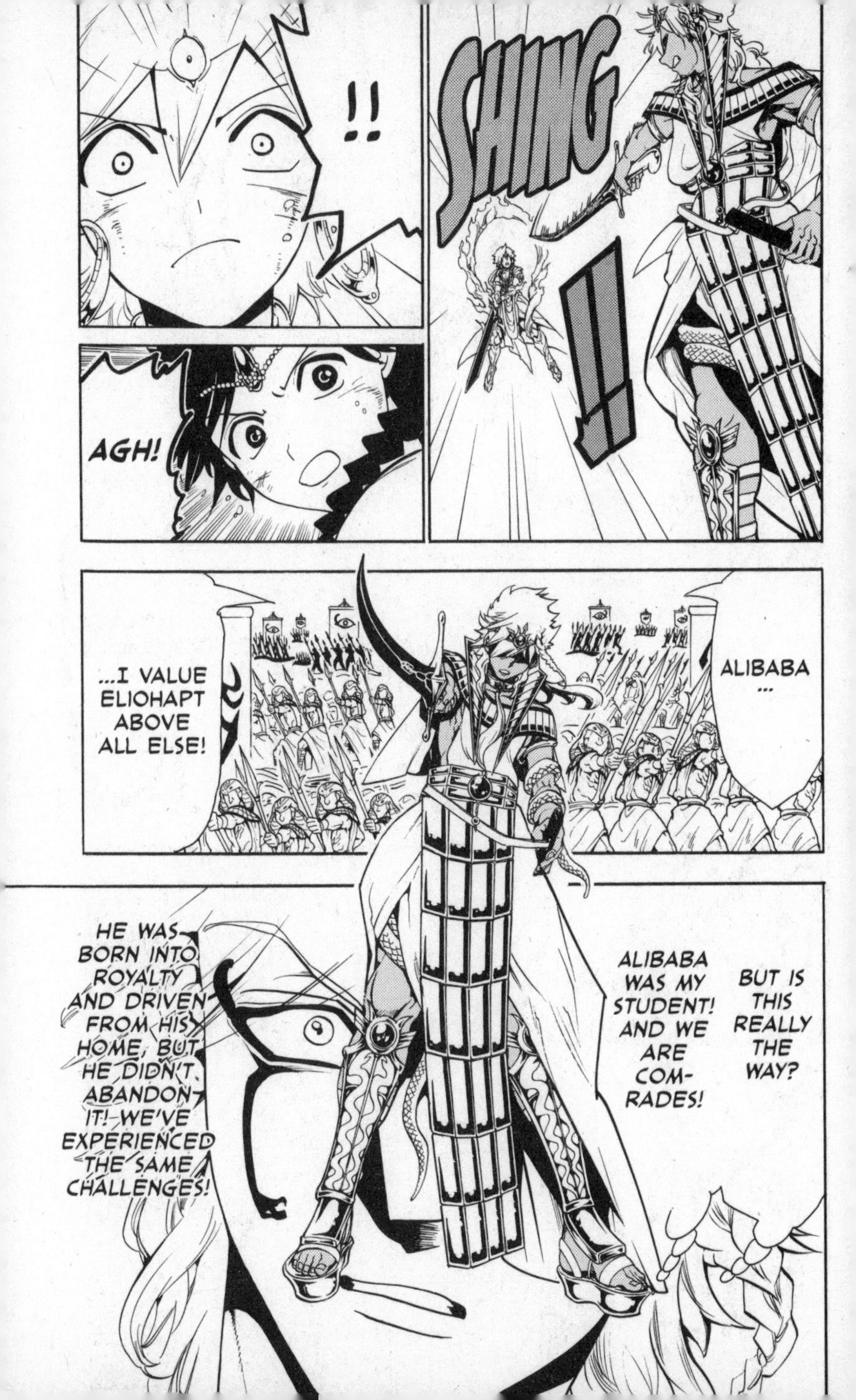
SHING
!!
!!
AGH!
ALIBABA ...
...I VALUE ELIOHAPT ABOVE ALL ELSE!
BUT IS THIS REALLY THE WAY?
ALIBABA WAS MY STUDENT! AND WE ARE COM-RADES!
HE WAS BORN INTO ROYALTY AND DRIVEN FROM HIS HOME, BUT HE DIDN'T ABANDON IT! WE'VE EXPERIENCED THE SAME CHALLENGES!

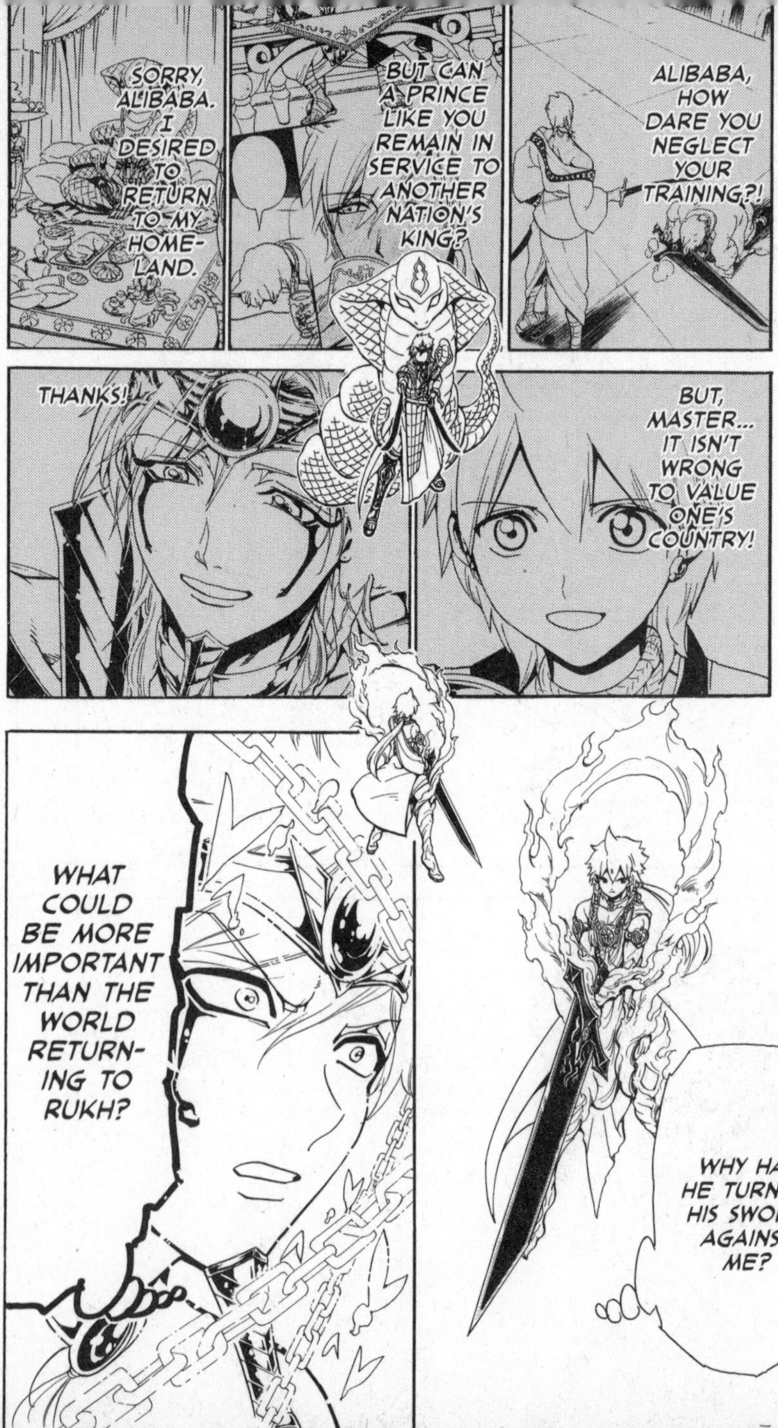
ALIBABA, HOW DARE YOU NEGLECT YOUR TRAINING?!
BUT CAN A PRINCE LIKE YOU REMAIN IN SERVICE TO ANOTHER NATION'S KING?
SORRY, ALIBABA. I DESIRED TO RETURN TO MY HOME-LAND.
BUT, MASTER... IT ISN'T WRONG TO VALUE ONE'S COUNTRY!
THANKS!
WHY HAS HE TURNED HIS SWORD AGAINST ME?
WHAT COULD BE MORE IMPORTANT THAN THE WORLD RETURN-ING TO RUKH?

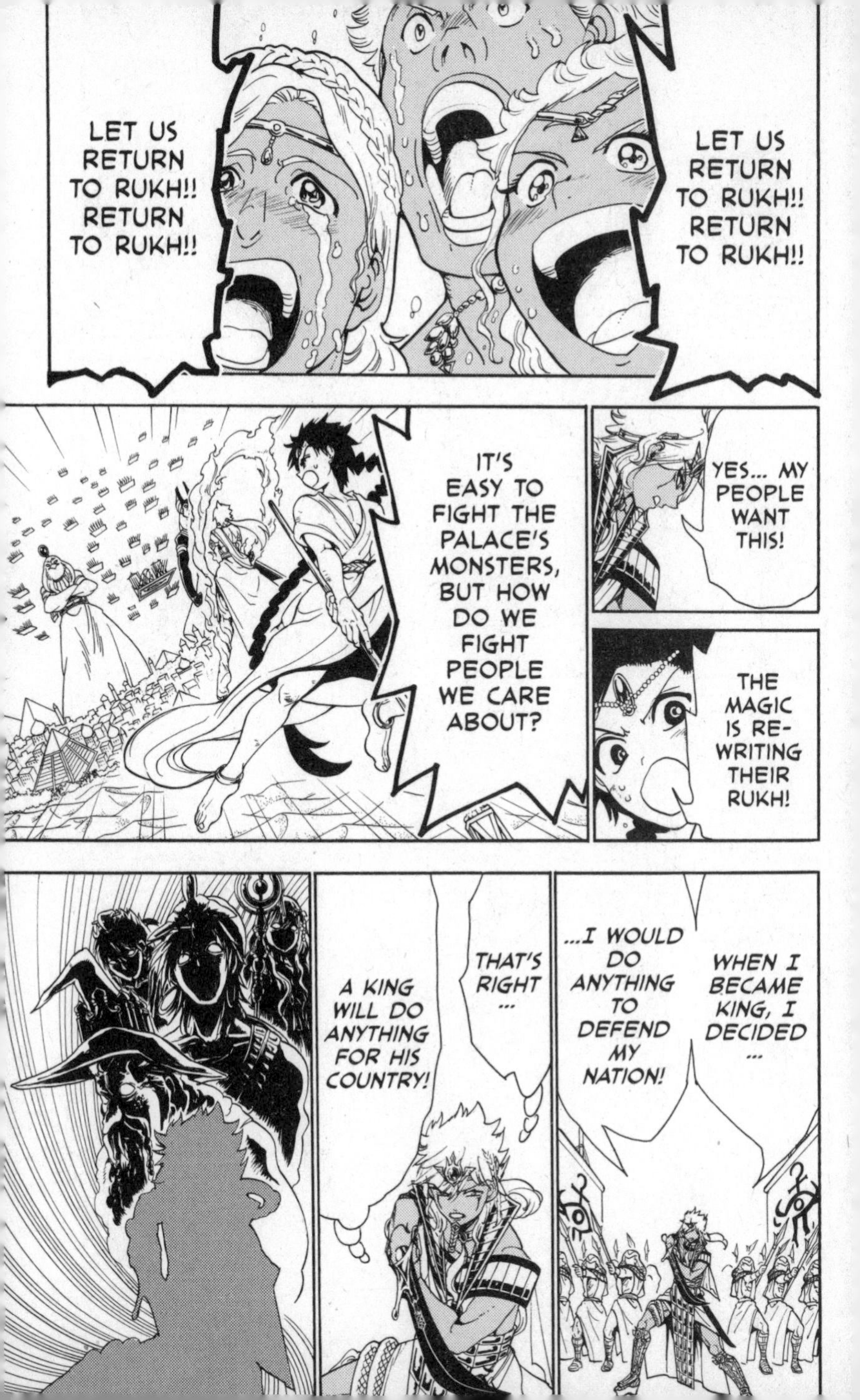
LET US RETURN TO RUKH!! RETURN TO RUKH!!
LET US RETURN TO RUKH!! RETURN TO RUKH!!
YES... MY PEOPLE WANT THIS!
THE MAGIC IS RE-WRITING THEIR RUKH!
IT'S EASY TO FIGHT THE PALACE'S MONSTERS, BUT HOW DO WE FIGHT PEOPLE WE CARE ABOUT?
WHEN I BECAME KING, I DECIDED...
...I WOULD DO ANYTHING TO DEFEND MY NATION!
THAT'S RIGHT...
A KING WILL DO ANYTHING FOR HIS COUNTRY!

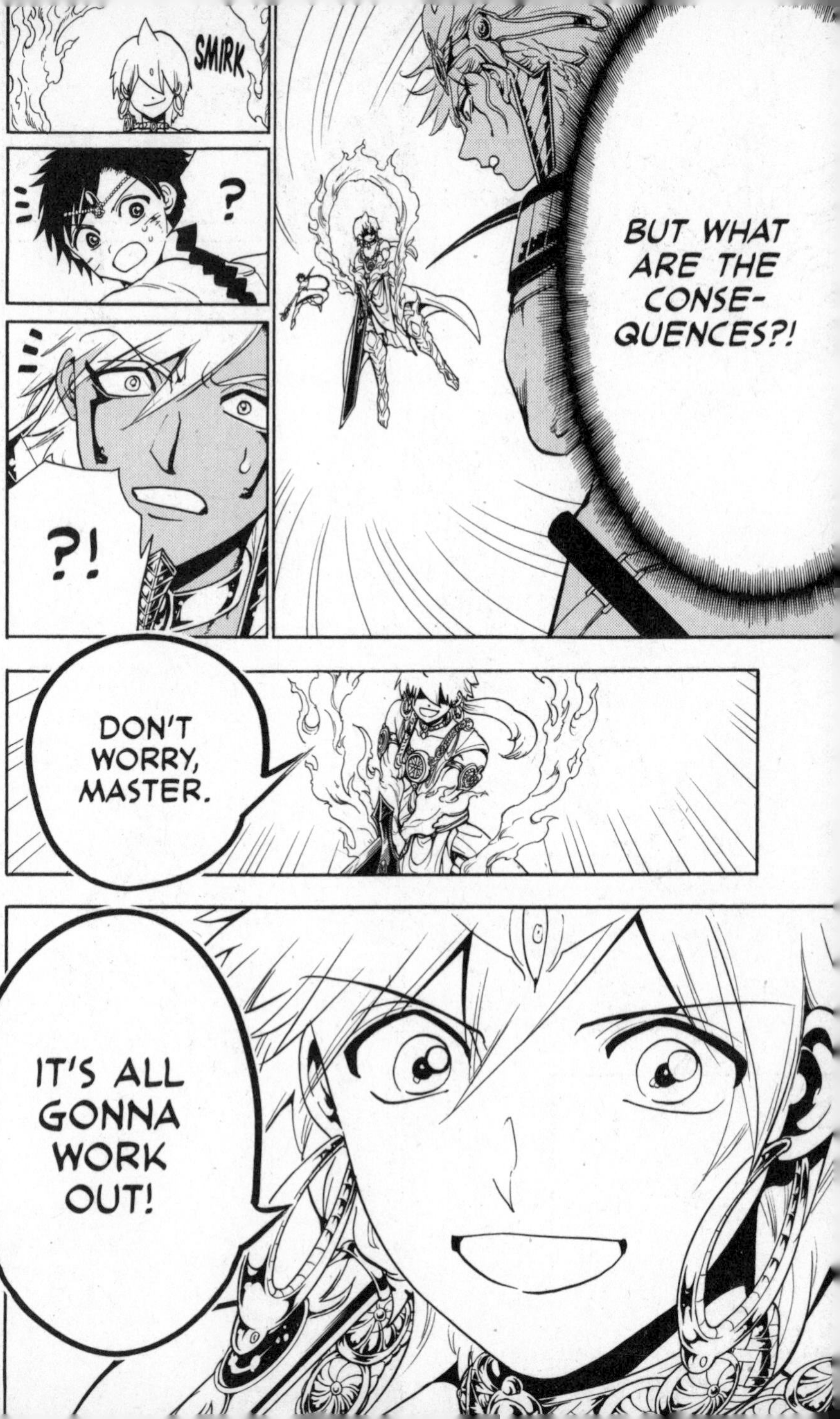
BUT WHAT ARE THE CONSE- QUENCES?!
SMIRK
?
?!
DON'T WORRY, MASTER.
IT'S ALL GONNA WORK OUT!

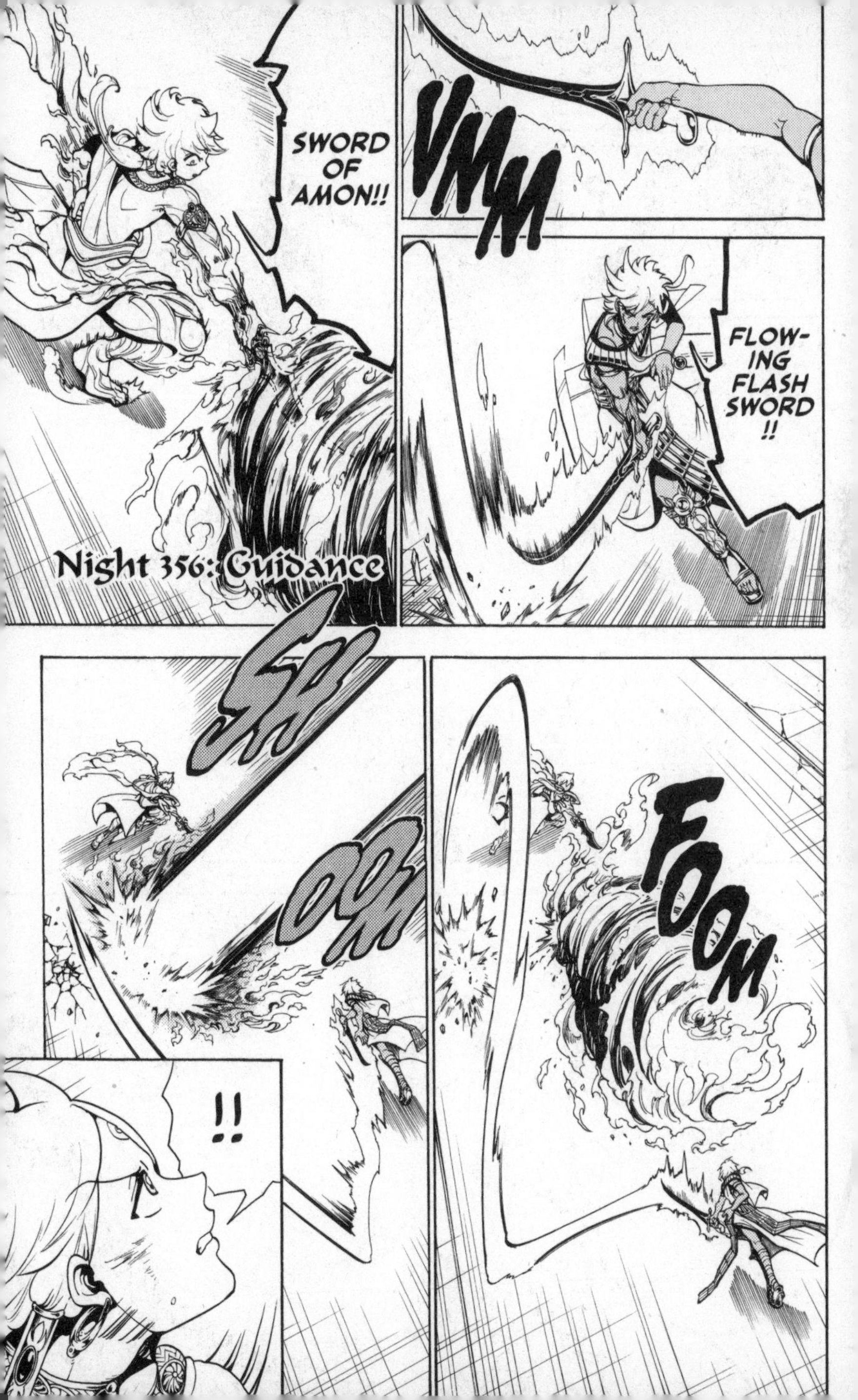
VMM
FLOWING FLASH SWORD!!
SWORD OF AMON!!
Night 356: Guidance
FOOM
SHOOM
!!

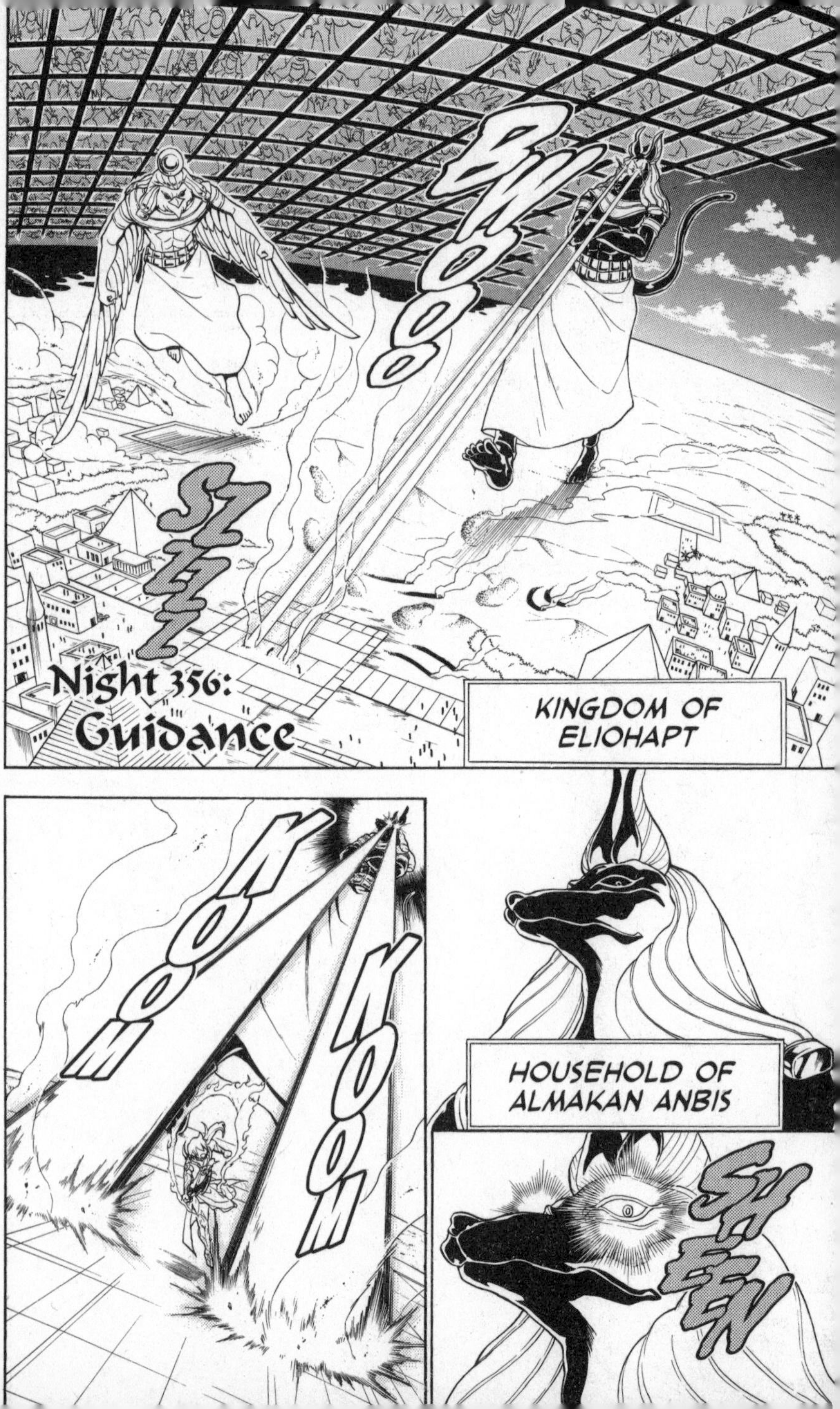
BWOOOOO
SIZZLE
Night 356: Guidance
KINGDOM OF ELIOHAPT
HOUSEHOLD OF ALMAKAN ANBIS
SHEEN
VWOOOM
VWOOOM

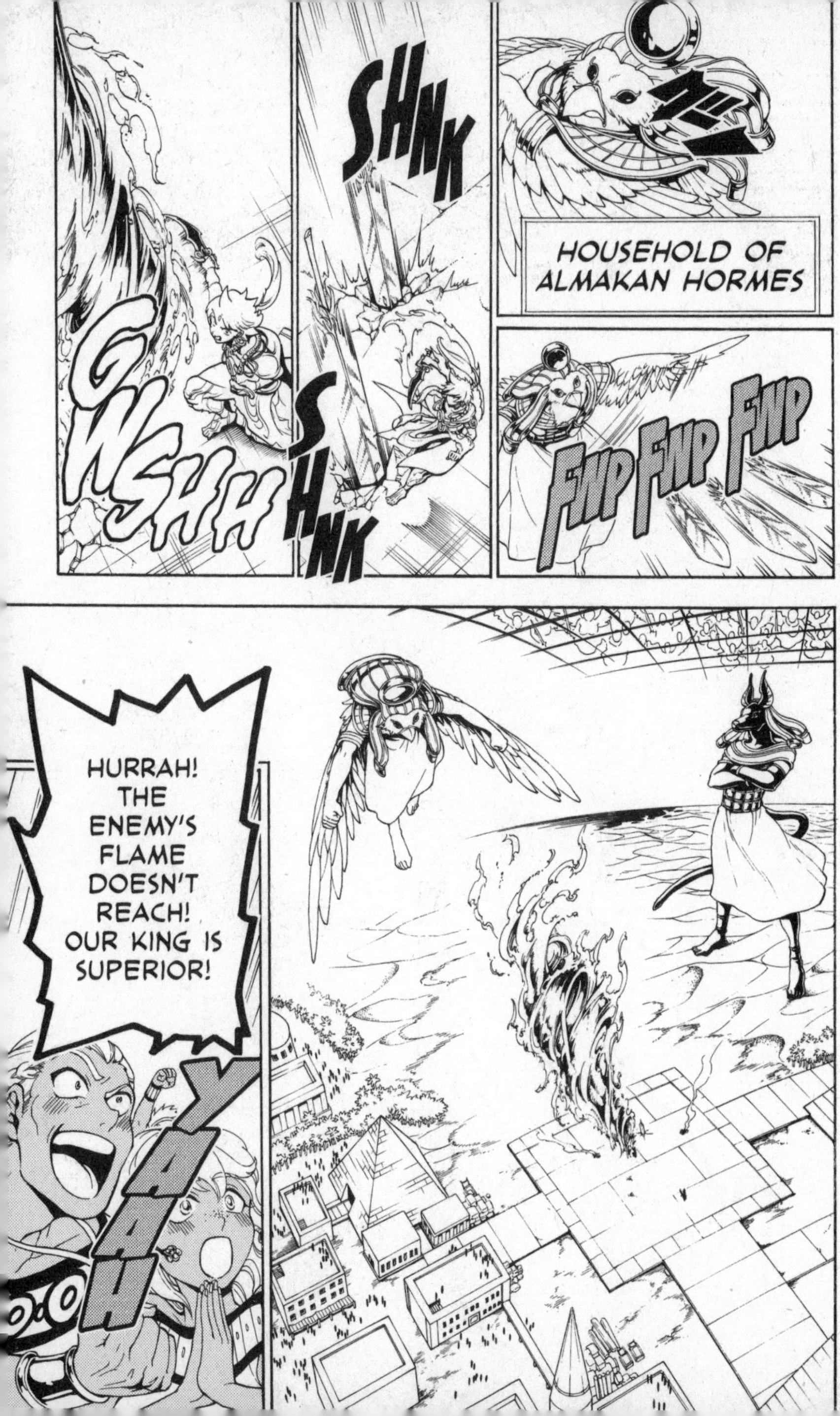
HOUSEHOLD OF ALMAKAN HORMES
FWP FWP FWP
SHNK
SHNK
GWSHH
HURRAH! THE ENEMY'S FLAME DOESN'T REACH! OUR KING IS SUPERIOR!
YAAAH

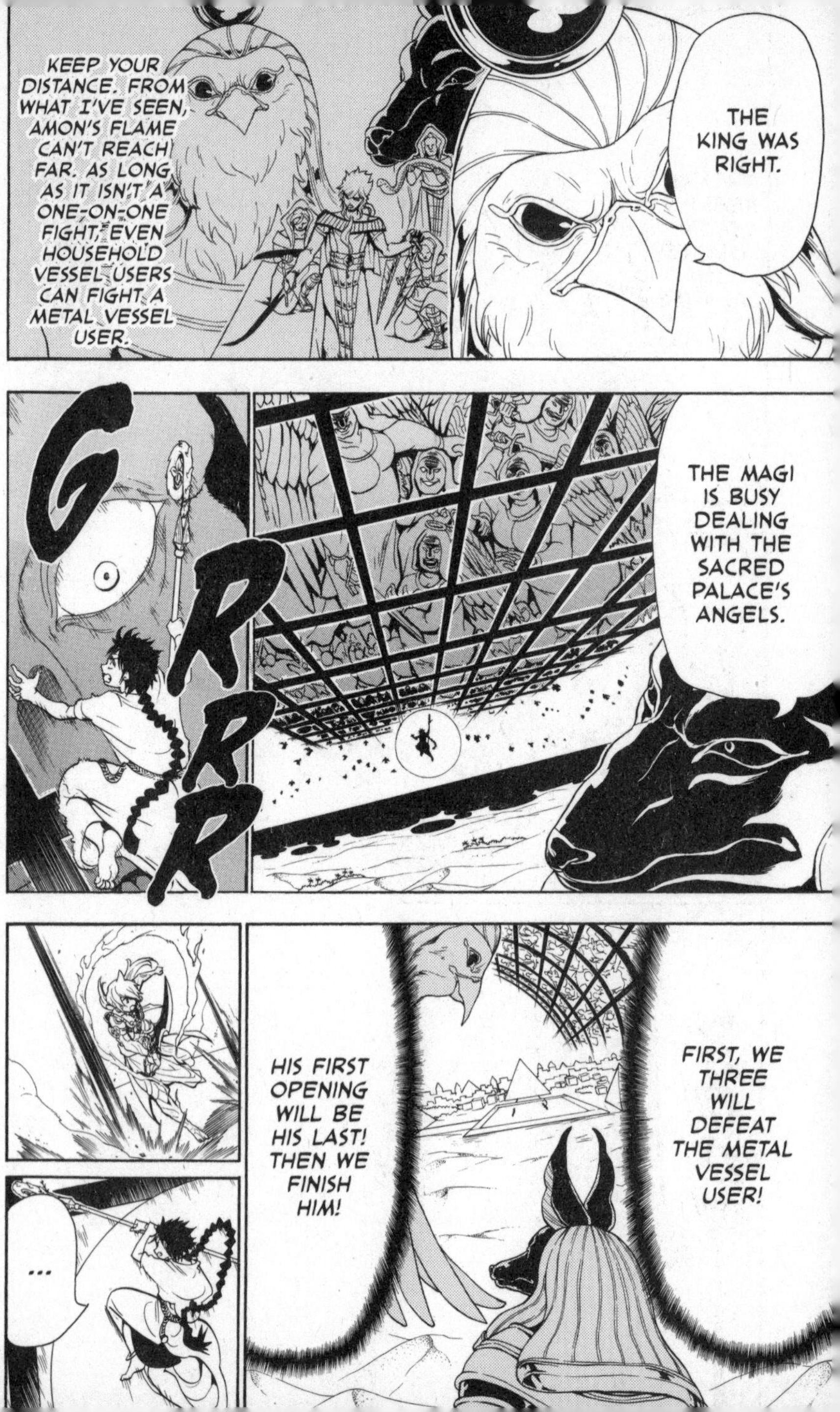
THE KING WAS RIGHT.
KEEP YOUR DISTANCE. FROM WHAT I'VE SEEN, AMON'S FLAME CAN'T REACH FAR. AS LONG AS IT ISN'T A ONE-ON-ONE FIGHT, EVEN HOUSEHOLD VESSEL USERS CAN FIGHT A METAL VESSEL USER.
THE MAGI IS BUSY DEALING WITH THE SACRED PALACE'S ANGELS.
GRRRR
FIRST, WE THREE WILL DEFEAT THE METAL VESSEL USER!
HIS FIRST OPENING WILL BE HIS LAST! THEN WE FINISH HIM!
...

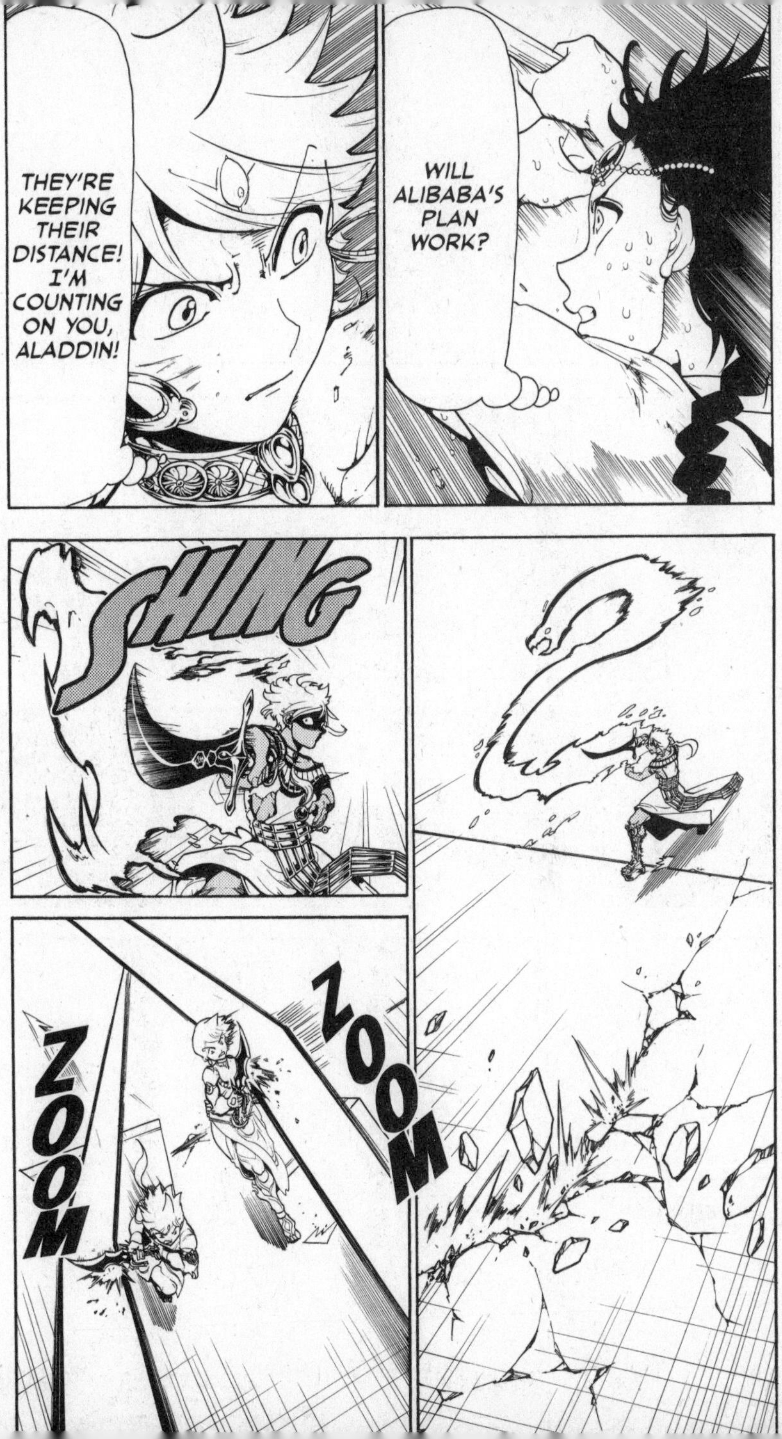
WILL ALIBABA'S PLAN WORK?
THEY'RE KEEPING THEIR DISTANCE! I'M COUNTING ON YOU, ALADDIN!
SHING
ZOOM
ZOOM

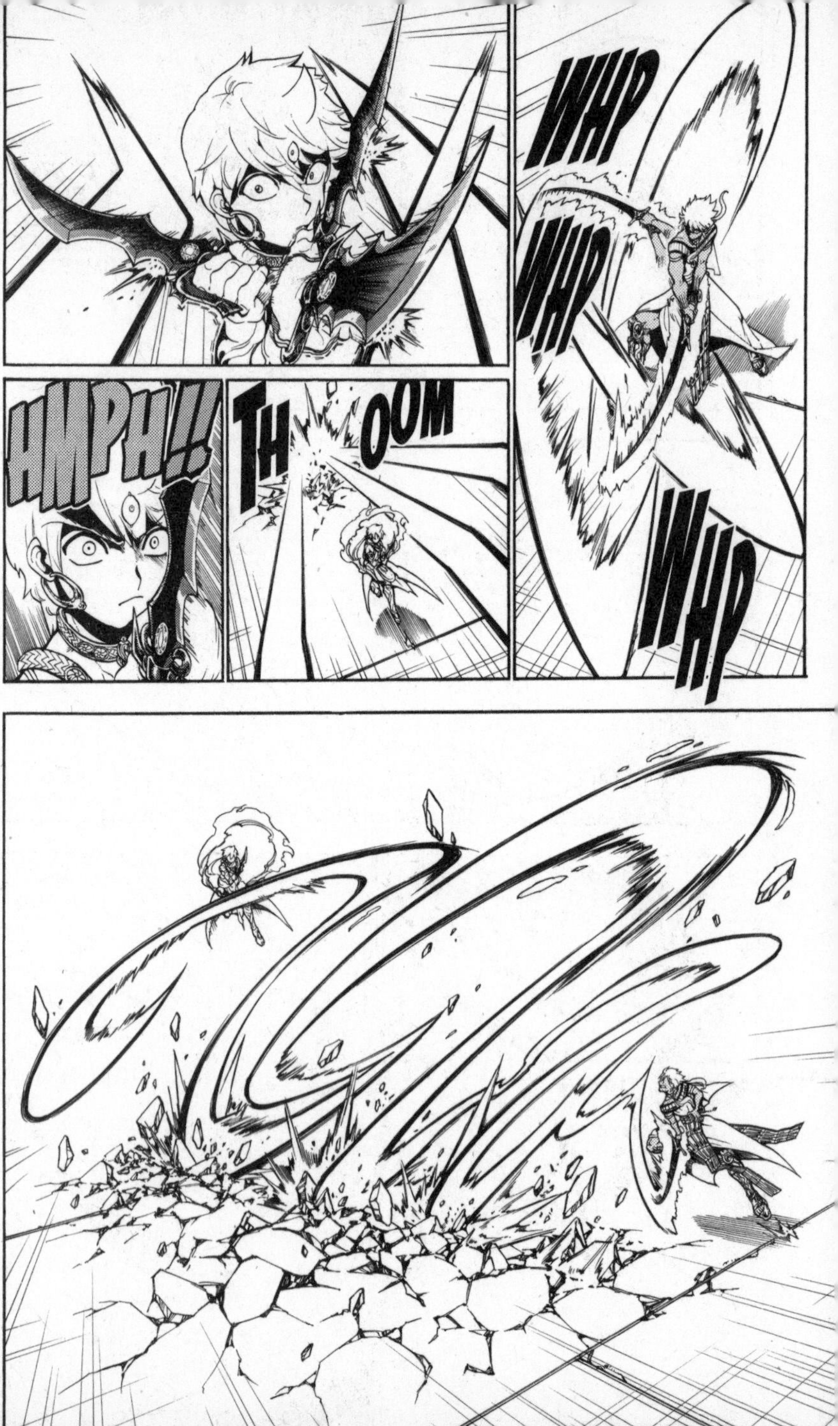
WHIP
WHIP
WHIP
THOOM
HMPH!!

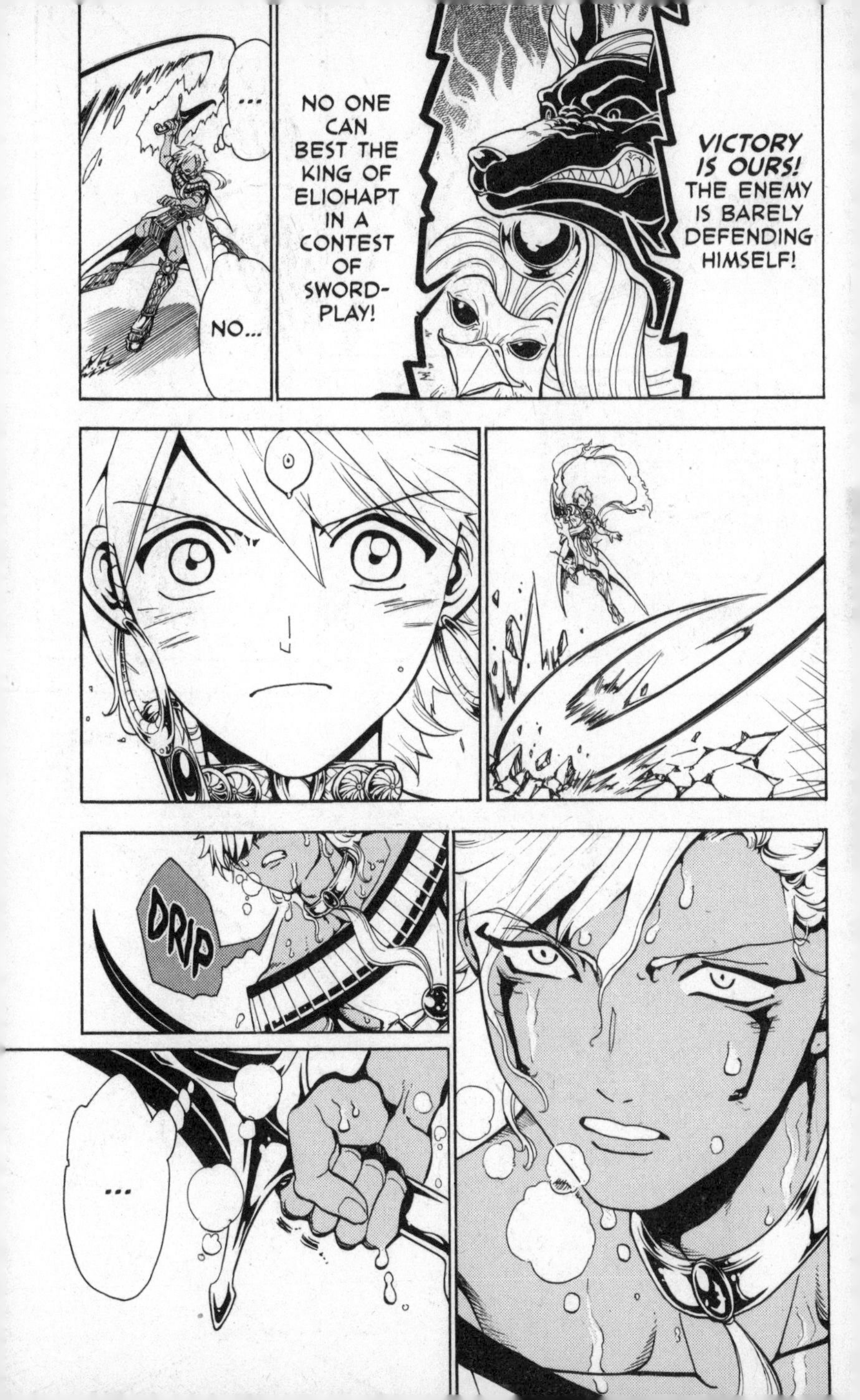
VICTORY IS OURS! THE ENEMY IS BARELY DEFENDING HIMSELF!
NO ONE CAN BEST THE KING OF ELIOHAPT IN A CONTEST OF SWORD-PLAY!
...
NO...
DRIP
...

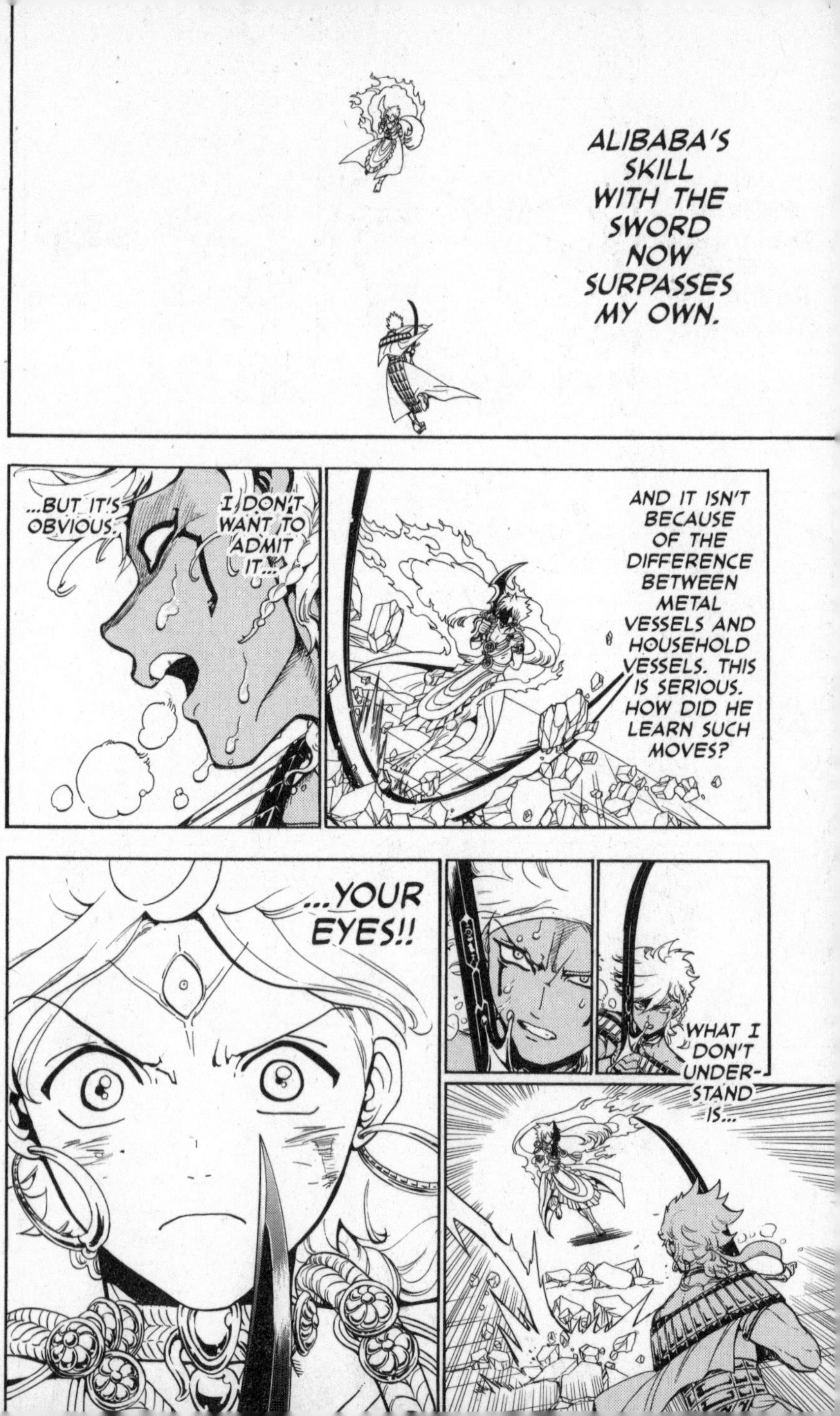
ALIBABA'S SKILL WITH THE SWORD NOW SURPASSES MY OWN.
AND IT ISN'T BECAUSE OF THE DIFFERENCE BETWEEN METAL VESSELS AND HOUSEHOLD VESSELS. THIS IS SERIOUS. HOW DID HE LEARN SUCH MOVES?
I DON'T WANT TO ADMIT IT...
...BUT IT'S OBVIOUS.
WHAT I DON'T UNDER-STAND IS...
...YOUR EYES!!

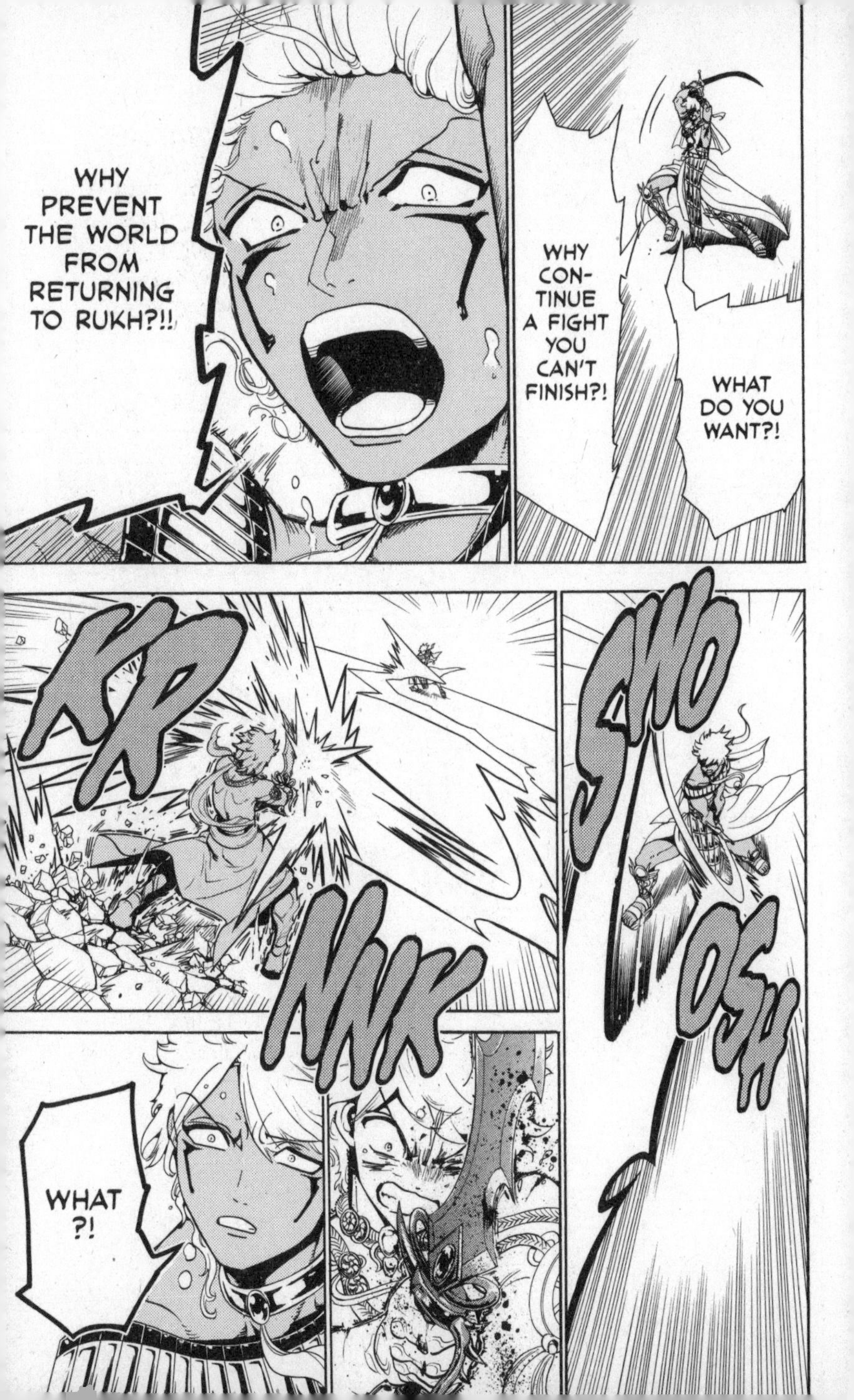
WHY CONTINUE A FIGHT YOU CAN'T FINISH?!
WHAT DO YOU WANT?!
WHY PREVENT THE WORLD FROM RETURNING TO RUKH?!!
SHOO
OSH
KR
NNK
WHAT ?!

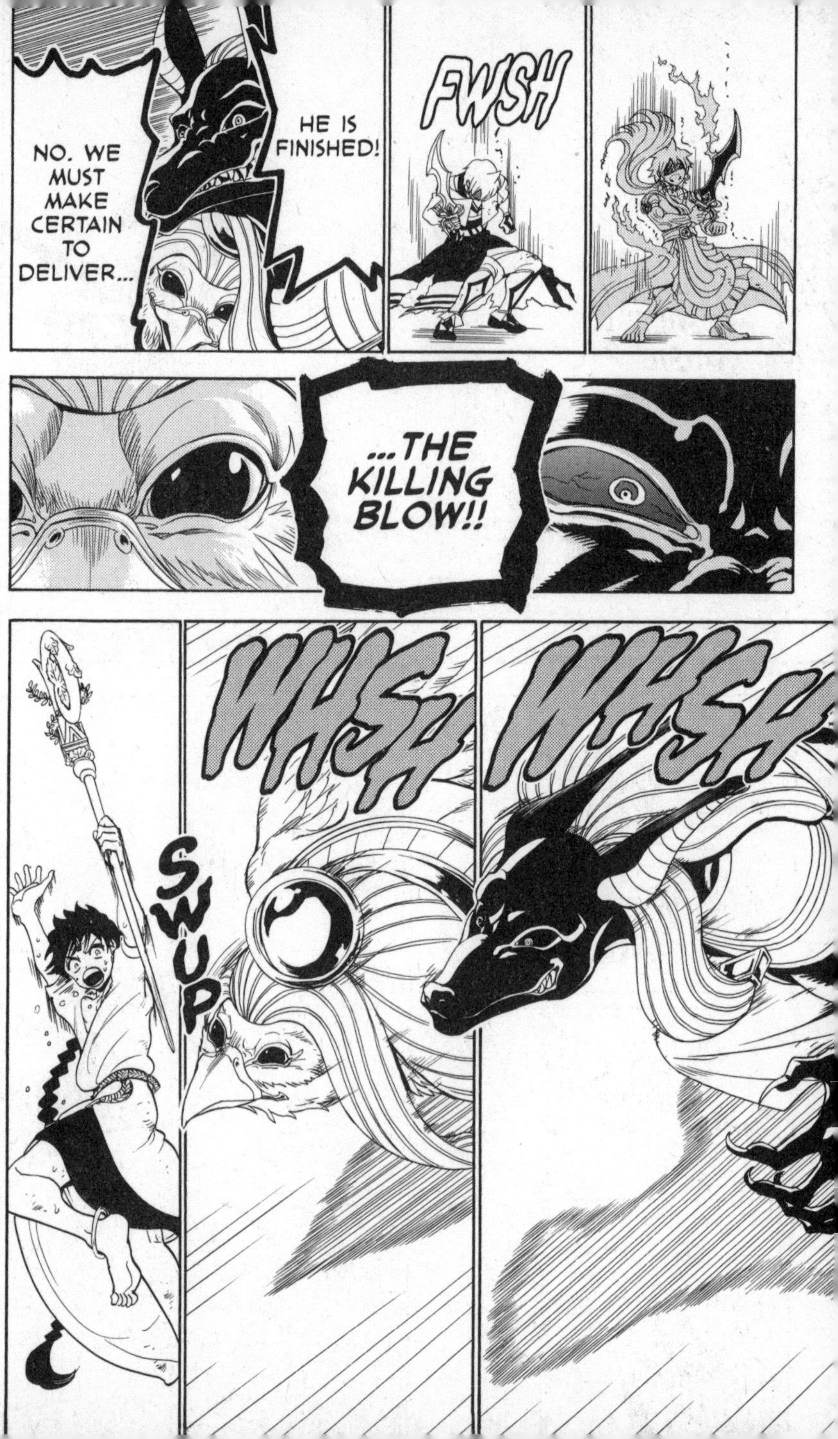
FWSH
HE IS FINISHED!
NO. WE MUST MAKE CERTAIN TO DELIVER...
...THE KILLING BLOW!!
WHSH
WHSH
SWUP

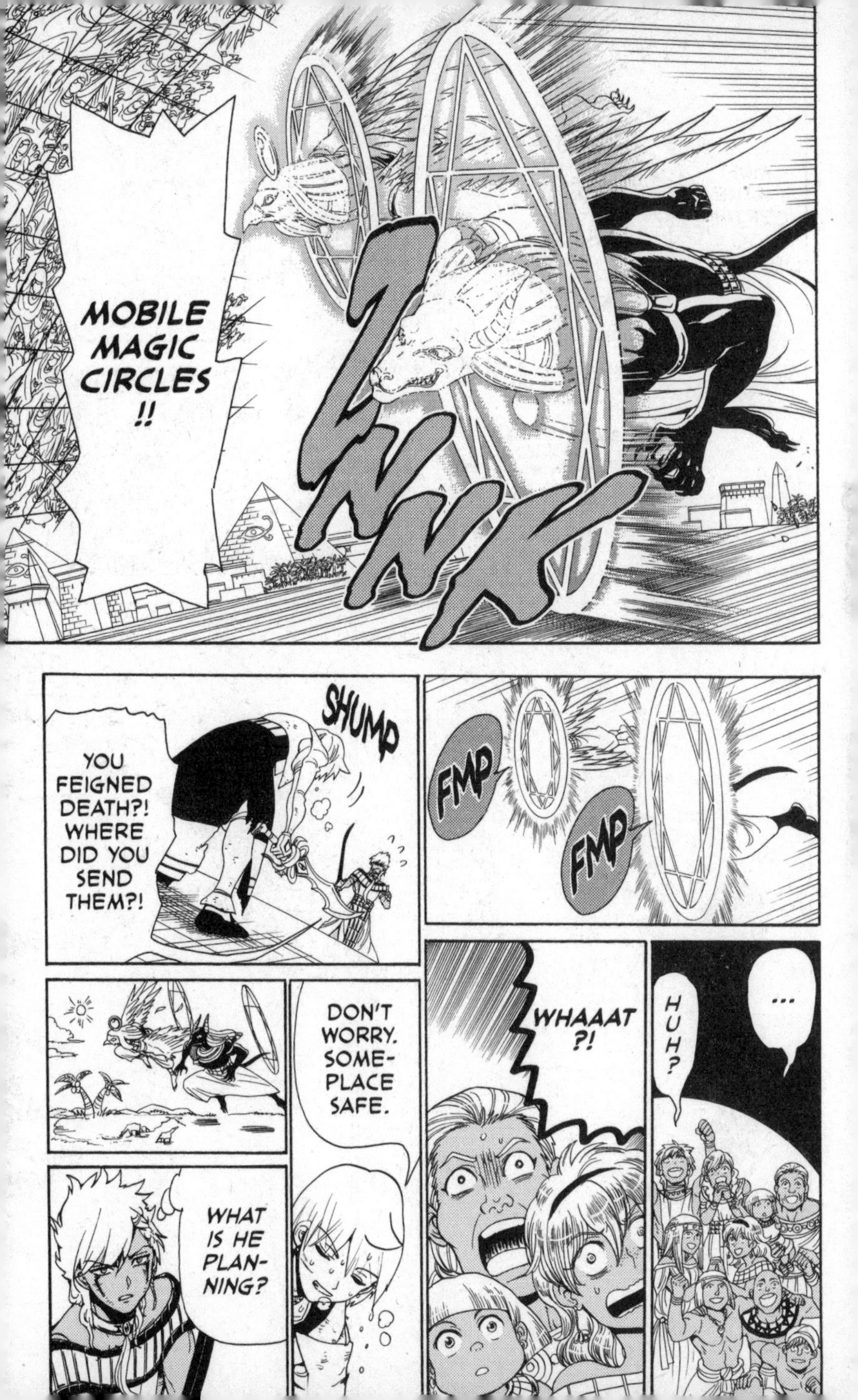
ZWNK
MOBILE MAGIC CIRCLES !!
FMP
FMP
SHUMP
YOU FEIGNED DEATH?! WHERE DID YOU SEND THEM?!
...
HUH?
WHAAAT ?!
DON'T WORRY. SOME-PLACE SAFE.
WHAT IS HE PLAN-NING?

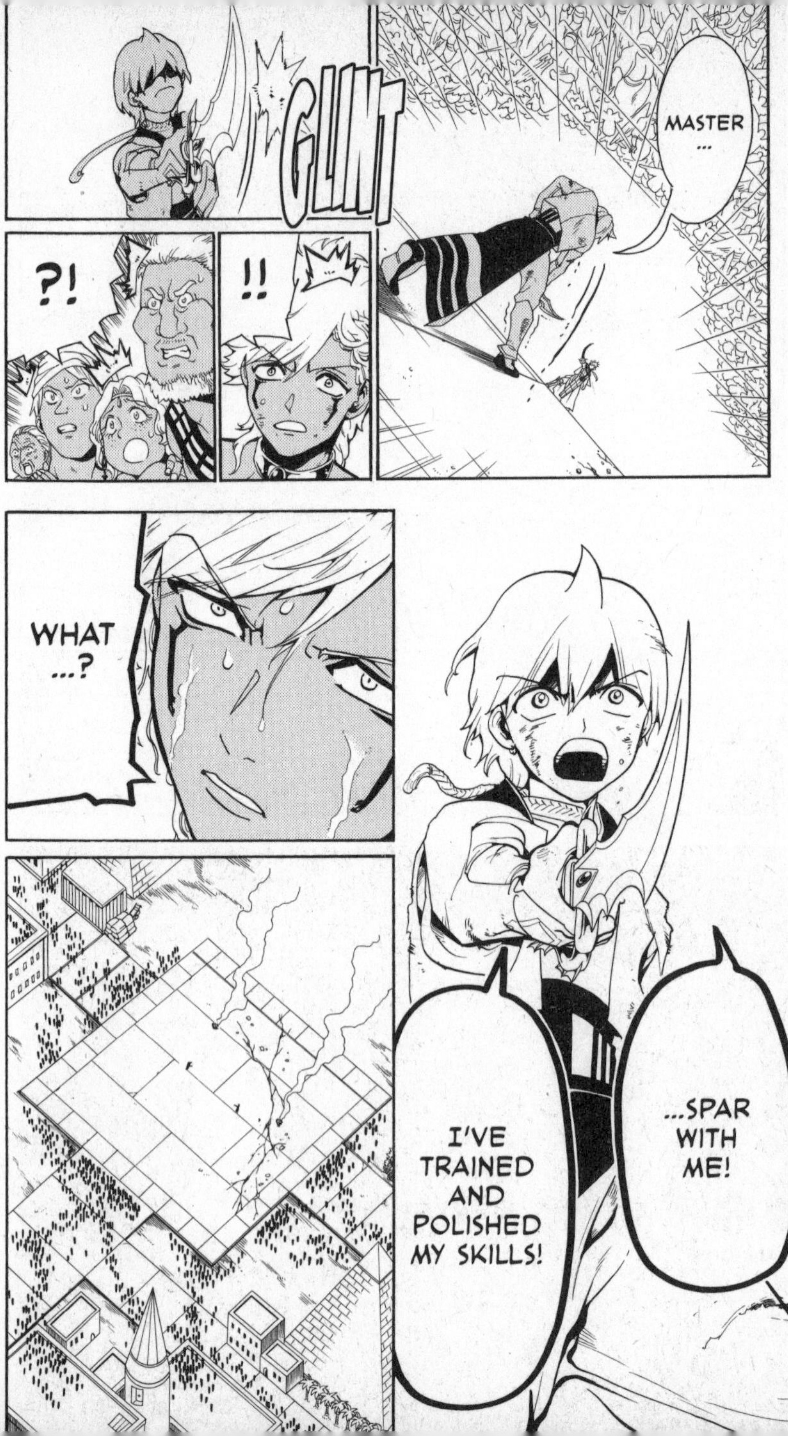
MASTER ...
GLINT
!!
?!
I'VE TRAINED AND POLISHED MY SKILLS!
...SPAR WITH ME!
WHAT ...?

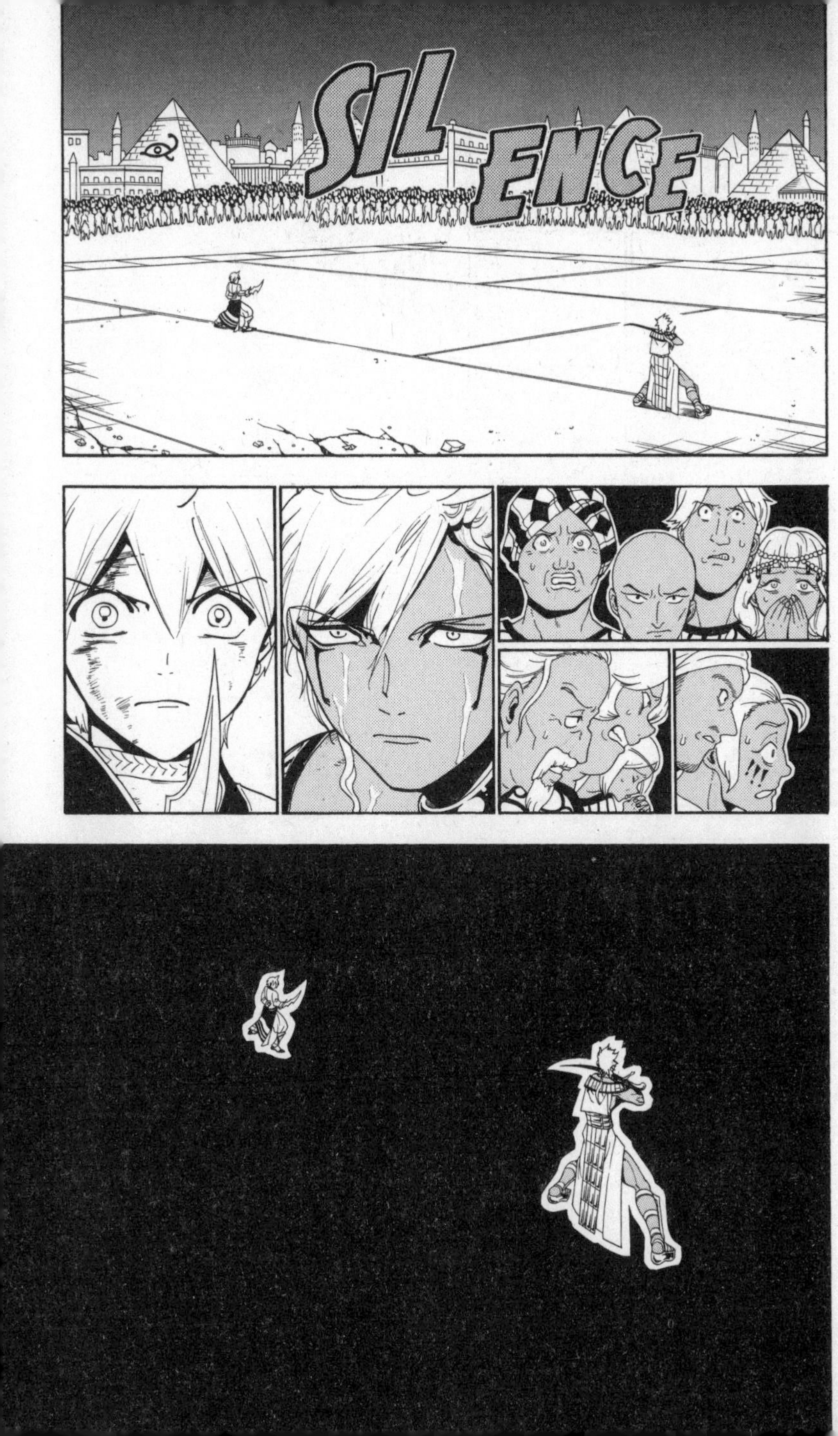
SILENCE

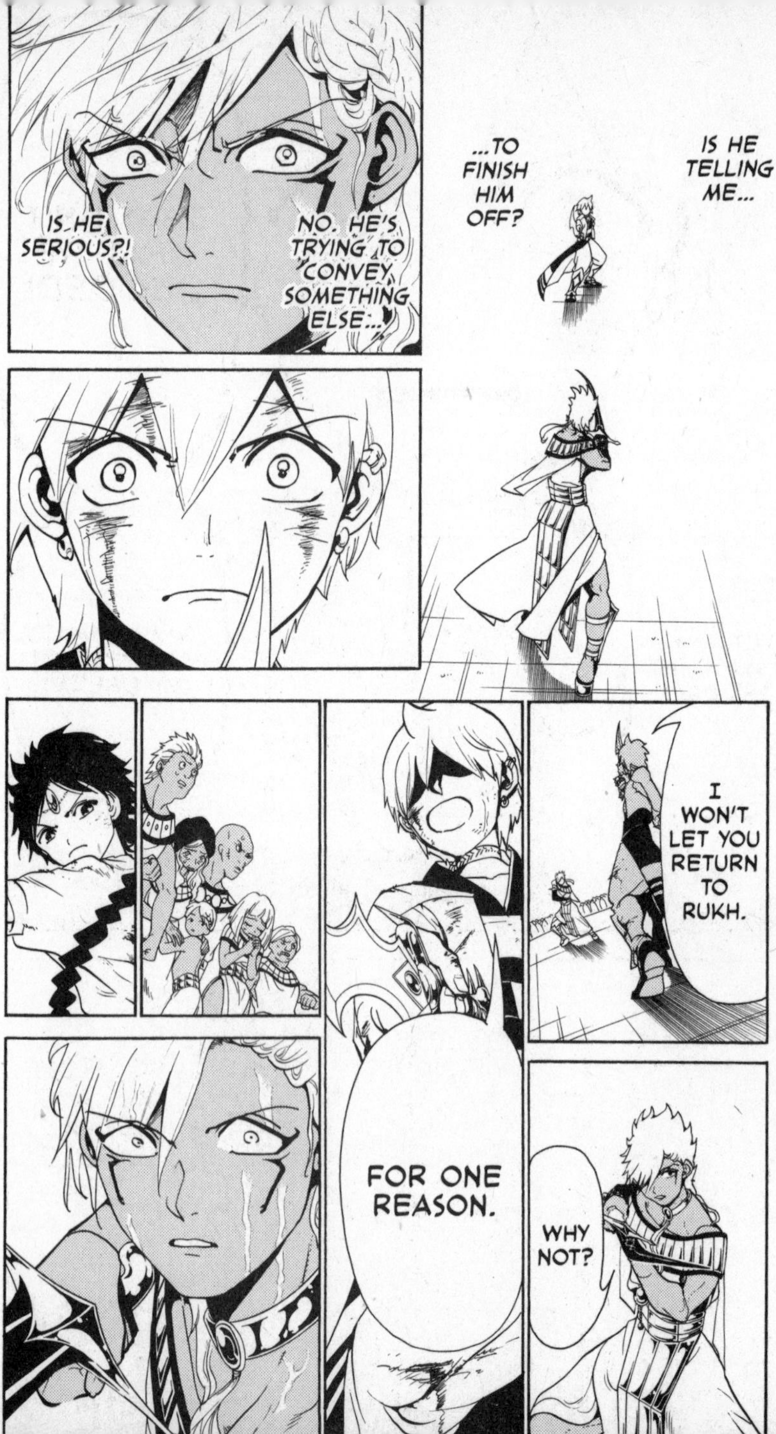
IS HE TELLING ME...
...TO FINISH HIM OFF?
NO. HE'S TRYING TO CONVEY SOMETHING ELSE...
IS HE SERIOUS?!
I WON'T LET YOU RETURN TO RUKH.
WHY NOT?
FOR ONE REASON.

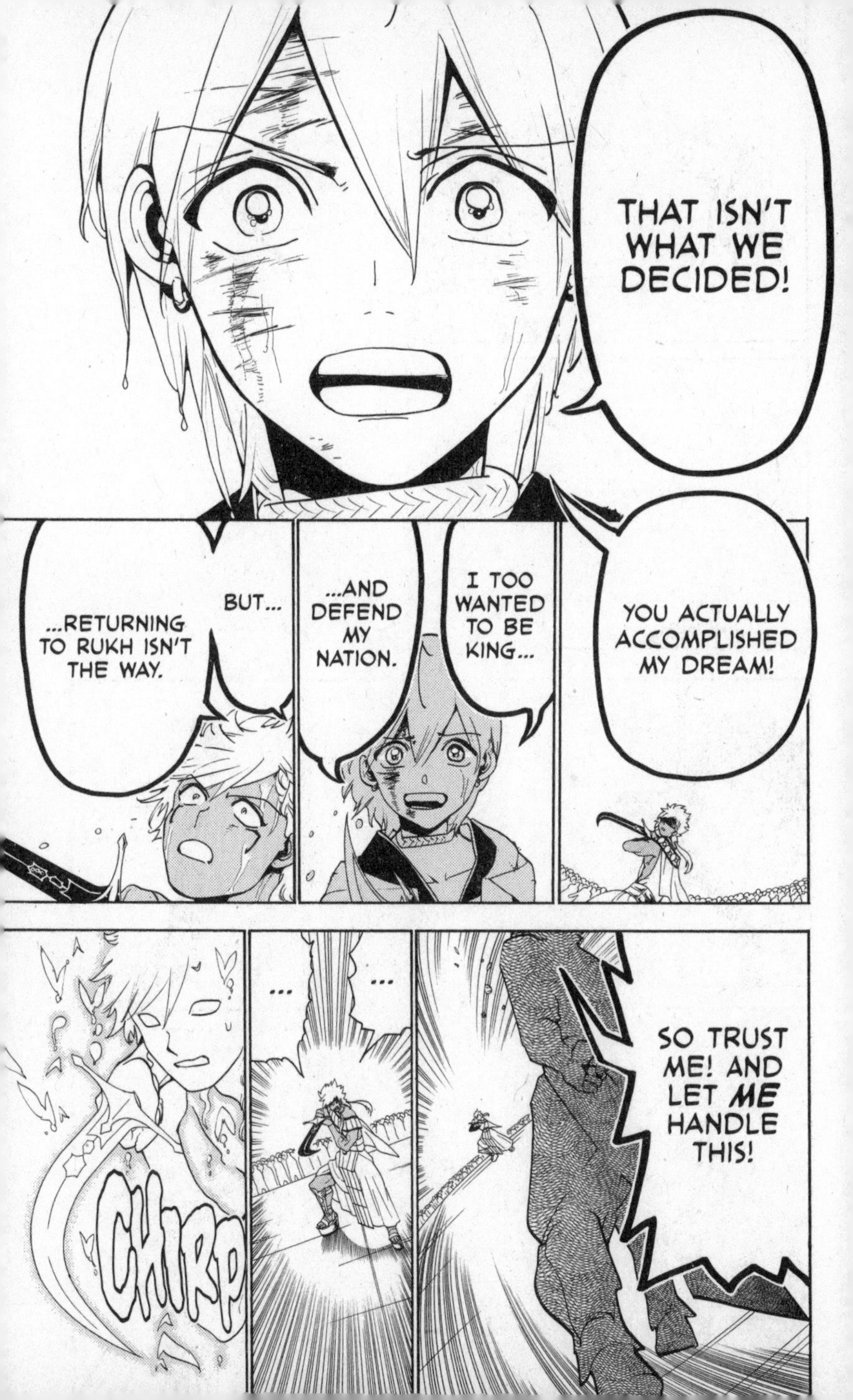
THAT ISN'T WHAT WE DECIDED!
YOU ACTUALLY ACCOMPLISHED MY DREAM!
I TOO WANTED TO BE KING...
...AND DEFEND MY NATION.
BUT...
...RETURNING TO RUKH ISN'T THE WAY.
SO TRUST ME! AND LET *ME* HANDLE THIS!
...
...
CHIRP

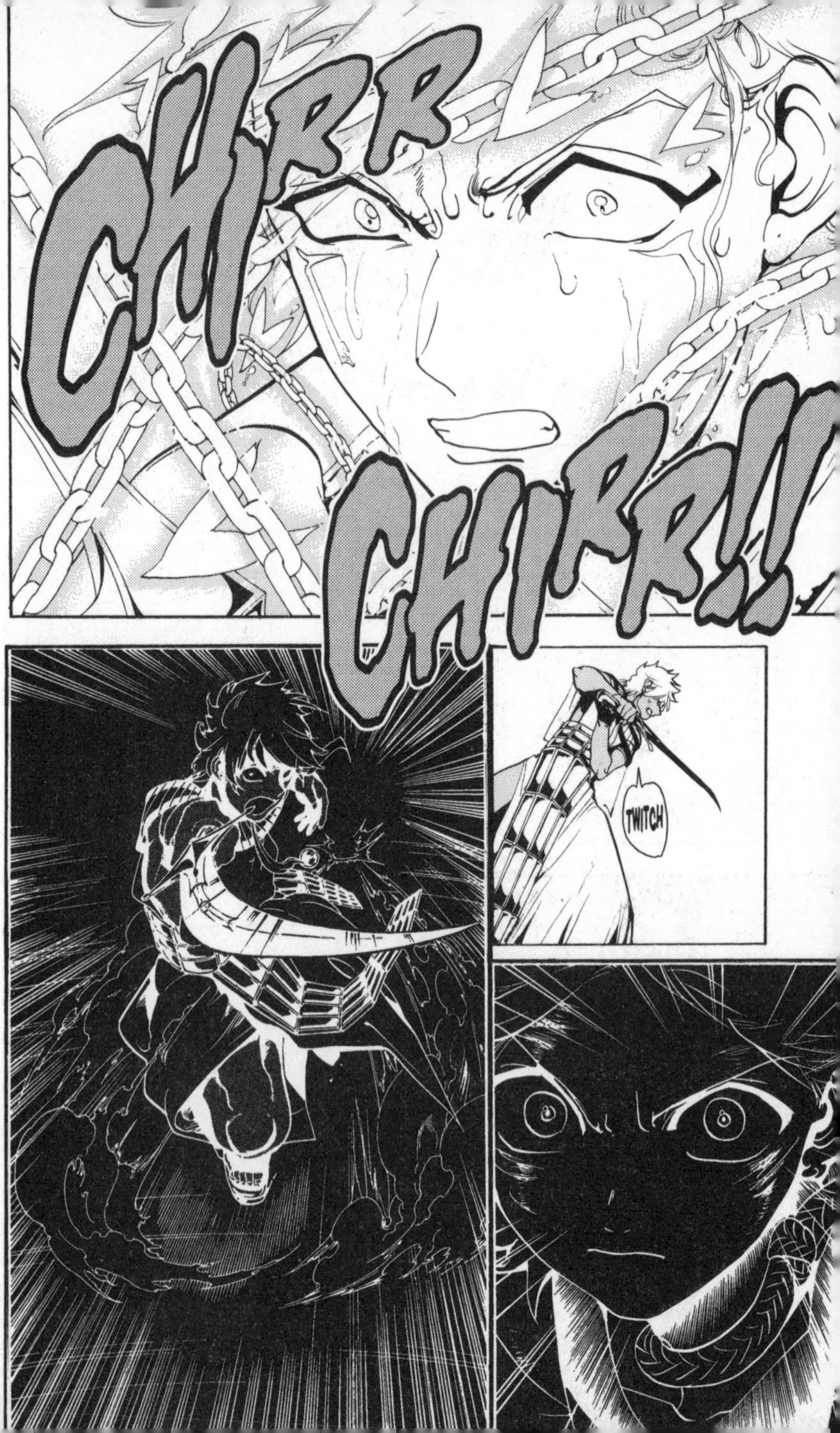
CHIRR
CHIRR!!
TWITCH

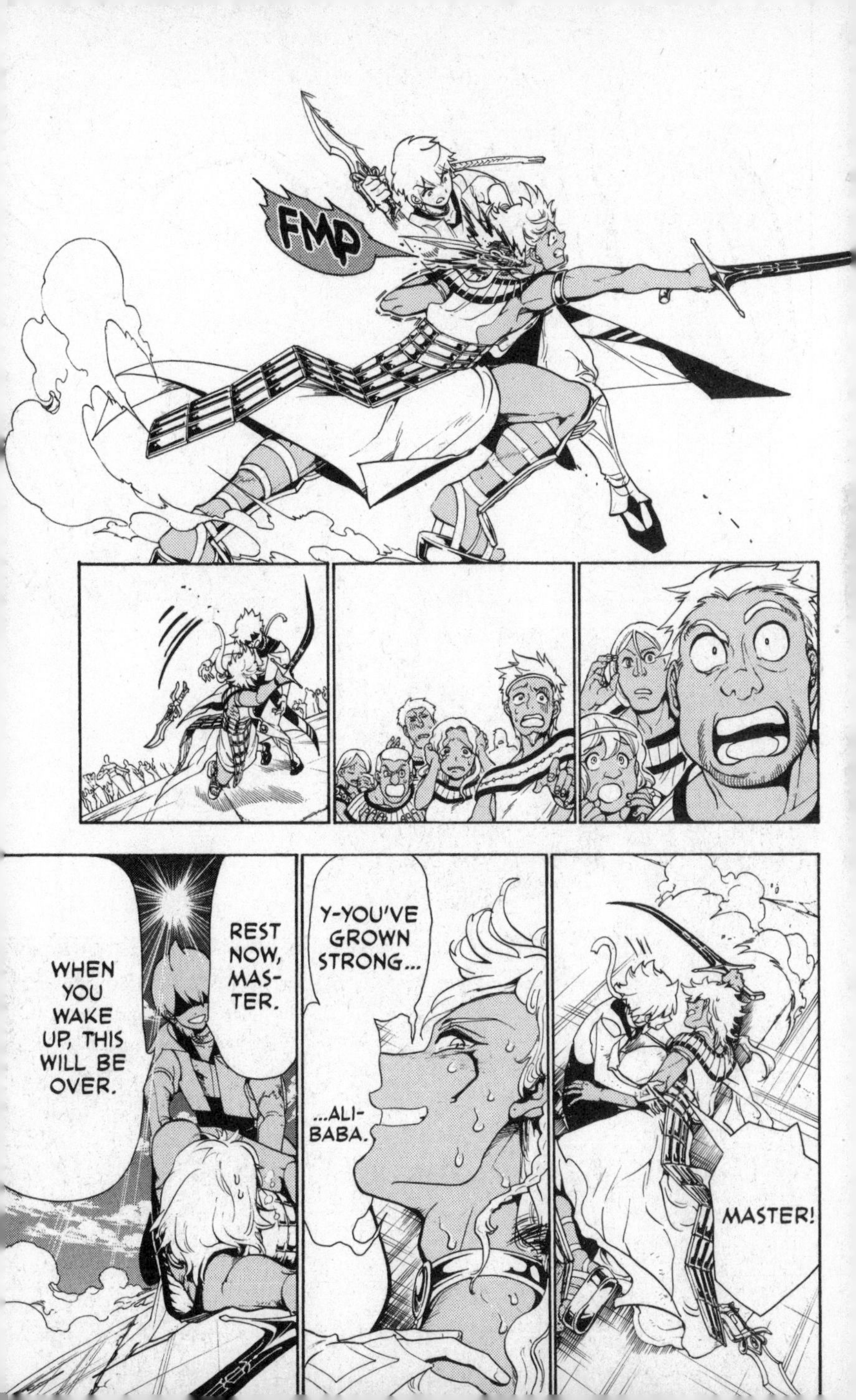
FMP
MASTER!
Y-YOU'VE GROWN STRONG...
...ALI-BABA.
REST NOW, MAS-TER.
WHEN YOU WAKE UP, THIS WILL BE OVER.

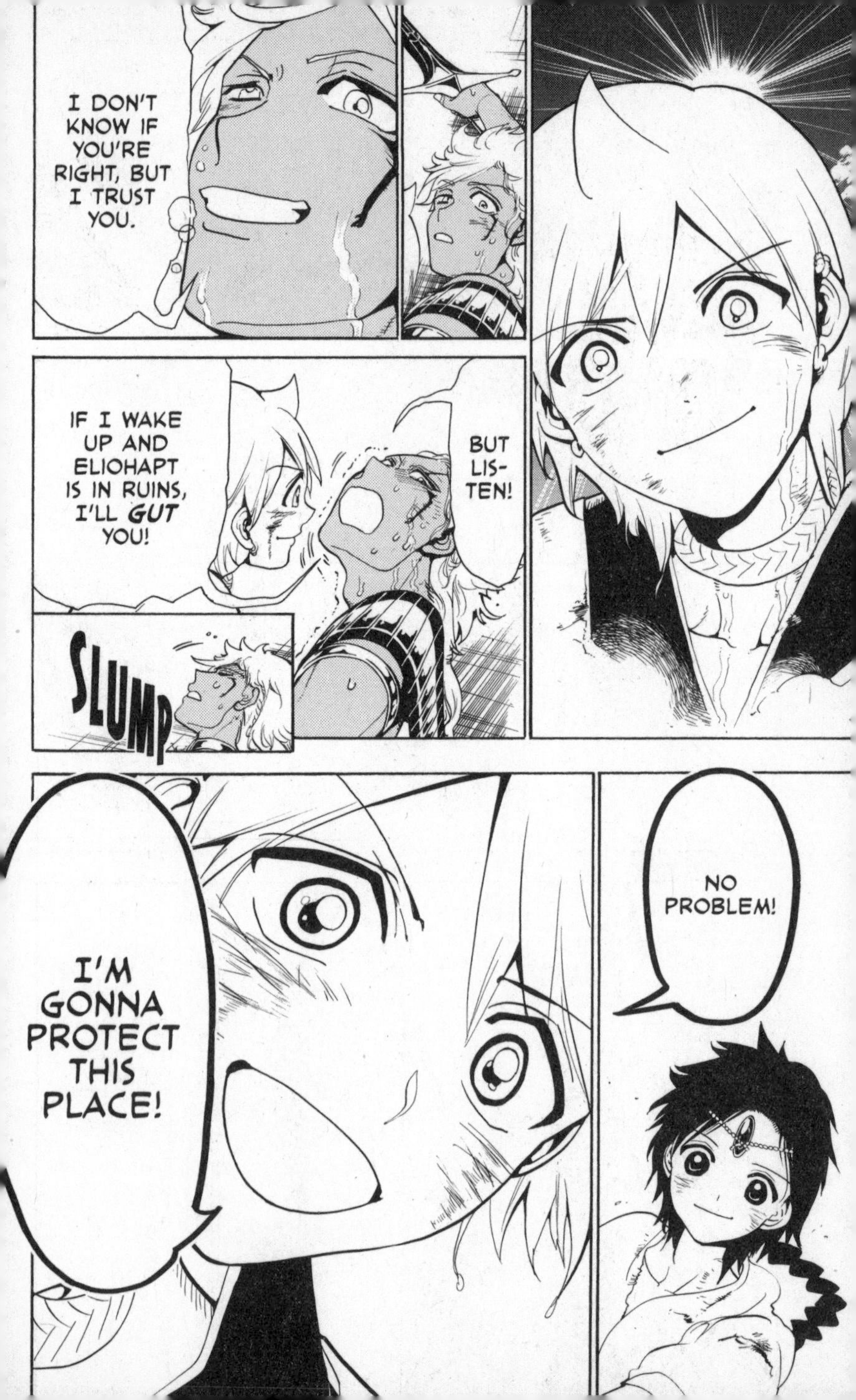
I DON'T KNOW IF YOU'RE RIGHT, BUT I TRUST YOU.
BUT LIS-TEN!
IF I WAKE UP AND ELIOHAPT IS IN RUINS, I'LL *GUT* YOU!
SLUMP
NO PROBLEM!
I'M GONNA PROTECT THIS PLACE!

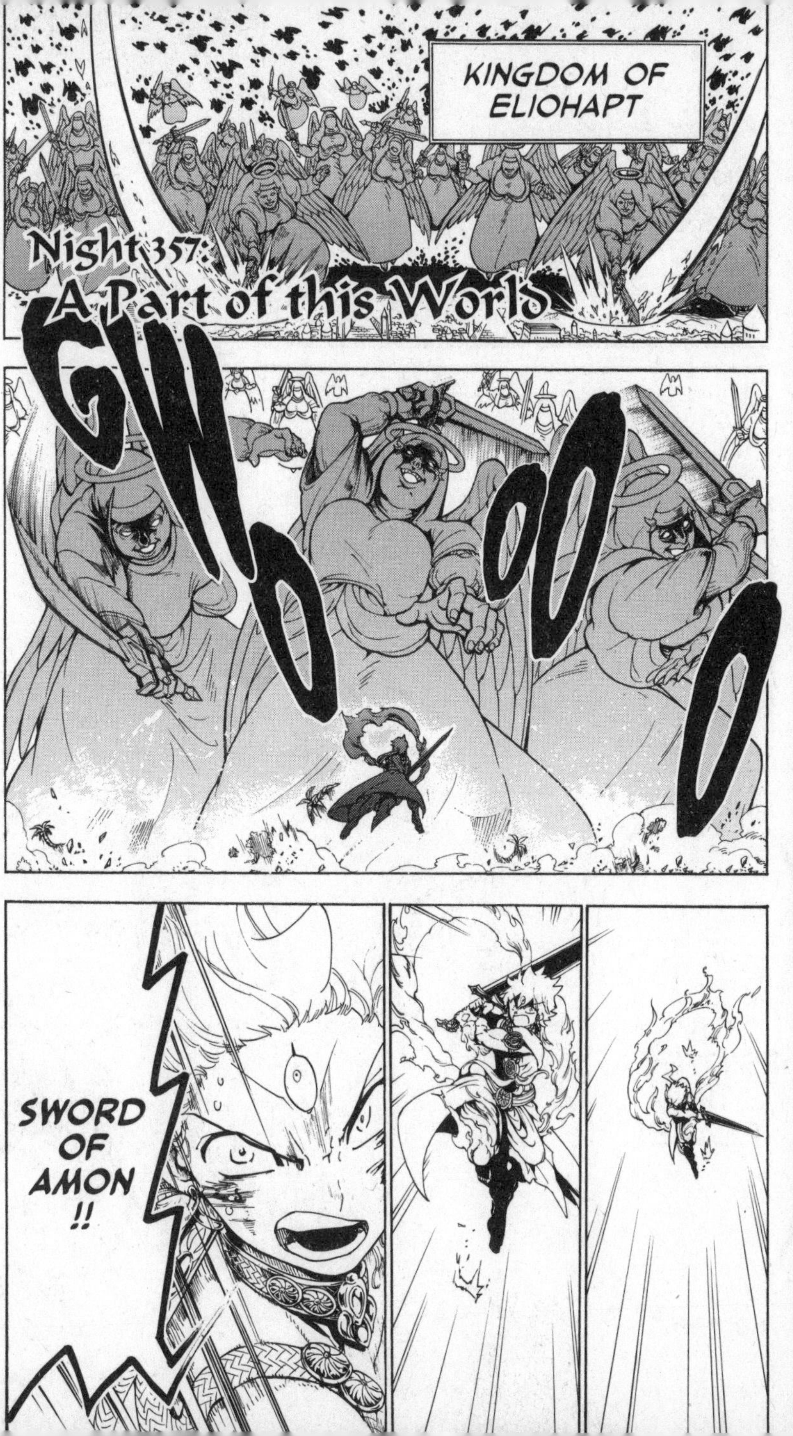
KINGDOM OF ELIOHAPT
Night 357: A Part of this World
GWOOOOO
SWORD OF AMON !!

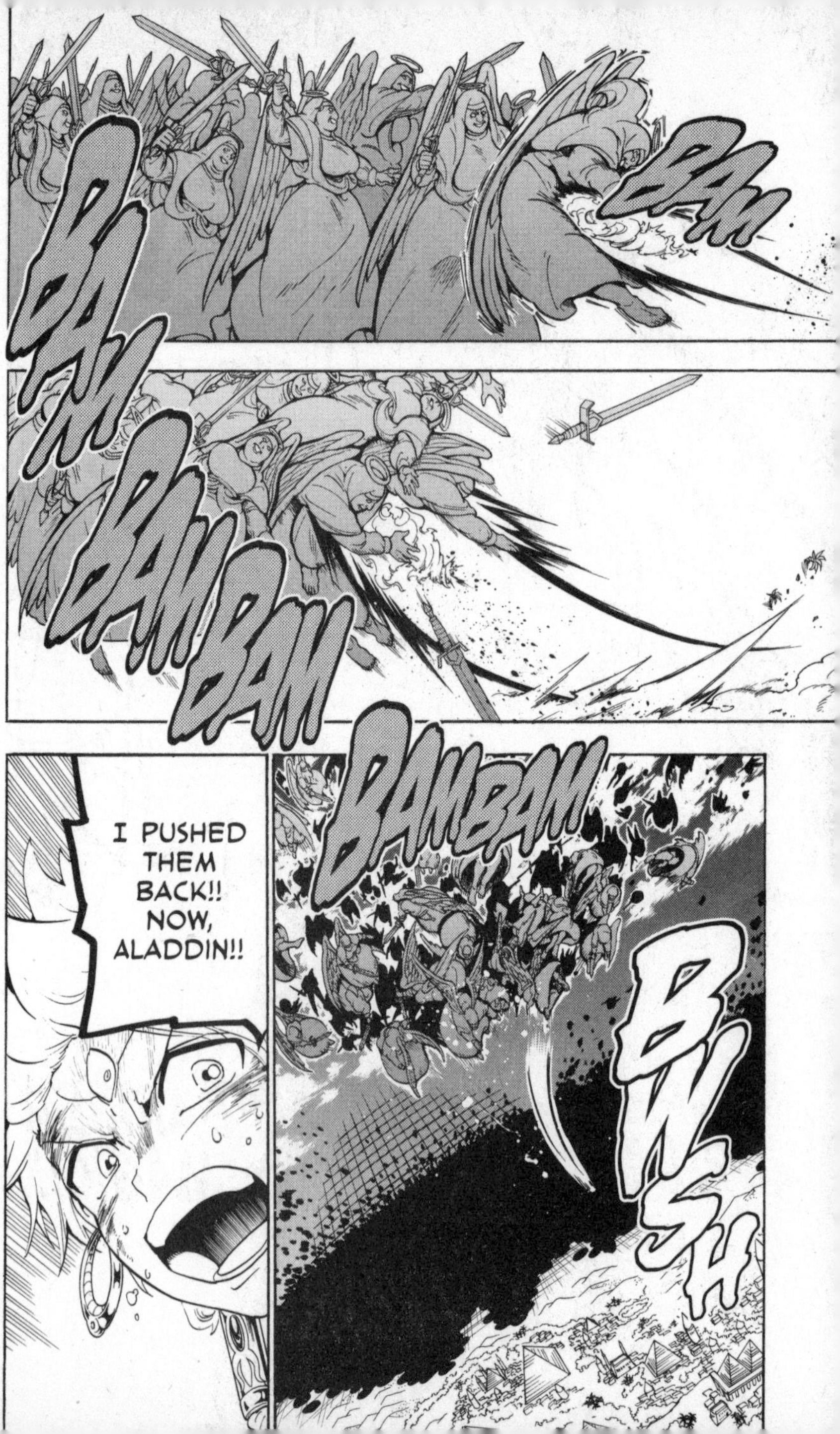
BAM
BAM
BAMBAMBAM
BAMBAM
BWSH
I PUSHED THEM BACK!! NOW, ALADDIN!!

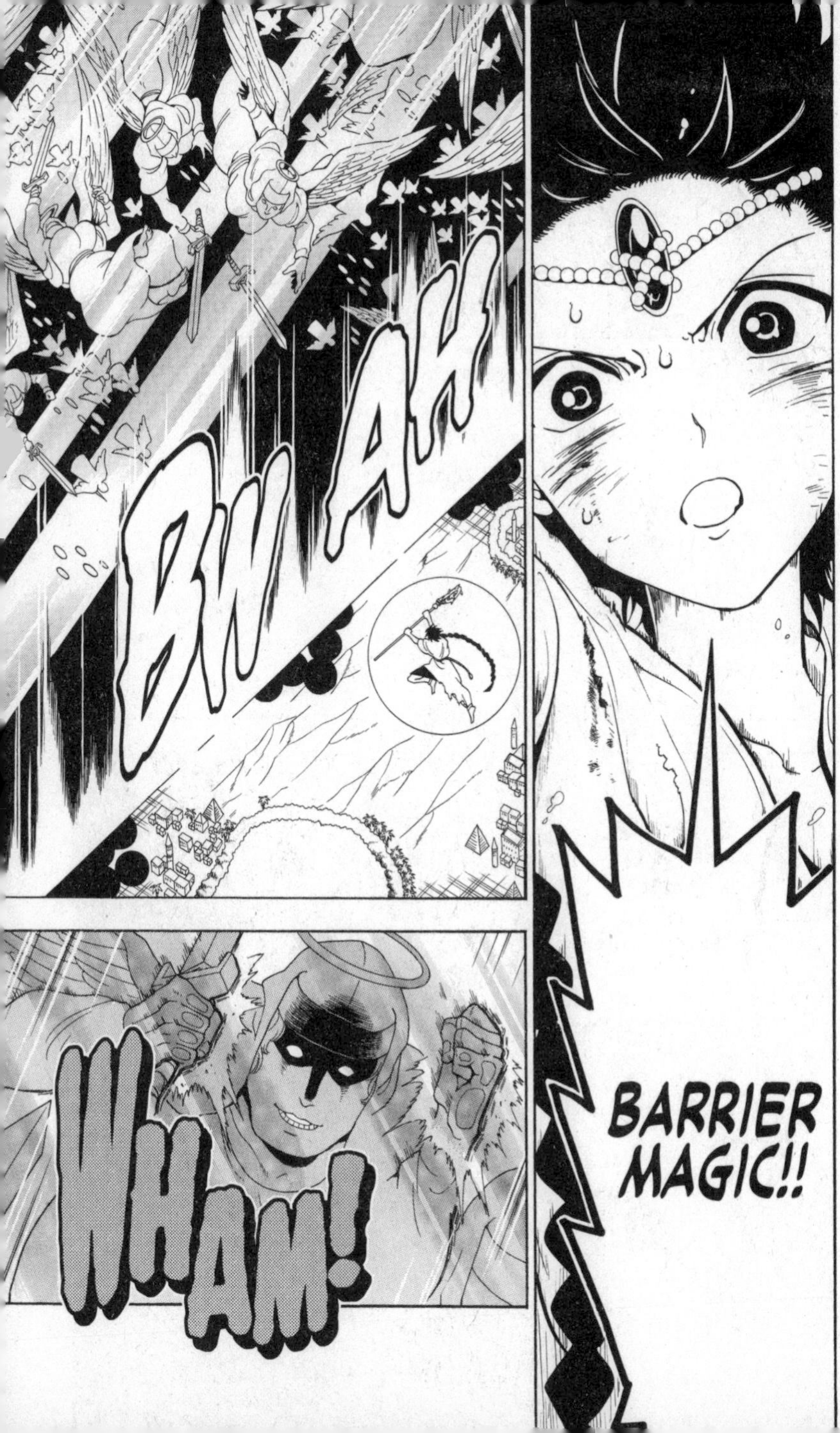
BARRIER MAGIC!!
BWAH
WHAM!

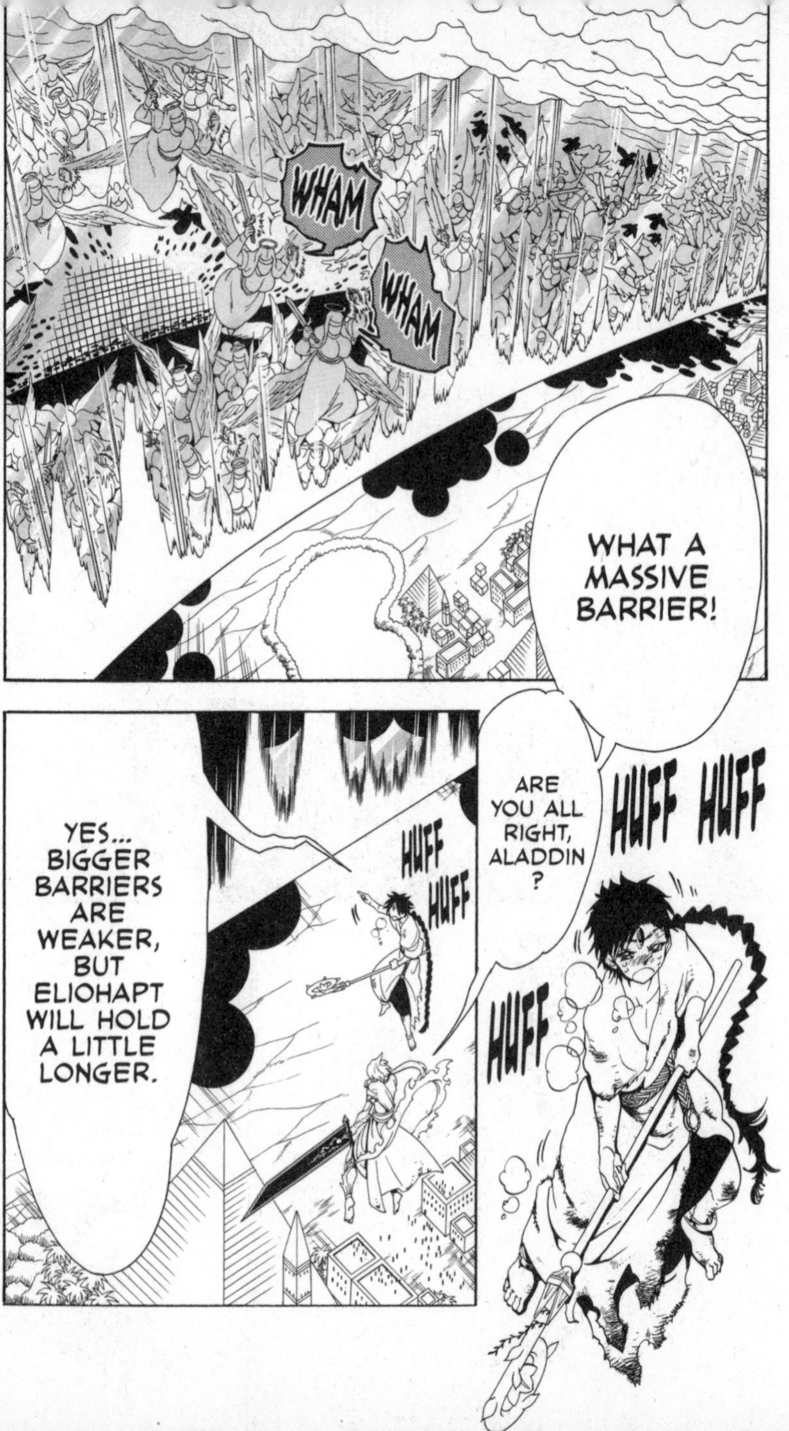
WHAM
WHAM
WHAT A MASSIVE BARRIER!
HUFF HUFF
ARE YOU ALL RIGHT, ALADDIN?
HUFF
HUFF HUFF
YES... BIGGER BARRIERS ARE WEAKER, BUT ELIOHAPT WILL HOLD A LITTLE LONGER.

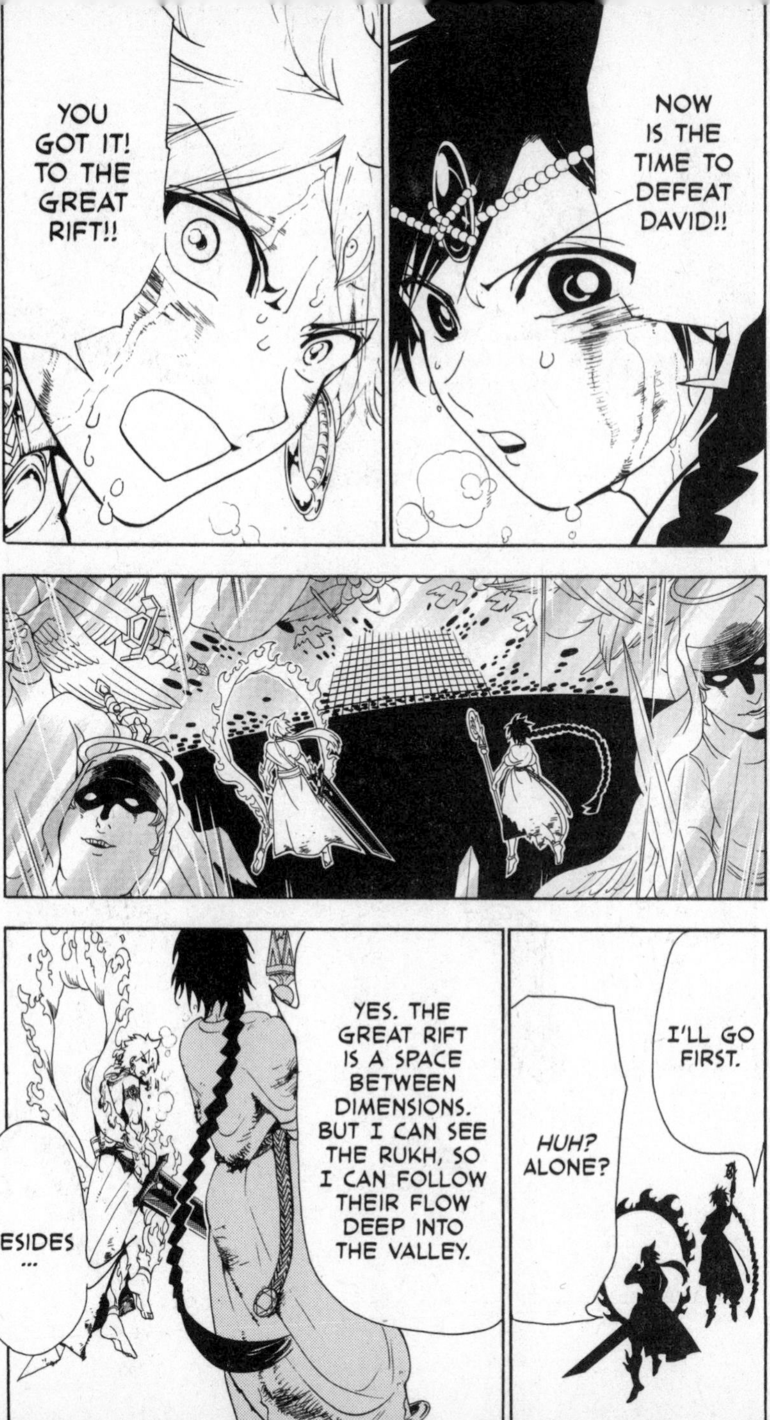
NOW IS THE TIME TO DEFEAT DAVID!!
YOU GOT IT! TO THE GREAT RIFT!!
I'LL GO FIRST.
HUH? ALONE?
YES. THE GREAT RIFT IS A SPACE BETWEEN DIMENSIONS. BUT I CAN SEE THE RUKH, SO I CAN FOLLOW THEIR FLOW DEEP INTO THE VALLEY.
BESIDES ...

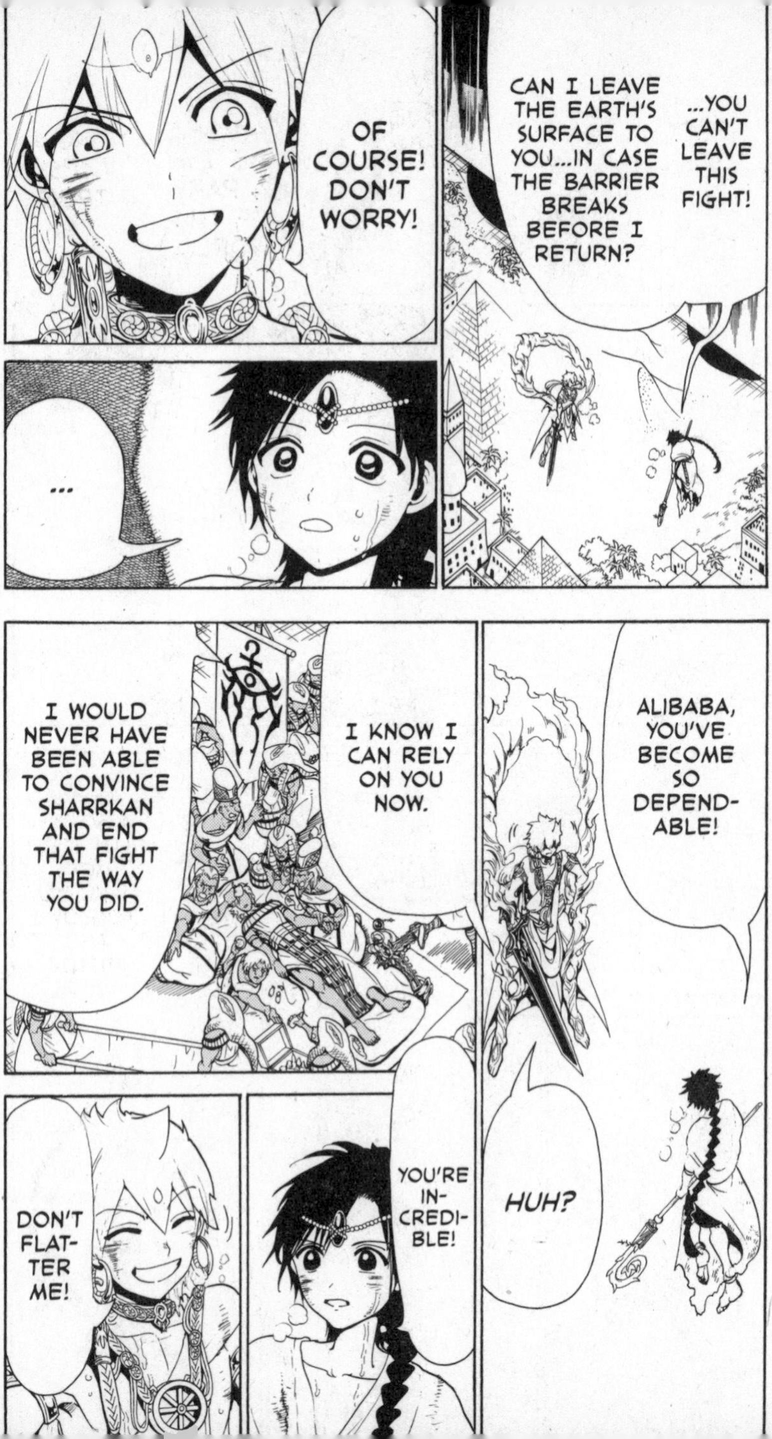
...YOU CAN'T LEAVE THIS FIGHT!
CAN I LEAVE THE EARTH'S SURFACE TO YOU...IN CASE THE BARRIER BREAKS BEFORE I RETURN?
OF COURSE! DON'T WORRY!
...
ALIBABA, YOU'VE BECOME SO DEPEND-ABLE!
HUH?
I KNOW I CAN RELY ON YOU NOW.
I WOULD NEVER HAVE BEEN ABLE TO CONVINCE SHARRKAN AND END THAT FIGHT THE WAY YOU DID.
YOU'RE IN-CREDI-BLE!
DON'T FLAT-TER ME!

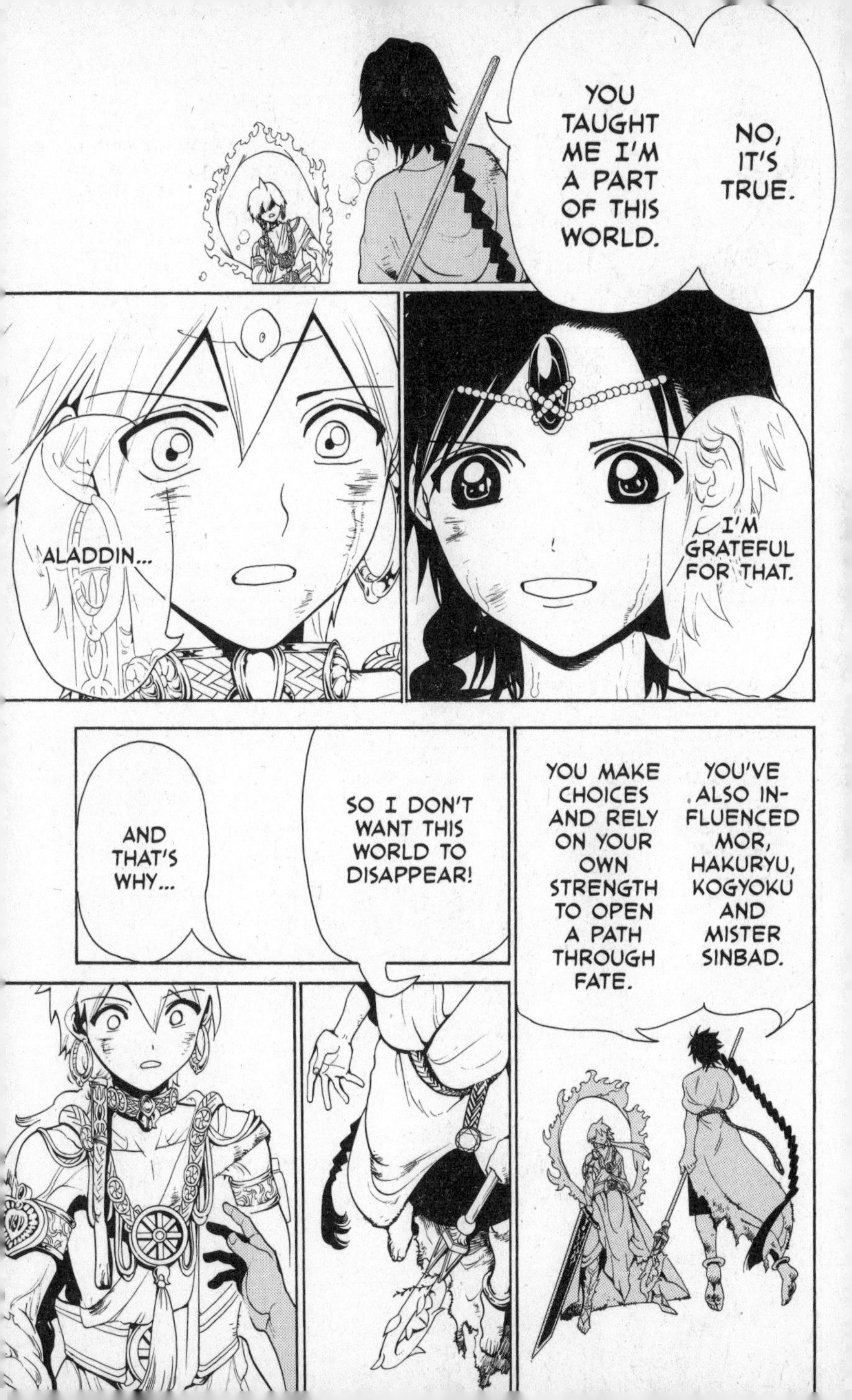
NO, IT'S TRUE.
YOU TAUGHT ME I'M A PART OF THIS WORLD.
I'M GRATEFUL FOR THAT.
ALADDIN...
YOU'VE ALSO IN-FLUENCED MOR, HAKURYU, KOGYOKU AND MISTER SINBAD.
YOU MAKE CHOICES AND RELY ON YOUR OWN STRENGTH TO OPEN A PATH THROUGH FATE.
AND THAT'S WHY...
SO I DON'T WANT THIS WORLD TO DISAPPEAR!

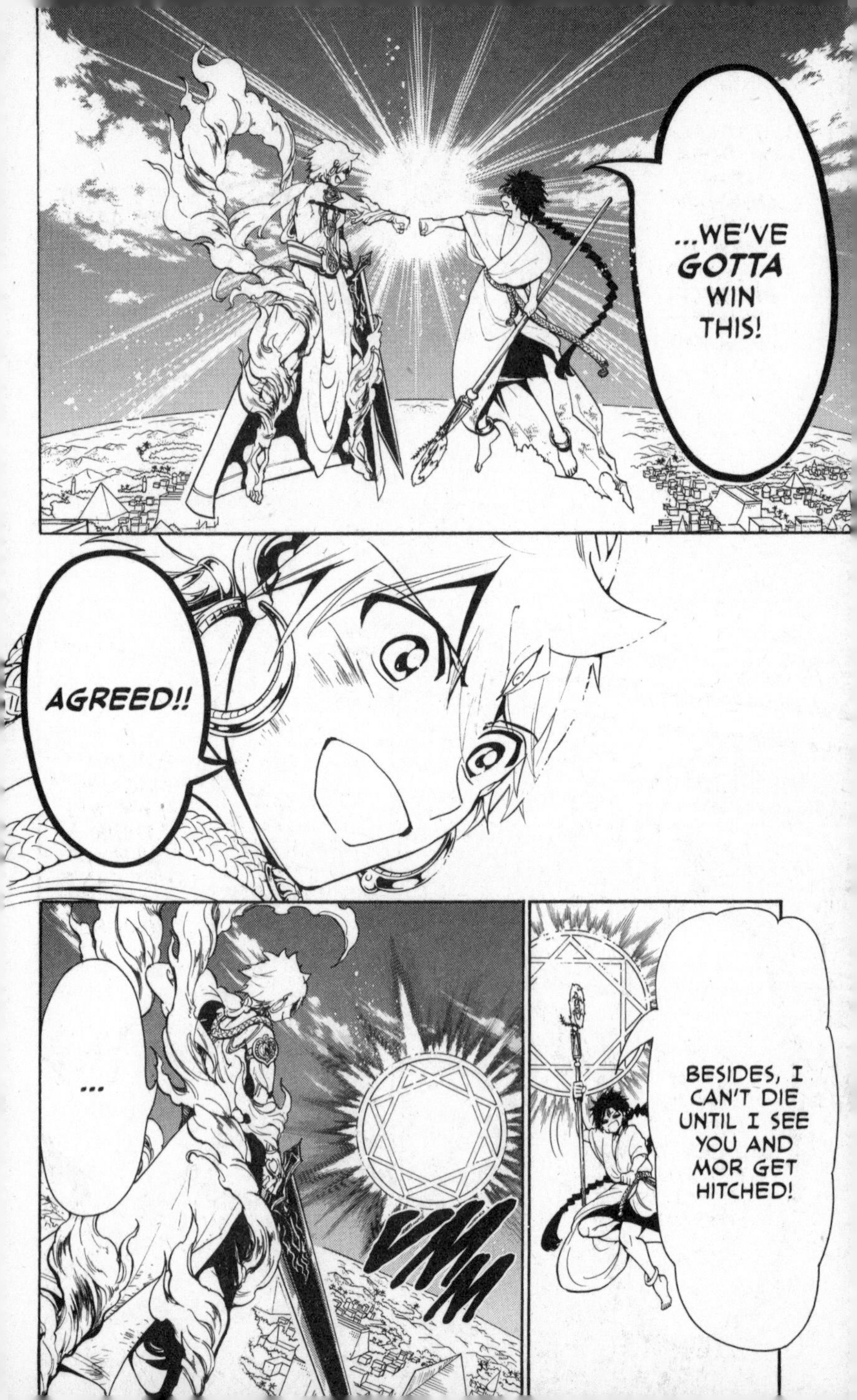
...WE'VE *GOTTA* WIN THIS!
AGREED!!
BESIDES, I CAN'T DIE UNTIL I SEE YOU AND MOR GET HITCHED!
...

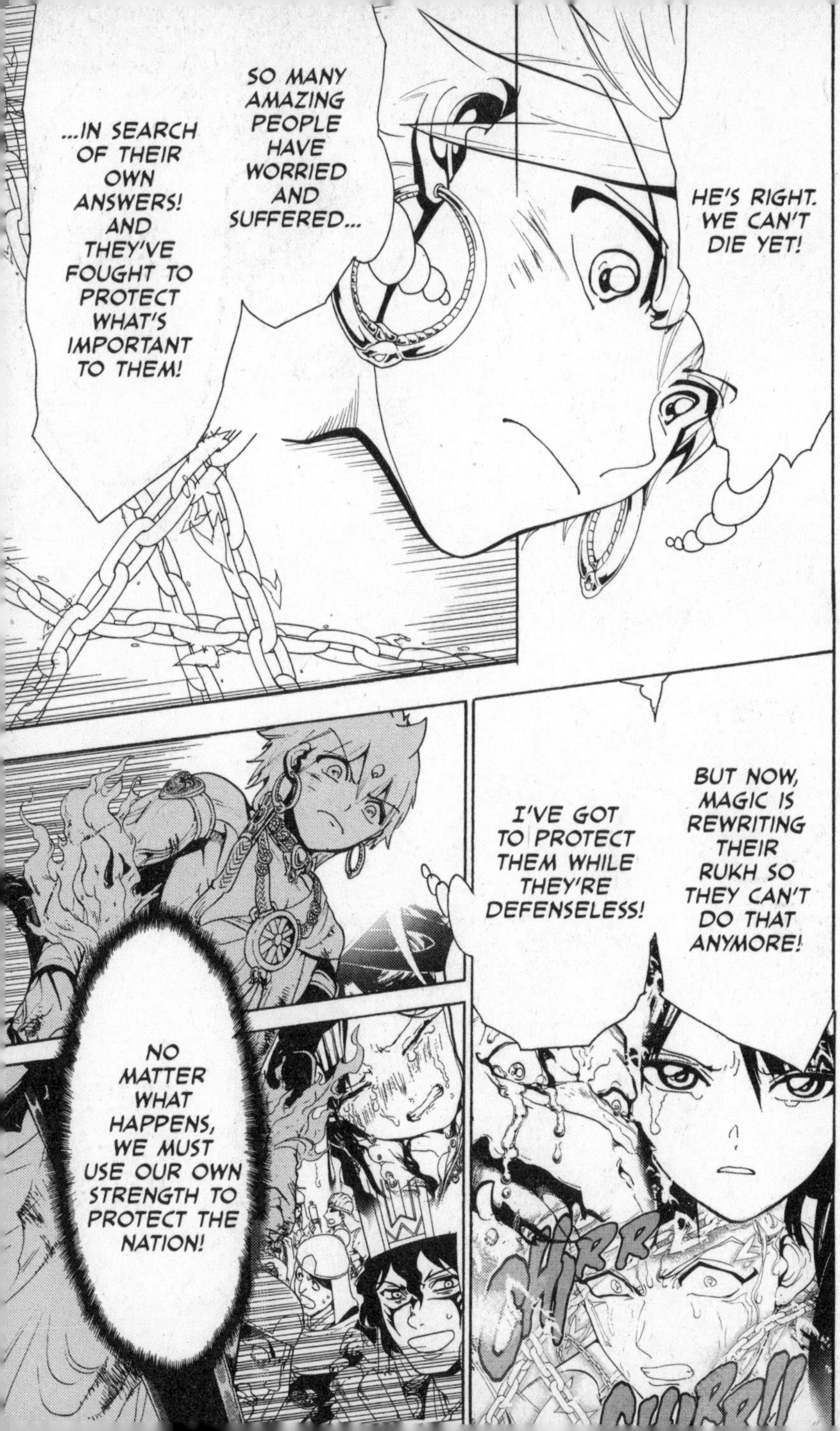
HE'S RIGHT. WE CAN'T DIE YET!
SO MANY AMAZING PEOPLE HAVE WORRIED AND SUFFERED...
...IN SEARCH OF THEIR OWN ANSWERS! AND THEY'VE FOUGHT TO PROTECT WHAT'S IMPORTANT TO THEM!
BUT NOW, MAGIC IS REWRITING THEIR RUKH SO THEY CAN'T DO THAT ANYMORE!
I'VE GOT TO PROTECT THEM WHILE THEY'RE DEFENSELESS!
NO MATTER WHAT HAPPENS, WE MUST USE OUR OWN STRENGTH TO PROTECT THE NATION!

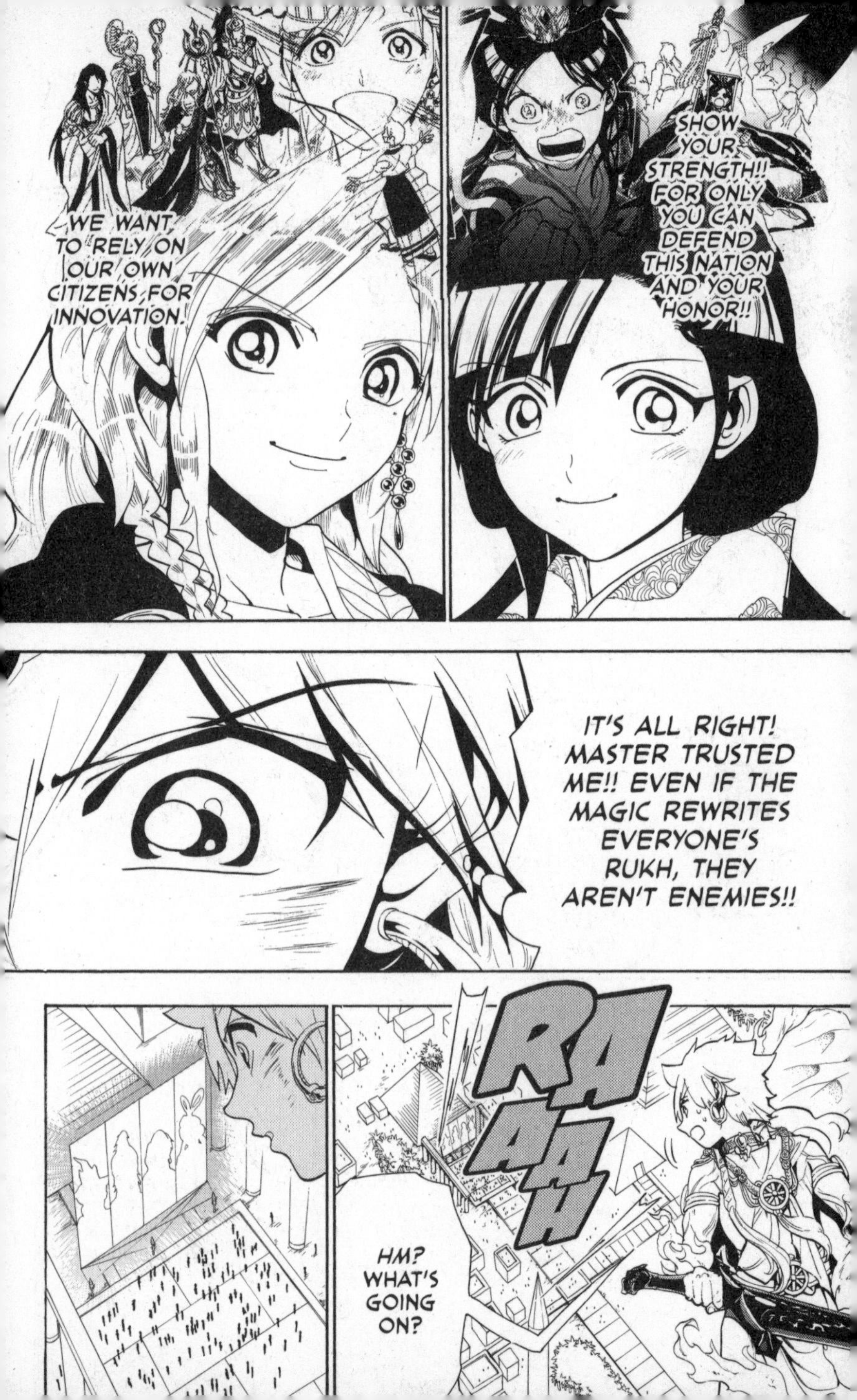
SHOW YOUR STRENGTH!! FOR ONLY YOU CAN DEFEND THIS NATION AND YOUR HONOR!!
WE WANT TO RELY ON OUR OWN CITIZENS FOR INNOVATION.
IT'S ALL RIGHT! MASTER TRUSTED ME!! EVEN IF THE MAGIC REWRITES EVERYONE'S RUKH, THEY AREN'T ENEMIES!!
RAAAH
HM? WHAT'S GOING ON?

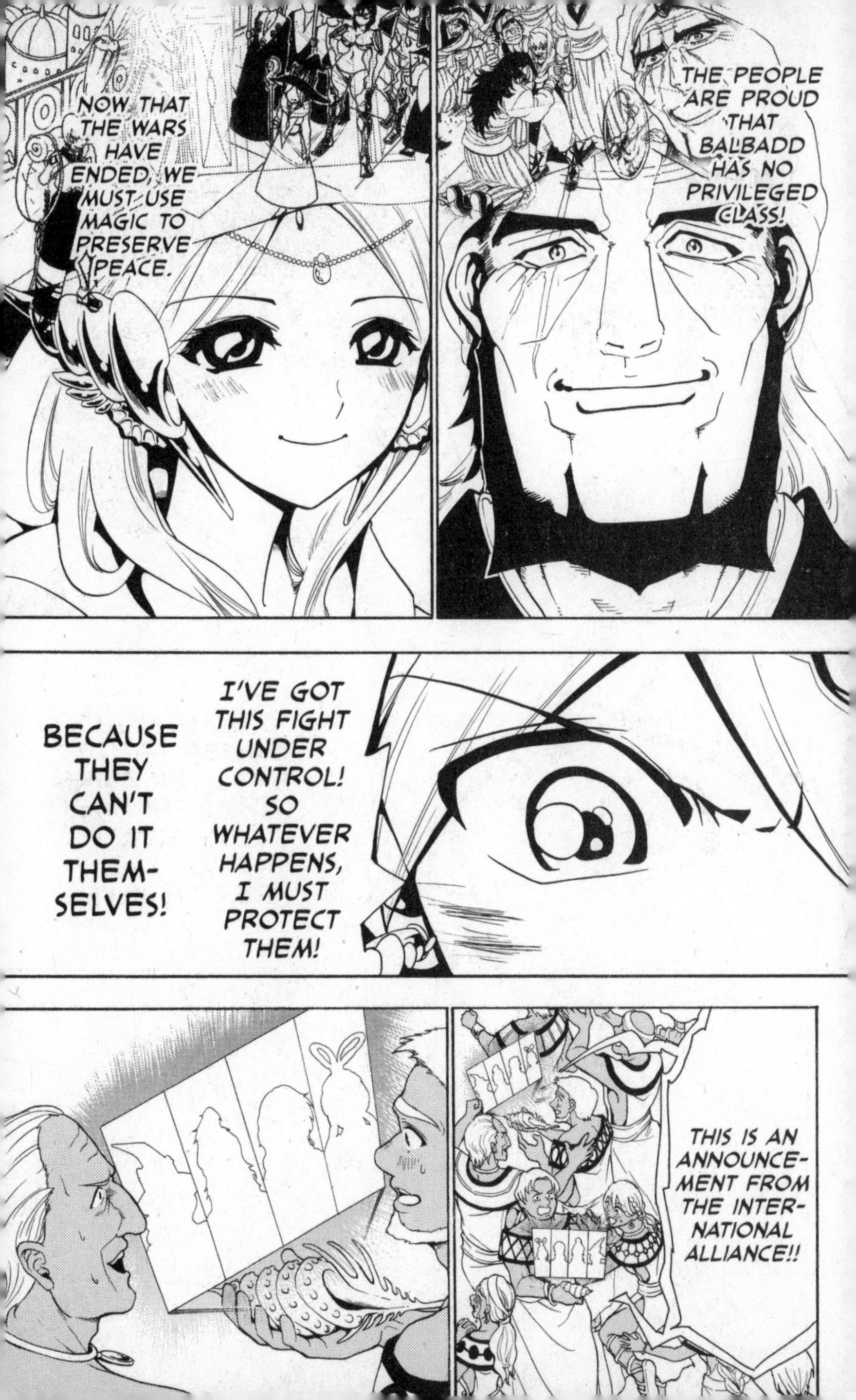
THE PEOPLE ARE PROUD THAT BALBADD HAS NO PRIVILEGED CLASS!
NOW THAT THE WARS HAVE ENDED, WE MUST USE MAGIC TO PRESERVE PEACE.
I'VE GOT THIS FIGHT UNDER CONTROL! SO WHATEVER HAPPENS, I MUST PROTECT THEM!
BECAUSE THEY CAN'T DO IT THEM-SELVES!
THIS IS AN ANNOUNCE-MENT FROM THE INTER-NATIONAL ALLIANCE!!

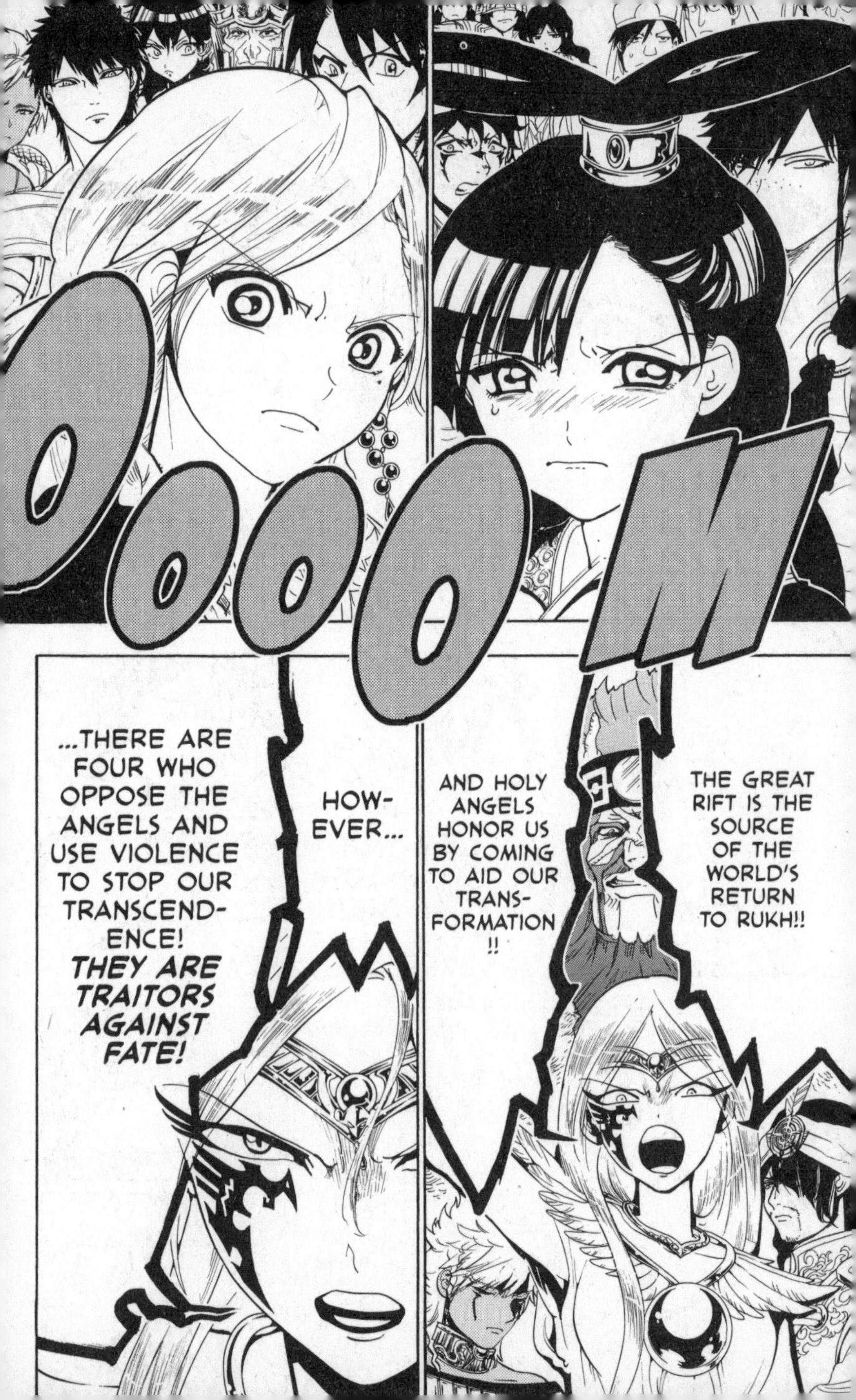
DOOOM
THE GREAT RIFT IS THE SOURCE OF THE WORLD'S RETURN TO RUKH!!
AND HOLY ANGELS HONOR US BY COMING TO AID OUR TRANS-FORMATION!!
HOW-EVER...
...THERE ARE FOUR WHO OPPOSE THE ANGELS AND USE VIOLENCE TO STOP OUR TRANSCEND-ENCE! *THEY ARE TRAITORS AGAINST FATE!*

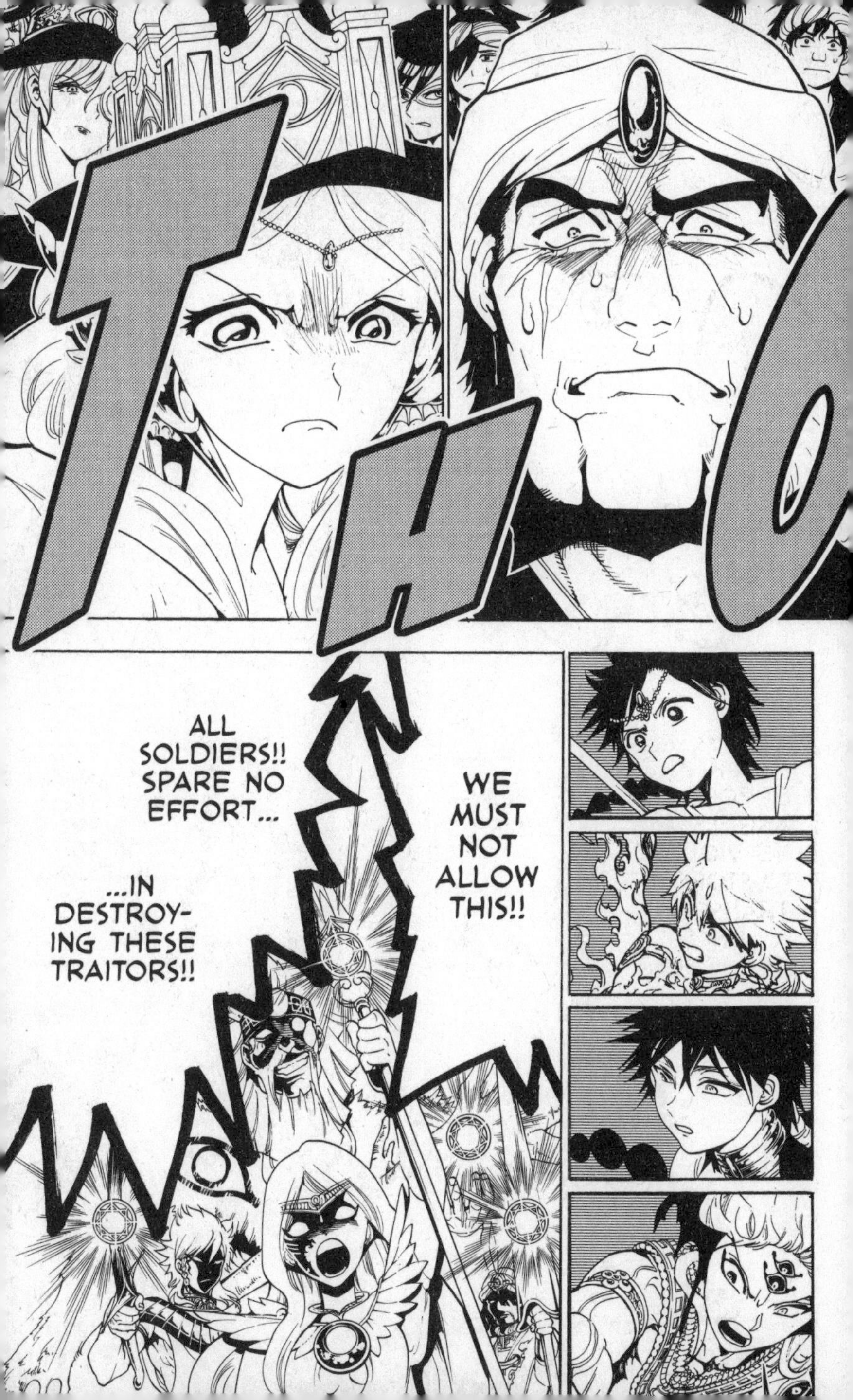
WE MUST NOT ALLOW THIS!!
ALL SOLDIERS!! SPARE NO EFFORT...
...IN DESTROYING THESE TRAITORS!!

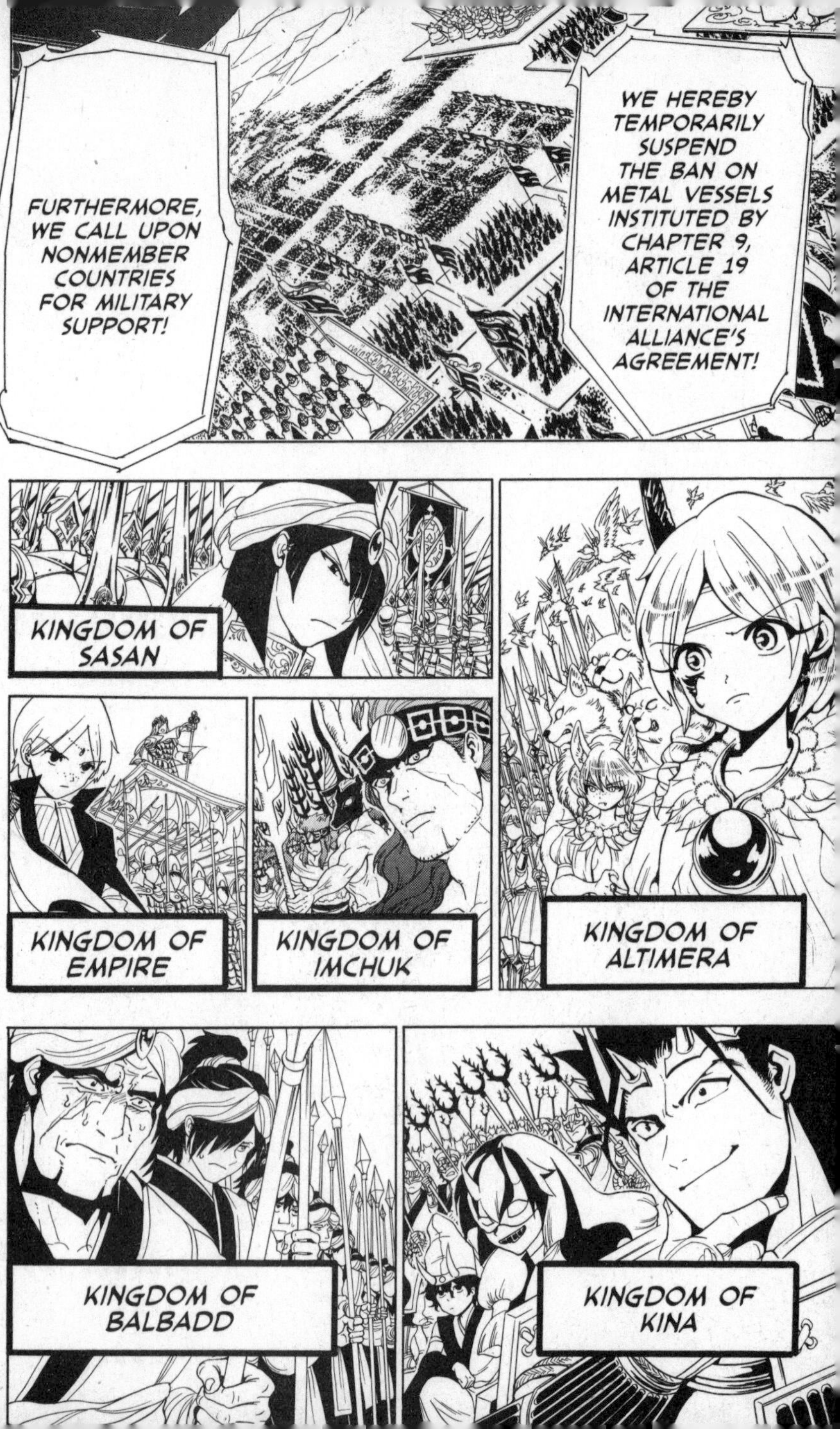
WE HEREBY TEMPORARILY SUSPEND THE BAN ON METAL VESSELS INSTITUTED BY CHAPTER 9, ARTICLE 19 OF THE INTERNATIONAL ALLIANCE'S AGREEMENT!
FURTHERMORE, WE CALL UPON NONMEMBER COUNTRIES FOR MILITARY SUPPORT!
KINGDOM OF ALTIMERA
KINGDOM OF SASAN
KINGDOM OF IMCHUK
KINGDOM OF EMPIRE
KINGDOM OF KINA
KINGDOM OF BALBADD

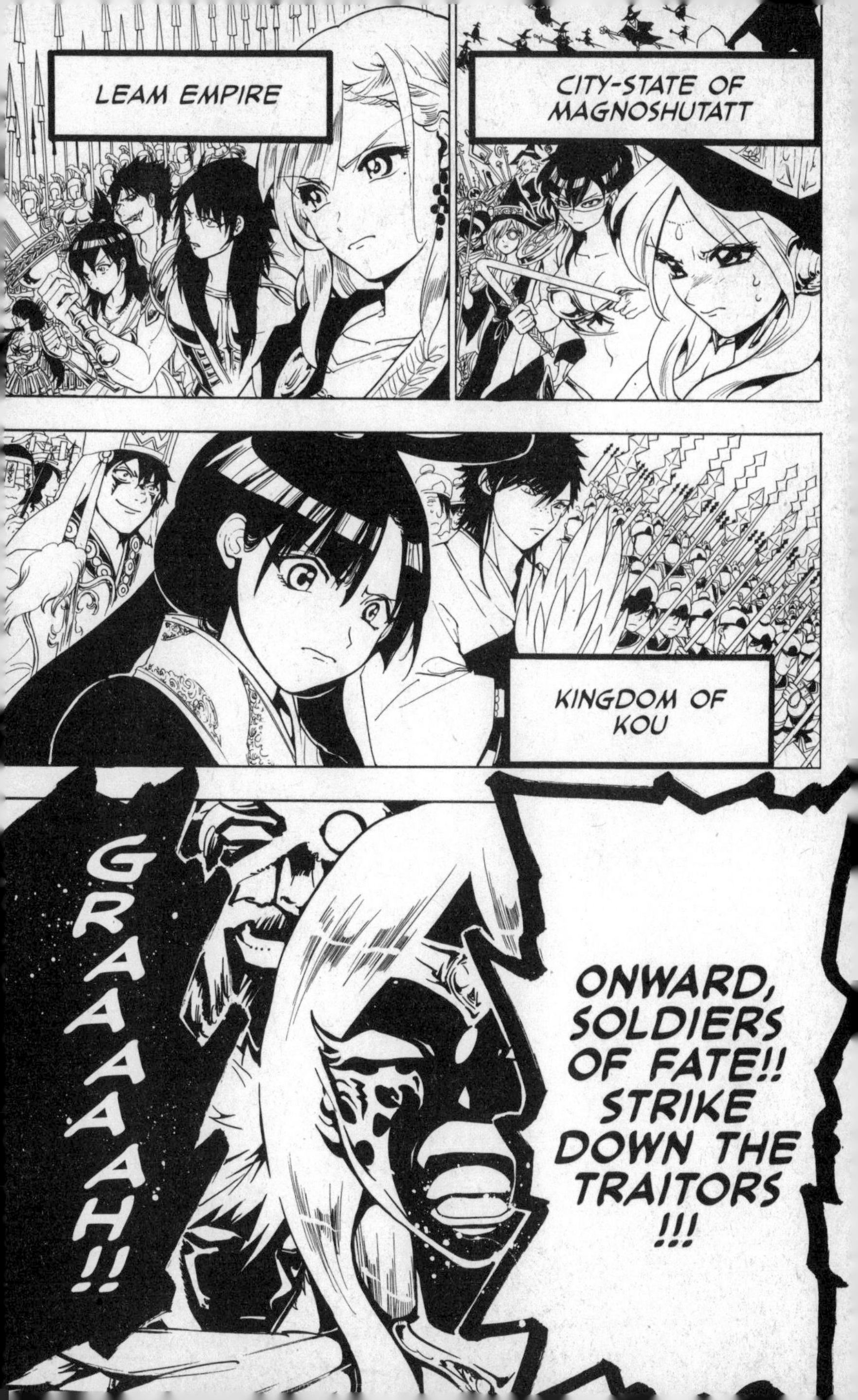
CITY-STATE OF MAGNOSHUTATT
LEAM EMPIRE
KINGDOM OF KOU
ONWARD, SOLDIERS OF FATE!! STRIKE DOWN THE TRAITORS!!!
GRAAAAAH!!

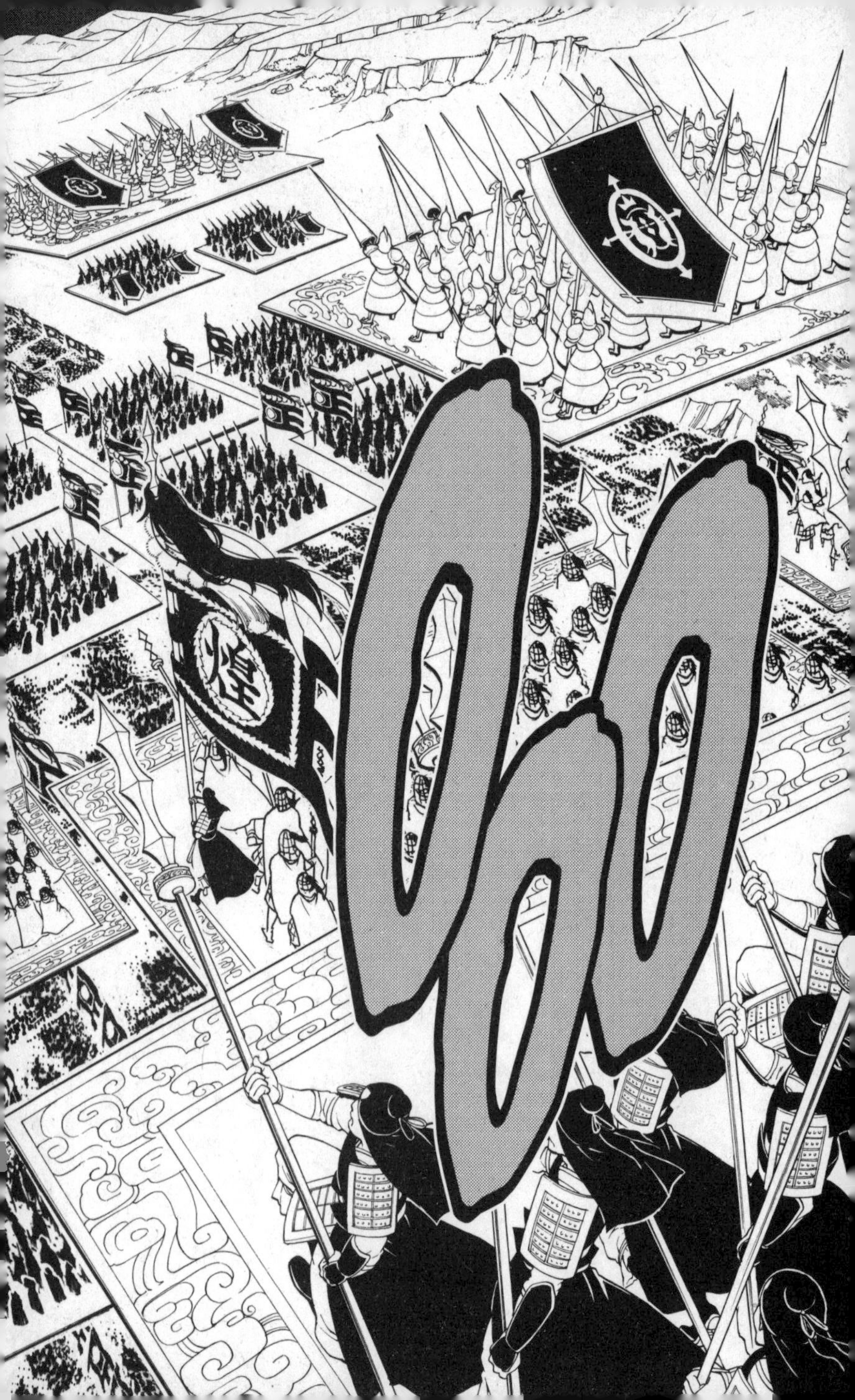
煌

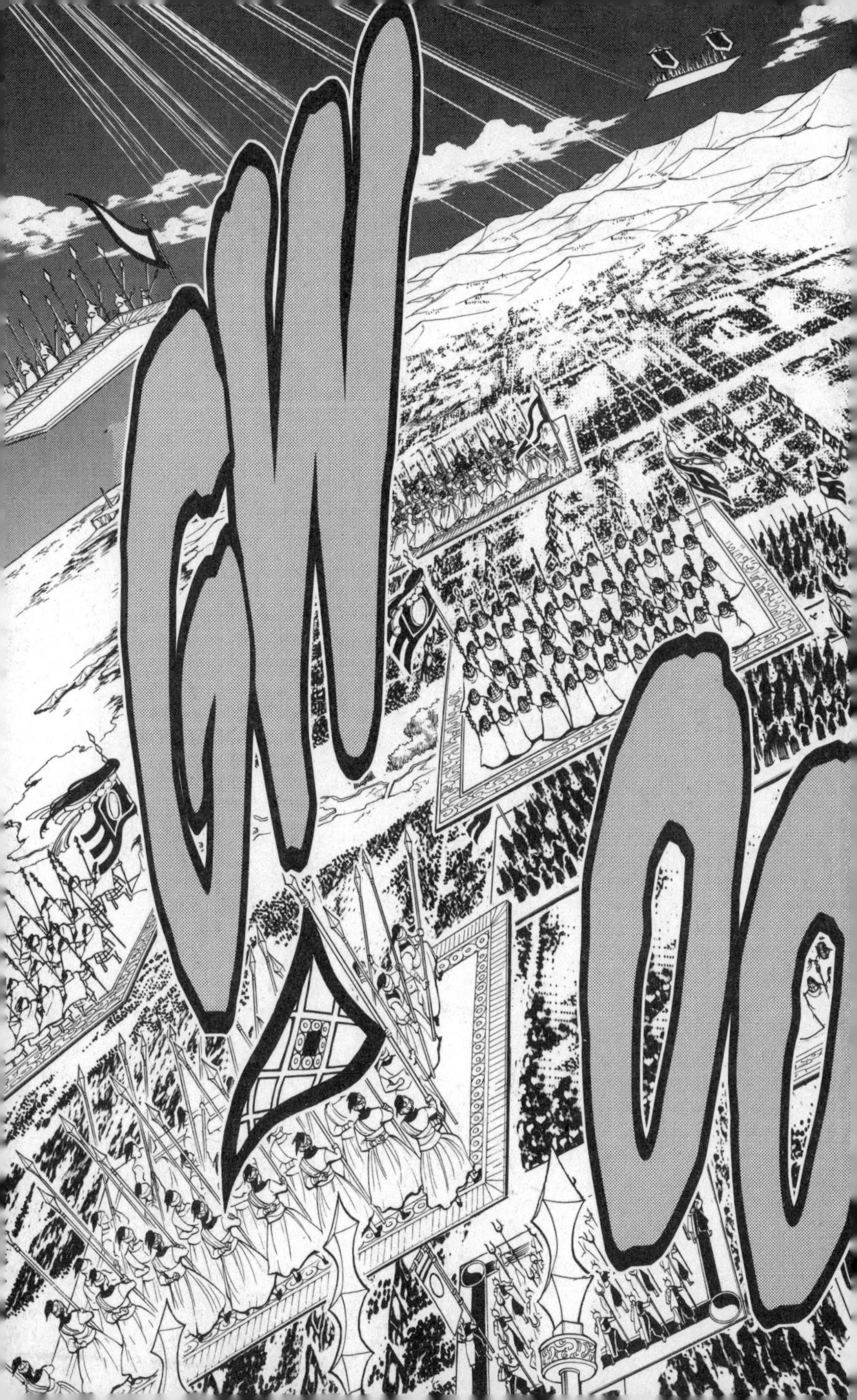

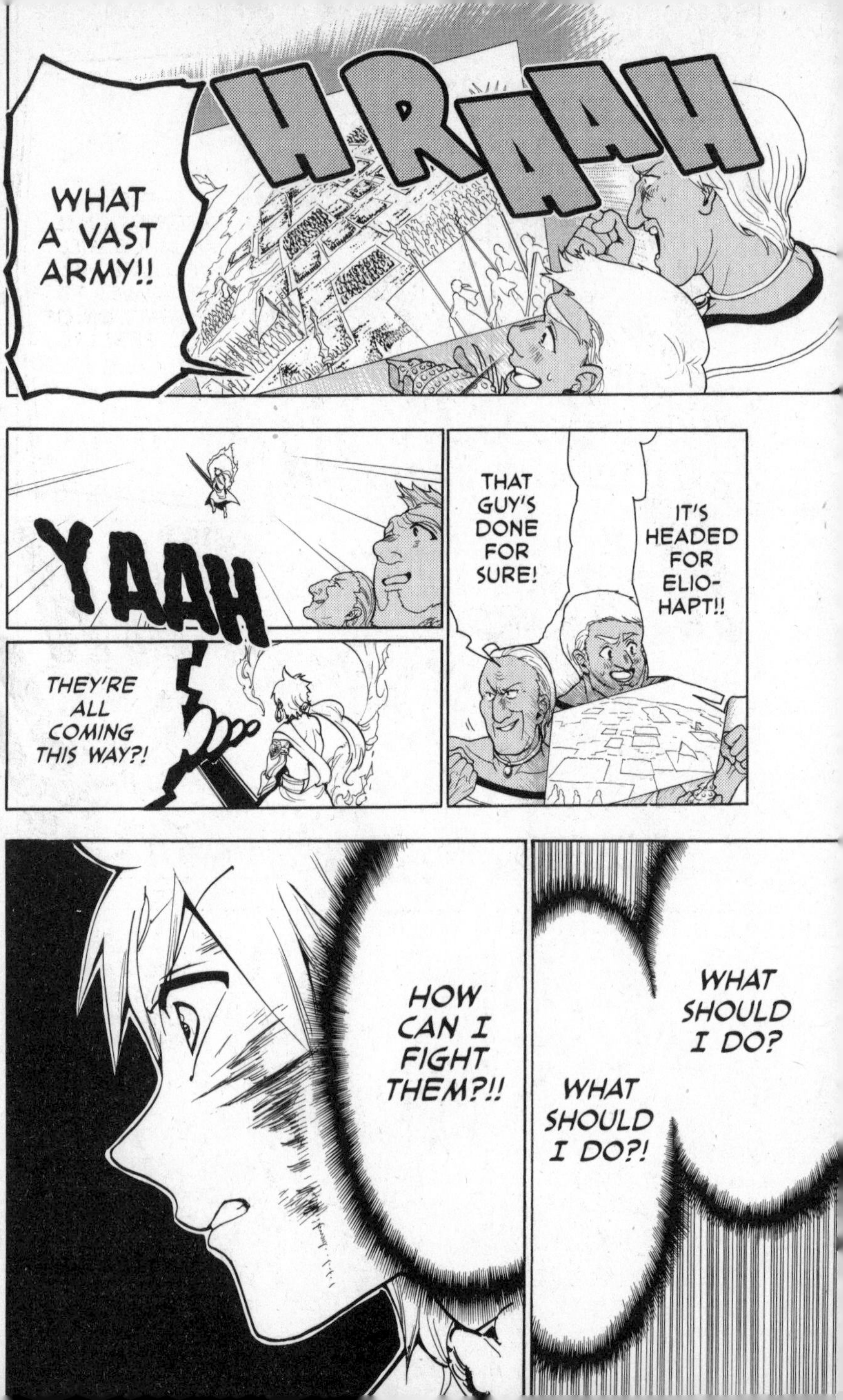
HRAAAH
WHAT A VAST ARMY!!
IT'S HEADED FOR ELIO-HAPT!!
THAT GUY'S DONE FOR SURE!
YAAH
THEY'RE ALL COMING THIS WAY?!
WHAT SHOULD I DO?
WHAT SHOULD I DO?!
HOW CAN I FIGHT THEM?!!

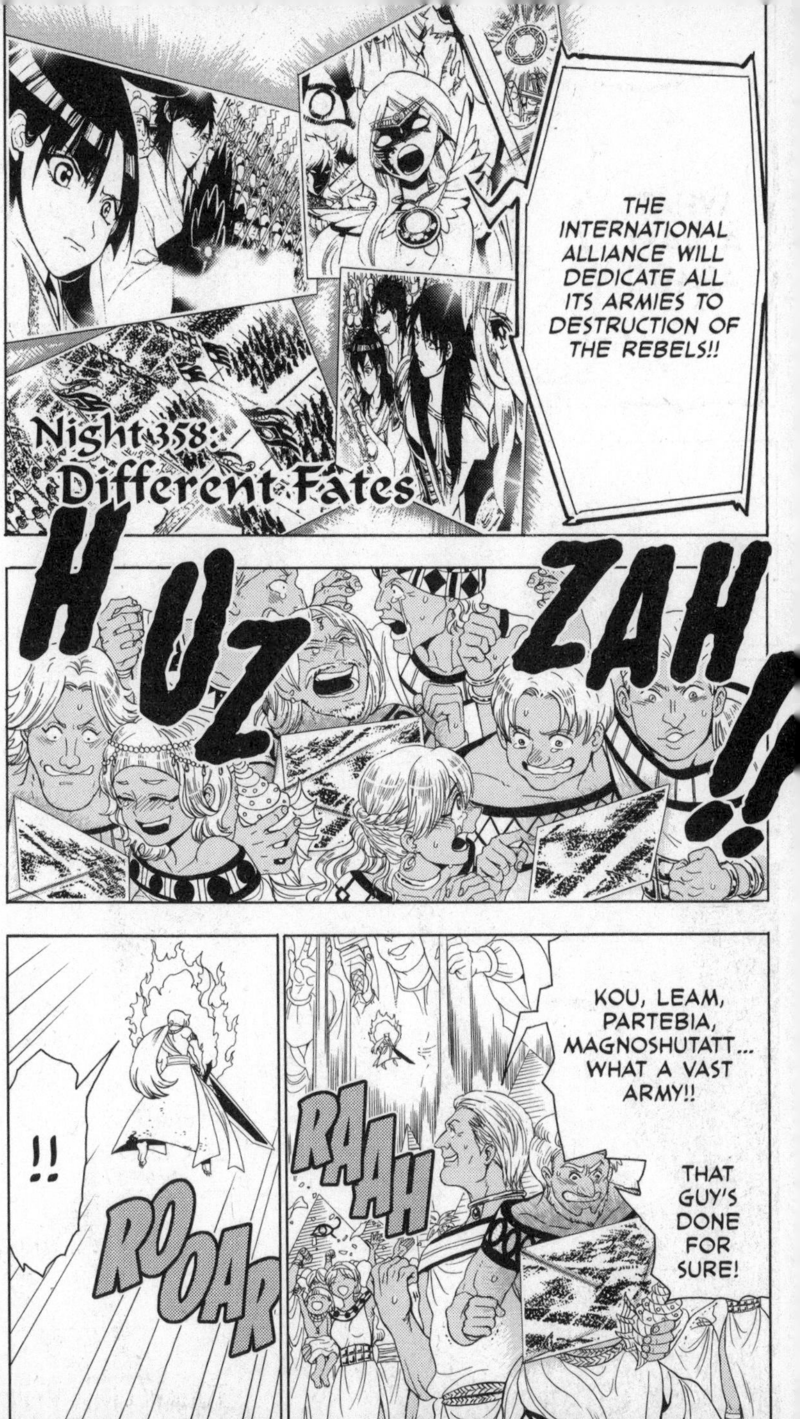
THE INTERNATIONAL ALLIANCE WILL DEDICATE ALL ITS ARMIES TO DESTRUCTION OF THE REBELS!!
Night 358: Different Fates
HUZZAH!!
KOU, LEAM, PARTEBIA, MAGNOSHUTATT... WHAT A VAST ARMY!!
THAT GUY'S DONE FOR SURE!
RAAAH
ROOOAR
!!

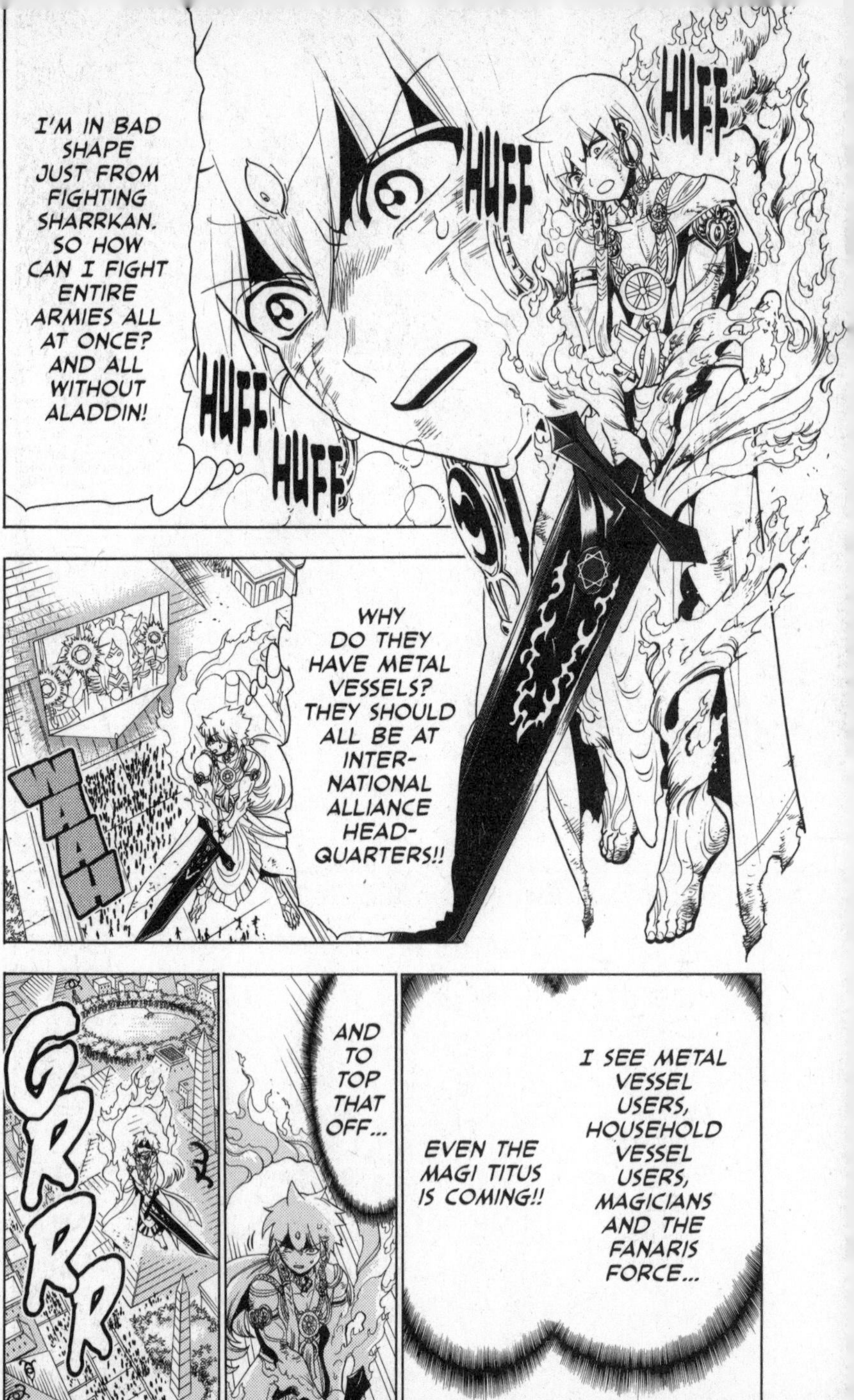
HUFF
HUFF
I'M IN BAD SHAPE JUST FROM FIGHTING SHARRKAN. SO HOW CAN I FIGHT ENTIRE ARMIES ALL AT ONCE? AND ALL WITHOUT ALADDIN!
HUFF HUFF
WHY DO THEY HAVE METAL VESSELS? THEY SHOULD ALL BE AT INTER-NATIONAL ALLIANCE HEAD-QUARTERS!!
WAAAH
I SEE METAL VESSEL USERS, HOUSEHOLD VESSEL USERS, MAGICIANS AND THE FANARIS FORCE...
AND TO TOP THAT OFF...
EVEN THE MAGI TITUS IS COMING!!
GRRR

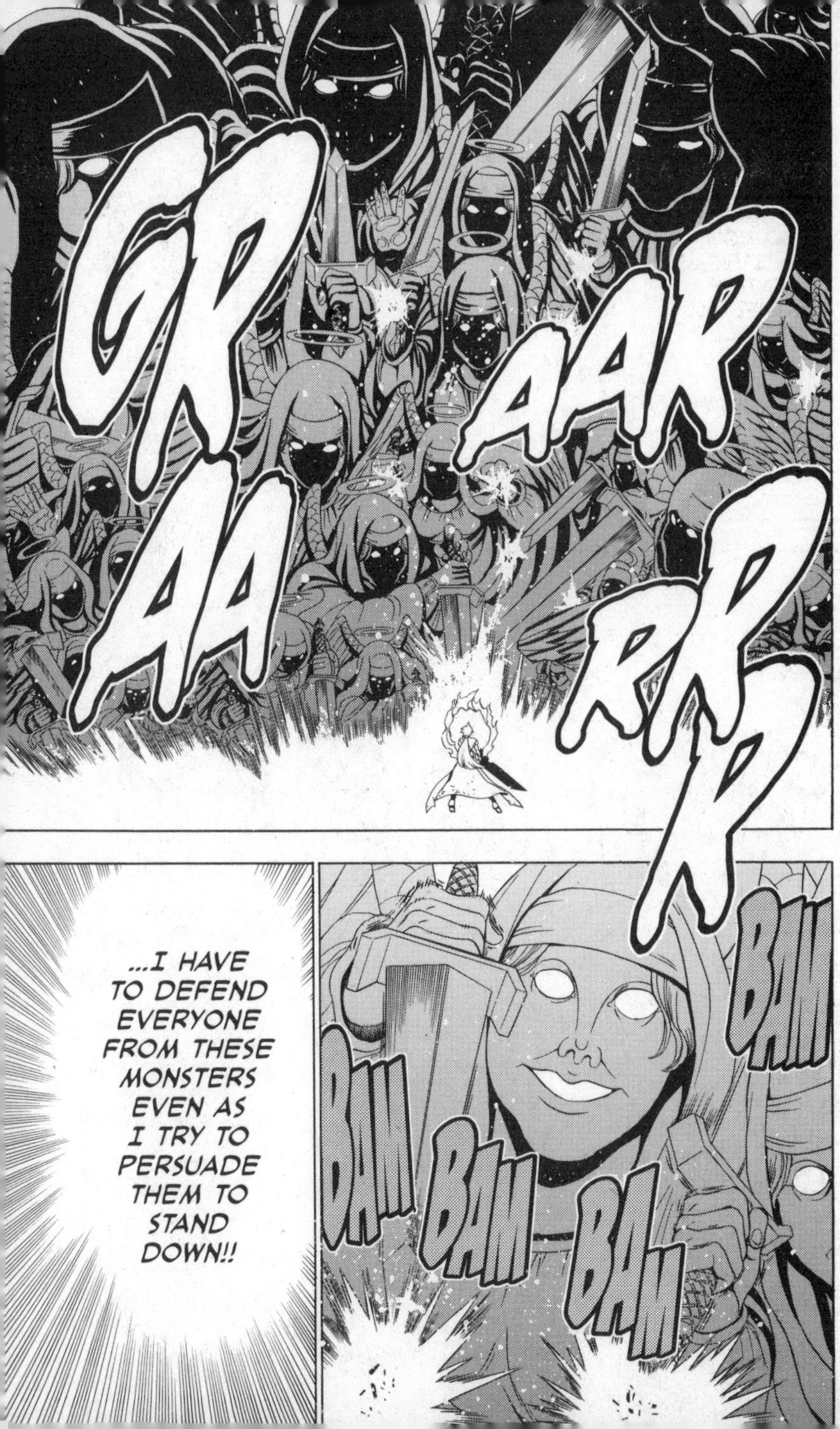
GRAAAARRRR
BAM
BAM
BAM
BAM
BAM
...I HAVE TO DEFEND EVERYONE FROM THESE MONSTERS EVEN AS I TRY TO PERSUADE THEM TO STAND DOWN!!

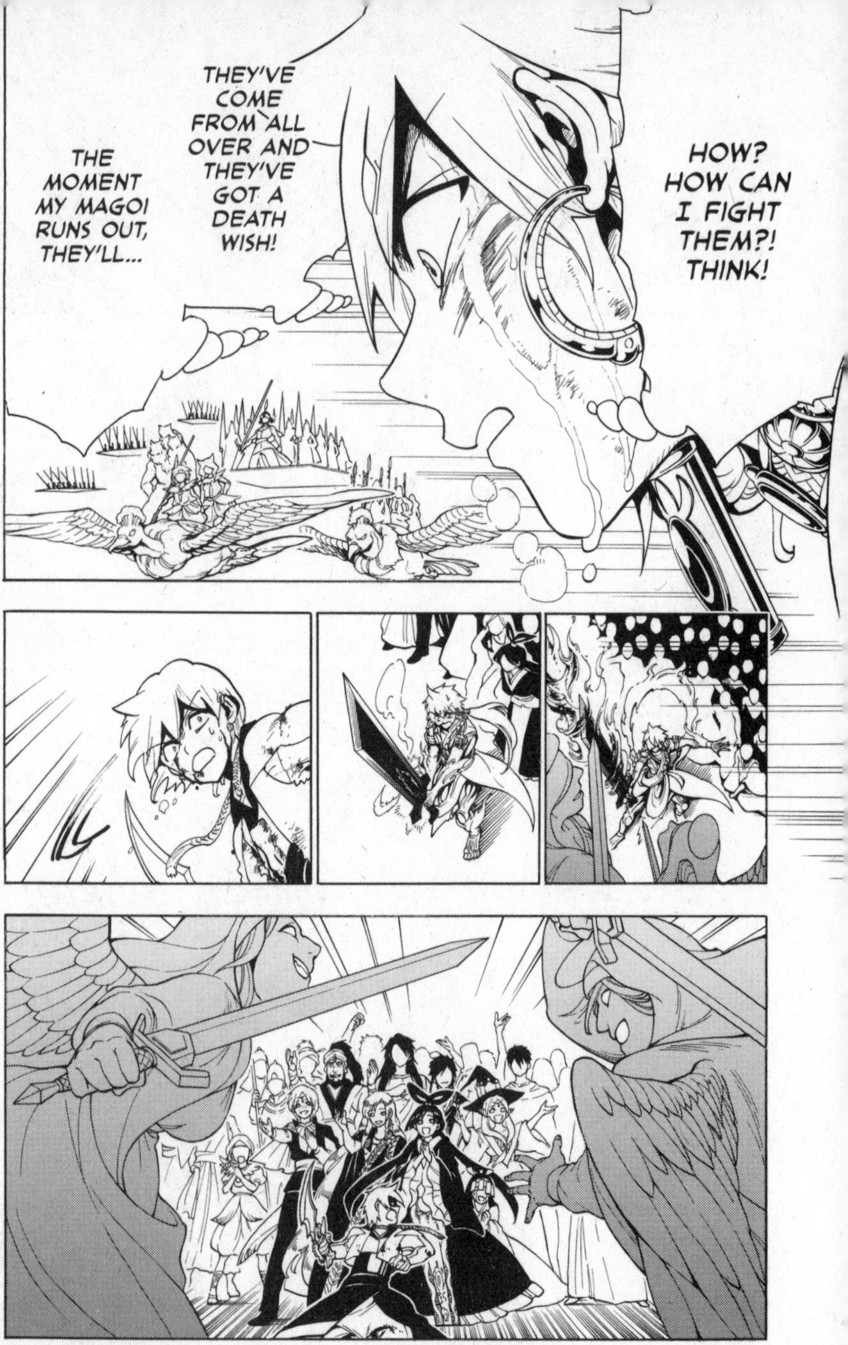
HOW? HOW CAN I FIGHT THEM?! THINK!
THEY'VE COME FROM ALL OVER AND THEY'VE GOT A DEATH WISH!
THE MOMENT MY MAGOI RUNS OUT, THEY'LL...

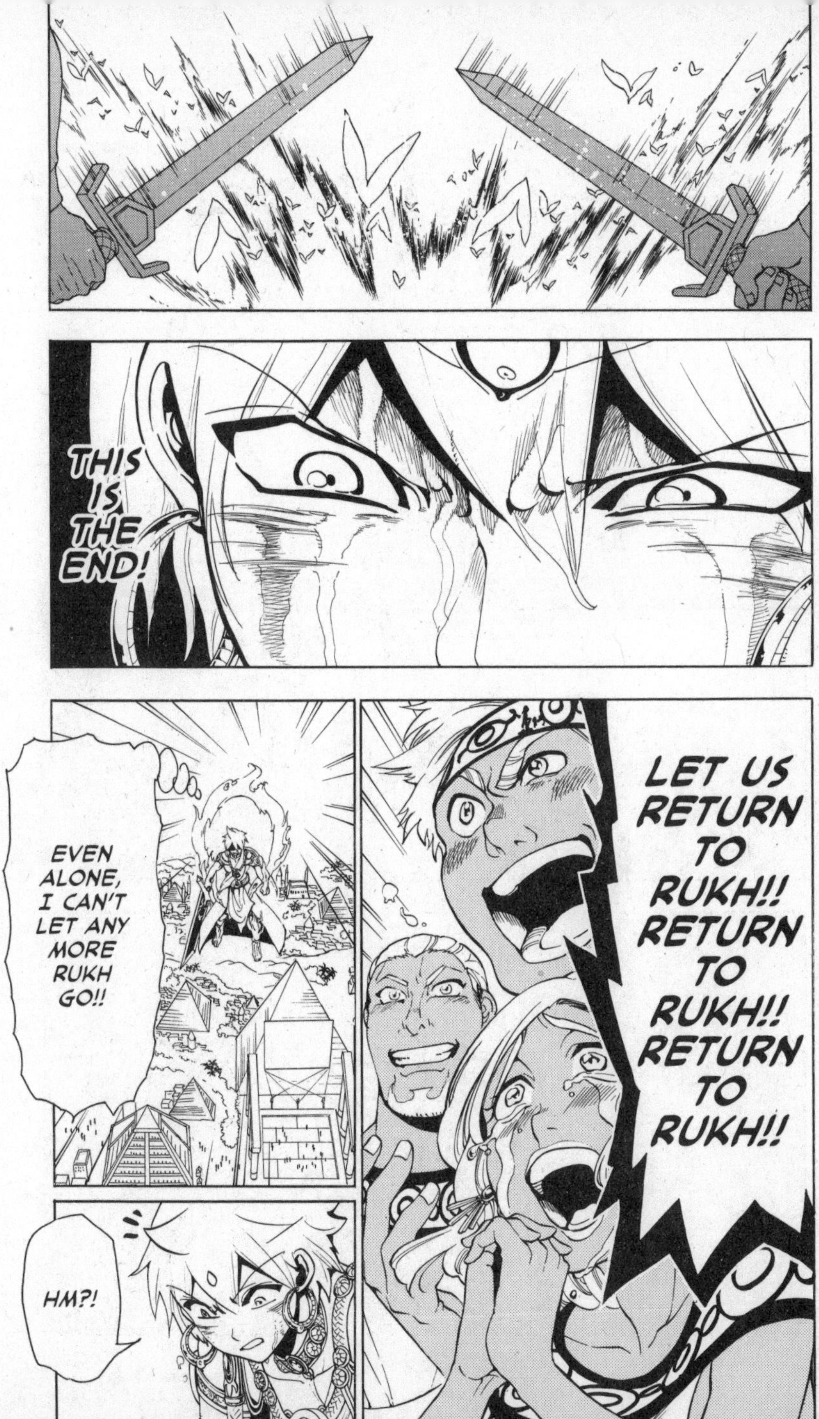
THIS IS THE END!
LET US RETURN TO RUKH!! RETURN TO RUKH!! RETURN TO RUKH!!
EVEN ALONE, I CAN'T LET ANY MORE RUKH GO!!
HM?!

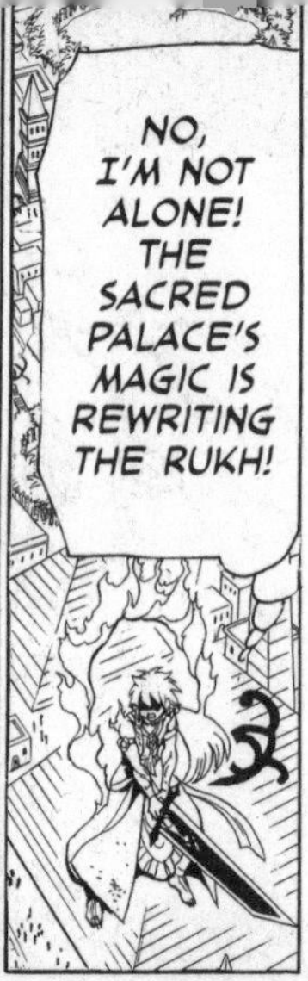
NO, I'M NOT ALONE! THE SACRED PALACE'S MAGIC IS REWRITING THE RUKH!
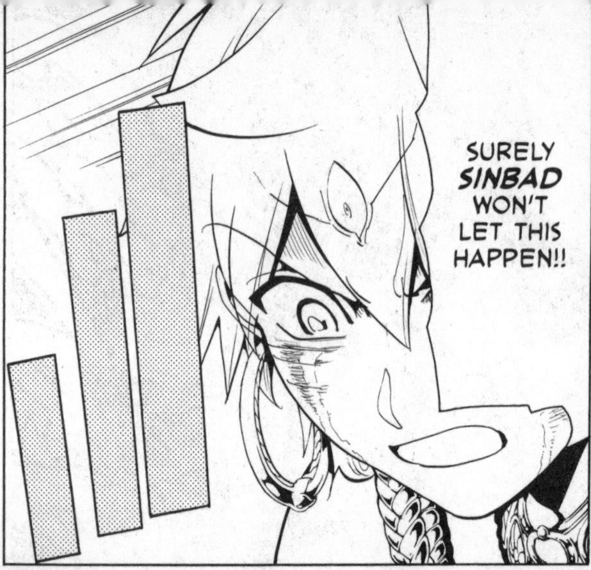
SURELY ***SINBAD*** WON'T LET THIS HAPPEN!!
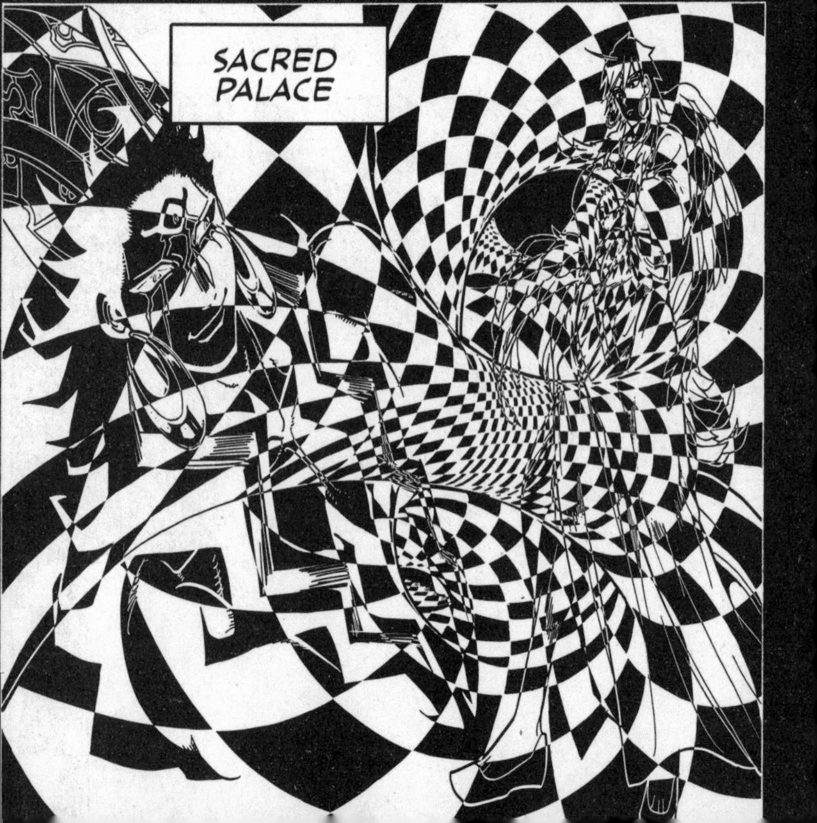
SACRED PALACE

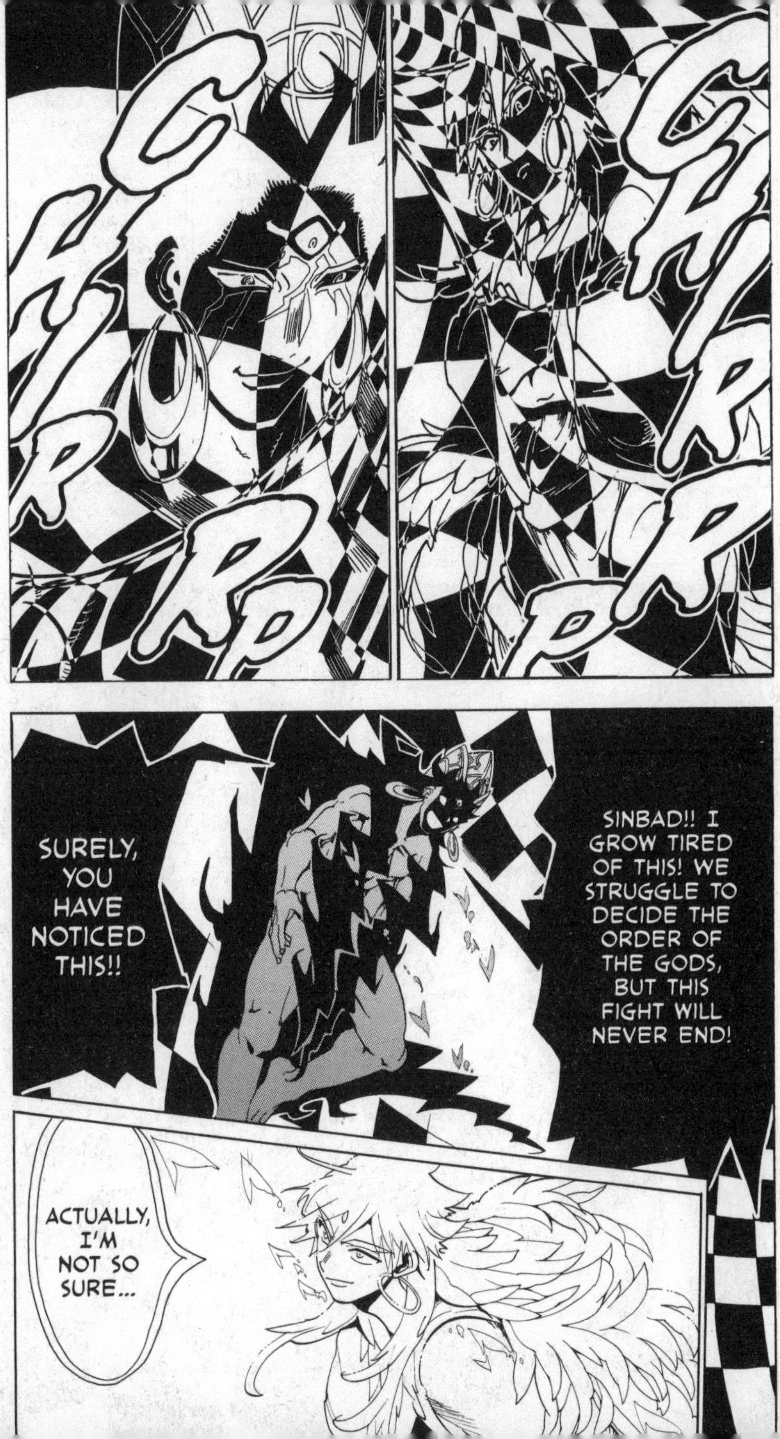
SINBAD!! I GROW TIRED OF THIS! WE STRUGGLE TO DECIDE THE ORDER OF THE GODS, BUT THIS FIGHT WILL NEVER END!
SURELY, YOU HAVE NOTICED THIS!!
ACTUALLY, I'M NOT SO SURE...

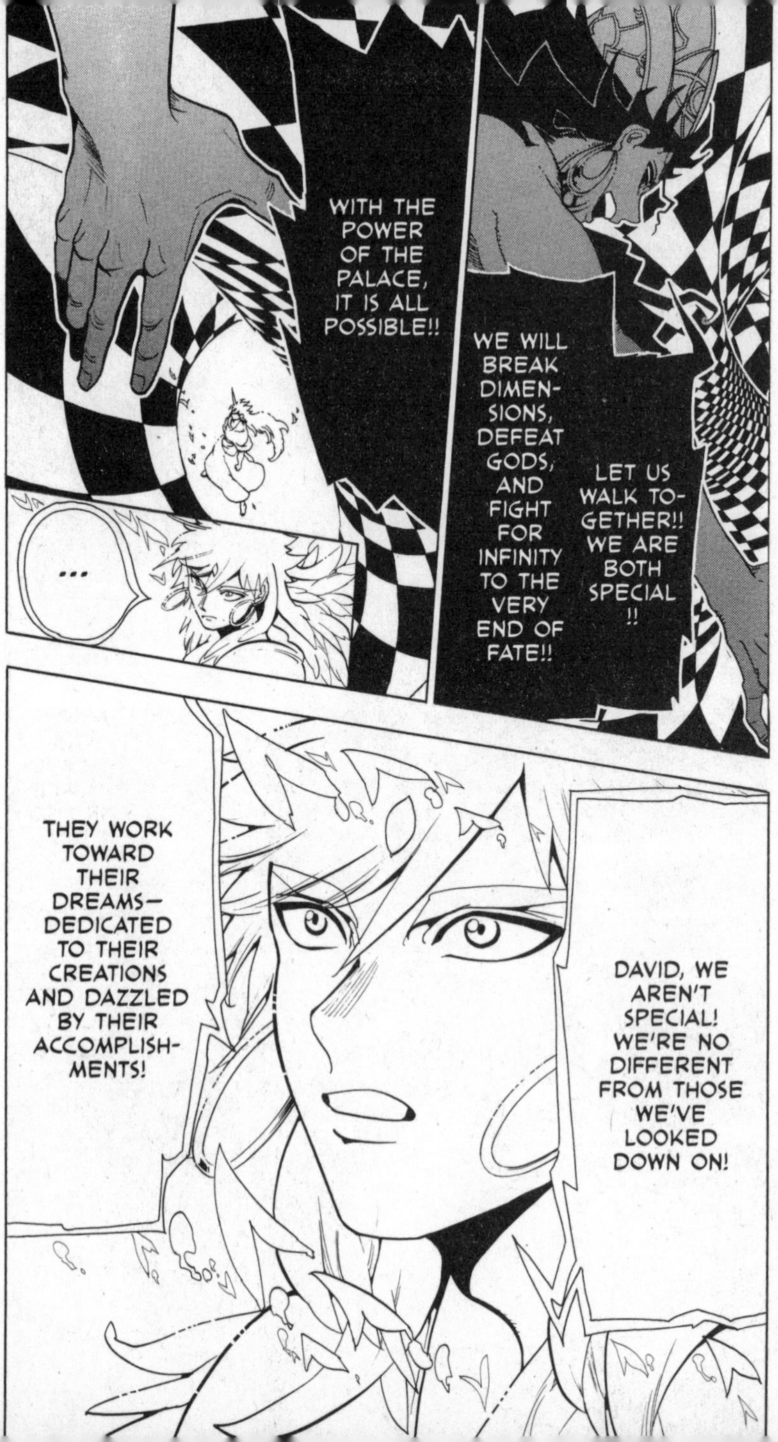

WE WILL BREAK DIMENSIONS, DEFEAT GODS, AND FIGHT FOR INFINITY TO THE VERY END OF FATE!!
LET US WALK TOGETHER!! WE ARE BOTH SPECIAL!!
WITH THE POWER OF THE PALACE, IT IS ALL POSSIBLE!!
...
DAVID, WE AREN'T SPECIAL! WE'RE NO DIFFERENT FROM THOSE WE'VE LOOKED DOWN ON!
THEY WORK TOWARD THEIR DREAMS—DEDICATED TO THEIR CREATIONS AND DAZZLED BY THEIR ACCOMPLISHMENTS!

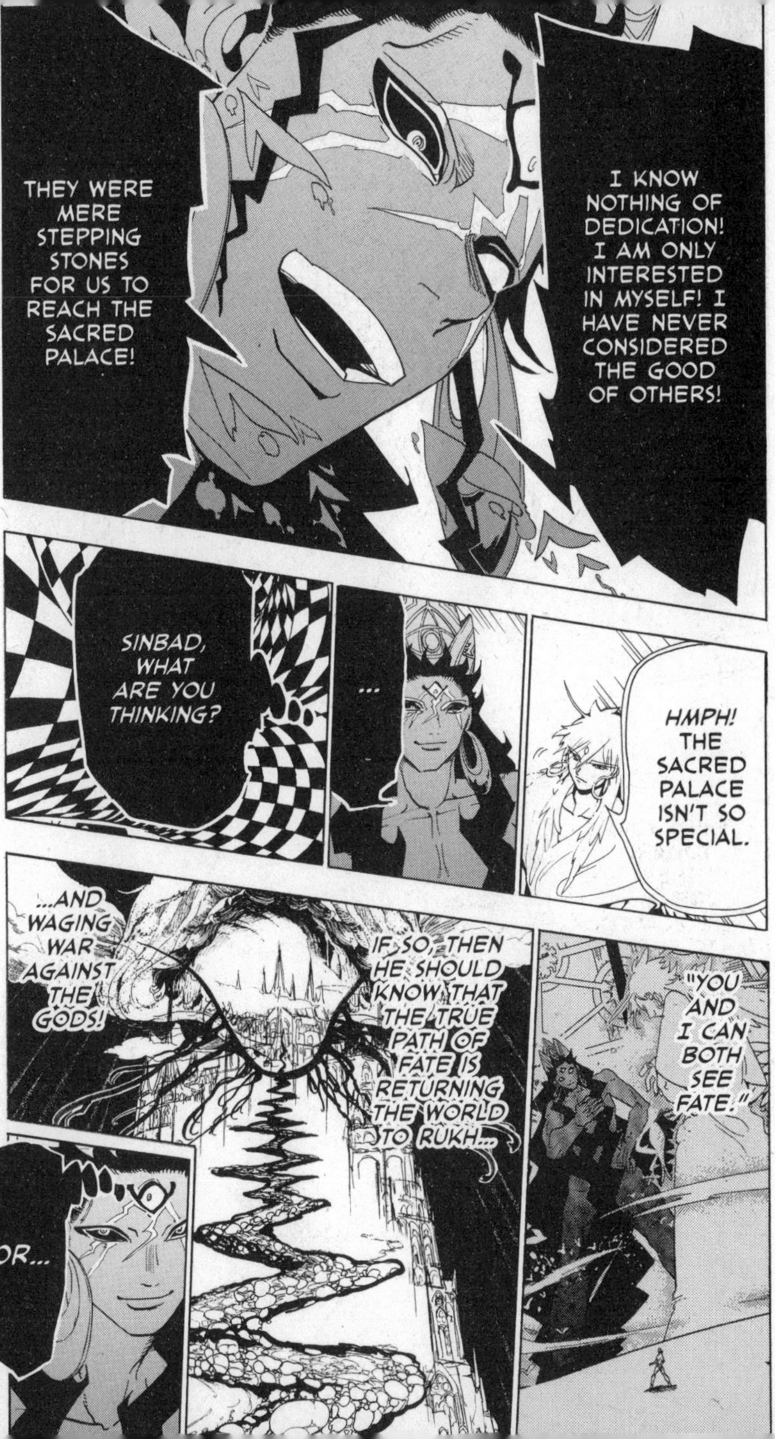
I KNOW NOTHING OF DEDICATION! I AM ONLY INTERESTED IN MYSELF! I HAVE NEVER CONSIDERED THE GOOD OF OTHERS!
THEY WERE MERE STEPPING STONES FOR US TO REACH THE SACRED PALACE!
HMPH! THE SACRED PALACE ISN'T SO SPECIAL.
...
SINBAD, WHAT ARE YOU THINKING?
"YOU AND I CAN BOTH SEE FATE."
IF SO, THEN HE SHOULD KNOW THAT THE TRUE PATH OF FATE IS RETURNING THE WORLD TO RUKH...
...AND WAGING WAR AGAINST THE GODS!
OR...

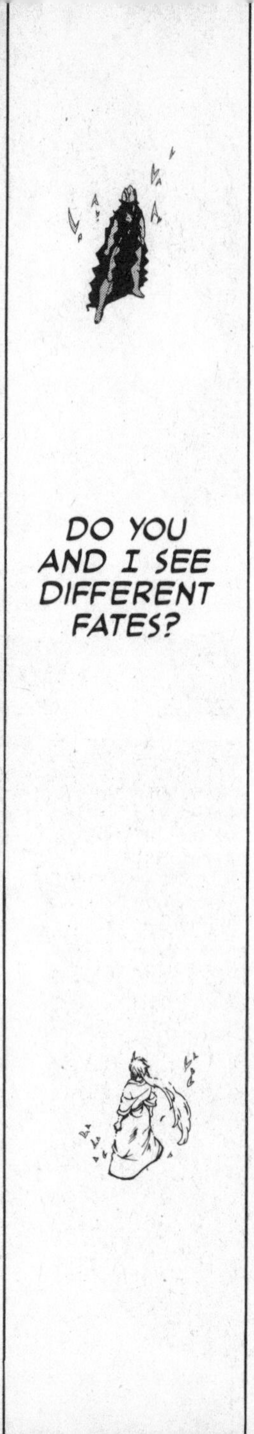
DO YOU AND I SEE DIFFERENT FATES?

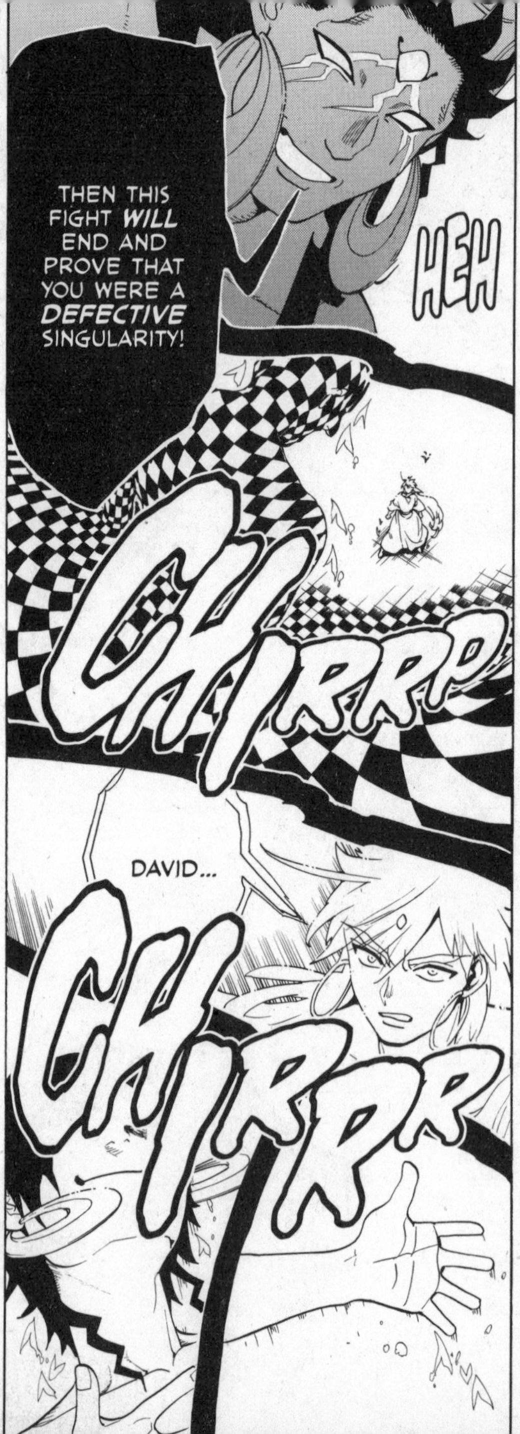
HEH
THEN THIS FIGHT *WILL* END AND PROVE THAT YOU WERE A *DEFECTIVE* SINGULARITY!
CHIRRP
DAVID...
CHIRRP

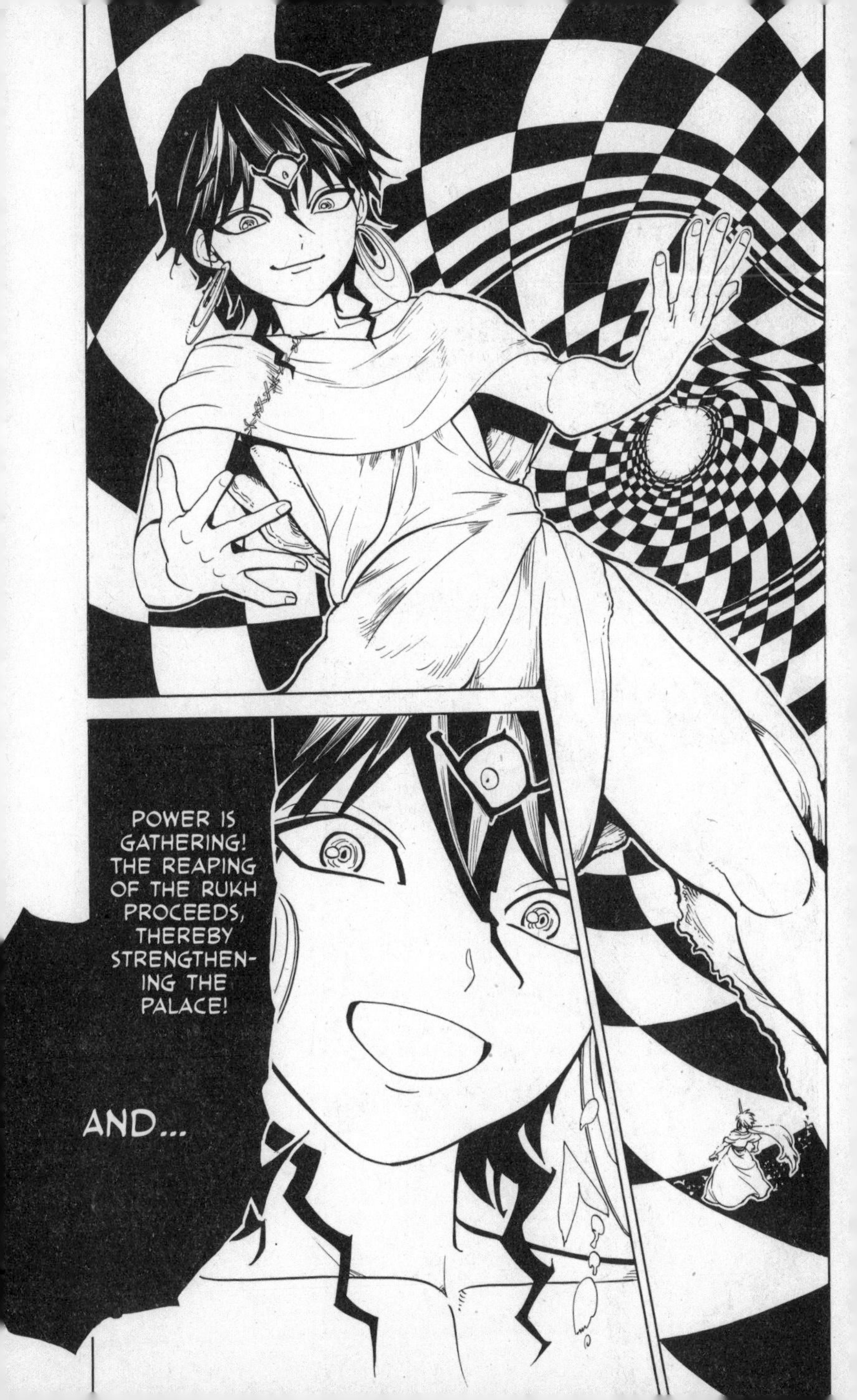
POWER IS GATHERING! THE REAPING OF THE RUKH PROCEEDS, THEREBY STRENGTHENING THE PALACE!
AND...

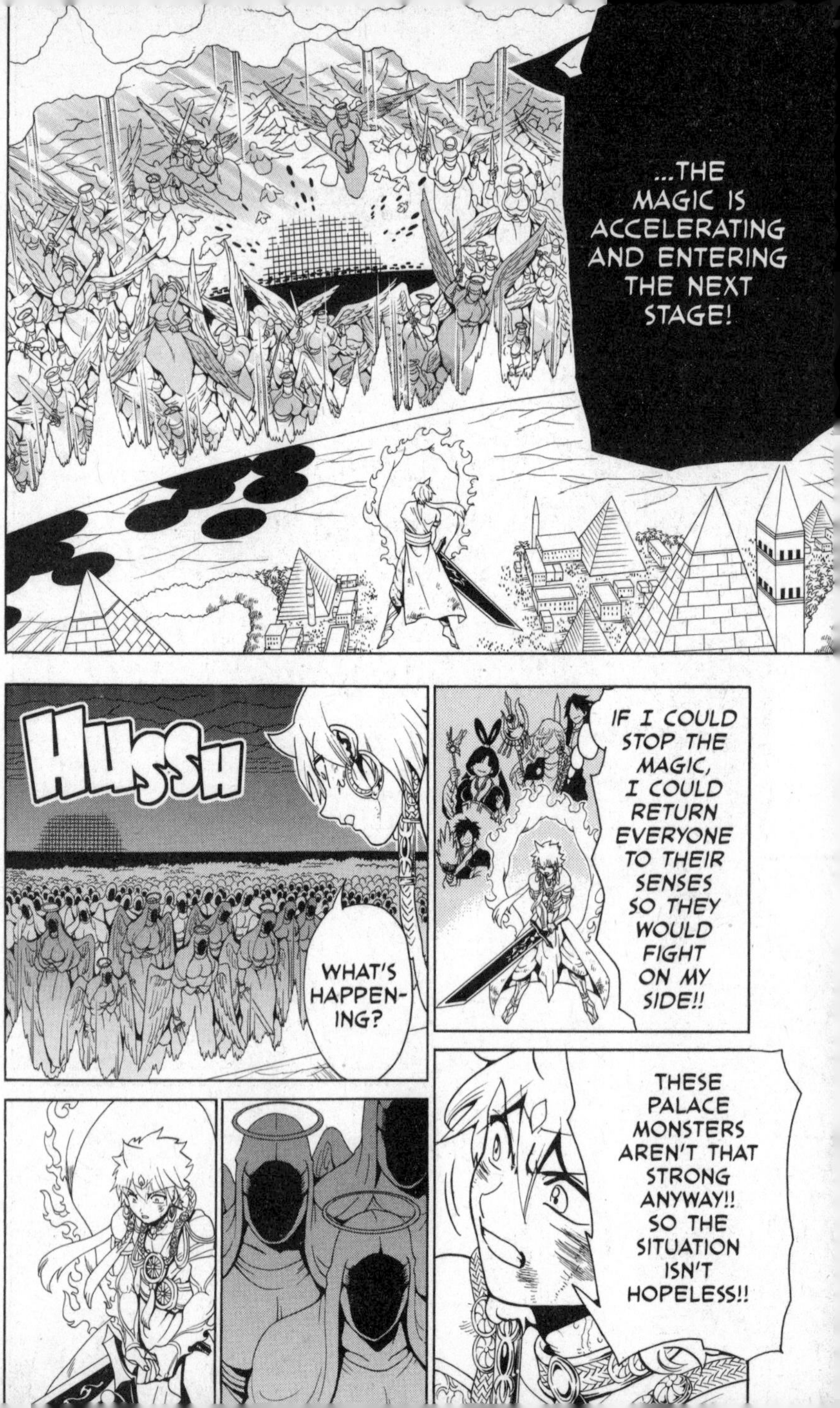
...THE MAGIC IS ACCELERATING AND ENTERING THE NEXT STAGE!
IF I COULD STOP THE MAGIC, I COULD RETURN EVERYONE TO THEIR SENSES SO THEY WOULD FIGHT ON MY SIDE!!
HUSSH
WHAT'S HAPPEN-ING?
THESE PALACE MONSTERS AREN'T THAT STRONG ANYWAY!! SO THE SITUATION ISN'T HOPELESS!!

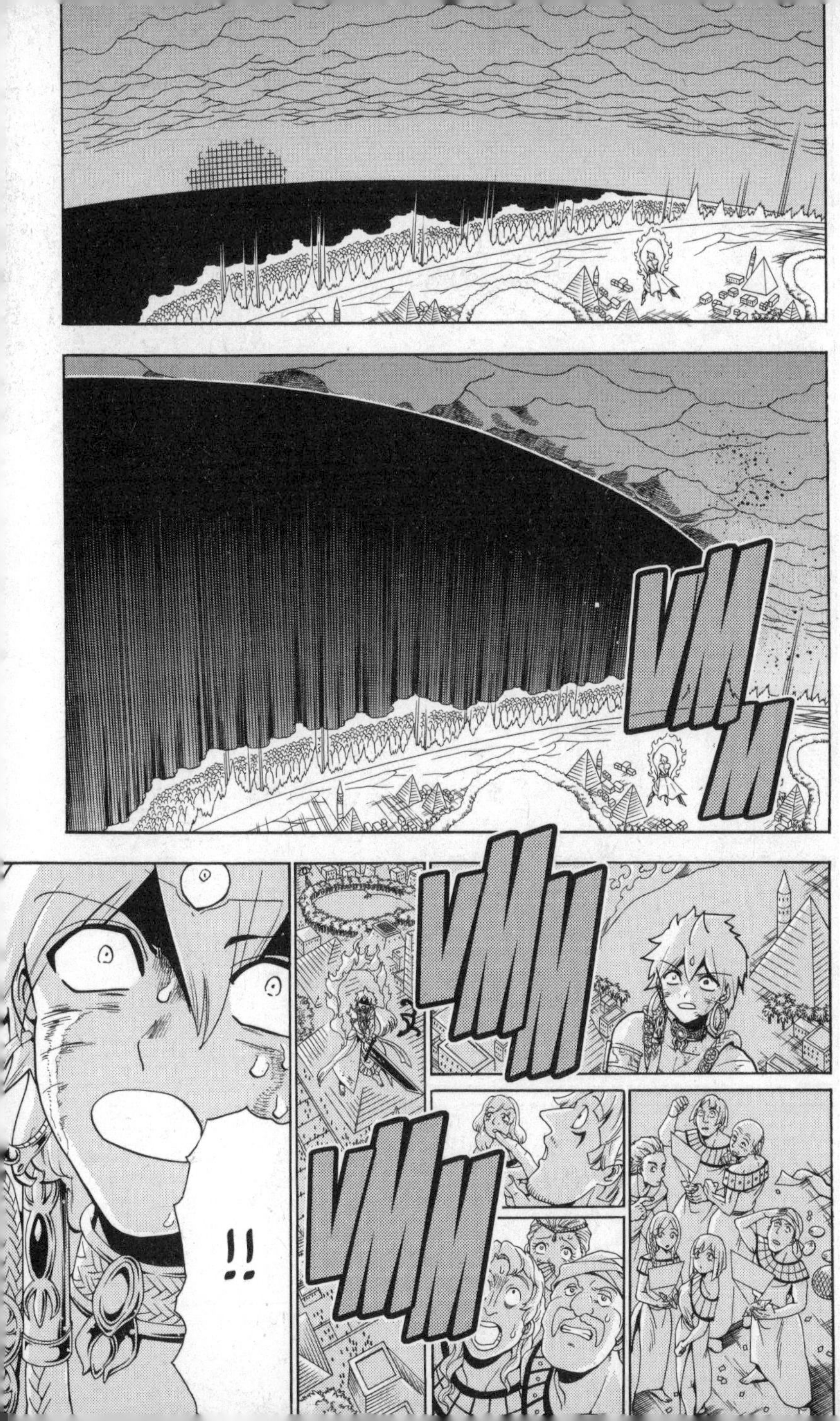
VMMM
VMMM
VMMM
!!

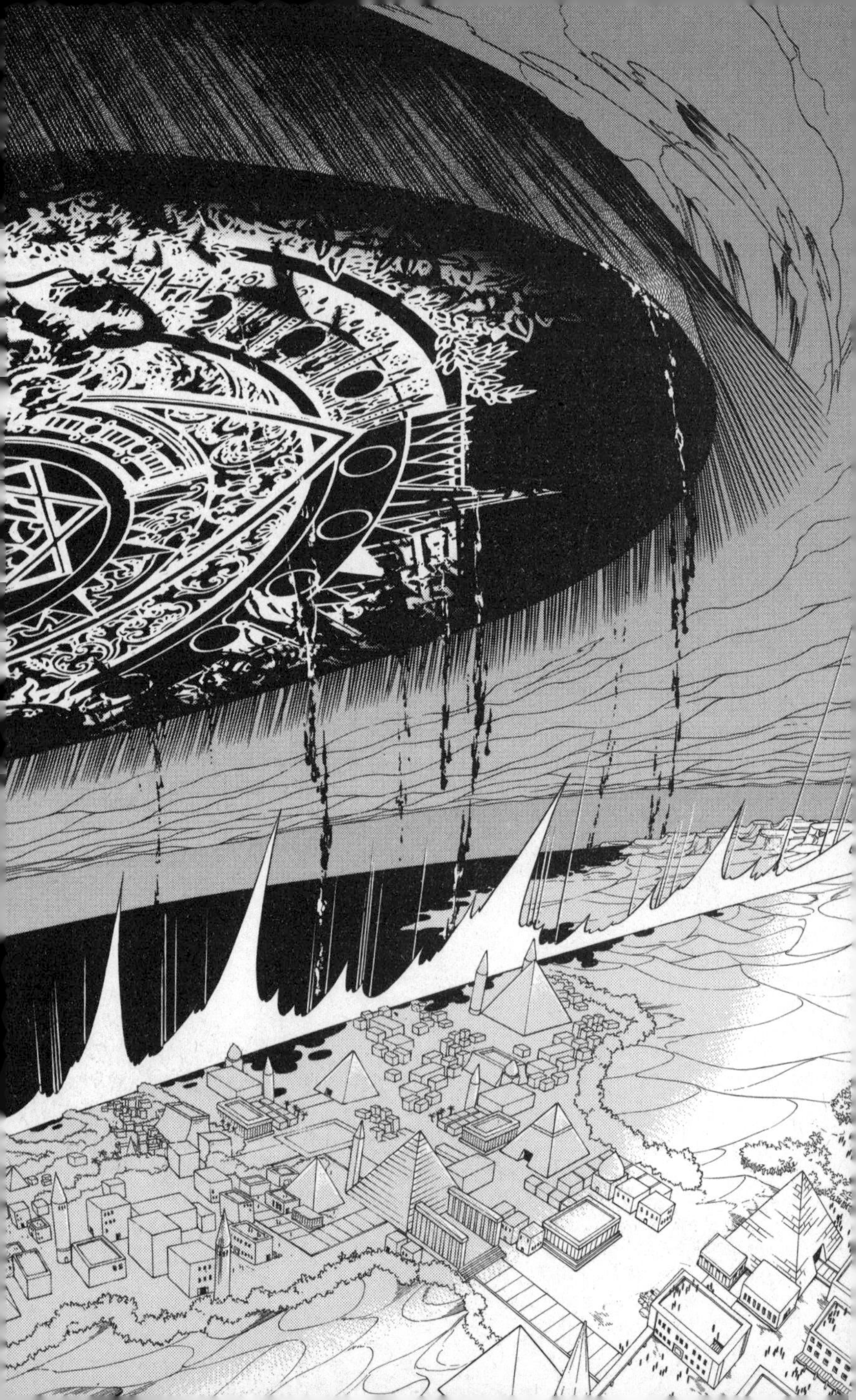

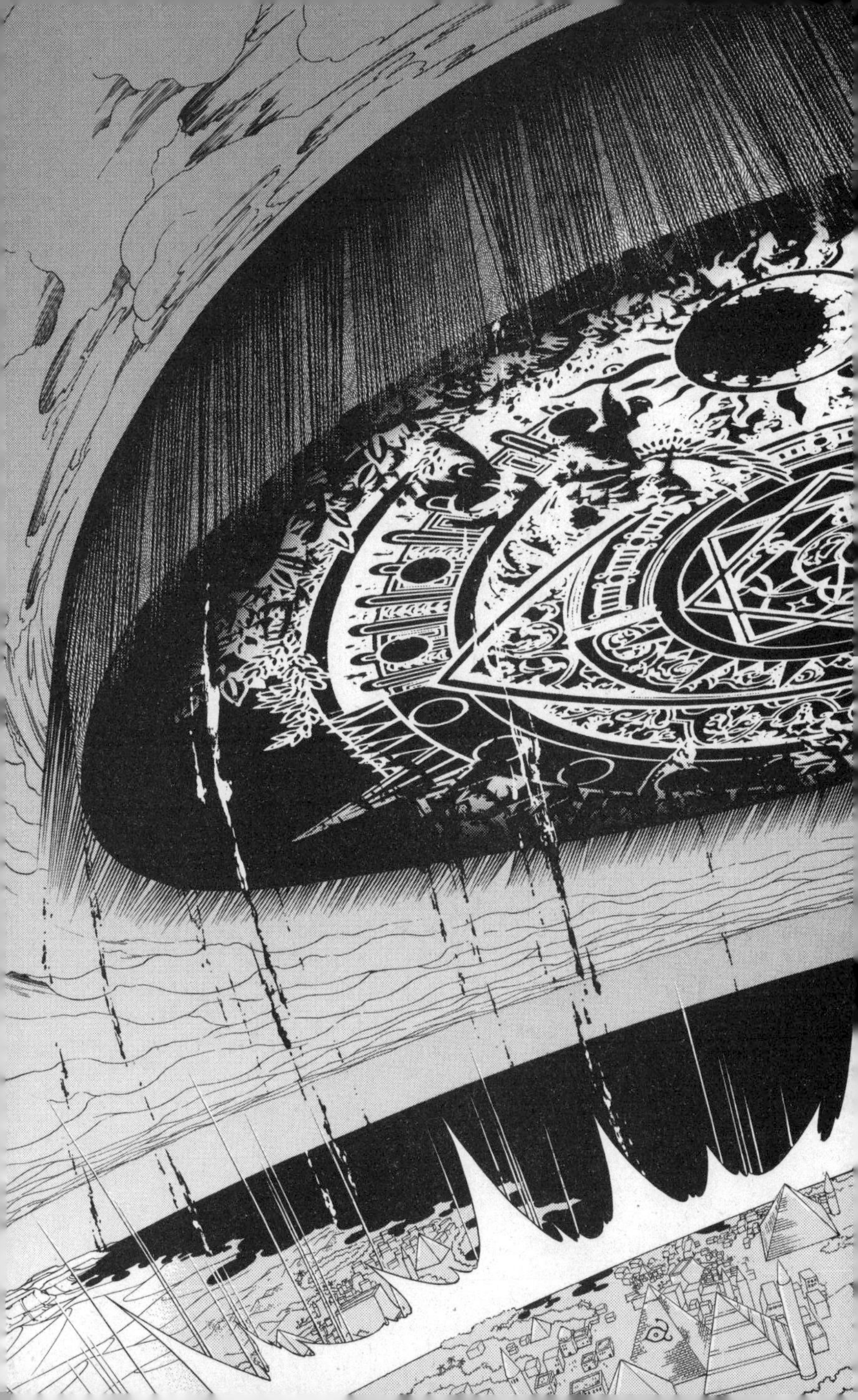

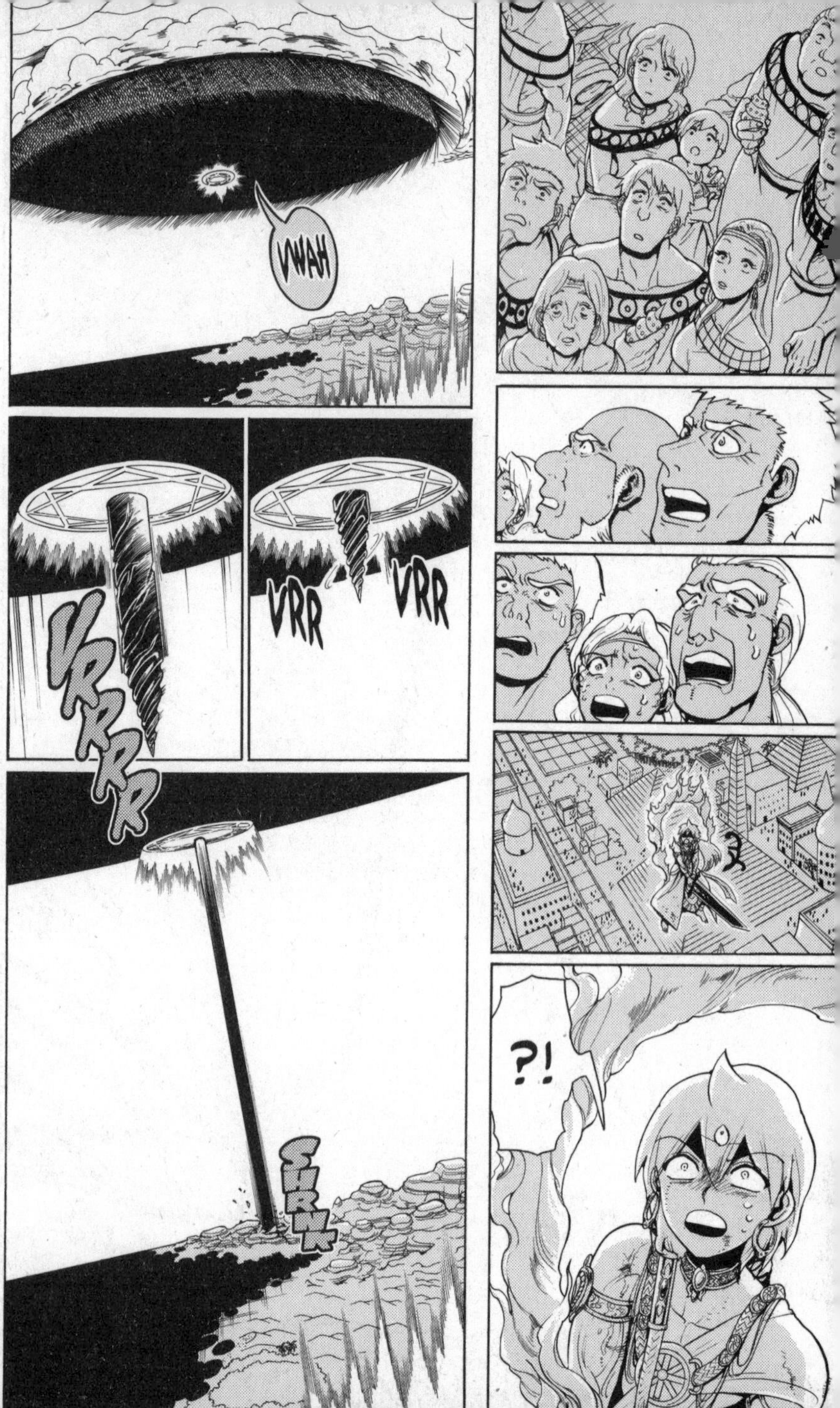
?!
VWAH
VRR VRR
VRRRRR
SHRNK

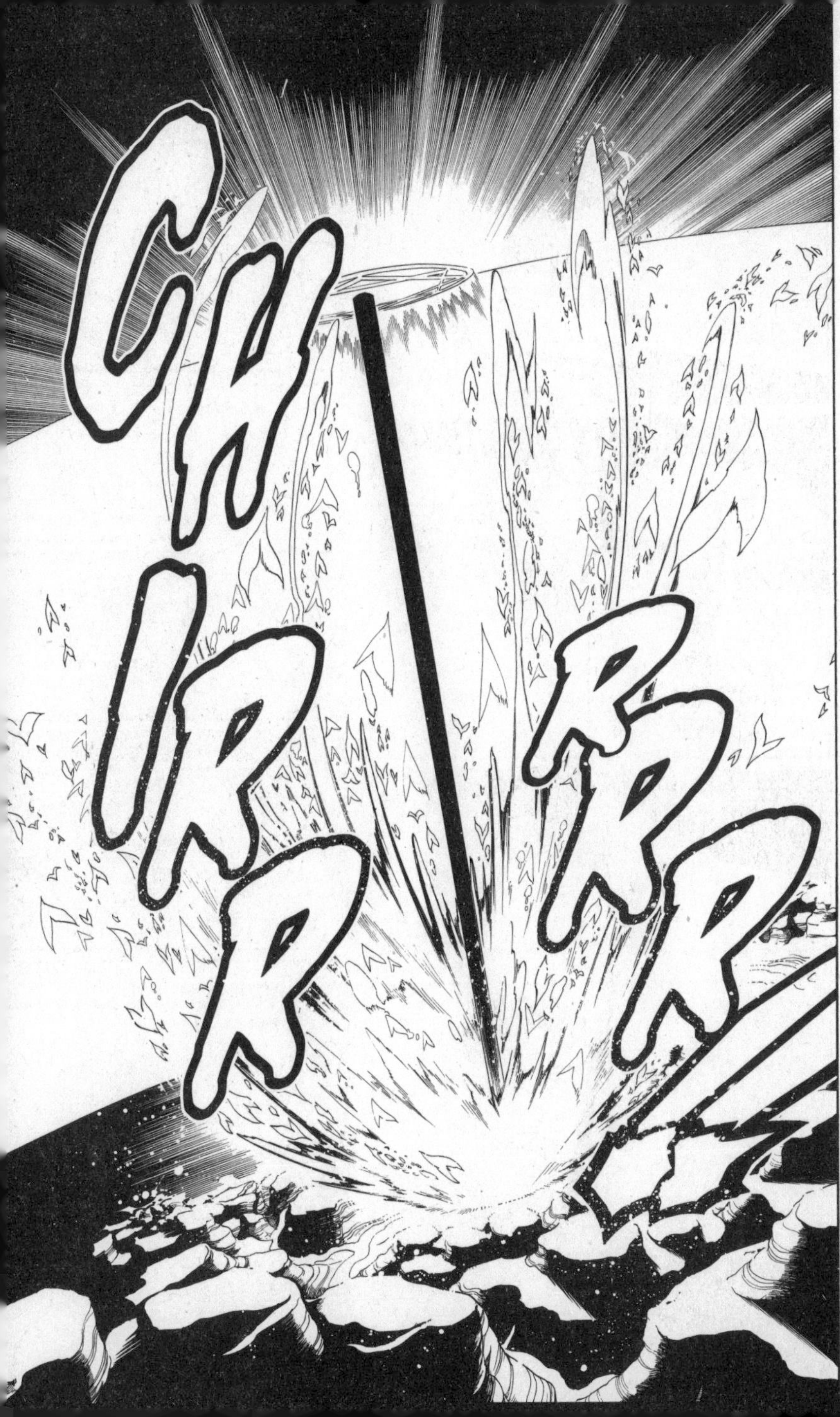
CHIRRRR

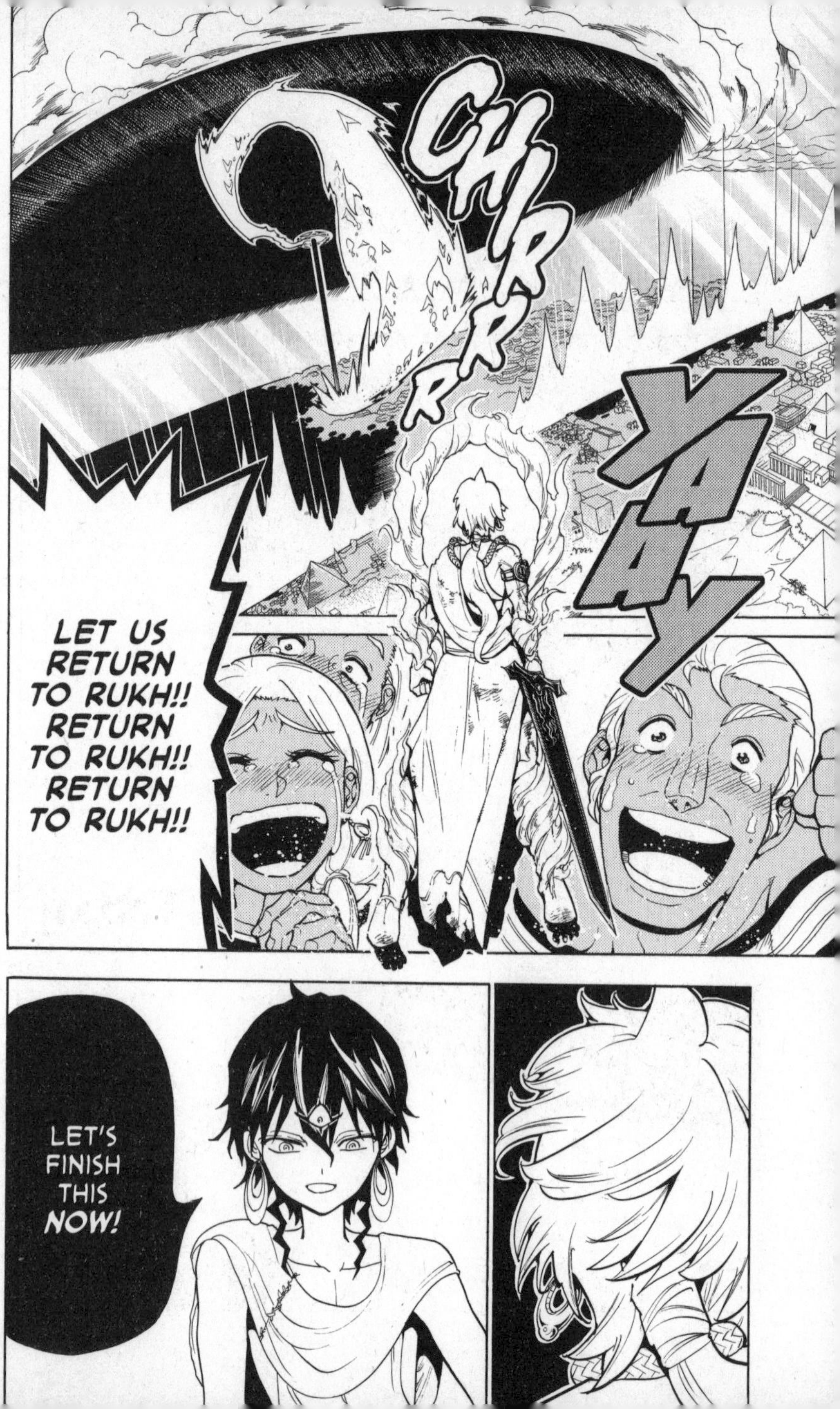
CHIRRR
YAAY
LET US RETURN TO RUKH!! RETURN TO RUKH!! RETURN TO RUKH!!
LET'S FINISH THIS NOW!

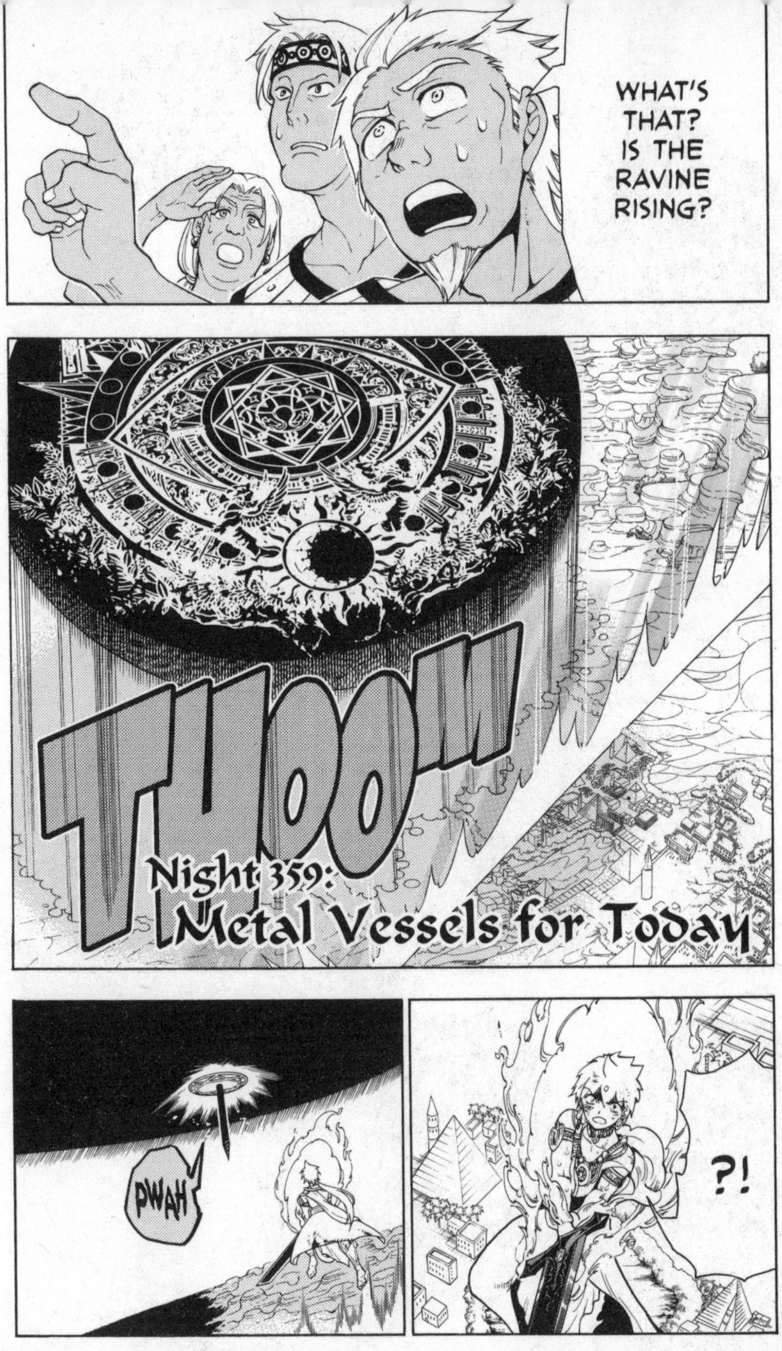
WHAT'S THAT? IS THE RAVINE RISING?
THOO
Night 359:
Metal Vessels for Today
?!
PWAH

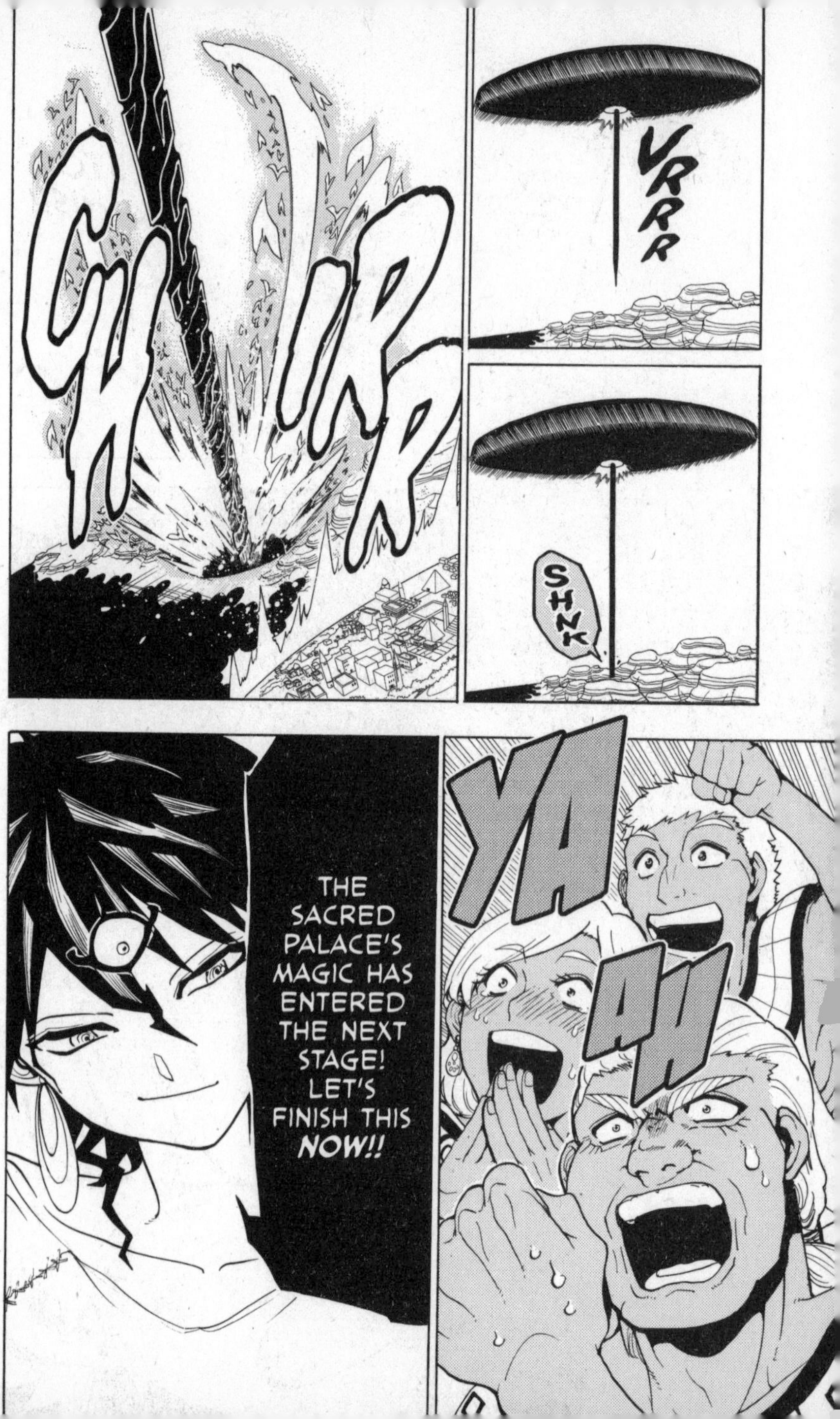
VRRR
SHNK
YA
AH
THE SACRED PALACE'S MAGIC HAS ENTERED THE NEXT STAGE! LET'S FINISH THIS *NOW!!*

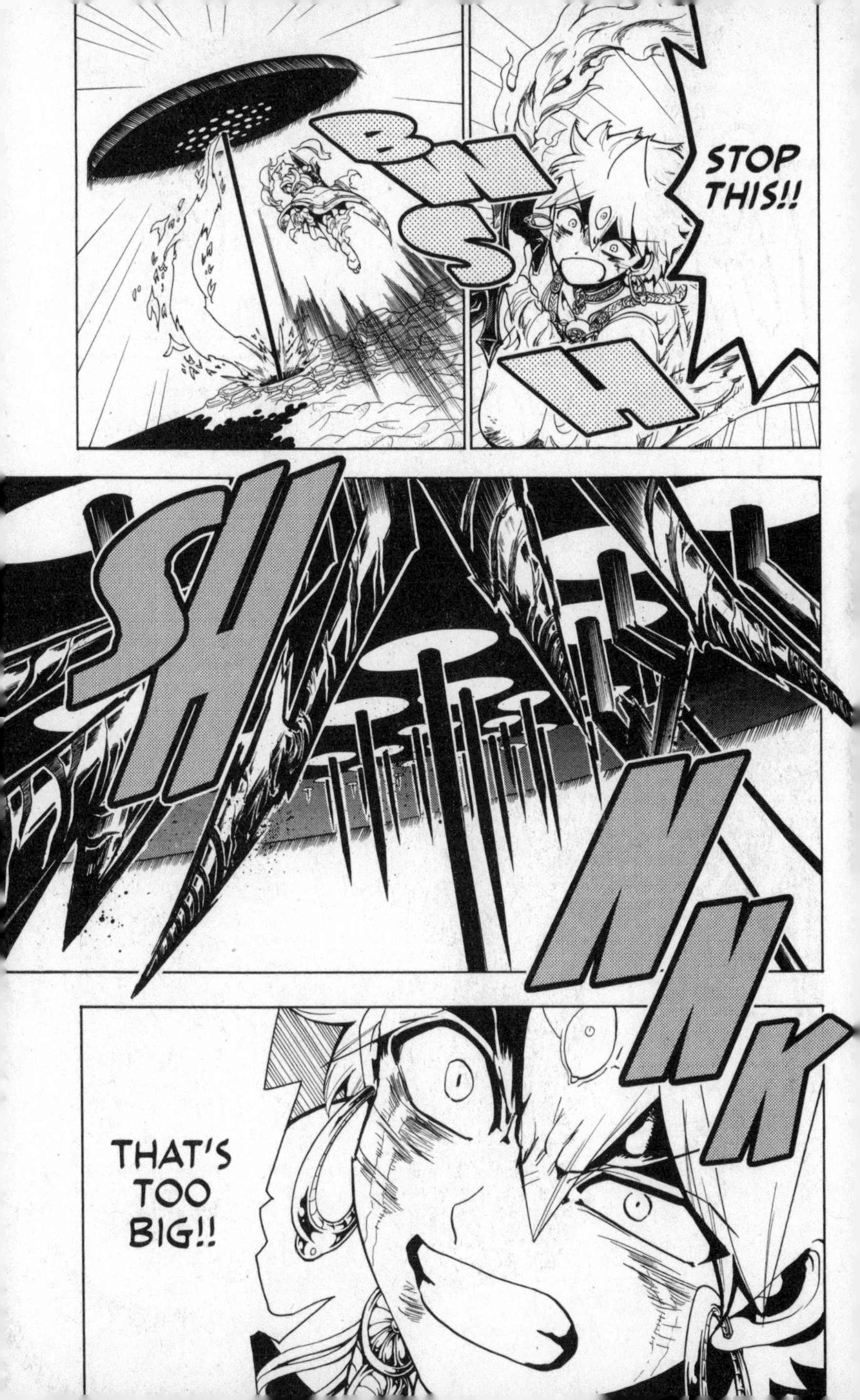
STOP THIS!!
BWSH
SHNNK
THAT'S TOO BIG!!

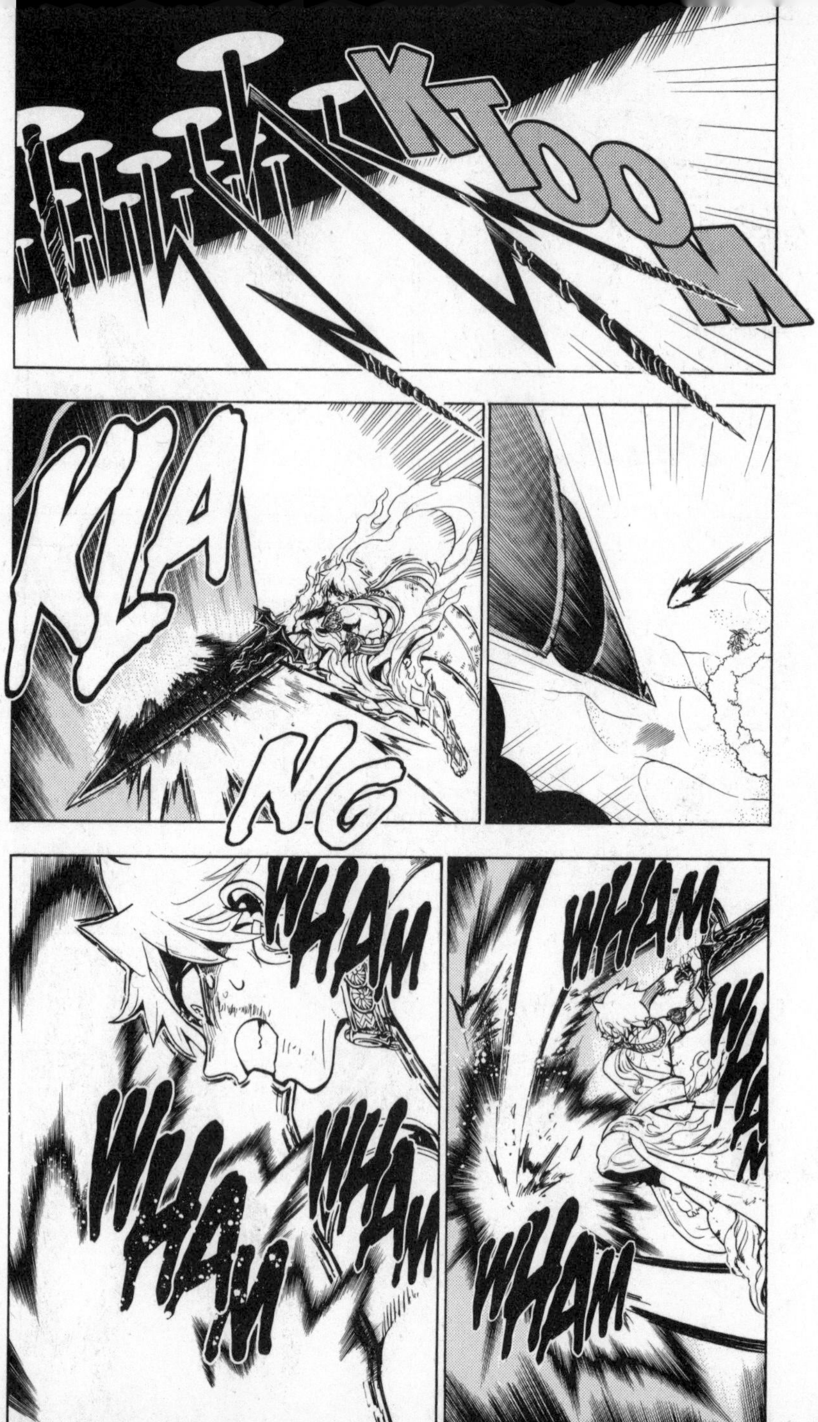
KTOOM
KLANG
WHAM
WHAM
WHAM
WHAM
WHAM
WHAM

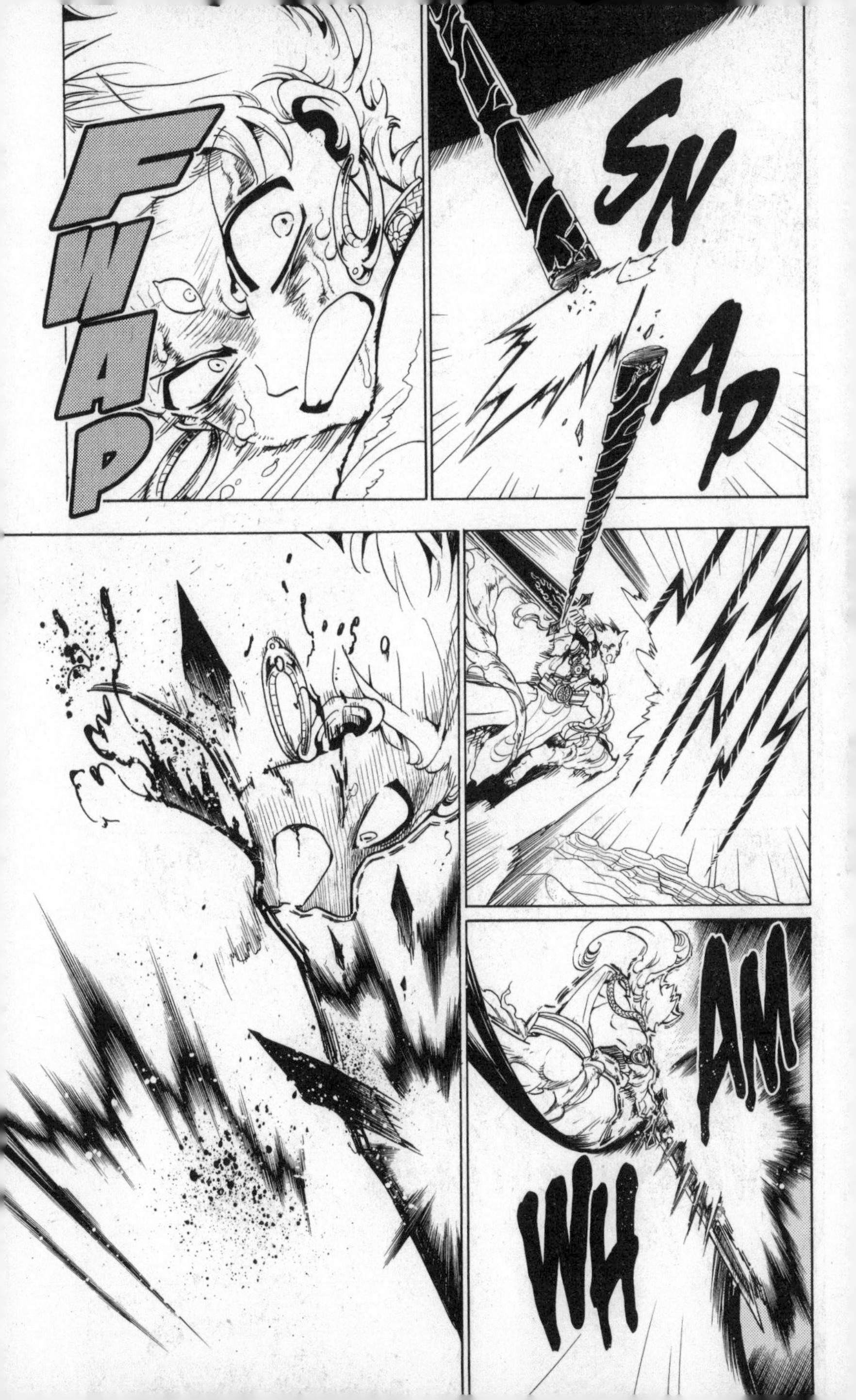
SNAP
FWAP
WHAM

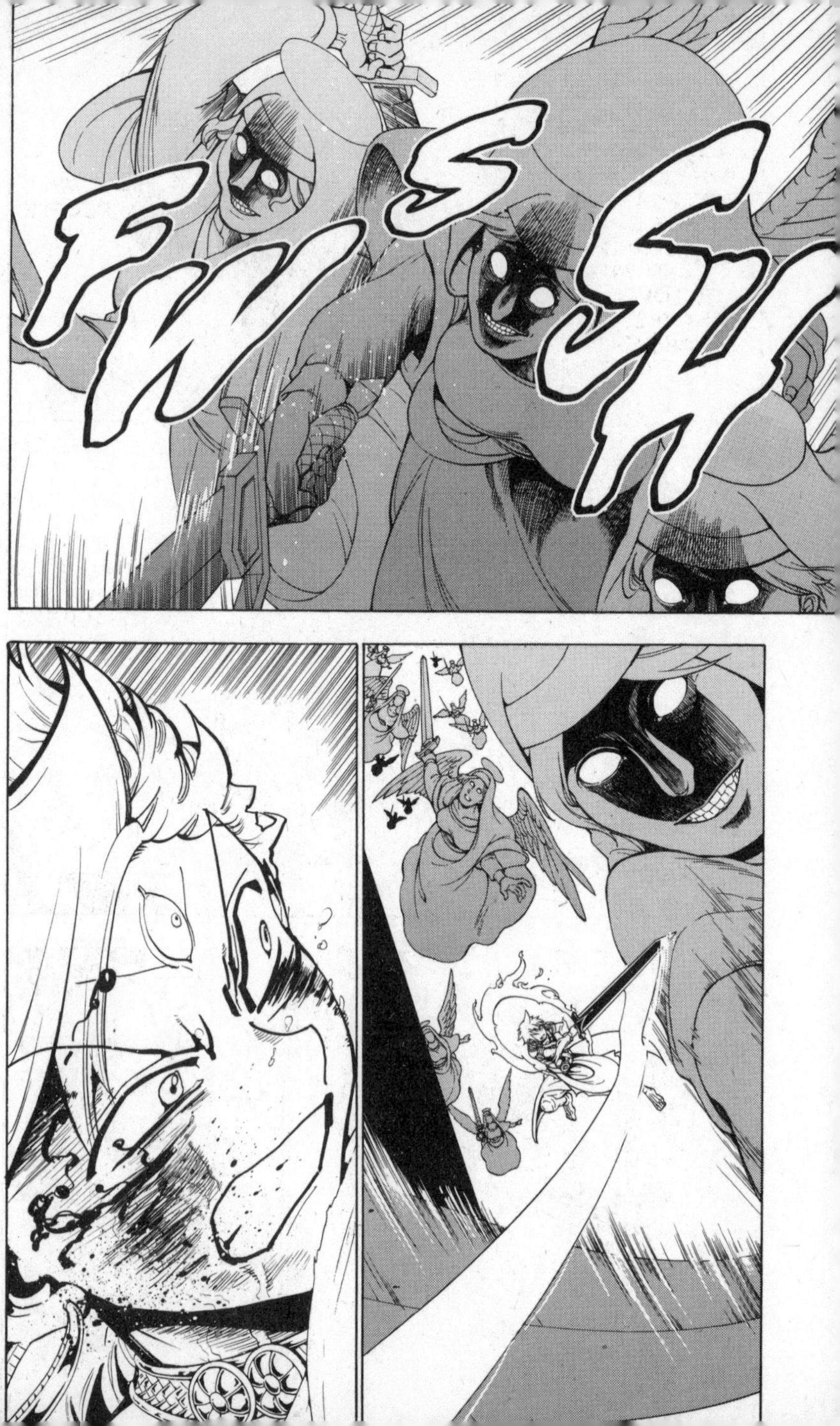
FWSSH

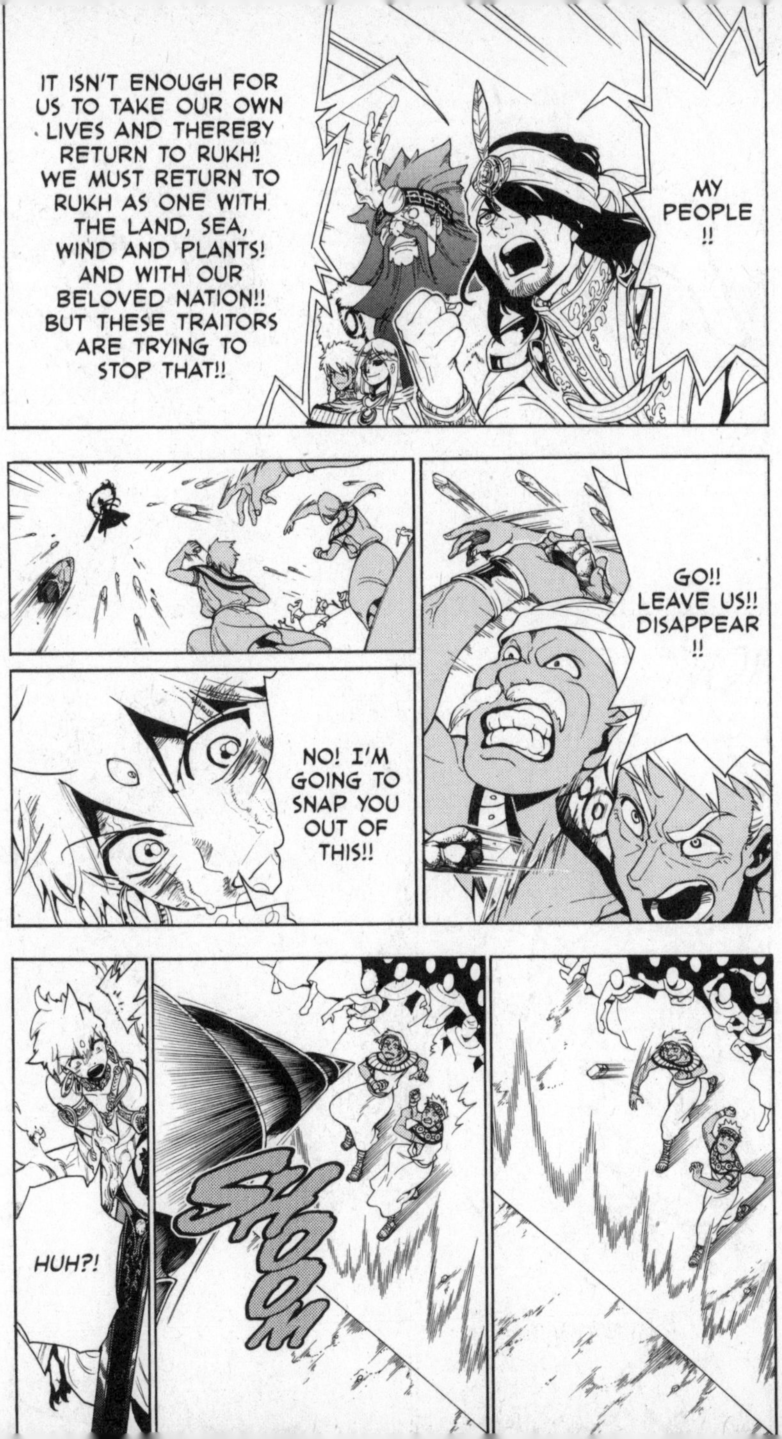
MY PEOPLE!!
IT ISN'T ENOUGH FOR US TO TAKE OUR OWN LIVES AND THEREBY RETURN TO RUKH! WE MUST RETURN TO RUKH AS ONE WITH THE LAND, SEA, WIND AND PLANTS! AND WITH OUR BELOVED NATION!! BUT THESE TRAITORS ARE TRYING TO STOP THAT!!
GO!! LEAVE US!! DISAPPEAR!!
NO! I'M GOING TO SNAP YOU OUT OF THIS!!
SHOOM
HUH?!

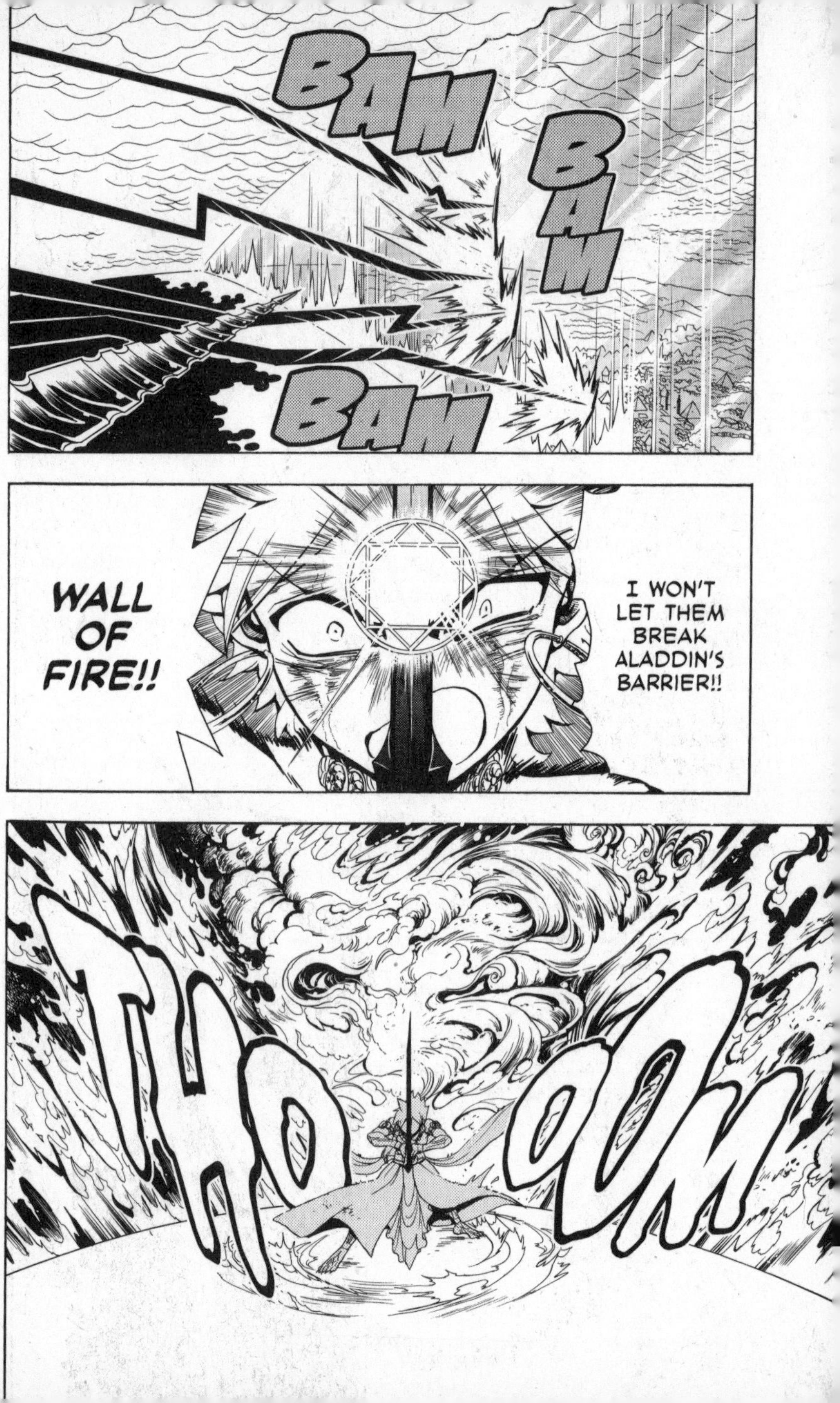
BAM
BAM
BAM
I WON'T LET THEM BREAK ALADDIN'S BARRIER!!
WALL OF FIRE!!
THOOM

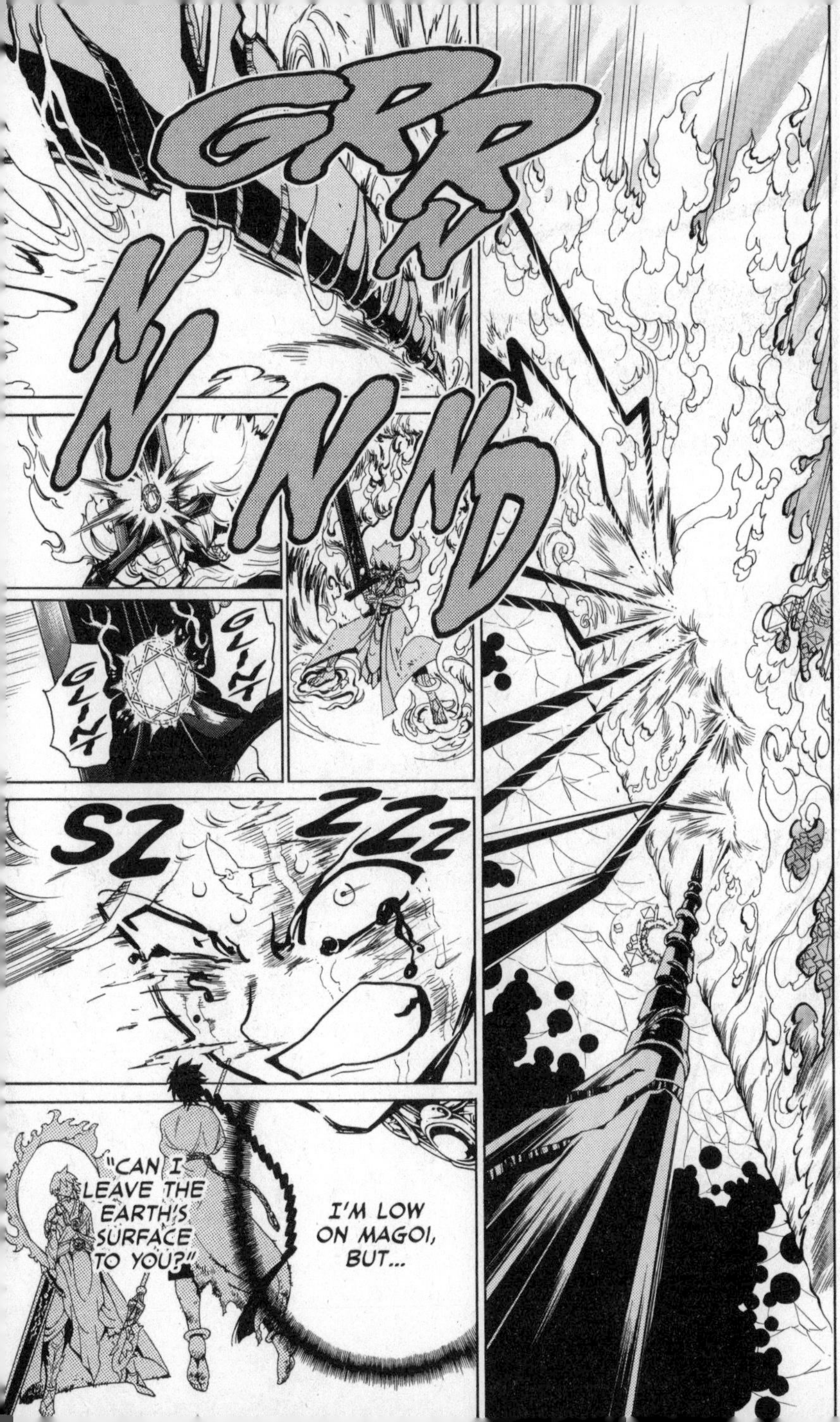
GRRNNNND
GLINT GLINT
SZZZZ
I'M LOW ON MAGOI, BUT...
"CAN I LEAVE THE EARTH'S SURFACE TO YOU?"

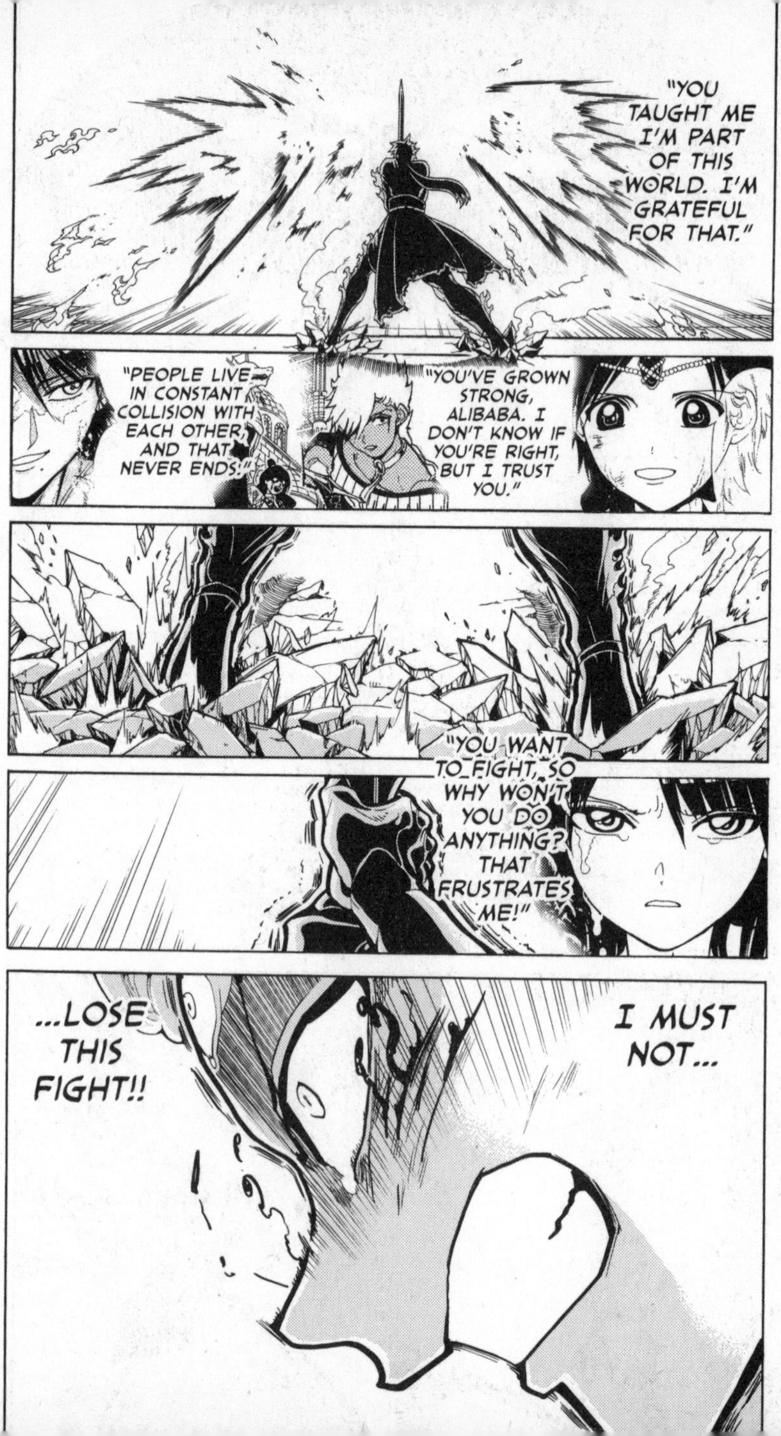
"YOU TAUGHT ME I'M PART OF THIS WORLD. I'M GRATEFUL FOR THAT."
"YOU'VE GROWN STRONG, ALIBABA. I DON'T KNOW IF YOU'RE RIGHT, BUT I TRUST YOU."
"PEOPLE LIVE IN CONSTANT COLLISION WITH EACH OTHER, AND THAT NEVER ENDS!"
"YOU WANT TO FIGHT, SO WHY WON'T YOU DO ANYTHING? THAT FRUSTRATES ME!"
I MUST NOT...
...LOSE THIS FIGHT!!

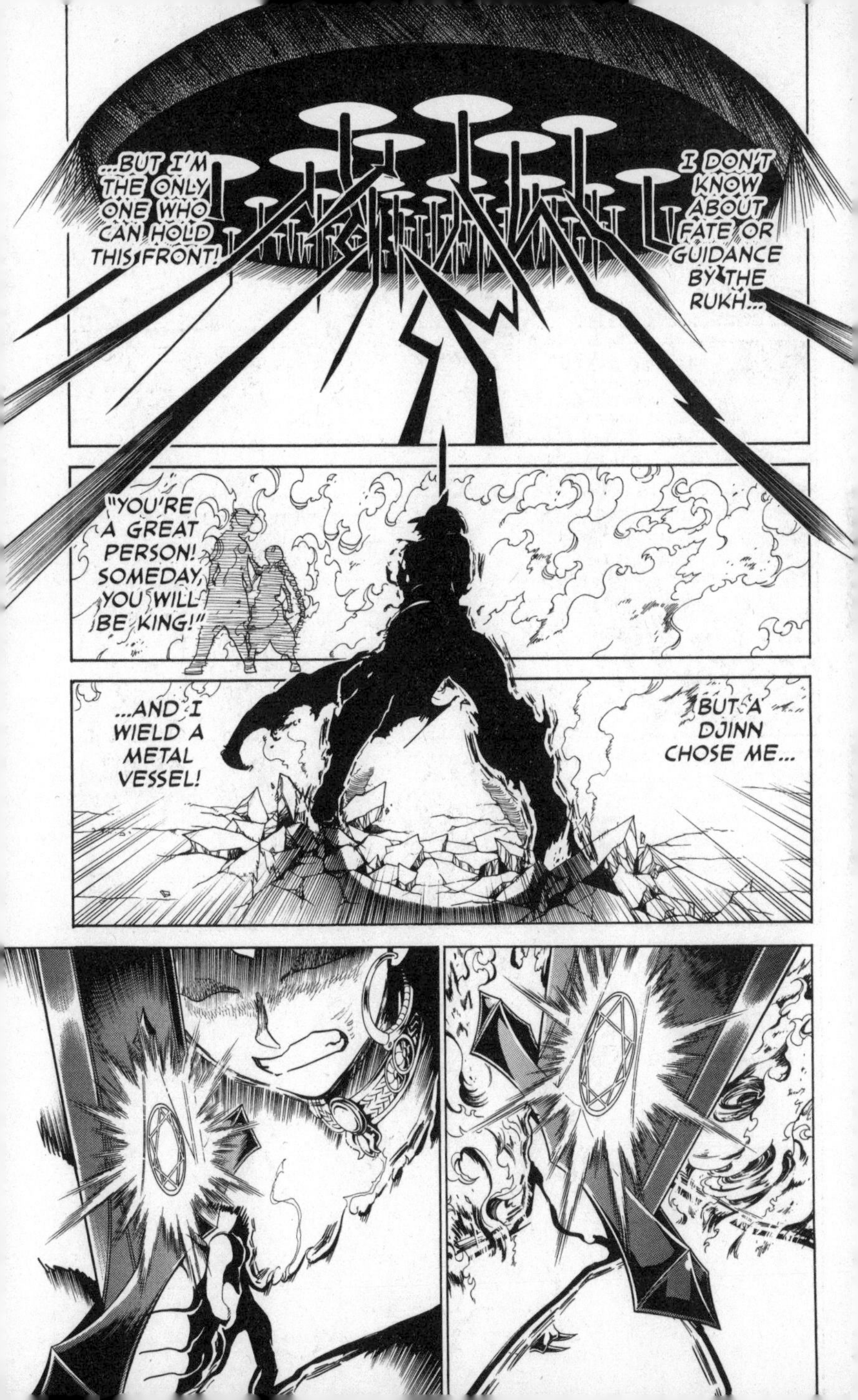
I DON'T KNOW ABOUT FATE OR GUIDANCE BY THE RUKH...
...BUT I'M THE ONLY ONE WHO CAN HOLD THIS FRONT!
"YOU'RE A GREAT PERSON! SOMEDAY, YOU WILL BE KING!"
BUT A DJINN CHOSE ME...
...AND I WIELD A METAL VESSEL!

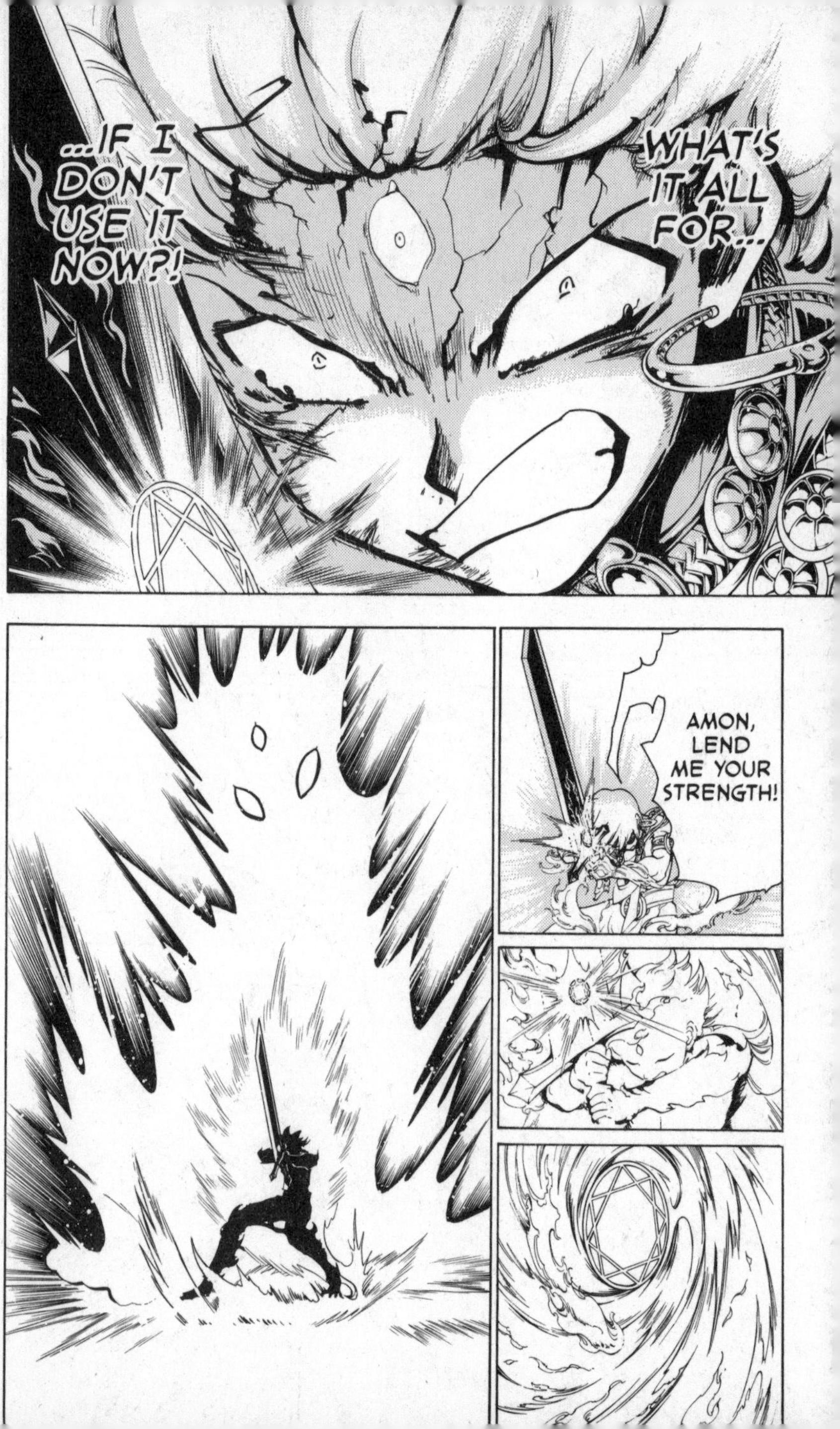
WHAT'S IT ALL FOR...
...IF I DON'T USE IT NOW?!
AMON, LEND ME YOUR STRENGTH!

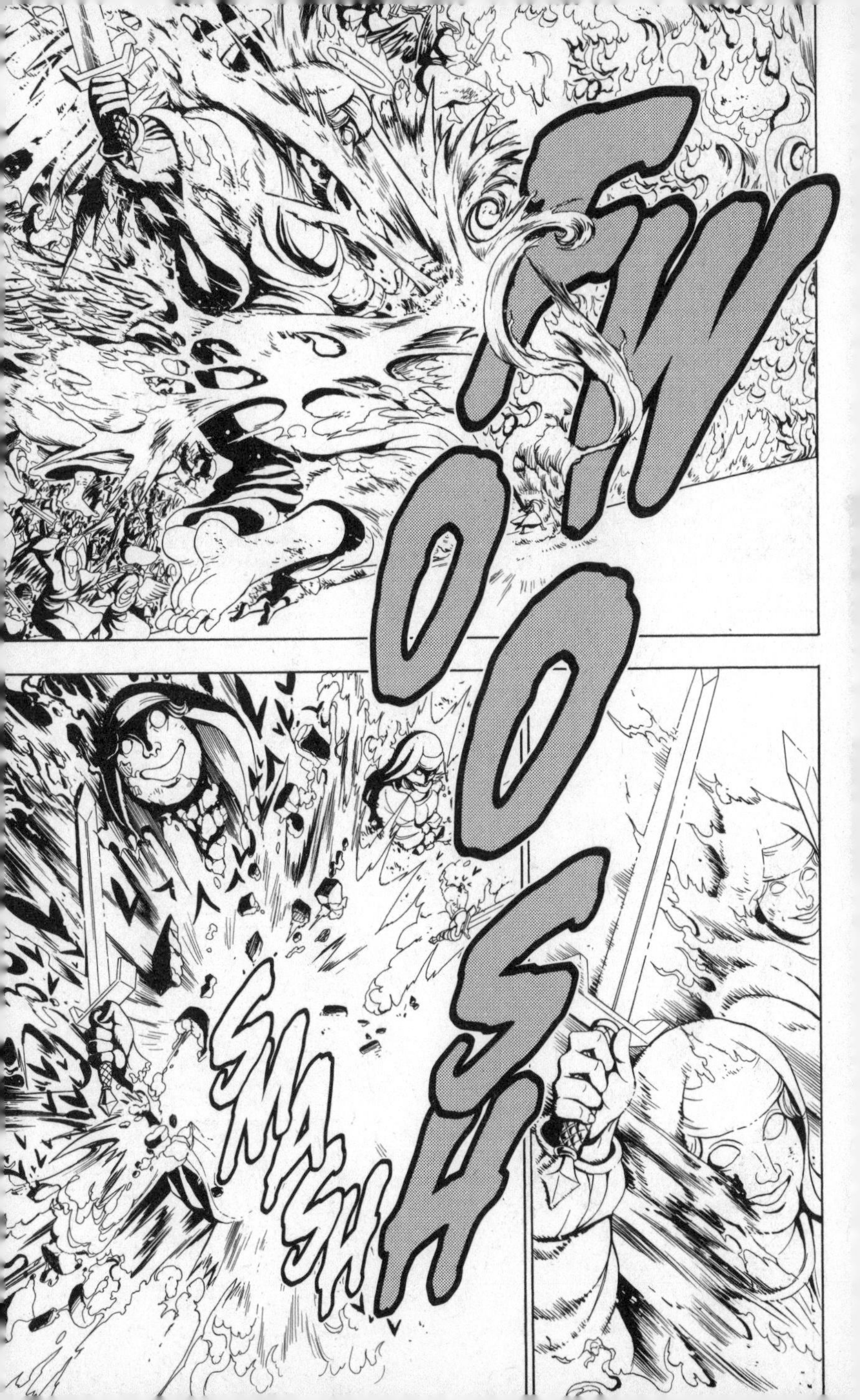
SWOOOSH
SMASH

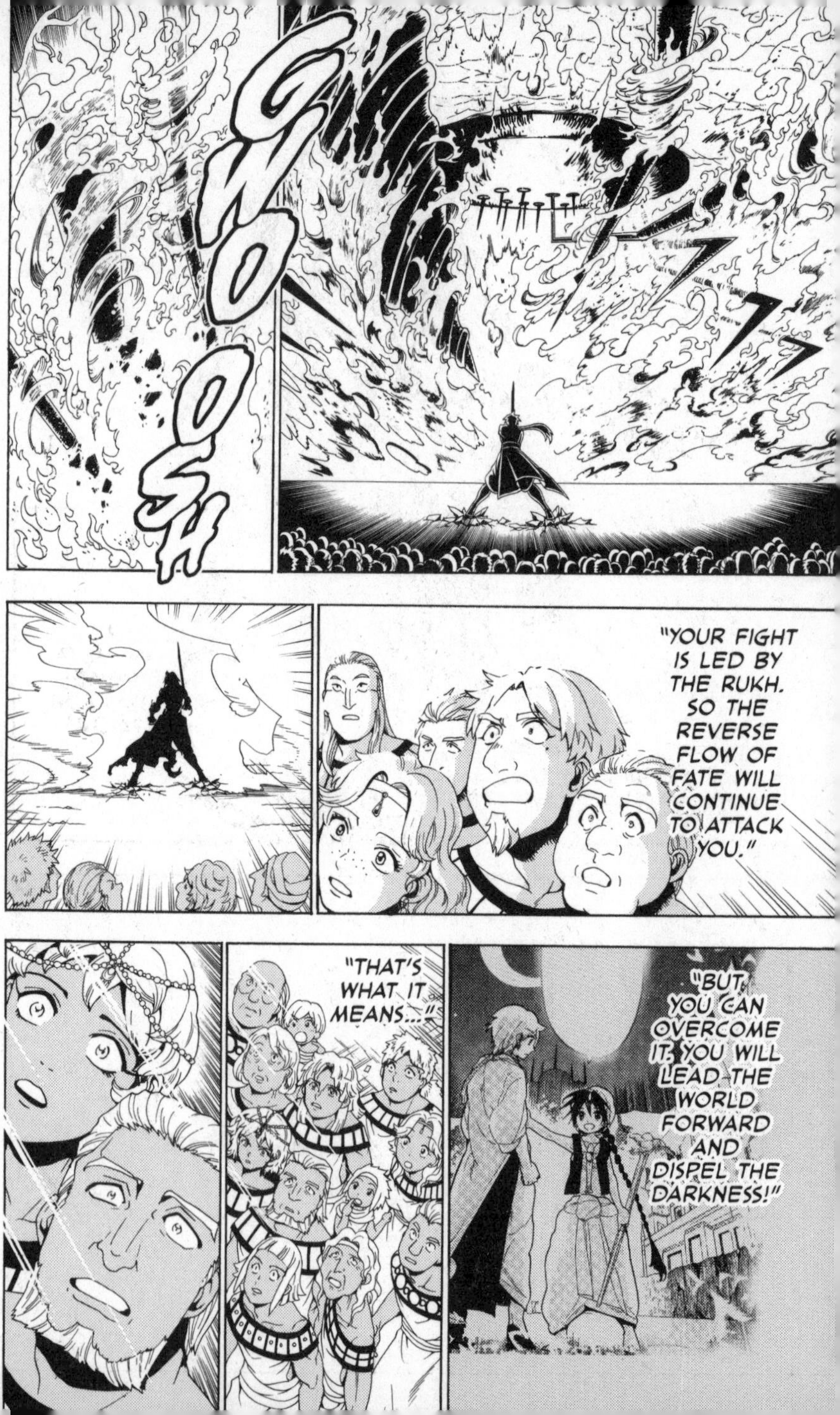
GWOOSH
"YOUR FIGHT IS LED BY THE RUKH. SO THE REVERSE FLOW OF FATE WILL CONTINUE TO ATTACK YOU."
"BUT YOU CAN OVERCOME IT. YOU WILL LEAD THE WORLD FORWARD AND DISPEL THE DARKNESS!"
"THAT'S WHAT IT MEANS...!!"

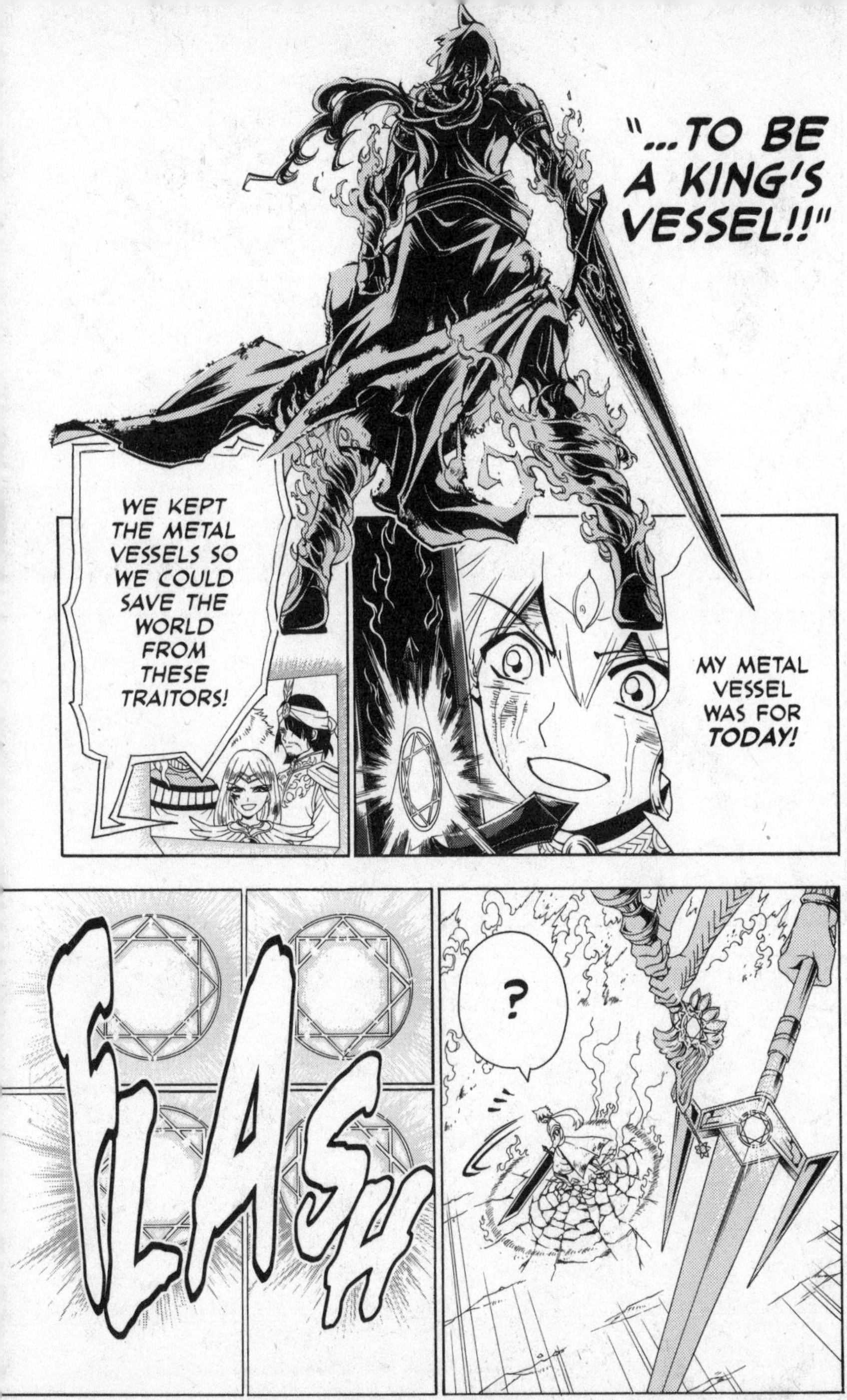
"...TO BE A KING'S VESSEL!!"
MY METAL VESSEL WAS FOR TODAY!
WE KEPT THE METAL VESSELS SO WE COULD SAVE THE WORLD FROM THESE TRAITORS!
?
FLASH

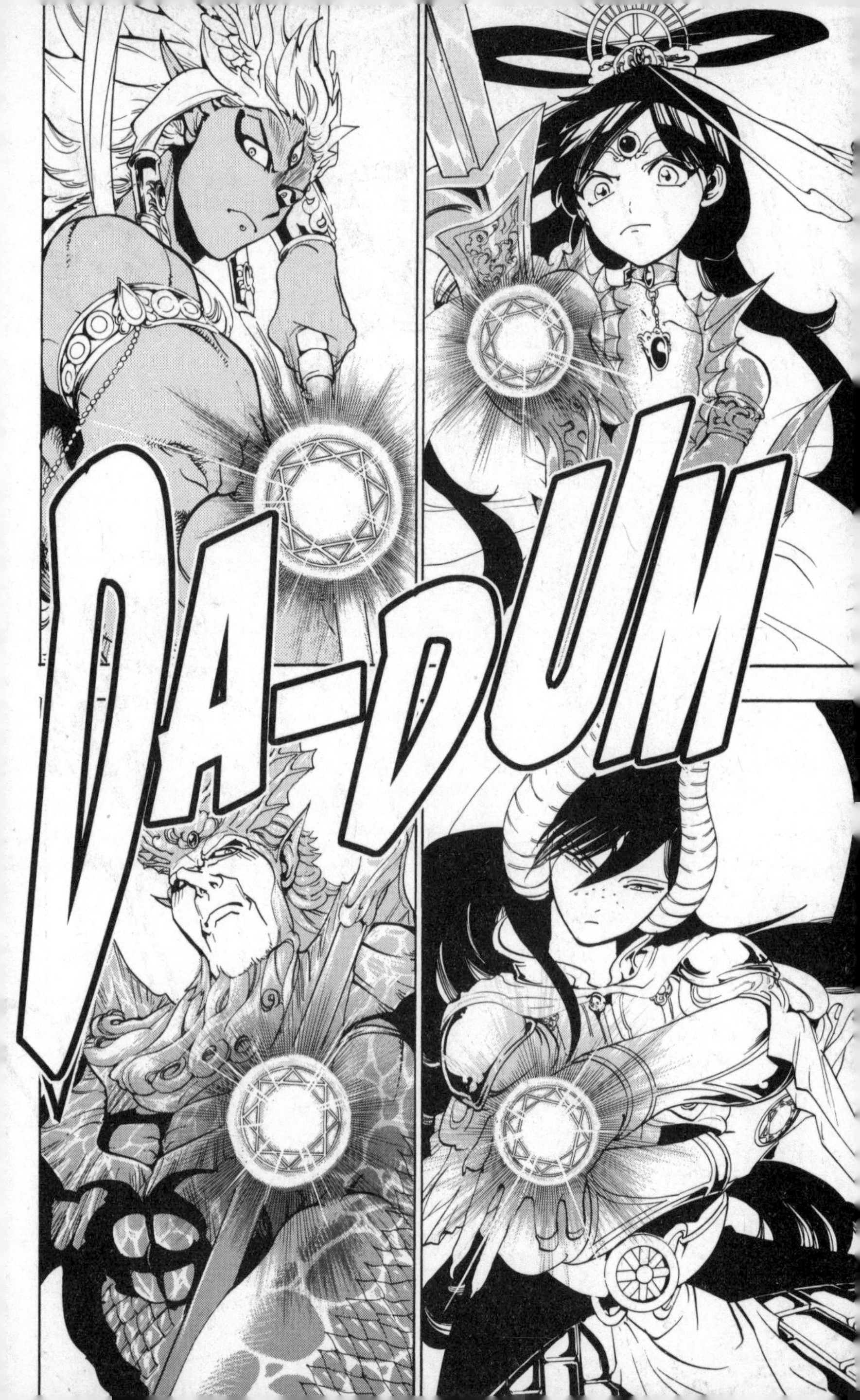
DA-DUM

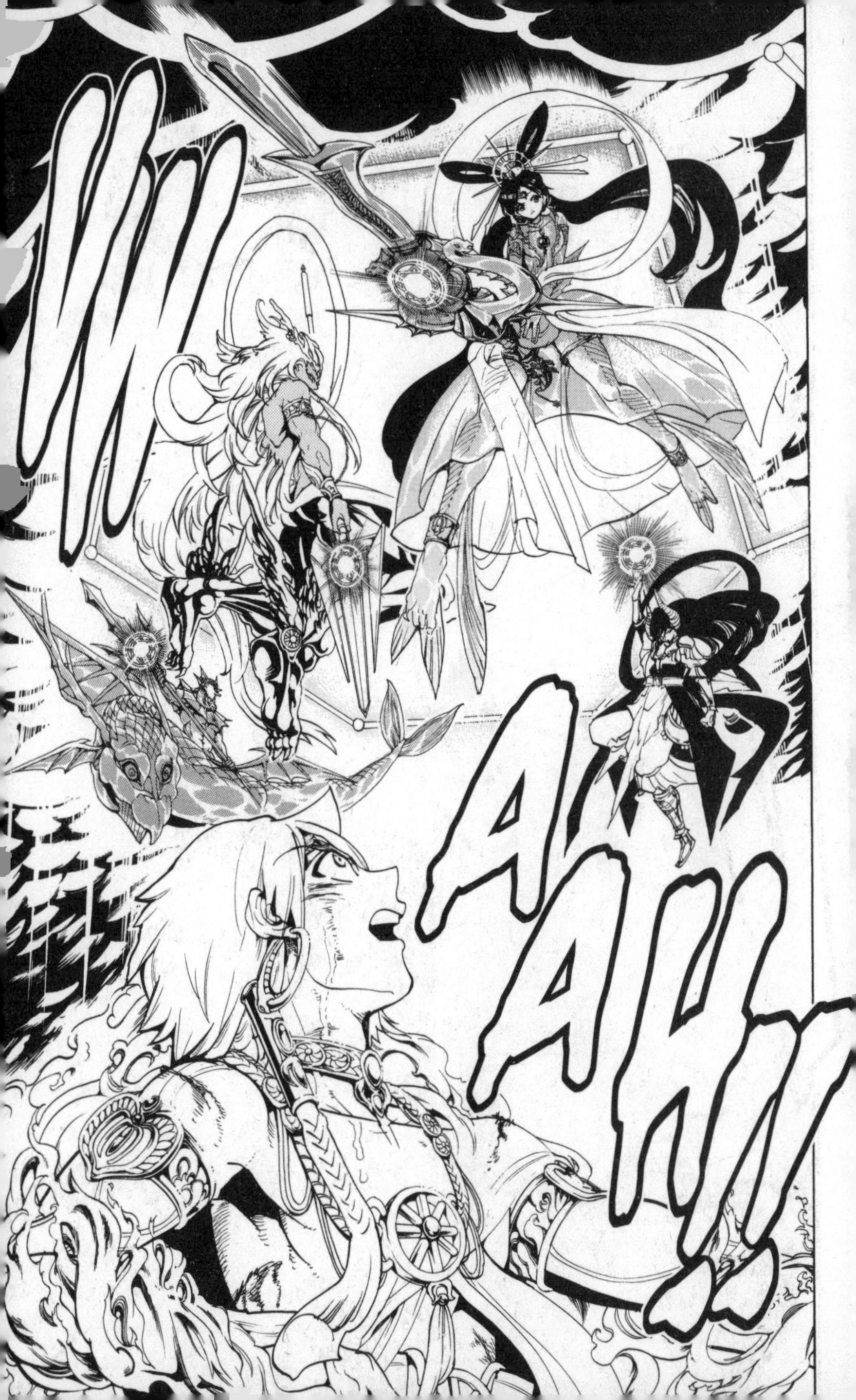
WM
AAAH!!

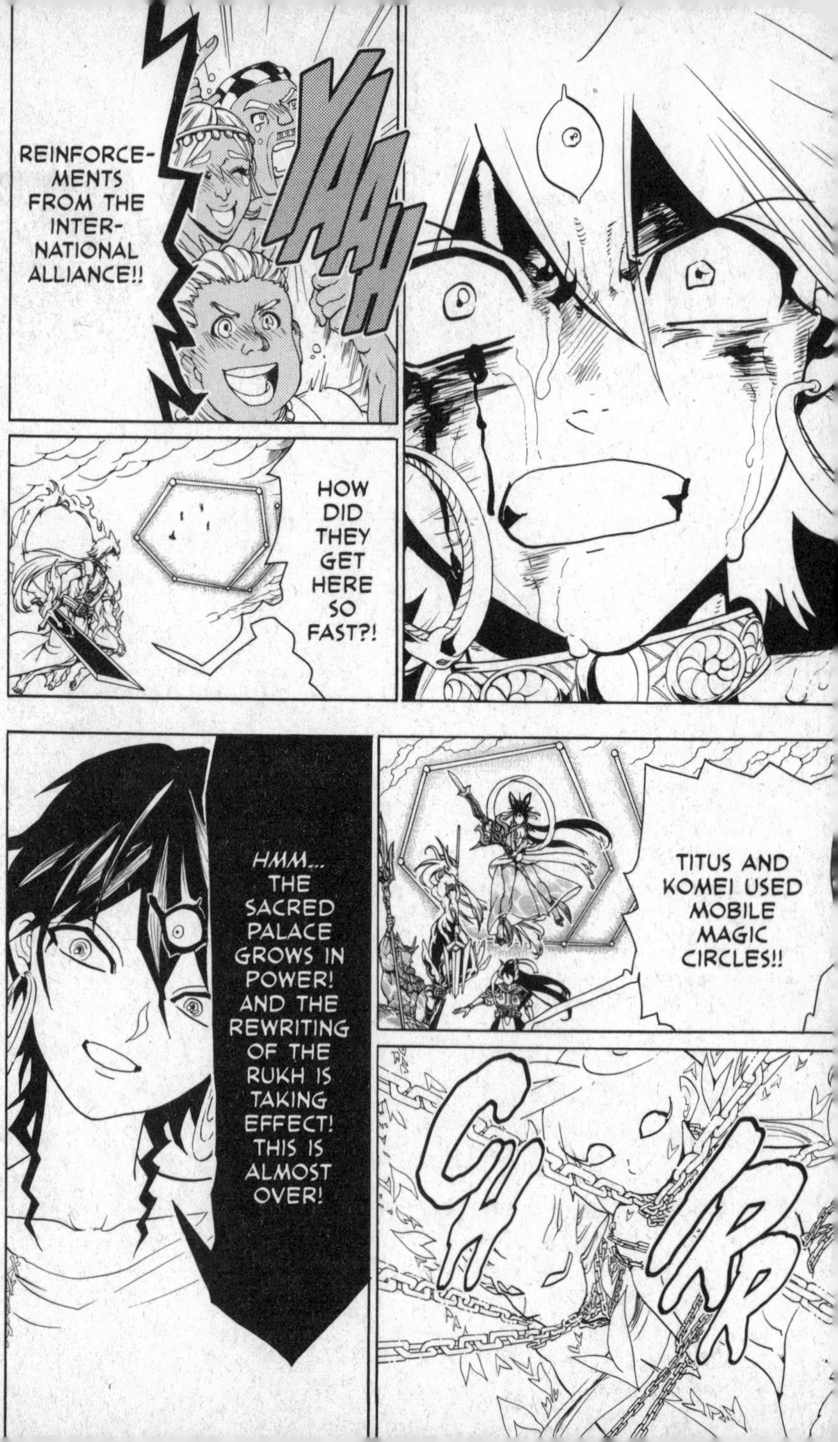
REINFORCEMENTS FROM THE INTERNATIONAL ALLIANCE!!
YAAAH
HOW DID THEY GET HERE SO FAST?!
TITUS AND KOMEI USED MOBILE MAGIC CIRCLES!!
HMM... THE SACRED PALACE GROWS IN POWER! AND THE REWRITING OF THE RUKH IS TAKING EFFECT! THIS IS ALMOST OVER!

MAGI
The labyrinth of magic

36

Staff

■ **Story & Art**

Shinobu Ohtaka

■ **Regular Assistants**

Hiro Maizima

Yuiko Akiyama

Megi

Aya Umoto

Mami Yoshida

Chidori Ishigo

■ **Editors**

Kazuaki Ishibashi

Makoto Ishiwata

Katsumasa Ogura

■ **Sales & Promotion**

Tsunato Imamoto

Asako Toita

■ **Designer**

Hajime Tokushige + Bay Bridge Studio

Magi Vol. 36 Bonus ①

Yunan's
Rukh Personality Test

Do you know what type of Rukh you're most compatible with? I've made a Rukh personality test based on my own arbitrary decisions and stereotypes, as well as in consultation with volume 14. Answer the questions to find your type of Rukh!

Read about your result on the next page!

A. What were you like as a child?

①I had good grades.
②I was no good at studying but had other skills.
③I was just average.

D. What kind of boss would you be?

①I would be strong and serious.
②I would be kind and supportive.
③I would treat everyone like friends and equals.

C. What are you like at a BBQ party?

①I eat as much as I'm offered.
②I take an active role, placing orders and grilling meat.
③I don't like parties, so I don't go.

H. Are you an only or youngest child?

①Yes ②No

You are Type 1

B. What are you like after a breakup?

①I get back up fast.
②I obsess for a long time.
③I've never experienced a breakup.

You are Type 6

You are Type 8

G. Are you the eldest child?

①Yes ②No

E. How do you spend sudden time off?

①I relax.
②One by one, I do all the things I've had on hold.
③I don't know what to do.

F. What do you do when sad?

①It takes time to recover.
②I search for the cause and solve it.
③I do other things and try not to think about it.

You are Type 2

You are Type 4

You are Type 3

You are Type 7

You are Type 5

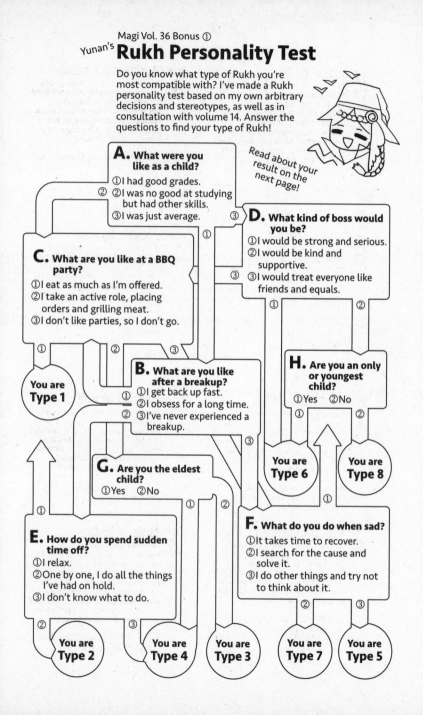

Type 1 Capricious Adventurer

You don't desire material goods or success. Instead, you work hard for others. That sounds great, but unfortunately this type has a ***vigorous sexual appetite.*** You're happiest when satisfying primal urges for food, sleep, etc.

Ex. Aladdin, Wahid, Masrur, Lolo, Toto

Type 2 Eccentric Explorer

You only pursue your own likes, and you ignore things (and people) that don't interest you. In a word, you're a nerd! And you're clueless when it comes to romance, so you don't notice when someone likes you.

Ex. Judar, Yamraiha, Ugo, Setta, Koen Ren

Type 3 Naive Popular Kid

You're good at asking favors and getting people to like you. You're naive, but you can also be calculating. Which means you should be overwhelmingly popular with the opposite sex! ***Hm? Alibaba, why do you look so glum?***

Ex. Alibaba, Pisti, Hakuren Ren, Perdinaus, Anis

Type 4 Hardworking Big Brother (Sister)

You're considerate toward others. And you're a serious person who is proud, fair, self-controlled, responsible and has a hard time cutting loose. You're an idealist with a realistic side, which can pull you in two directions. ***I get a kick out of teasing such people!***

Ex. Mu, Isnan, Drakon, Sharrkan, Koha Ren, Hakuei Ren

Type 5 Cool Idealist

You look low-key and relaxed. In fact, you may even look cold, but you're a romantic on the inside. People say they don't know what you're thinking. In your cynicism and self-suppression, ***you often lose sight of what you really feel.*** In other words, you're difficult to heat up and difficult to cool down!

Ex. Yunan, Komei Ren, Laylah, Ignatius, Fatima

Type 6 Harmonious Pacifist

You're warm, faithful and dependable—and you worry a lot. You're also perceptive and cooperative, so you value friends, family and peers above all else. ***In other words, you're a good person.*** But try to be more self-assertive, okay?

Ex. Spartos, Hinahoho, Dunya, Marga, Sahsa

Type 7 Charismatic Genius

You're the courageous and kingly type—a leader who inspires awe and respect in others. Which sounds perfect, but this type strikes me as having a ***dark side.*** In your obsession, you may head in the wrong direction.

Ex. Sinbad, Solomon, Cassim, Mogamett, Hakuryu Ren, Hakuyu Ren, Gyokuen Ren

Type 8 Explosive Romantic

You're kind and loving. With all that emotion, you go through a lot of ups and downs. You value relationships, so you enjoy helping others. You're also single-minded and self-sacrificing. ***Just the type to have a hard time...***

Ex. Morgiana, Ja'far, Falan, Scheherazade, Titus, Sphintus, Kogyoku Ren

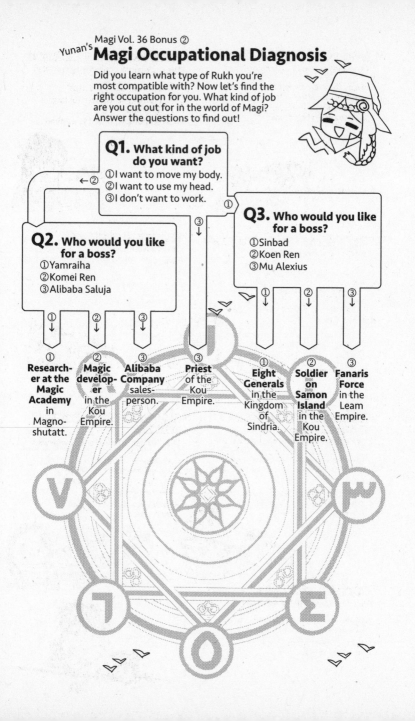

Magi Vol. 36 Bonus ②

Yunan's Magi Occupational Diagnosis

Did you learn what type of Rukh you're most compatible with? Now let's find the right occupation for you. What kind of job are you cut out for in the world of Magi? Answer the questions to find out!

Q1. What kind of job do you want?
① I want to move my body.
② I want to use my head.
③ I don't want to work.

← ②

Q2. Who would you like for a boss?
① Yamraiha
② Komei Ren
③ Alibaba Saluja

Q3. Who would you like for a boss?
① Sinbad
② Koen Ren
③ Mu Alexius

① **Researcher at the Magic Academy** in Magnoshutatt.

② **Magic developer** in the Kou Empire.

③ **Alibaba Company** salesperson.

③ **Priest** of the Kou Empire.

① **Eight Generals** in the Kingdom of Sindria.

② **Soldier on Samon Island** in the Kou Empire.

③ **Fanaris Force** in the Leam Empire.

Alibaba Company Salesperson
They're interested in working with you!

- Enjoy the lively atmosphere of a venture company!
- Open to anyone who can put up with Alibaba when he's drunk.

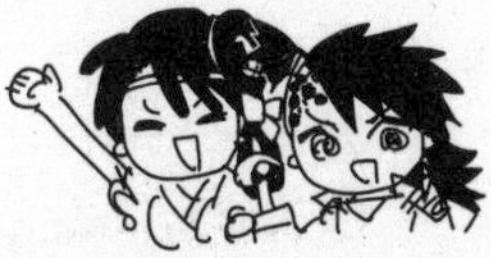

Fanaris Force in the Leam Empire
They're interested in working with you!

- Three meals a day and naps!
- Polygamy is encouraged for large, lively families!
- Safety not guaranteed in wartime.

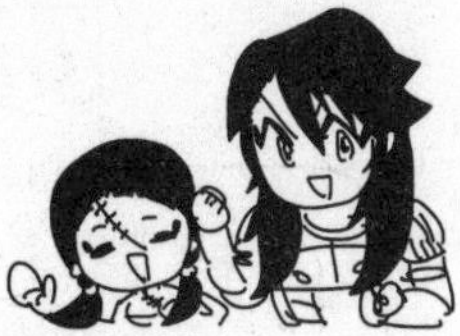

Magic Researcher in the Kou Empire
They're interested in working with you!

- Leisurely research magic beneath the earth!
- Win Lord Komei's praise!
- Use a Preservation Seal to work after death! Keep at it until you literally fall apart!

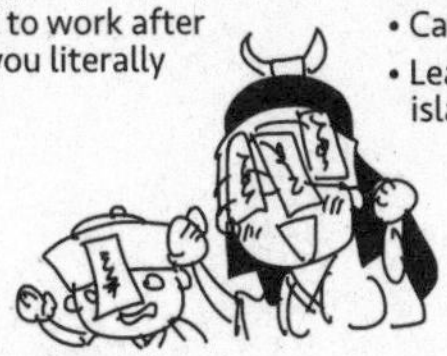

Soldier on Samon Island in the Kou Empire
They're interested in working with you!

- Learn survival skills!
- Care for Lords Koen and Koha!
- Leave the clamor of the city for island life!

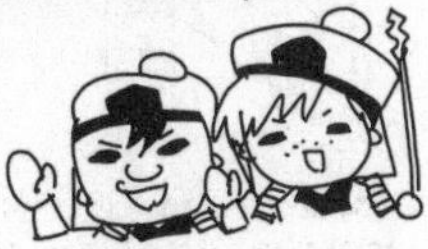

Scholar at the Magic Academy in Magnoshutatt
They're interested in working with you!

- Leisurely research magic beneath the earth!
- Win Lord Komei's praise!
- Use a Preservation Seal to work after death! Keep at it until you literally fall apart!

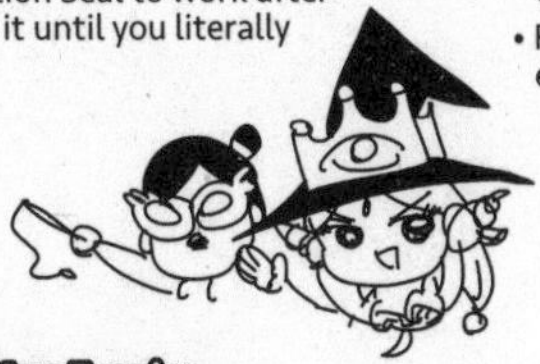

Eight Generals in the Kingdom of Sindria
They're interested in working with you!

- As older members advance, younger members move up!
- The current Eight Generals are the third generation.
- Follow your beloved Sinbad everywhere!

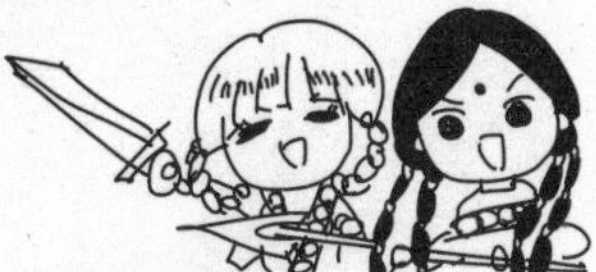

Priest of the Kou Empire
He's interested in dragging you in!

- Waste time hanging out and munching on peaches!
- Eat the meals Hakuryu prepares to relieve stress.

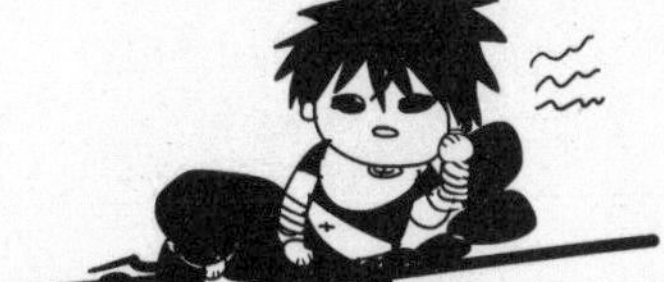

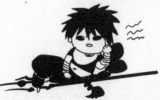

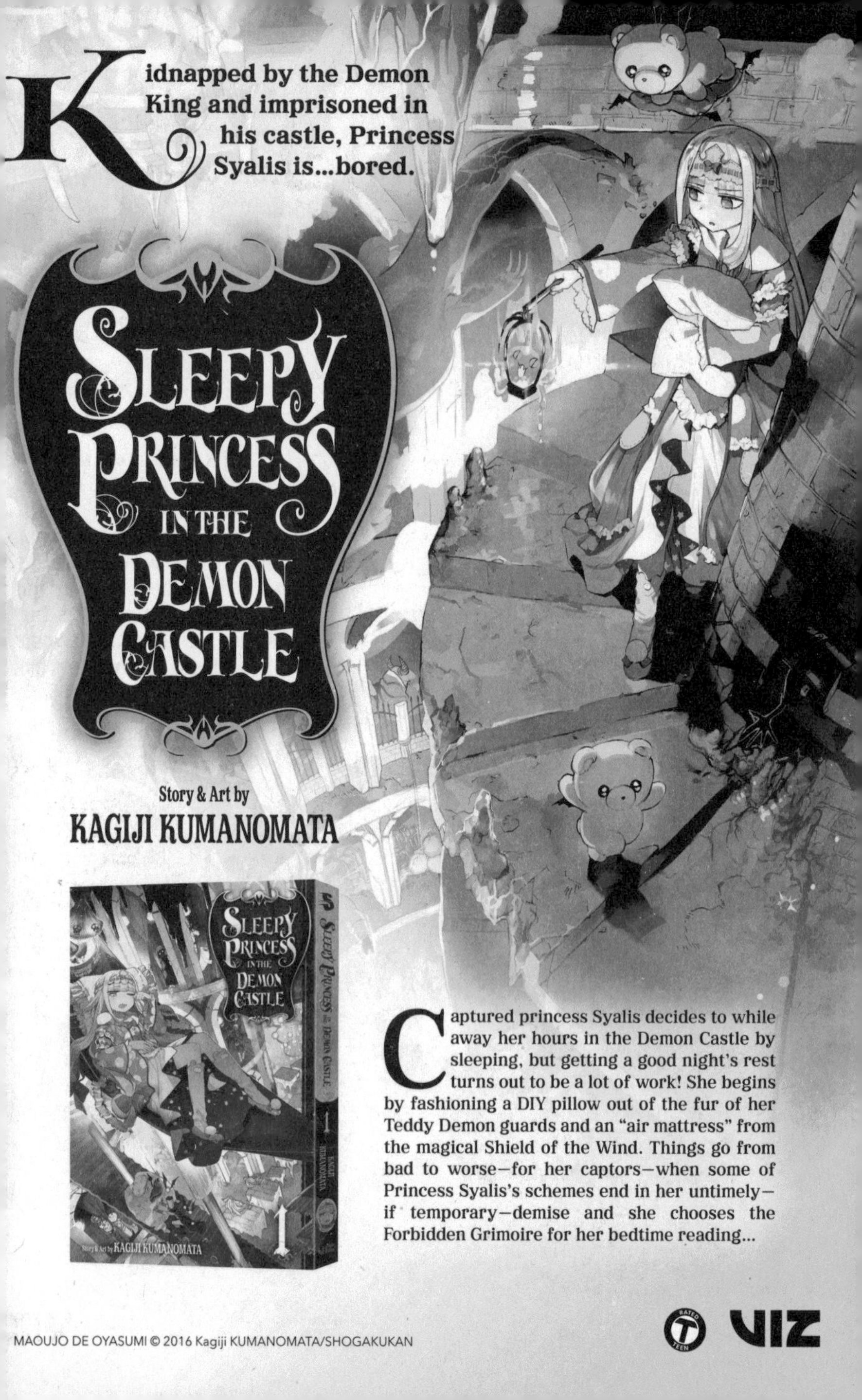
Kidnapped by the Demon King and imprisoned in his castle, Princess Syalis is...bored.
SLEEPY PRINCESS IN THE DEMON CASTLE
Story & Art by
KAGIJI KUMANOMATA
SLEEPY PRINCESS IN THE DEMON CASTLE
1
Story & Art by KAGIJI KUMANOMATA
Captured princess Syalis decides to while away her hours in the Demon Castle by sleeping, but getting a good night's rest turns out to be a lot of work! She begins by fashioning a DIY pillow out of the fur of her Teddy Demon guards and an "air mattress" from the magical Shield of the Wind. Things go from bad to worse—for her captors—when some of Princess Syalis's schemes end in her untimely—if temporary—demise and she chooses the Forbidden Grimoire for her bedtime reading...
MAOUJO DE OYASUMI © 2016 Kagiji KUMANOMATA/SHOGAKUKAN
T RATED TEEN
VIZ

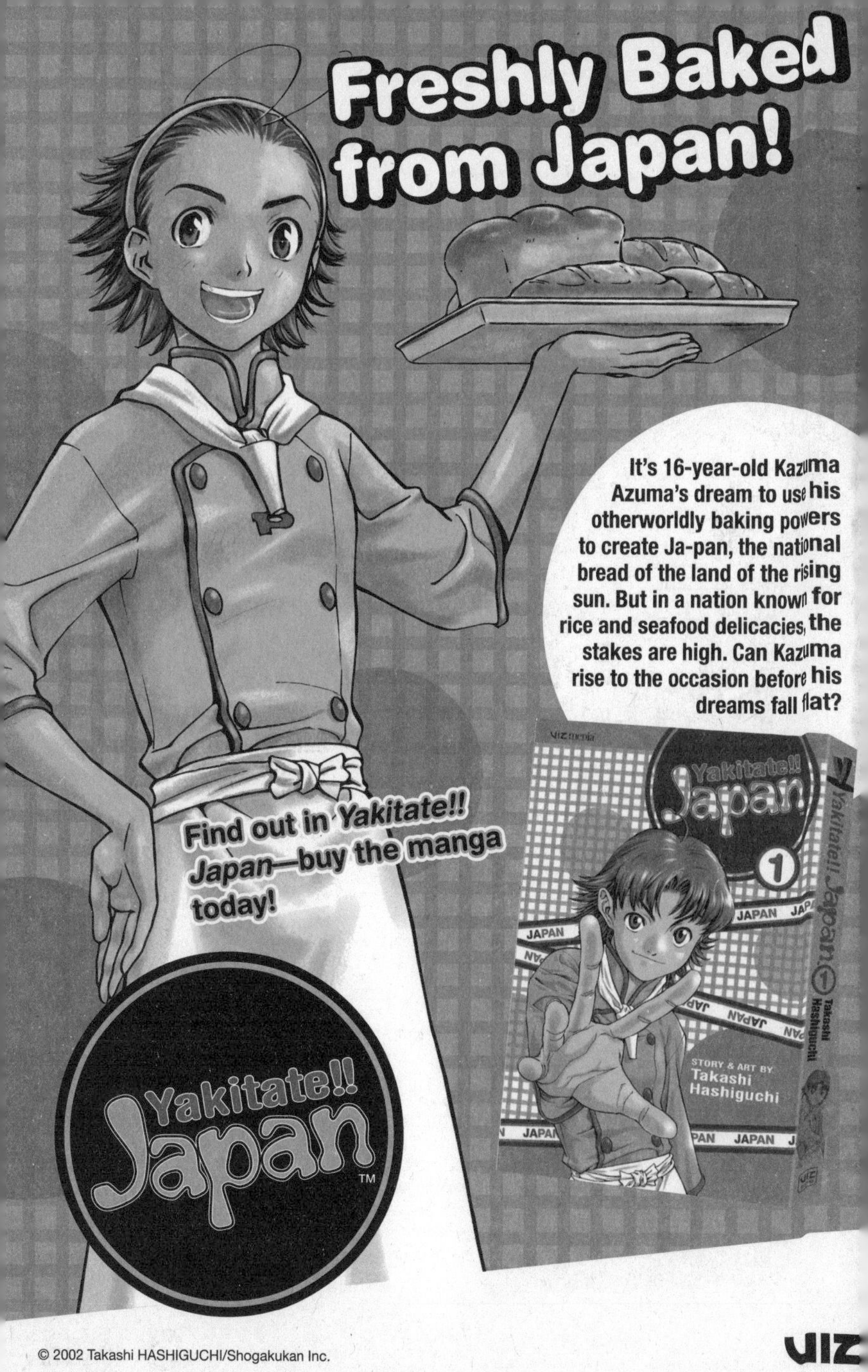
Freshly Baked from Japan!
It's 16-year-old Kazuma Azuma's dream to use his otherworldly baking powers to create Ja-pan, the national bread of the land of the rising sun. But in a nation known for rice and seafood delicacies, the stakes are high. Can Kazuma rise to the occasion before his dreams fall flat?
Find out in Yakitate!! Japan—buy the manga today!
Yakitate!! Japan™
Yakitate!! Japan 1
STORY & ART BY Takashi Hashiguchi
VIZ

You're reading the
WRONG WAY

MAGI reads from right to left, starting in the upper-right corner. Japanese is read from **right** to **left**, meaning that action, sound effects, and word-balloon order are completely reversed from English order.

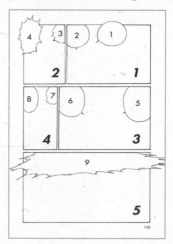